The War of Words

The War of Words

A Glossary of Globalization

Harold James

Yale UNIVERSITY PRESS
New Haven & London

Published with assistance from the Mary Cady Tew Memorial Fund.

Yale University Press books may be purchased in quantity for educational, business, or promotional use. For information, please e-mail sales.press @yale.edu (U.S. office) or sales@yaleup.co.uk (U.K. office).

Set in Galliard Old Style type by IDS Infotech Ltd., Chandigarh, India.
Printed in the United States of America.

Library of Congress Control Number: 2021932832
ISBN 978-0-300-25829-5 (hardcover : alk. paper)

A catalogue record for this book is available from the British Library.

This paper meets the requirements of ANSI/NISO Z39.48-1992 (Permanence of Paper).

10 9 8 7 6 5 4 3 2 1

To Maximilian, Marie-Louise, and Montagu,
and the world's next generation

Contents

Preface

This book originated from a powerful sense that the fierce discussion about globalization has not been grounded in clear thinking about the basic concepts generally used to describe it. As someone who has thought about globalization and its discontents for over thirty years, I am convinced that much of the confusion has arisen from imprecise vocabulary. Particular terms—most recently *neoliberalism, globalism,* and *geopolitics*—pop up everywhere, but aren't adequately defined. To address the problem, I take a broad view in this book, offering historical information as well as contemporary context. The goal is to help all of us who want to advance these essential policy conversations to at least speak the same language.

Some chapters are drawn in part from previous articles. I thank the editors of *Capitalism* for permission to use a modified version of Chapter 12, taken from "Neoliberalism and Its Interlocutors," *Capitalism: A Journal of History and Economics* 1, no. 2 (Spring 2020), Copyright © University of Pennsylvania Press. Parts of Chapter 1 appeared as my chapter "Finance Capitalism" in Jürgen Kocka and Marcel van der Linden, eds., *Capitalism: The Reemergence of a Historical Concept* (London: Bloomsbury Academic, an imprint of Bloomsbury Publishing Plc., 2016); parts of Chapter 4 appeared as "International Order after the Financial Crisis," in *International Affairs* 87, no. 3 (May 2011): 525–537, © 2014 The Royal Institute of International Affairs by permission of Oxford University Press; and parts of Chapter 11 appeared as "Deglobalization: The Rise of

Disembedded Unilateralism," in *Annual Review of Financial Economics* 10 (2018): 219–237, © 2018 by Annual Reviews.

I should like to thank the organizers of several seminars and conferences at which I presented parts of the arguments advanced here, including David Bell at the Davis Center for Historical Studies and Markus Brunnermeier at the Bendheim Center for Finance in Princeton; Wolfgang Quaisser at the Akademie für Politische Bildung; Piotr Pysz at the Konrad Adenauer Foundation Warsaw; Liz Mohn, Wolfgang Schüssel, and Joerg Habich at the Bertelsmann Stiftung Trilogue; Daniel Gros at CEPS, Brussels; Andrew Lo and Robert Merton's Annual Review of Financial Economics conference at NYU's Stern School; Anne Deighton and Oxford University's Cyril Foster Lecture series; Jeffrey Edward Green at the University of Pennsylvania; Adam Posen at the Peterson Institute; and Mary Lewis at Harvard. I have also benefited from comments on some sections by Michael Bordo, Luís António Vinhas Catão, Marc Flandreau, Jürgen Kocka, Jurgen Reinhoudt, and Daniel Rodgers. Joshua Derman gave the whole text a highly perceptive reading.

Seth Ditchik at Yale University Press gave me very helpful guidance and advice. Anna Vinitsky provided absolutely first-rate research assistance and opened up some Russian-language sources. Julie Carlson copyedited the manuscript with exceptional thoughtfulness. Chapters 6 and 7 were written together with Marzenna James, of the Princeton Politics Department, to whom I owe infinite debts. Our children, Maximilian, Marie-Louise, and Montagu James, also gave invaluable inputs.

The War of Words

Introduction: How Words Become Arguments

We are currently experiencing a radical reorientation of economy, society, and politics through the dramatic clash of two principles or philosophies. *Globalism, cosmopolitanism, internationalism, multilateralism:* there are many alternative ways of describing a commitment to openness. On the other side are *particularism, localism,* and *nationalism.* Adding to the intensity of the argument, a globally contagious virus in 2020 became the face—the realization—of globalization. The coronavirus pandemic accelerated many developments that were already well advanced: on a broad scale, it pushed the application of technology into new, and often more personal, areas of daily life, even as it intensified a (provisional) backlash against globalization. It produced economic and social strains, as well as new and peculiar psychic burdens.

Crises are a time for rethinking and reorientation: for going back to basics. Can history tell us anything about what to expect next, and how to think about it? This book starts from the notion that moments of profound social transition spark new questions and inspire new vocabularies. A vocabulary is a way of summing up ideas, and ideas package our collective visions of reality. They translate experiences from an individual perspective into a more general, or even universal, understanding. Ludwig Wittgenstein famously made a central point of his philosophy that "the limits of my language mean the limits of my world."[1] Humans have always been divided by languages: one of our most powerful myths is the story of the Tower of Babel, or how God destroyed an edifice that would create a universal language or understanding because that would give the humans power themselves to be God ("let us make us a name, lest we be scattered abroad upon the face of the whole earth").[2] Since then, there have been attempts to create a universal language—Esperanto and Volapük—but they have been largely forgotten. Instead we have largely assimilated the idea that translation is possible, even if it involves the loss of all sorts of nuance. In particular, in trying to understand how people express their thoughts about states and governments—and how an international society is created by interactions among states as well as clashes of ideas—particular languages are continually being translated, frequently poorly or inadequately. The losses in translation, though enormous, are also often not fully recognized.

Translation is often presented as an easy exchange, much like trading with money, which establishes equivalences between goods, services, or even promises. But words that are standardly fired as munition in today's culture, policy, and economic wars—*capitalism, socialism, democracy, imperialism* and *hegemony, multilateralism, geopolitics, populism, technocracy, the politics of debt, globalism, globalization,* and *neoliberalism,* to take just a few examples—have become so indistinct that they are used not for exchange, but instead to blur the arguments and blame those with opposing views. All the terms examined in the book, then, have long histories during which they have been batted back and forth between advocates and critics. After their original success as ways of capturing the predicament of the moment, their meanings snowballed, picking up more and more connotations until they either became icy or began to melt. They are no longer precise analytical tools.

A remarkable and still timely essay by the great Russian writer Alexander Solzhenitsyn targeted this kind of obfuscation in terms. He saw the lie as not a simple untruth, but the consequence of the distortion and misrepresentation of labels: "If we did not paste together the dead bones and scales of ideology, if we did not sew together rotting rags, we would be astonished how quickly the lies would be rendered helpless and would subside. That which should be naked would then really appear naked before the whole world."[3]

Over a century ago, the philosopher William James created widespread outrage when he suggested that the test of ideas lay in how they were evaluated, or in what he provocatively called "truth's cash-value in experiential terms."[4] Ideas had no innate quality for individuals, but only generated their worth by being accepted in a broader environment, in other words through a general circulation in a marketplace. The presentation was excoriated by Princeton philosopher (and future university president) John Grier Hibben, who claimed—immediately after the destructive financial crash of 1907—that it "would certainly precipitate a panic in the world of our thinking as surely as would a similar demand in the world of finance."[5] The debate is just as current today, and many people are panicking.

Just like currencies, the terms emerged from centers of influence. In monetary history, the nineteenth century was dominated by Great Britain, and the later twentieth century by the United States. Ideas also come from centers of production and distribution—places where ideas emerge, clash, and are refined and distorted. During the first half of the nineteenth century, in the aftermath of the great Revolution, France, especially Paris, was the creator of malleable terms like *nation, socialism,* and *democracy.* In the late nineteenth century, as Germany rose to a new political role, it, too, became an intellectual powerhouse. Fascinated in the past by its osmotic adoption of French political vocabulary, German thinkers evolved a new terminology that included *Machtpolitik* and *Geopolitik.*

In the mid-twentieth century, much of the German vocabulary crossed the Atlantic and was placed in a new crucible. The bearers of the terms were often victims of Nazi persecution—a system produced in part by the terms that they too had internalized. In the United States these terms became part of the new language for a nascent superpower thinking about its concept of world order.

We inherit from the past (and from past producers of ideas) the language that we use to contest and interpret our views. In particular, two eras have molded much of today's conceptual framework of politics, including the responses to successive shocks delivered by the process of globalization. The first of these eras of verbal innovation occurred around two hundred years ago, after the end of the great disturbances of the French revolutionary and Napoleonic wars. The aftermath of the twin upsets of the French Revolution and the Industrial Revolution produced a new political language focused on nation and democracy, and then on capitalism and socialism. The great German intellectual historian Reinhart Koselleck considered this period the *Sattelzeit,* or saddle time (from a mountain saddle, where travelers can look over two contrasting landscapes in two different valleys). The word expresses the movement of people through time as well as place. The early nineteenth century was when the key concepts of political modernity were born: apart from *nation* and *nationalism,* there were *conservatism, liberalism, socialism, capitalism,* and *democracy. Democracy,* the last term, is of course much older, but it was rediscovered in a new way that depended on a different sort of organization, large-scale elections instead of lotteries for office, that made the democratic debate quite different than that of ancient Athens or late medieval Italian city-states. The *-isms* are the terms in which we still conduct our debates. Because of the way they originated, the concepts are curiously intertwined and complexly interdependent. They share the same intellectual oxygen.

As an example of this symbiosis of terms, *socialism* and *capitalism* are conceptual antonyms, a yin and yang. Socialism developed out of a critique of a new concept, capitalism, that was invented to describe the uncomfortable features of a changing world. Old-style artisans, new industrial workers, but also an aristocracy whose wealth might be dissipated, and intellectuals whose social capital might be eroded: all felt vulnerable in the face of a new juggernaut. They did not necessarily want socialism, but they deplored capitalism, and people who appealed to a collectivist impulse could attract supporters. The two antonyms remained intertwined, and in the late twentieth century, apologists for capitalism justified their position easily by speaking of the failures of socialism. There is an old Soviet joke that perfectly exemplifies the interdependence of the two concepts: What is the difference between capitalism and communism? Capitalism is the exploitation of man by man. With communism, it's the other way around. As we will see, the converging or merging of these two concepts has been accelerated by cheaper and more readily available information.

The terms *capitalism* and *socialism,* as they were used after their emergence in the nineteenth century, were complex. They were used in different settings and for different purposes. They described continually evolving ways of understanding how the world was, and should be, organized. Capitalism was recognized very early as a phenomenon that crossed state borders, becoming a global reality. Socialism, like its mirror image, was also international. But with socialism, the place for realizing the political order was dictated by the character of the state system, which increasingly relied on a belief that the nation-state was the normal form of existence. National politics and the international or cross-border phenomenon of capitalism or socialism, then, lived in constant tension with each other. In order to understand the troubled relationship of all these different ways of describing social organization, it's helpful to revisit the debates that took place when the concepts were born.

Capitalism began as the description of a system that facilitated exchanges—of property, of labor—and increasingly commoditized the subjects of those transactions in a way that broke down traditions. As more was exchanged, capitalism as a principle became increasingly diffuse, permeating every aspect of individual behavior. Market principles were applied to dating behavior, spousal choices, sports management, cultural production, and so on. Everything looked as if it had financial equivalents. Money served as a mechanism for translation, or a way of storing memories—and much like a language, it was, and is, being continually reinvented. There was a further paradox: capitalism relies on decentralized decision-making, but as capital becomes increasingly concentrated, decisions look as if they are made in a few central nodes: does that open the way to planning?

Socialism developed as a response to the organizational challenge of how to humanize capitalism. It developed in two different directions, one toward a concept of overall planning, another concerned with the redistribution of proceeds to create a more just society. Despite its claims to internationalism, both these strands in socialist thinking were best realized in the context of existing states, so that the relationship between practical socialism and internationalism was always strained.

The *nation-state*, controlled by popular politics or democracy, responded to the challenge of delocalized capitalism. It became increasingly associated with efforts to manage the economy and promote economic growth and development, a fixation that made it vulnerable and dangerous in times of economic setback or turmoil. The same thinking, about the rationalization of national existence through an economic goal, was applied to transnational modes of organization—most strikingly in the European case. The European Community and then the European Union became vulnerable because they looked as if they had been built primarily around a narrowly economic purpose.

By the end of the nineteenth century, the question of the dominance of one state over another—as *hegemony,* or as *imperialism*—came to be the central organizing feature of international relations. Hegemony was a complex phenomenon because it relied on power, but required more than simple force. The hegemon was required to make some investment, shoulder some burden, or pay a price. And the exercise of hegemony produced not increasing costs, but an increasing backlash, so that an incipient dehegemonization set in.

Those living a hundred years ago, after another period of revolutionary conflict that included the First World War and the Bolshevik Revolution, experienced another *Sattelzeit*—a new challenge to global connectedness. The certainties of the pre-1914 world seemed to have been destroyed, but at the same time many felt nostalgic about the prewar world and wanted to get back to its better features. John Maynard Keynes, in his *Economic Consequences of the Peace,* gave a famous and brilliant evocation of the economics of pre-1914 civilization in which the world was interconnected, before describing how political shortsightedness was destroying opportunity for the new generations. Nationalism, socialism, capitalism, even democracy, all seemed to have become much more violent, and much less rational. The ideas developed then—technocracy, geopolitics, multilateralism, globalism, neoliberalism—were supposed to lead away from the obsolete concepts of the previous century. They laid down the markers for the rest of the century, even when, after 1945 and the defeat of European fascism, normality and order seemed to return. By the end of the twentieth century, a new buzzword, *globalization,* had been born. It seemed to be another way of describing the oppressive juggernaut that was changing individual choice and making national policies more difficult and complex.

Might there be a new mechanism for bringing a large number of states together to work for common goods: peace, freedom from hunger, human well-being, and limiting the damage from environmental insults and climate change? The concept of *multilateralism* arose as a reaction to *hegemony,* but also as a challenge to the increasingly popular vision of *geopolitics,* in which the world is shaped by interactions based primarily on physical geography.

The entanglements of the early twentieth century were so complex because they were amplified by financial ties. The question of dominance related also to the politics of debt. During the nineteenth century, capitalism had led to the marketization of international debt on a novel scale, and debt could be used as an instrument of power. Sometimes the influence was unintended, in that a large debtor could exercise substantial pressure on the creditor by threatening not to repay. Debt and its politics became critical shapers of modern politics.

In the early twentieth century, another term emerged: *technocrat*. Technocrats have particular skills, or expert knowledge, that set them apart from politicians, who are typically generalists. In the use of the terms *technocrat* and *technocracy*, there is often also an implication that unlike politicians, who will evade unpleasant choices, technocrats are in a better position to discern long-term developments clearly, and consequently identify what—often painful—decisions or sacrifices need to be made in the present. This vision is often realized in exceptional times, when there are unprecedented (a favorite technocratic term) challenges (another favorite) that demand some new approach.

Just as capitalism and socialism looked like conjoined twins, on the other side of technocrats are populists, who want to reassert a general principle of popular control and take power back from technocrats or functional elites.

An extreme form of hegemony was *globalism,* in which any discussion of what linked countries was recast as the attempt by one country to exercise domination, by military, economic, political, or cultural pressure and influence. Globalism came to be discussed more in the late twentieth century, as the world embarked on a new era of globalization, one that echoed some features of nineteenth-century globalization. Thus the old themes of dominance and the abuse of power returned.

Neoliberalism as conceived in the interwar period held out a promise of turning back the development of large-scale power, whether in the national context of the creation of large concentrations of economic power, or in the international context of the quest for hegemony. But so successful—or so corrosive—was the analysis of hegemonic practice that neoliberalism also came to be regarded as a new and more potent form of the application of power and hegemony.

With the Global Financial Crisis that began in 2007, and even more with the coronavirus pandemic, the new ideas of a century ago—technocracy, globalism, globalization, or neoliberalism—all looked problematic. There was a near universal perception that many different aspects of society were all in a state of crisis—but a crisis that could not be resolved. All the terms attracted eloquent denunciations that became an element of political rhetoric that was simply taken for granted. The world turned against these terms, even at a time when the basic problems (health, environment, as well as the economy and well-being) were seen as clearly global; and we are now looking for new ways to describe how we should organize society, politics, and the economy. Some influencers have announced that they are looking for a "successor ideology" to the current impoverished options, one that could counteract "what happens when ideas meant to encourage critical self-reflection become a part of an echo chamber and grow increasingly divorced from reality."[6] In 2001, when I wrote a book on "the end of globalization," I wrestled with the same predictive problem, and concluded then that the alternatives to the mainstream analytic vocabulary were too incoherent, allusive, or postmodern.[7] We are now drowning in clashing ideas formulated in incoherently used words.

The best understanding of a liberal, open society relies on the concept of a marketplace of ideas. According to that vision, everyone should be free to develop, express, examine, revise, contradict, refute, and confound ideas. Debate becomes a testing ground, in which approval raises the price or value of ideas, and makes them more attractive and compelling, while confusion or contradiction lowers their acceptance and worth.

If this approach were correct, it should lead inexorably to a victory of superior ideas, and the world would be a better governed—perhaps a generally better—place. There would be a gradual tweaking of the prevalent framework of belief as circumstances change, and—very occasionally—radical epistemic breaks, in which a new mental world would arise, one that appeared to have a better correspondence with reality. John Stuart Mill thought that "as mankind improve, the number of doctrines which are no longer disputed or doubted will be constantly on the increase; and the well-being of mankind may almost be measured by the number and gravity of truths which have reached the point of being uncontested."[8] It does not take much familiarity with history to see that this picture is completely unrealistic, and that many very bad and destructive ideas have won out, at least for substantial periods of time. In the battle of ideas, the best do not necessarily or usually win. The twentieth century was a vast experimental field in which the marketplace did not seem to serve humanity well at all.

The experience of the twenty-first century is equally distressing. An increasingly obvious feature is that debate—which is essential to the marketplace concept—has become impossible. In deeply polarized discussions in many countries—about Trump, or Brexit, or EU austerity programs, or Erdoğan, or Putin, or the anti-drug program of the Philippines—there is no room for any nuanced exchange of ideas. There is simply antagonism. The world is divided into friends and enemies, in the manner that the twentieth-century anti-liberal German philosopher Carl Schmitt thought to be characteristic of politics and the political process. Schmitt will appear regularly in these pages, not so much as a guide but rather to provide a supreme example of a rhetorically seductive thinker whose thought relies on dichotomous characterizations of the world.[9]

The new divisiveness may be technologically driven. Instead of a national or universal media, reality is more and more filtered selectively, with competing demands to explain and resolve crises. There are informational and ideational bubbles. People derive their information and their views from sources that they have chosen because they are a good fit with their own views and prejudices; and increasingly from platforms that are driven by algorithms to identify the precise patterns of wants and needs in the consumer. In this way people get exactly the news, and the views, that bolster their own inclination and their own identity. Interpretation becomes nothing more than an extension of smart advertising. That sort of selectivity into self-referential bubbles is not new, but it has become more obvious, and more widely discussed.

Liberal politics requires debating and contesting; anti-liberal politics rests on mutual demonization as an outcome of that contestation. That imperative sets up a massive trap for liberals: if they fall into the demonization of their opponent, aren't they fundamentally asserting the dualistic worldview and confirming all the suppositions of the figures against whom they are fighting? It is by now well established that militant anti-Trumpism simply energized the substantial part of the population that found the president's assault on a liberal political and cultural elite appealing. The biggest argument for Brexit had less to do with the problems of EU regulation; instead it was founded on suspicion of, and hostility toward, those experts who made arguments about EU regulation.

And then there's the role of the "state of emergency," a political phenomenon that is perhaps desirable for dealing with a dramatic crisis, but also opens the way for tremendous mischief, disorder, and damage. It is intended not only to override rules and established processes, but also to subvert language. Historically, declarations of emergency were at the heart of democracies' responses to both the Great Depression and the Second World War. In contemporary terms, the state of emergency also returned as an injunction after the Global Financial Crisis, with the invocation of "big bazookas," "shock and awe," and "whatever it takes"—and perhaps even more dramatically in the 2020 COVID-19 pandemic. It would be foolish to deny that an emergency requires an exceptional response, or to claim that societies can deal with calamities simply by continuing business as usual. But it is also true that short-circuiting traditional institutional protective devices can lead to a bonanza of irregularity, corruption, and corporate welfare that threatens long-run organizational legitimacy and viability. In interwar Europe, Schmitt made himself into the preeminent theoretician of the state of emergency: he saw it as the progenitor of a new politics. He began his *Political Theology,* which first appeared in 1922, in the middle of the inflation and hyperinflation crises that challenged the Weimar Republic, with a striking redefinition of sovereignty: "Sovereign is he who decides on the state of exception [*Ausnahmezustand*]. Only this definition can do justice to the concept of sovereignty as a delimiting concept [*Grenzkonzept*]."[10]

These historical observations lead to a number of possible conclusions. One is that the whole concept of the liberal society and the marketplace of ideas is fundamentally flawed, and the market leads to the absurd succession of overvaluation and booms and then undervaluation and busts that characterizes the sort of markets that economists study. The market needs regulation. But in the case of ideas, who would do the regulating, and on what basis? Isn't that notion itself a very bad idea that would lead quickly to tyranny and injustice?

A second conclusion is the premise for this book. The marketplace doesn't work because the ideas cannot correctly be valued. They are too much in flux, too uncertain. The marketplace does not work because there are no prices at which exchange can take place. The price is the meaning, but the meanings of each term aren't clear. So there is no way of ascertaining a price.

The terms have been batted about between countries, between quite peculiar national traditions of meaning and understanding that are then used to shape and pervert usage elsewhere. But they are all themselves linked to the idea of spillovers between different political orders. Something of that spillover effect may explain the peculiarity of why those countries that were at the center of an idea of global order in the twentieth century have had the most severe and peculiar reaction. The Brexit referendum and the election of Donald Trump brought a new style of politics, one that constitutes a major challenge to the liberal international order that was constructed after the defeat of Nazism in 1945 and strengthened after the collapse of the Soviet system between 1989 and 1991. While the United States and the United Kingdom were the main architects of the post-1945 order, with the creation of the United Nations system, they now appear to be pioneers in the reverse direction, steering an erratic, inconsistent—and domestically highly contested—course away from multilateralism.

In the twentieth century, the international language of ideas became American: the mantle was passed from the French and Germans, who had dominated in the previous century. Walter Lippmann, the inspiring figure usually considered the father of modern political journalism, who was also a key influence on Woodrow Wilson's carrying the United States onto the world political stage, was a fertile inventor of terms. Unlike Carl Schmitt, he did not see terms as always polarizing. He saw that analysis required usably packaged concepts, and he supplied many of them himself. He introduced the notion of *stereotype*, for which these terms might easily lend themselves, as well as of *Cold War*, which provided a backdrop to the initial polarization and mobilization of political language. He himself moved through different ideas quite rapidly, from a youthful socialism to a supreme faith in science, to an embrace of Wilsonianism, to skepticism about majoritarianism and democracy, to renunciation of Wilsonianism, moving to a final attempt to combine realpolitik with an overall religion, even though skepticism about organized religion ran through his life. Immediately after the 1929 crash, he concluded: "What is most wrong with the world is that the democracy, which at last is actually in power, is a creature of the immediate moment. With no authority above it, without religious, political or moral convictions which control its opinions, it is without coherence or purpose. Democracy of this kind cannot last long."[11] Lippmann is also associated with the term *neoliberalism,* which came into use after a colloquium organized in Paris in 1938, on the eve of the Second World War, to celebrate his ideas. He also often articulated a critique of *globalism.* Globalism looked as if it was a way of understanding the connections that drew together the world. Part of undoing modern stereotypes might mean going back to the underpinnings of Lippmann's definitions, and rethinking them.

The terms examined here started with a precise focus and definition. But once they achieved a certain cachet and appeal, it became almost irresistibly tempting to use them more widely, and to introduce quasi-metaphorical meanings. In the new conceptual universe, it becomes hard to distinguish between the original and the metaphor, and the meaning of the term is extended and distended. Morality and moralism are injected into the vocabulary, so that the words become easy labels, usually of condemnation. It is easy to pull many of the expressions that originally delimited concrete political or social phenomena into a description of mental states. Paradoxes emerge and generate political confusion: the terms infect the political debate and become demon words.

The verbal confusion engendered by our political debate suggests an analogy with inflation, the extension of credit and the expansion of money. I will consider, then, the way in which money is linked to information and ideas, and consequently how changes in monetary practice, arising out of profound shocks to economic processes, may produce new ways of organizing our social world. In the course of treating multilateralism, I will identify a key flaw of financial and monetary multilateralism: its fixation on one national currency, the US dollar. What would happen in a world of genuine currency diversity, with easy equivalences that lead to more seamless translation, or exchange? Might that enable a more general flexibility in social and political categorization, in the context of a globalization now driven by information as well as money?

Globalization and its problems are described using many terms, and readers may find that their favorite globalization word does not appear as a chapter in this analysis of a global vocabulary. Some concepts are important, but their usage is not in itself controversial. The theme of inequality appears in many of the discussions of other terms, but there is here no chapter on inequality, which is also the subject of illuminating and highly influential recent work by Thomas Piketty, Tony Atkinson, and Branko Milanovic.[12] Trade and commerce, or financial flows, are part of the standard analysis of globalization, and are here treated as such.

At the other extreme, some words are so fluid that they have become conceptually elusive. Some very frequent, highly inflated terms in the political vocabulary are treated here only in passing where they impinge on the other terms: *fascism* in particular has become an omnipresent term of abuse. Trump is widely called a fascist, and then in turn regularly calls his opponents left-wing fascists.

Another very frequently used term is central to the conception of the book. *Liberalism,* which for some is a vague badge of honor, and for others a vitriolic term of abuse, requires debate, but one supported by a nuanced, contextualized definition of the word. Helena Rosenblatt recently constructed a fine history of the vagaries of the term: how the Atlantic revolutions of the late eighteenth century took a Roman ideal and "Christianized, democratized, socialized and politicized" it so that it could be used to describe the aspirations of the revolutionaries.[13] From then it became so ubiquitous that the American historian Jill Lepore can describe liberalism simply as "the belief that people are good and should be free, and that people erect governments in order to guarantee that freedom."[14]

Some other often-used terms also overlap or bear a close relationship to other terms: thus I will discuss *imperialism,* a key part of the story of globalization, but also now used flexibly (in the sense that informal ideas of empire have been added to the study of the extension of formal rule) in the context of hegemony.

The problem of how to define each term is in fact central to our current dilemmas. The uncertainties about their meaning have become an obstacle to productive debate, and to the application of rigorous logic. To solve pressing problems, each term needs to be rethought in what can be thought of as an act of intellectual decluttering. The lifestyle guru Marie

Kondo created a highly successful practice of cleaning up people's homes, achieving a minimalist aesthetic. She holds that items that no longer "spark joy" should be discarded. The Kondo principle involves families collectively sifting through items left by previous generations. Applying this method to intellectual hygiene would mean that the family cleanup would become a national as well as an international debate—leading to a decluttering, a way to create more room for those ideas that truly "spark creativity." To quote Mill again: "when we turn to . . . morals, religion, politics, social relations, and the business of life, three-fourths of the arguments for every disputed opinion consist in dispelling the appearances which favour some opinion different from it."[15]

We should start by looking at how the ideas evolved, and why they became generalized and globalized, but we should finish by considering how the meaning and usefulness that drove the original conceptualization might be recovered. Negotiating the gaps between different understandings, which arose across countries and over time as communities responded to technical change and the acceleration of life experience, can bring us back to basics. That means reflecting not only on the roots of social cohesion and political organization, but also on the terms (political language) and the instruments (money) that we use to translate our own experiences into our ideas about the experiences of others. Getting back to what really matters will require revisiting an earlier era, to learn what was at stake before the conceptual lexicon became so cluttered.

1

Capitalism

Capitalism defines much of modern life, and the past thirty years have been uber-capitalist. In 1989, capitalism was widely supposed to have triumphed. But what exactly won out when Soviet communism collapsed? A great deal of the debate about capitalism has been over how it should be defined. If we think of it as simply an outcome of Adam Smith's "propensity to truck and barter," it is a pretty universal feature of human life. (Indeed, a substantial number of non-human animals also display capitalistic behavior. Penguins in the Antarctic, for instance, collect rounded pebbles—a sort of capital accumulation—that they then trade for sex.) Chronicles depict hoarding and bartering in almost every human society, even in extreme circumstances such as prisons or concentration camps. Capital accumulation occurs when people hoard. *Capitalism* is when they can exchange their hoarded goods or products. It is inherently decentralized, and not subject to centralized control.

Capital is thus an elastic concept, capable of being expanded quite widely. For some analysts, the stretching process is a vigorous intellectual exercise. The French sociologist Pierre Bourdieu tried to distinguish four types of capital: to the familiar economic notion of capital, he added symbolic, social, and cultural capital. He thought of the economic discussion as artificially limiting: "Economic theory has allowed to be foisted upon it a definition of the economy of practices which is the historical invention of capitalism; and by reducing the universe of exchanges to mercantile exchange, which is objectively and subjectively oriented toward the maximization of profit, i.e., (economically) *self-interested,* it has implicitly defined the other forms of exchange as noneconomic, and therefore *disinterested.* In particular, it defines as disinterested those forms of exchange which ensure the *transubstantiation* whereby the most material forms of capital . . . can present themselves in the immaterial form of cultural capital or social capital or vice versa."[1] Symbolic capital may often depend on the customs and traditions of a particular society, and is less easily obviously bought and sold via a distinctively market mechanism.

Symbolic and cultural capital have become ever more important in thinking about capitalism, especially as capitalism has become triumphalist. These forms of capital might help explain why a process that is innovative, creative, and destructive might eventually perpetuate existing inequalities. They may also illuminate how capitalism develops, since capitalism is no longer seen as requiring an initial and large-scale raising of capital, as in Marx's vision of "primitive capital accumulation." The historian Joyce Appleby, for example, describes how "the accumulation of cultural capital, especially the know-how and desire to innovate in productive ways, proved more decisive in capitalism's history" than has accumulation of physical capital. Medieval cathedrals were enormous investments in terms of physical capital, but didn't unleash a capitalist revolution.[2] The economic historian Joel Mokyr, too, reckons that "what counts for economic history was the beginning of a long and drawn-out rise in the belief in the transformative powers, social prestige, and virtuousness of useful knowledge."[3]

Two paradoxes mark the history of capitalism, and they have emerged with great clarity since 1989. First, capitalism depends on decentralized decision-making to aggregate millions of separate decisions, but capital gets concentrated, and with it decision-making. Second, the effective operation of capitalism depends on an external order provided usually by governments, but the concentration of capital means that large capitalists will try to capture the government (in a phenomenon often called *crony capitalism*).

Institutionalizing the Act of Exchange

Capitalism depends on frequent exchanges, and the mechanisms for these exchanges can become more complex or institutionally sophisticated, though money is required. Doubts or uncertainty about a monetary standard impede the process of exchange, and may make that exchange look more illegitimate—closer to robbery than a voluntary trade.

Definitions of capitalism have not only an empirical part, but also sometimes an element that is normative, though often ambiguously so. Concepts that are designed as criticisms can quickly flip to become neutral or even celebratory, and may then flip back again. In the mid-nineteenth century, *capitalism* arose as a term used by revolutionaries and social critics to describe the inhuman subjection of mankind to abstract forces. By the end of the century, however, in the analysis of Max Weber, it had become a simple description of a new rationalized form of conduct, the institutionalization of exchange and the stripping away from exchange of traditional values (including symbolic capital).

Normative accounts emphasize—if they are negative—how this model is at odds with basic traits of human nature, to the extent that the trading of claims is a process of "alienation" that wrecks human relationships by subjecting them to a one-dimensional and anti-human vision. This sort of critique originally came from Marx's analysis of capitalism, but it is not confined to that tradition. Thus, for instance, the teaching of the Catholic Church as formulated in the 1991 encyclical *Centesimus annus:* "The historical experience of the West, for its part, shows that even if the Marxist analysis and its foundation of alienation are false, nevertheless alienation—and the loss of the authentic meaning of life—is a reality in Western societies too. This happens in consumerism, when people are ensnared in a web of false and superficial gratifications rather than being helped to experience their personhood in an authentic and concrete way. Alienation is found also in work, when it is organized so as to ensure maximum returns and profits with no concern whether the worker, through his own labour, grows or diminishes as a person."[4] The neo-Aristotelean philosopher Alasdair MacIntyre speaks of the "moral impoverishment of advanced capitalism."[5]

The normative accounts that, by contrast, paint a positive or celebratory vision of capitalism start from the propensity of humans to truck and barter. Smithian versions suggest that there is always a market of some kind, and that if the natural signals of the market are suppressed, the result is not only a loss of efficiency, but also a loss of humanity as individuals substitute violence and coercion for mutually agreed-on bargains.

A society may be more or less capitalistic. The usefulness of an abstract term depends on our ability to use it to judge the extent or scale of a phenomenon. Speed: what is the velocity? Good: is something more or less good? Capitalism and related concepts such as globalization can be used in this way: How globalized is an economy? How capitalist is a society? Can capitalism be mixed with other social or organizational forms, and how do the values that those other organizational forms generate affect the trading that goes on in capitalist processes?

Industrial capitalism, in a modern form, with large numbers of workers bound by labor contracts with fixed rates, is not the only form of market exchange for labor. It has often been contrasted with serfdom or slavery, with fixed and involuntary labor obligations, but those forms of contractual obligation had prices too—slaves and serfs were bought and sold. There was no wage in the sense of a price for labor, but the operation of serf or slave estates was subject to calculations of gain and loss. A great deal of historical writing over the past fifty years has been devoted to demonstrating the market, or capitalist, rationale behind slavery. The expansion of capitalism, as Elizabeth and Eugene Genovese make clear, "conquered, absorbed, and reinforced servile labor systems throughout the world."[6] "In the narrow sense perhaps the slave plantations could not have been run any more capitalistically than they were."[7] The practices of the past left legacies for subsequent market processes. Workers in a factory setting or in a modern service economy are often separated into distinct groups—by age, gender, race—which then operate in separated market systems. The different systems are thus much less clearly differentiated than is conventionally thought.

The initial mercantile capitalists developed production systems that depended on involuntary labor. Italians, from the time of the First Crusade, were involved in the colonial and export-oriented production of sugar with Muslim slave labor in the Levant. Venetian-controlled Crete and Cyprus became major centers of this trade. The Genoese later developed Madeira with imported slaves from West Africa. The Portuguese plantations in Brazil simply expanded on a system pioneered elsewhere.[8] That was then in turn a model for the American South.

Conversely, voluntary labor was frequently a good deal less voluntary than it might legally appear. In Britain, the first modern industrial country with only very small agricultural employment by the late nineteenth century, there were labor contracts, but until 1875, breach of contract by the worker (but not by the employer) was treated as a criminal issue.[9] And in many societies, especially in rural settings, a great deal of work—farm work, but also domestic manufacture in the "putting out" system—was done by unpaid family members.

For much of the twentieth century, the world lived with competing economic systems (from market-oriented societies to central planning, with many intermediate stages). During the postwar decades, a number of influential analysts, from James Burnham to John Kenneth Galbraith, maintained that convergence of systems in some kind of mixture, characterized by a high degree of planning, would take place. They saw the corporation as a way of avoiding high costs and inefficiencies associated with market processes. Meanwhile socialist reformers such as Ota Šik in Czechoslovakia and Yevsai Lieberman in the USSR wanted to use prices in order to make planning more efficient. At this time, both the planned and the market systems were supposed to deliver growth, and the analysis of patterns of growth became a major focus of research. During the 1970s there was an emphasis on resource constraints and environmental issues, and how they might be overcome by different systems. One philosophy claimed that only more centralized and globalized planning could deal effectively with scarce resources, while another view held that, with properly judged incentive systems in place, markets offered the only way of evolving rational responses to ecological questions. In the 1980s a new topic in international issues emerged: the dynamics of debt and development in poorer countries that were embarking on an economic catch-up. Sharply opposed ideological responses shaped assessments of how best to approach the question of development and how to avoid "lost decades," during which the cost of debt service would take away chances for a better future.

Following the collapse of communism between 1989 and 1991, the clash of systems has eased. But the intellectual baggage created in debates about systems has continued to influence attempts to think about the institutions and characteristics of both markets and economies. Some of the ideas about different styles of capitalism, for example, linger in approaches that stress the different institutional characteristics of Asian, "Rhineland," and "Anglo-Saxon" capitalisms (and sometimes make claims about differences in their performance).[10] Some of the most contested issues have involved the extent to which different models of legal organization, corporate structure, regulation and supervision, and competition policy can be transferred from one setting to another: can this be a subject of globalization, and if so, what would be the costs and benefits? Aspects of particular entrepreneurial and managerial styles are constantly being transferred and imitated across borders: in the 1990s, Europeans rushed to adopt American approaches to shareholder value; now Americans like European vocational training traditions; and trust-based Asian models look as if they handle adaptation to consumer demand and consumer loyalty more effectively. Can particular cultural patterns really be taken up elsewhere, or are they always bound to the specific environment that produced them in the first place? One known effect of globalization is to diminish or devalue symbolic and traditional capital by pointing out that it cannot be traded.

Origins and Meanings of the Word

The literature on capitalism has been marked by two contrasting tendencies. One is to assert that capitalism is something very specifically modern, and that the economic phenomena of antiquity, or the European Middle Ages, or pre-colonial Africa, cannot be considered capitalist. Karl Polanyi, whose *Great Transformation* is still hailed as a guide to the creation of the modern economy, begins his account of the pre-modern world by stating that "eighteenth century society unconsciously resisted any attempt at being made into a mere appendage of the market. No market economy was conceivable that did not include a market for labor; but to establish such a market, especially in England's rural civilization, implied no less than the wholesale destruction of the traditional fabric of society."[11] This is simply nonsense, a sentimentalization on a grotesque scale of "merrie England" of cakes and ale: long before the eighteenth century there was a labor market, and wages and conditions of work responded to a market logic.[12]

The second tendency is much more persuasive: to argue that the capitalist instinct is deeply embedded in the human psyche and is thus practically universal. The Christian socialist economic historian R. H. Tawney rightly noted that "the 'capitalist spirit' is as old as history, and was not, as has sometimes been said, the offspring of puritanism." He was thinking of the debate launched by Max Weber's famous thesis on the "Protestant ethic" and early modern capitalism. In Tawney's reformulation, a religious mind-set, seventeenth-century Puritanism, merely provided a "tonic" that encouraged a new formulation of the inherent logic of a market or capitalist process.[13]

A key to understanding the debate is to think of the circumstances in which the term arose. While it is absurd to suggest that there was no capitalism before the nineteenth century, the term itself originated then, and with it a rather different conceptual framework of how to interpret economic reality. It was not the market that was being created, far from it, but a way of thinking about the market.

The early classical economists Adam Smith and David Ricardo, however, did not use the term. By the nineteenth century, a debate had developed in western Europe about a new kind of society that seemed more capital-istic than anything that had gone before. The *Oxford English Dictionary* gives the first occurrence in a British newspaper, *The Standard,* in 1833: "Whatever tended to paralyse British industry could not but produce cor-responding injury to France; when the same tyranny of capitalism which first produced the disease would be at hand to inflame the symptoms by holding out promises of loans, &c." Just after the Europe-wide revolutions of 1848, capitalism appeared as a way of describing a new society. In the revolutionary year the *Caledonian Mercury* deplored "that sweeping tide of capitalism and money-loving which threatens our country with the horrors of a plutocracy," linking capitalism unambiguously to a specifically financial phenomenon.

One of the earliest French references to capitalism occurs in 1839, in a critique of contemporary conditions in France by the Marquis de Villeneuve. This reactionary figure considered the vices of the time to be journalism and capitalism: "one dissipates the fortunes which it claims to consolidate, the other evaporates the instruction which it aims to spread: both are pre-cious when used well, but formidable when abused."[14] In 1850 the French socialist leader Louis Blanc defined "capitalism" as "appropriation of capital by some to the exclusion of others." A German economist, Johann Karl Rodbertus, wrote in 1869 that "capitalism has become a social system." In 1870 another German economist, Albert Schäffle, published a book entitled *Kapitalismus und Sozialismus,* defining capitalism as a "national and international organism of production under the leadership of 'entrepreneurial' capitalists competing for highest profit."[15] In Schäffle's work, socialism and capitalism are conceptual twins.

Capitalist as a noun describing a person was an older usage. The 1845 novel *Sybil,* a powerful plea for "one nation" by the romantic Tory politician Benjamin Disraeli, castigated social division and the separation of society into classes. Disraeli described how "the capitalist flourishes, he amasses immense wealth; we sink, lower and lower; lower than the beasts of burthen." The classical economist Nassau Senior has a discussion of how the concept of "capitalist's share" of the proceeds of production was used "familiarly" by economists.[16]

The mid-nineteenth-century usage was quite specific, and generally associated *capital, capitalist,* and *capitalism* with financial accumulation, not with manufacturing or industrial activity as a whole. In this way the initial condemnations took up many older discussions of usury. An 1845 description of various types of English personality includes an essay on the "Capitalist": "His politics are the wonder and sphynx's riddle to the vulgar and the uninitiated. A Capitalist, and the opponent of government? Bound to the aristocracy by wealth and connection, and yet a decrier of the corn-laws? An advocate of the Reform Bill; and, ay, even for the Ballot? Rich and expensive: refined in taste, and fastidious as to connections; yet the defender of mobs, and the promoter of tumultuous petitions? He bewilders the country gentlemen; he beguiles the multitude; he is an enigma. The newspaper sages are even puzzled; they know not what to predicate of him; today he votes for equality and cheap bread; and tomorrow for high prices and despotism. . . . But he is still consistent to one principle; and that is his own principal."[17] The essence of finance was its easy transferability or ubiquity. The British peer Lord Brougham, a key figure in the making of the Reform Act that extended the franchise, explained to the House of Lords: "A capitalist does not like to send his capital to a country where a doctrine like this might be established on the model of another so very similar which has already been set up there."[18] Meanwhile an Austrian chemist, trying to explain basic terms in an encyclopedia of science, explained that "the capitalist only receives his determined interest, it is all the same to him how his capital is used as long as capital and interest is secure. The increase in product only brings losses, not a profit."[19]

Finance and financial capitalism thus play a particular role in this story. The peculiarity arises because financial institutions involve a degree of organization that serves to camouflage or obscure the market process. The extent of financialization can be measured; but often the growth in scale of financial institutions means a camouflaging or even suppression of basic market signals. Banks, which are at the center of finance capitalism, have consequently puzzled many observers. Banks are conceptually a black box, in which the outsider—the depositor—does not really know much about how his money is being used; consequently, they are subject to panics and runs as some depositors come to believe that their funds may not be safe, and as other depositors realize that a run means that all liabilities cannot be paid, so it is advantageous to be first in line to make a withdrawal.[20] Modern banks have increased their complexity, and hence become less transparent. In the recent financial crisis, observers were astonished to find that in a panic, price signals no longer operated to clear markets, and it was impossible to determine the worth of complex derivative products.

The same problem of opacity plagues the other great modern feature of capitalism: the corporation with a personality of its own (with the term *corporation* taken into modern economic life from a medieval and very non-capitalist theory of fellowship).[21] Corporations collectivize property rights, as well as substitute a hierarchical authority for voluntary transactions. The innovation was usually justified as a way to save on the cost of transactions: if a manufacturer had to buy parts from many individual contractors, he would be less able to control quality effectively and cheaply.[22] Employing workers and subjecting them to factory discipline removed that source of uncertainty.

In this regard, financial capitalism is something of a paradox. (Marxists used to love the term "contradiction" when thinking about capitalism.) Finance facilitates the trading of derivatives of capitalist innovation (claims on the future), but at the same time it functions so effectively by suppressing some aspects of the price signaling effect that is crucial to the operation of capitalism.

Types of Capitalism

Finance capitalism plays an increasingly important part in some phases of the capitalist narrative. Almost every analysis of capitalism from Smith and Marx onward includes a notion of stages. Fernand Braudel identified four cycles, around geographic hegemonic cores (Genoa, Amsterdam, London, New York), with a progressive process of transformation from real to financial assets in each cycle.[23] It is striking that the last two, but not the first two, coincide with the story of "the rise and fall of the great powers" as told by the historian Paul Kennedy, where Spain anticipates British and then American hegemony.[24] The Italian city-states and the Dutch Republic needed to operate a complex, universal, and intensely rule-based financial system without being able to impose a global security order.

An equally striking—and necessary—role is played by the government. The essence of market transactions depends on there being a capacity to measure equivalences, or prices, which are measured in terms of a safe asset. For centuries, a clash of interpretation that goes back to Aristotle disputed whether that safe asset was generated by a social or market logic, out of the interactions of merchants, or by the imposition of the government, because money arose out of the fiscal needs of governments. There were undoubtedly self-sustaining trading systems that existed outside the control of single judicial authorities, but governments almost always played the central role in setting the terms on which coins were used and traded. Having more secure, government-provided assets made capitalist transactions easier.

Here a slightly different breakdown of types of capitalism in stages or historical periods, with rather loose dating, is proposed:

Mercantile/commercial capitalism, 1300–1690
Mercantile capitalism with secure (government) assets, 1690–1800
Industrial capitalism, 1800–1890
Finance capitalism, 1890–1914
Managerial (organized) capitalism, with different types (liberal versus coordinated market economies, sometimes also thought of as a contrast between market-dominated "Anglo-Saxon" economies and a more negotiated Rhineland model of capitalism), 1914–1990
(Hyper- or globalized) finance capitalism, 1990–2008

And then what? The years after 2008 have been revolutionary, and not simply due to fallout from the Global Financial Crisis, which led to a widespread questioning of financialization, the role of banks in the economy, and the ability of authorities to regulate and supervise financial institutions. At the same time, radically new technologies appeared: 2007, the year of the first signs of financial strain, was also the year in which the iPhone was introduced, and when the payments system MPesa was first launched, in east Africa. The consequence was that finance was democratized at the same time as it was questioned and even demonized. Instead of attacking capitalist hierarchies through protest movements such as Occupy Wall Street, millennials realized that they might use cheap and widely available platforms such as Robinhood against hedge funds and the financial establishment.

By now, there exist a wide variety of private-payment mechanisms, many but not all of them linked to traditional currencies. For example, there are currently an estimated $1.6 billion held on Starbucks customer cards and $20 billion in PayPal accounts. By comparison, the physical stock of US currency, most of which is probably held outside the United States, is of course much larger: currently $1.7 trillion. One reason that this trend away from the use of traditional cash and of old-style banking facilities is likely to proceed at an increasingly rapid pace—and lead to a tipping point—is that the cost of e-transactions is falling rapidly, while many banking services have become considerably more expensive. This is a development analogous to the widespread replacement of managed funds in the investment world by low-cost exchange-traded funds (ETFs).

Both the development of new kinds of money and the creation of new investment practices bring clear regulatory challenges. The use of private-payment platforms raise financial stability questions—might they be subject to runs?—as well as the question of whether AliPay or PayPal might contemplate their own monetary policies. Many such financial and monetary stability concerns will be fanned and played up by existing institutions, which rightly perceive themselves to be under threat by these radically different technologies. Two very recent challenges have underlined the urgency of the challenge: on the one hand, Facebook's proposal for a digital currency, Libra (now renamed Diem), pegged to a basket of major currencies; and on the other, China's development of a widely available digital currency as an explicit challenge to the US dollar. The best way of describing this new form of capitalism is *information capitalism*.

Institutional Developments

Two developments have been crucial: banks as credit institutions, and the limited liability joint stock corporation as a mechanism for organizing banking activity. Credit creation is the driving force of the modern monetary economy, and the joint stock company permits a scale that would not be possible in the limited world of family banking and partnerships that characterized finance until the mid-nineteenth century.

First, let's consider the emergence of banks that engaged primarily in the business of credit and lending. For a long time, lending at a fixed interest rate was regarded as problematic because of religious prohibitions on usury. International banking evolved as an outgrowth of transactions with bills of exchange or bills of trade that related strictly to flows of goods. The foundations were laid in the fourteenth-century era of mercantile capitalism, as Italian city-states spread their commercial networks first across the Mediterranean and then over the European continent. The standard ninety-day form reflected the origins of the instrument in the wool and textile trade of medieval times, when wool from England took around three months to reach Florence, and the same time was required for Florentine cloth to travel to England or Flanders. Most of the early Florentine banks worked primarily on discounting bills and avoided the morally problematic business of lending to individuals. What lending business they did do was secondary: as part of their search for trade expansion, the great banking houses lent to governments, the Bardi and the Peruzzi lending above all to the king of England so he could obtain permission to export English wool and import Florentine cloth, and the Medici to the papacy, in order to develop the alum trade but also to influence the politics of the Italian peninsula.

The next great center of European capitalism, the Netherlands, had powerful trading houses, and by the eighteenth century was home to banks that engaged in large-scale financing of foreign governments, but (unlike early modern England) no real credit-creating banks. The most important bank in Amsterdam, the Wijsell Bank, was modeled instead on the Venetian Rialto bank, a girobank or payments bank whose main function was to facilitate customers' transfers of deposits from one account to another; it did not include a credit-creating mechanism. In the late seventeenth century, by contrast, a number of London goldsmiths developed a very substantial lending business. Here lay the origins of modern banking, but as long as the activity was based on the partnership form, it was necessarily limited in scope. The son of a Scottish goldsmith, John Law became one of the greatest modern theorists of banking operations—as well as the deviser of one of the most destructive experiments in the management of currency.[25]

Analyses of the time stressed the general advantages that could follow from financial activity. As John Houghton, a fellow of the English Royal Society, put it in 1692 at the beginning of the English financial revolution: "Without doubt, if those Trades were better known, 'twould be a great Advantage to the Kingdom; only I must caution Beginners to be very wary, as there are many cunning Artists among them."[26]

The second major device that was essential for the development of finance capitalism is the limited liability principle as applied to the corporation. The new approach evolved in the Netherlands, in the context of the debate about the relative responsibilities of shareholders and managers in the Dutch East India Company (VOC).[27] In the early eighteenth century, with these two devices in place, there was an explosion of joint stock companies in England, mostly connected with managing state debt.

The limited-liability innovation was associated, too, with a broader financial revolution, in which a new approach to banking and the management of the government debt created the underpinning for an increasingly solid web of confidence. Government debt, managed since 1694 by the Bank of England—another joint stock corporation—provided a secure asset, one that lay at the base of a financial system that made credible promising a real possibility. This financial order dramatically reduced borrowing costs in Britain. It gave a strategic as well as a commercial advantage that was envied on the other side of the English Channel, but could not be emulated until after the French Revolution.[28]

The change in government finance laid a basis for private-sector financial developments. The two long dominant British insurance companies, the Royal Exchange Assurance and the London Assurance, were both founded in a single year, 1720, when financial speculation ran wild in England and in France, with the simultaneous promotion of South Sea Company stock and John Law's scheme for revolutionizing French finance by assuming the debt of the French state through the Mississippi Company. The Royal Exchange Assurance had its origins in 1717 in a proposal to create a large subscription for marine insurance. The sum was so vast that it required a charter as a joint stock company, but that was only possible if the new company would also offer a scheme to take over a part of the English national debt, as the Bank of England had done in 1694 and as the South Sea Company was also promising to do. The same speculative year that produced so many joint stock companies had the same effect in the Netherlands, where the Rotterdamsche Maatschappij van Assurantie was established. Gigantic amounts of capital flooded into the new offerings, though the price quickly collapsed with the end of the speculative bubble.

For some time after the extreme financial turbulence of 1720, the joint stock company model was discredited, and new companies were either completely prohibited (in England) or required a complex chartering process (in France). Banks shared in the obloquy: the economist Charles Kindleberger records—with some exaggeration—how in France, in a "classic case of collective financial memory," there "was hesitation in pronouncing the word 'bank' for 150 years."[29] When the idea resurfaced in Europe as a result of the new demands for security produced by the technical changes of the Industrial Revolution, those countries with liberal incorporation laws—notably the new Kingdom of Belgium—had substantial advantages. Belgium in particular experienced an explosion of corporate activity, much of it concerned with providing new services to French and German businesses.

That year of exuberant financial innovation—1720—is a kind of litmus test of attitudes about capitalism. It is worth contrasting two perspectives on the relationship of 1720 to the modern age. Consider first that of the Austrian physician and economist Rudolf Hilferding, who discussed in a flowery passage the "reduced role of speculation" as business became more and more organized.

> Those mass psychoses, which speculation produced at the beginning of the capitalist era, those blessed times in which every speculator felt himself to be God, creating a world out of nothing, all that seems irretrievably lost. The tulip swindle with its idyllic underpinning of poetic flower-fancying, the South Sea swindle with

its adventuresome and stimulating fantasies of unheard of discoveries, the Law scheme with its prospect of world conquest, all these give way to the undisguised chasing of arbitrage opportunities which found an end in the *Krach* of 1873. Since then belief in the wonderworking power of credit and the stock exchange has waned, the beautiful Catholic cult has waned despite Bontoux [author of a scheme for a Catholic bank in France, the Union Générale, that failed in 1882], and has been replaced by a sober Enlightenment that does not want to believe in the Immaculate Conception through the Spirit of Speculation, but takes the natural naturally and leaves faith to the stupid, who aren't quite all there yet. The stock exchange has lost its faithful, and only retained priests who make their business out of the faith of others. Since faith has turned into business, the business of belief gets ever smaller. The beautiful madness has flown, the tulips faded and the coffee only generates a commercial profit, but no speculative gains. Prose has defeated the poetry of profit.[30]

Hilferding, like his near contemporary Max Weber, saw a world of increased rationalization, in which wild, undisciplined capitalism no longer had a sense of purpose, but needed the discipline of the routine. What a contrast can be found in the works of more recent authors! The most erudite and wide-ranging historians of the Dutch Republic, Jan de Vries and Ad van der Woude, reach an exactly opposite conclusion. In their view, "it is undeniable that the financial institutions and practices of this first modern economy left much to be desired." But they further argue that "the 'irrational' speculative manias—involving tulips, hyacinths, VOC shares, and English funds—hardly qualify as serious indictments. On the contrary, they only underscore the modern character of the economy."[31] Finance capital is thus creative and expansive, but also deeply destabilizing and potentially destructive.

The modern joint stock bank as a business model emerged in the setting of post-independence Belgium: a small state, part of which (Flanders and Brabant) had once been with the Italian city-states the most dynamic part of Europe, but which after 1572 had lapsed into two and a half centuries of relative stagnation compared with the now more dynamic North Netherlands (the United Provinces). After independence in 1830, Belgium looked for a

way of promoting growth, and found it in what was called, quite characteristically, the general company, Société Générale. Its entrepreneurial
governor, Ferdinand de Meeûs, propagated the idea of the *société anonyme*
as a replacement for family businesses that could not raise enough capital
and thus could not innovate adequately in the new industrial environment.[32]
The Belgian model of company formation proved very attractive, and French
and German entrepreneurs were soon incorporating in Brussels. Eventually,
other states followed suit. The breakthrough in Great Britain came with the
limited liability provisions of 1855. France introduced a new law permitting
joint stock companies in 1867. In 1843, Prussian law had been changed to
allow the creation of joint stock companies, but only where they served the
"higher interest of the common good," and where the goal of the company
could not be realized in any other way: the legislation was above all intended
to promote railroad building. In practice, a more liberal law of 1870 was
what prompted a flood of new corporations.

Both banks and joint stock companies were seen as the major enemy by
many nineteenth-century entrepreneurs, who detested what they referred
to as "capitalists." The German coal and engineering pioneer Franz Haniel, for instance, was outraged by his partners' suggestion to convert a
partnership into a joint stock company, an *Aktiengesellschaft,* which smacked
of the financial dealing that he had always greatly suspected and detested,
and he threatened simply to break up the company into three parts. He
concluded: "as a consequence, the swindle with shares was prevented and
the works and the company still remain. How much unpleasantness I have
experienced in the course of my almost sixty year long most selfless and
strenuous activity for the company, but ingratitude is the reward of the
world."[33] The steelmaker Alfred Krupp wrote that "by preference, we
should avoid the assistance of banks—systematically!"[34] Banks, however
they developed, in Krupp's eyes constituted a constant threat not only to
entrepreneurial dynamism, but also to patriotic engagement. In July 1873,
in the middle of a major crisis for his company—and for the whole German
economy—Krupp set out his life philosophy: "Not speculation or gambling,
but rather the deliberate non-observance of the principles of a commercial
entrepreneur, who is always trying to draw the highest dividend from his
capital, and the creation of a work which in a certain measure is inseparable from the idea of the development and importance of the state."[35]

The hostility of entrepreneurs and businessmen to banks had a considerable intellectual tradition. Adam Smith in the *Wealth of Nations* devoted a great deal of his analysis to a demonstration of the perverse incentives created by joint stock companies. His notable target was the East India Company, and its scandalously overpaid managers and directors. Its increase in fortune, he wrote in words that prefigure the modern critique of capitalism, "only served to furnish their servants with a pretext for greater profusion, and a cover for greater malversation." But Smith saw a useful function for joint stock companies in the unentrepreneurial basic provision of standardized services, in short, for utilities, including standardized banking: "The only trades which it seems possible for a joint stock company to carry on successfully without an exclusive privilege are those of which all the operations are capable of being reduced to what is called a routine, or to such a uniformity of method as admits of little or no variation. Of this kind is, first, the banking trade; secondly, the trade of insurance from fire, and from sea risk and capture in time of war; thirdly, the trade of making and maintaining a navigable cut or canal; and, fourthly, the similar trade of bringing water for the supply of a great city."[36] The economist Joseph Schumpeter followed Smith in seeing the entrepreneur—idealized as the source of innovation and dynamism—as fundamentally distinct from the capitalist. The banker, for Schumpeter, was simply an "ephor," a controller.[37]

Another critique came from conservatives who saw the rise of financial forms of organization as undermining or destroying traditional social values. Marx and Engels were quite prepared to take up this right-wing critique when they too pointed out how capitalism was destroying the family. From the point of view of the conservatives, the debate occurred with respect to the joint stock corporation, where the managerial and bureaucratized form eroded the financial and commercial pressures that had held families together as business units in the early nineteenth century. The historian Otto von Gierke complained that "if the joint stock company ruled alone it would lead to the despotism of capital."[38]

Why was the family so important to the old order? Businesses had been continually trying to lure skilled workers away from their rivals, and industrial espionage had evolved into a major ancien-régime activity. The best defense mechanism against defecting craftsmen was to restrict the most important secrets to sons or even daughters: the sons would be locked into the business, and the daughters would be a useful bargaining chip in the strategic game of dynastic marriage. The widespread institution of joint stock corporations not only radically changed the way Europeans did business, but also revolutionized the way they conducted their personal lives. The modern corporation posed a new threat to family businesses because of the greater efficiencies and economies of scale it could provide. It also gave new opportunities for families to use those efficiencies. On the one hand, it held out the possibility of dispersing ownership more widely, and gave entrepreneurs incentives, in that they could exit from their achievements by selling their stock on the secondary securities markets and thus be immediately rewarded for having taken risks.[39] It was this novel advantage that gave rise to the impression that the path from the individualistic entrepreneur working to develop the market to the atomized ownership of a bureaucratized corporation that would control the market was a one-way street.

On the other hand, the corporation gave families a means of institutionalizing themselves that appeared especially attractive as the passage of generations meant larger and more distant families, with members less immediately connected by personal memory to the founder generation. The rise of the managers also meant the separation of ownership from control: what the progressive economists Adolf Berle and Gardiner Means later referred to as "splitting the atom of property."[40] For the family, it offered a way of replacing trust (which could be problematic, especially as families got larger) with contract. With the contractual relationship, there was no need to enforce trust by restricting the choice of marriage partners.

The French social reformer (and social conservative) Frédéric Le Play linked the popularity of the joint stock corporation to the issue of partible inheritance (dividing an inheritance almost equally among heirs), instituted by the *Code Napoléon,* which he saw not only as a dissolvent of the family but also as a cause of national decline: "In France, joint stock companies are multiplying beyond the actual needs of our day; but rather than seeing this as a regular movement, it should be seen as a tacit reaction of all the interests against the consequences of Forced Partition [partible inheritance]."[41]

The financialization of assets—of which the share was the primary example—was thus interpreted as a way of undermining individual human interactions (for instance, in the family setting) and replacing them with anonymous trades on the bourse as well as non-market controls. That alienation or reification of transactions frequently led to an identification of capitalism with a sinister outside force. Often the search for enemies led to a specific identification of capitalism, notably with Jews. The German academic who introduced the term *capitalism* to the mainstream of economic debate, Werner Sombart, in 1911 wrote what he conceived as an answer to Max Weber's celebrated identification of the Protestant spirit with the ethic of capitalism. Sombart's work *The Jews and Economic Life* argued that the Jews' "lack of a sense of the organic, the natural grown, presents no obstacle since in the capitalist world there is nothing organic, natural, historically developed but only what is mechanical, artificial and created."[42] Sombart's book gave an academic sheen to a popular commingling of anti-capitalism and anti-Semitism, a powerful and destructive ideology that now had its prophet.[43] The association was much older. Some scholars suggest that Karl Marx in his notorious early work *Zur Judenfrage* (On the Jewish question) used *Judentum* as a euphemism for capitalism because he feared censorship if he openly wrote about capitalism.[44]

Effects of the Modern Financial System

Financial intermediation played a major role in generating nineteenth-century economic growth. Consequently, some analysts see it as a central part of the process. The economist Raymond Goldsmith pioneered the modern analysis of the growth of financial intermediation as an impetus to development. He showed a close link between increases in real income and wealth and the extent of what he termed "the financial superstructure." Although he was careful to avoid any clear causal link, he was prepared to claim that the financial superstructure "accelerates economic growth to the extent that it facilitates the movement of funds to the best user, i.e. to the place where the funds will yield the highest social return."[45] Goldsmith calculated a financial intermediation ratio between financial assets and overall national wealth, which he thought would trend toward substantially increasing national wealth in the early phase of economic growth, but would then stabilize as the social or economic benefits from increased financialization petered out.

The economic historian Alexander Gerschenkron provided a modified version of this approach, when he tried to explain how banks could be a factor in mobilizing savings in poorer ("backward") countries, and how what he thought of as the German model of a universal bank collected savings but also engaged in industrial promotion and the reorganization and reordering of business life.[46] The Gerschenkron hypothesis has been a fruitful spur to research on the engagement of banks in business life, and in particular on how banks of that era could overcome coordination problems. Banks brought companies together through patterns of interlocking directorates, and they directly promoted company mergers.[47] On the whole, this sort of description portrays the activities of banks as stabilizing and beneficial, with credit creation playing only a small part in banks' innovations. In debates at the time, the continental European model was held up for emulation in other societies: for instance, in Italy, where the German universal banking model was applied in the early 1890s in the wake of a financial crisis and bank failures, and in the United States after the crisis of 1907, when the National Monetary Commission examined the German universal banks as well as the central banking support mechanism as a potential inspiration for US financial reform.[48] Some German writers tried to make this a comparative point: Adolf Wagner and Franz Oppenheimer, for instance, claimed in the middle of the First World War that Britain had lost "to more powerful German competition" because of "the clumsiness and backwardness of British banking and of the organization of the London stock exchange."[49] Some recent literature also makes the point that banking, and the internationalization of the bankers' viewpoint, were forces that made for peace and were a counterweight to the atavistic nationalism of old European aristocratic and military elites.[50]

By the interwar period, the assessment of the role of the banks had become rather more negative. Central European banks had been weakened by the aftermath of wartime finance and by hyperinflation. In the stabilization of the European economies, the big banks were reconstructed with a small—and as it proved inadequate—capital basis. They attracted large inflows of borrowed money, on the basis of which they expanded their balance sheets. Some of the most colorful adventures occurred in Austria, where the old banks of the prewar monarchy resumed their activities in the great confines of the new Austrian Republic. Camillo Castiglioni, briefly the wealthiest man in Central Europe, used a bank in order to build up a vast industrial complex.[51] Jakob Goldschmidt, the head of the Darmstädter Bank in Germany, was a vociferous and articulate proponent of how bank-driven capitalism was transforming the world and making it better. As he put it: "The private quest for profit is the main driver of economic activity and will lead with the rise of the individual to a higher stage of development of human cooperation." Individuals could be subsumed in a larger organization. The story as he told it focused centrally on the ability to borrow money, on credit. Germany needed to restore confidence in the private economy so that foreign creditors would lend more. In his view, the international economy was a tool that Germans could use to enrich themselves, since "we are dependent on the world's credit."[52]

The house of cards that was built around the banks created by Castiglioni and Goldschmidt collapsed, and that financial collapse was instrumental in turning a cyclical downturn into the Great Depression. The 1931 crisis was an obvious accident waiting to happen. It stemmed from a fundamental fragility of the institutions of banking, especially when faced with a deflationary spiral. Its immediate consequences were much more severe than the US stock market crash of 1929. A series of contagious banking and currency crises brought down one central European country after another. The chronology begins with the apparently unique case of the Austrian Creditanstalt, which collapsed on May 11, 1931. The panic then spread to Hungary, and more significantly to Germany, where the collapse of the Darmstädter Bank on July 13, 1931, in turn precipitated a crisis in Great Britain and forced Britain off the gold standard on September 21, 1931. Speculation turned against the United States, had a desperately destructive effect on US banking, and only stopped in April 1933 when, under the new regime of Franklin Roosevelt, the United States also left the gold standard. In a sad and prolonged aftermath of the Depression, the remaining gold standard countries, notably Belgium, the Netherlands, and Switzerland, continued to be buffeted by financial panic and the threat of bank failures until in September 1936 the so-called Gold Bloc finally disintegrated.

It was during the interwar period, in the aftermath of the monetary disorders brought about by the First World War, that credit creation was presented as not only the driver of the system, but also as a central source of the disorder that had undermined and destroyed markets. It should not be surprising that the most influential critiques of the world built on credit came from Austria. Friedrich Hayek in the early 1930s preached about the perils of credit creation: "the only practical maxim to be derived from our considerations is probably the negative one that the simple fact of an increase of production and trade forms no justification for an expansion of credit, and that—save in an acute crisis—bankers need not be afraid to harm production by overcaution."[53]

Hayek was not alone, and there are parallel efforts to describe the problem created when some institutional mechanism drives the market rate of interest below the natural rate (the terminology of a natural rate, in which investment corresponded to saving, was taken by both Hayek and Keynes from the Swedish economist Knut Wicksell). The consequence of an artificially depressed market rate is to promote overinvestment in the basic and investment goods industries, which generates chronic overcapacity and leads to deflation. These efforts resemble the interpretations of Marxist economists, who also at the time focused on the way in which investment goods capacity drove economic cycles. An analogous concern appears prominently in John Maynard Keynes's 1930 work *A Treatise on Money,* where the analysis is driven by a concern with how credit cycles drove large fluctuations in prices and output. There was in his view an irrational and speculative element: "The pace at which a circle of financiers, speculators and investors hand round one to another particular pieces of wealth, or titles to such, which they are neither producing nor consuming but merely exchanging, bears no relation to the rate of current production. The volume of such transactions is subject to very wide and incalculable fluctuations, easily double at one time what it is at another, depending on such factors as the state of speculative sentiment; and, whilst it is possibly stimulated by the activity and depressed by the inactivity of production, its fluctuations are quite different in degree from those of production."[54] Booms got out of hand because of overly lax monetary policy: "Booms, I suspect, are almost always due to tardy or inadequate action."[55] Keynes consequently in this work sees the banker as not only a source of instability but also—as his biographer Robert Skidelsky felicitously puts it—an "economic therapist."[56]

Neither Keynes's *Treatise* nor Hayek's *Prices and Production* have found great acclaim among economists. Both focus on how what are apparently market mechanisms in the credit-creation process end up destroying the capacity of markets to operate effectively and efficiently. Both works have the reputation of being confusing and confused. Keynes himself wrote in the preface that he felt "like someone who has been forcing their way through a confused jungle." In his later and more influential *General Theory of Employment Interest and Money* (1936), it is not the banker or the central banker acting on credit who is glorified as the therapist; instead the state acting on aggregate demand provides the better therapy.

The 1930s were characterized by deleveraging, deglobalization, and an increasing renationalization of finance. States became more interventionist, and financial institutions focused increasingly on the uncomplicated business of recycling depositors' funds into state securities. The setbacks to financialization and globalization were only very slowly themselves reversed.

At the end of the twentieth century, financial activity exploded. In a new formulation of Goldsmith's approach, the economists Òscar Jordà, Moritz Schularick, and Alan Taylor showed how bank assets relative to GDP rose at a much faster rate than did bank loans relative to GDP (see Figure 1), indicating that the social usefulness of banks (credit) was not keeping up with the banks' ability to grow their own balance sheets.

The greater relative size of financial transactions and new financial instruments, coupled with an ability of large banks to tap into one national source of funds and pass them on to users of capital elsewhere, contributed to what was seen in the 2000s as a "frictionless" global financial system. Cross-border transactions soared, with capital flows rising from 4 percent of world GDP in 1980, to 5 percent in 1990, 13 percent in 2000, and 20 percent by 2007 (the flows plunged abruptly in the Global Financial Crisis, and though they recovered were only 6 percent of GDP in 2012).[57] Large financial institutions became central mediators of international capital movements because in practice they alone could provide "markets" for their customers—pension and trust fund managers—who required counter-parties for exchanging complex financial products for which there was no obvious or natural market. The effect of regulation was to drive big institutions' financial activity off their balance sheets and into off-balance-sheet conduits or investment vehicles that they controlled. In practice, a relatively small number of institutions (termed after 2008 SIFIs,

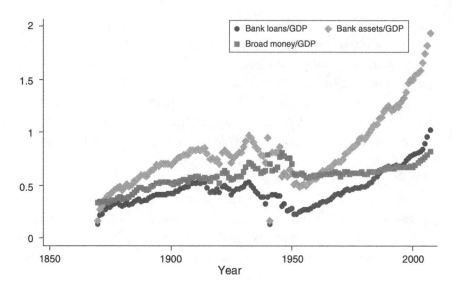

Figure 1. Global financial activities in relation to world gross domestic product (GDP). *Source:* Moritz Schularick and Alan M. Taylor, "Credit Booms Gone Bust: Monetary Policy, Leverage Cycles, and Financial Crises, 1870–2008," *American Economic Review* 102, no. 2 (2012): 1035, Copyright American Economic Association; reproduced with permission of the American Economic Review.

or systemically important financial intermediaries) became central in market-making. It later emerged that some of the critical signals on which the market depended—notably the widely used interest rate LIBOR, or London inter-bank offered rate—had been set not by a normal market process, but rather by collusion among a handful of key players.

The dominance of banks became celebrated in popular writing: a landmark is Tom Wolfe's novel of 1987, *The Bonfire of the Vanities,* which popularized the phrase "masters of the universe." In the same year, Oliver Stone's film *Wall Street* had as its anti-hero a financier Gordon Gekko, who rapidly became a cultural icon. Gekko, played by Michael Douglas, was best remembered for his speech: "I am greedy. But most people misunderstand greed. Greed is a powerful driving force. Throughout history, mankind's greatest achievements were driven by men that wanted to better their positions. Driven by greed. Greed, for lack of a better word, is good."[58]

As the financial sector expanded, academics became increasingly interested in the phenomenon of credit. Initially Hyman Minsky, who gave a deeply historically rooted but rather under-mathematized picture of the key role of financial panics, was relatively alone in his views. James Tobin in 1989 described him as "the most sophisticated, analytical, and persuasive of those contemporary economists who believe that leverage is the Achilles heel of capitalism."[59] By that time, the analysis of credit was entering the mainstream, chiefly as a result of articles by Ben Bernanke and a number of co-authors, including Alan Blinder and Mark Gertler, which developed the idea that financial institutions transmitted monetary policy through the "credit channel," in which a "financial accelerator" operated.[60] The result was sometimes called "creditism" by Bernanke's critics.[61] The idea was influential in academic circles, but also as a policy approach, especially since Blinder was vice chair of the Federal Reserve Board from 1994 to 1996 and Bernanke, after being appointed a governor of the Fed in 2002, was in 2006 appointed chair under President George W. Bush, a tenure he continued under President Barack Obama. The major implication of this strand of the literature was that central banks could and should consider the credit channel in designing a monetary policy that would counter fragilities produced by the banking system and by the pro-cyclical effect of collateral policy.

The view that credit bubbles and asset price inflation might be a source of instability was restricted to a few academic analysts. Some noted that major crises had been preceded by periods of unusually rapid credit growth. The Bank for International Settlements, the central bankers' central bank, warned of the contemporary implications of credit booms. Claudio Borio and others revived elements of the Hayekian analysis of credit cycles.[62]

There was also some criticism of the joint stock company as a source of moral hazard. In 2009 the German economist Hans-Werner Sinn identified the principle of limited liability as the crucial cause of distorted incentives in financial institutions, and reflected on the consequences of formerly private banks going public, with the giant Goldman Sachs taking this step in 1999.[63] By the 2000s, and especially after the outbreak of the 2007–2008 Global Financial Crisis, a reversal had started, with some influential companies (such as Dell and Heinz) making the decision to go private. Financialization had created wrong or misleading signals, and to that extent it frustrated and obstructed the process of the allocation of resources for future collective benefit and dynamic growth. After the crisis, a broad and generalized anti-capitalism flourished.

The longer-term outcome of the Global Financial Crisis is likely to be a world in which there is more normal banking, less financial innovation, lower profitability for financial institutions, and greatly increased uncertainty. A new variety of capitalism is emerging: after a succession of early modern commercial or mercantile capitalism, nineteenth-century industrial capitalism, turn-of-the-century finance capitalism, mid-twentieth-century managed capitalism, and then turn of the millennium hyper-finance capitalism, my guess is that we will see a shift to information capitalism. Physical goods will be moved less frequently, and in lower volumes. Instead, ideas, processes, services—immaterial goods—will be traded so as to reallocate production more locally (a theme I take up later). This chronology of different types of capitalism accords a critical role to finance capitalism, with finance capitalism flaring up, exploding, and then disappearing in a repeated cycle. Thus chronology and prediction depend on a positivist typology of capitalism (what is), but we also might think about the development in terms of the normative approaches (what could or should be). Might the information economy promote a broader range of human hopes and aspirations, and contribute to their fulfillment, better than finance capitalism has done?

2

Socialism

Just as anti-capitalism is a powerful driver of today's politics, with accusations that capitalism is the origin of inequality and conflict and so should be controlled, anti-socialism features prominently in the political clash. At the Republican National Convention in 2020, Donald Trump, as he accepted the nomination to run for reelection, blasted his rival as a "Trojan horse for socialism" who would not have "the strength to stand up to wild-eyed Marxists."[1] What socialism was supposed to be was left completely undefined.

Planned utopias have long excited the human imagination. Plato, Saint Francis, Thomas More, and Tommaso Campanella imagined various utopias in conceiving of a better path for humankind. But modern socialism is unambiguously a product of modern capitalism. The previous visions of collectivism frequently depended on a spiritual, even a mystic, connection that would draw people together. Socialism, by contrast, arose out of a concatenation of two circumstances: the development of large-scale factory production, which was an economic advance; and a world that seemed increasingly interconnected, which was a cultural development. It was Karl Marx's peculiar genius that he could tie these two together in an elegant but complex knot, which he could explain by claiming with some plausibility that economic changes (such as production methods or communications technologies) might drive cultural development. He then added the political fire provided by France's revolutionary tradition.

The new doctrine also had an inherently universalist message: everything that created socialism crossed national political boundaries. This was a world of mobility in which ideas were traveling. Capitalism was creating an international economy, with an international division of labor. The culture was full of borrowings and learnings. And the French revolutionary tradition was aggressively international. But at the same time, the problem of how socialism could be implemented looked more and more like one that belonged to particular, territorially delimited, political societies—that is, taking over the means of production could only happen via a specific political framework of control. Later, an alternative tradition developed, *social democracy*, that emphasized much less the practical control of industry, and more the principle of redistribution through a tax and welfare system. And that redistribution would always be almost entirely national, not international. The story of implementing socialism thus always stood in some tension with the universalist or cosmopolitan inspiration.

Practical socialism depends on describing clearly and concretely how—short of some religious inspiration—large numbers of people can be organized collectively. At the beginning of the 1800s, the models for big collective organizations were armies, or—even more abhorrently—slave plantations in warm climates. Neither looked like an appealing template for a utopian vision. But over the course of the nineteenth century, as workshops became larger and were replaced by factories, the factory looked like a model that could be operated in a different way. The old models were wrong, and something needed to be found to replace them. Joseph Livesey, the son of a mill owner, wrote of the early workers of the Industrial Revolution: "They were apprenticed to a system to which nothing but West Indian slavery can bear any analogy."[2] There was surely a way to organize a better and more human future.

A Way to Organize Labor

The most prominent early socialists were thus intimately concerned with industrial organization, and it is only a superficial paradox that they were also business leaders. Robert Owen, a successful textile entrepreneur in New Lanark, Scotland, is perhaps the most interesting. His efforts at improving the living conditions of the mill workers were also an attempt to raise efficiency and productivity through cooperative effort. He thought what he had done in a microcosm at the cotton mill, by encouraging rationality, enlightenment, thrift, and provision for old age, could also be done on a national scale, and would make for a stronger economy and polity: "The efficient strength of a state governed by laws founded on an accurate knowledge of human nature, in which the whole population are well trained, will greatly exceed one of equal extent of numbers, in which a large part of the population are improperly trained, and governed by laws founded in ignorance."[3]

Henri de Saint-Simon, an Enlightenment French aristocrat who participated in the French Revolution and later was imprisoned in the lunatic asylum of Charenton, was a very unusual figure in the early history of socialism. He became a source of inspiration to Marx and Engels, to twentieth-century strategists of national development, as well as to followers of French Bonapartism in the nineteenth century and Gaullism in the twentieth. He initially wanted to establish a doctrine of *industrialism*, in which there would be an administration of objects rather than a government of people. He was one of the first to use the word *proletarian*. And he saw a future in which bankers, intellectuals, and artists would overthrow an outdated theological and feudal system. He wanted the banks to support industry, writing: "The most productive and active of stimulants pushes the heads of the first Paris banks to establish the industrial flag."[4] Some of his followers indeed established banks dedicated to large-scale industrialization.[5] He was as much of a capitalist as he was a theoretician of socialism.

The development of socialism was also decisively shaped by its origins in what was in some ways a pre-industrial but international political revolution, in 1848–1849. There were factory workers involved in that revolution, but they were a small minority.

The revolutions of 1848 looked at their outset as if they were an extension of an international movement against despotism rather than capitalism. In the years after the end of the Napoleonic wars and the Congress of Vienna, "Young" movements had arisen in every country as a challenge to autocracy. Young Italy, Young England, and Young Germany had viewed each other as sympathetic siblings and united in solidarity behind heavily oppressed nations: Greece in the 1820s or Poland after the revolution of

1830. Goethe in his late old age started to develop a theory of *Weltlitera-tur* (world literature), and there was a trend toward cultural globalization. The failure of 1848–1849 brought an end to the dream of the solidarity of nations. The revolutions were undone in part because of the lack of support from other national groupings: the Czechs and the Poles, for instance, were unenthusiastic about supporting Germans in the newly created and short-lived Frankfurt assembly. The Croats in particular provided the armies that allowed the Habsburg dynasty to suppress Czech, German, Italian, and Hungarian national movements. The young German Friedrich Engels, another businessman, wrote of how the southern Slavs constituted "this residual fragment, which is . . . extremely confused, sees its salvation only in a reversal of the whole European movement, which in its view ought to go not from west to east, but from east to west, and that for it the instrument of liberation and the bond of unity is the Russian knout—that is the most natural thing in the world." And he prophesied, in a bloodcurdling way, that "the next world war will result in the disappearance from the face of the earth not only of reactionary classes and dynasties, but also of entire reactionary peoples. And that too is a step forward."[6]

In the aftermath of 1848, socialists were torn between the idea of international solidarity and the practical aspects of enacting political solutions where—more and more—the national setting mattered. It was a difficult balancing exercise. Socialists who strayed too close to nationalism and the nation-state looked as if they were compromising themselves by associating with the class enemy. Ferdinand Lassalle, who built up one of the movements that eventually merged into the German Socialist Party, was one who consistently placed much more emphasis on the national than did the internationally oriented Karl Marx. A highly romantic figure, Lassalle would perish prematurely in a characteristically upper-class and distinctly non-proletarian ritual, the duel, after challenging the fiancé of a young girl with whom he wanted to elope. But before his death, he held fast to a romantic vision of the state, and what it might achieve, as well as a pragmatic sense that the Prussian minister-president Otto von Bismarck was open to bold experiments in social and political organization. Lassalle thought that the existing state—particularly if it supported a project of national consolidation—could implement reformist legislation. He talked to Bismarck and may well have been responsible for persuading him to introduce a universal male suffrage in order to obtain support for the wars of unification.[7] Yet the idea that the transnational working class could defeat and overthrow governments, and stop capitalist or imperialist wars, looked increasingly implausible as states were consolidated and strengthened; as they developed their formidable bureaucracies, police systems, and armies; and as they started to educate populations and form a new national consciousness.

Socialist Internationalism

Karl Marx had from an early point in his intellectual development seen capitalism and socialism as international developments. His vision of economic development provides a striking contrast with his contemporary Friedrich List, who had seen capitalism as preeminently a national development. The two thinkers represent the alternative poles in a debate that remains current to this day.[8] Marx's *The German Ideology,* written in 1845–1846, describes how "nationality is already dead."[9] In 1846, attacking the French socialist anarchist Pierre-Joseph Proudhon, he asked rhetorically, "Is the whole inner organization of nations with all their international relations anything other than the expression of a particular division of labor? And must not these change when the division of labor changes?"[10]

Capitalism was creating a vision of the world as a general system. In *A Contribution to the Critique of Political Economy* (1859), Marx wrote: "Just as money develops into world-money so the commodity owner develops into a cosmopolitan. The cosmopolitan relation of men is originally only a relation of commodity owners."[11] The *Communist Manifesto* explained how "Modern industry has established the world market." "The need of a constantly expanding market for its products chases the bourgeoisie over the entire surface of the globe. It must nestle everywhere, settle everywhere, establish connections everywhere. The bourgeoisie has through its exploitation of the world market given a cosmopolitan character to production and consumption in every country. To the great chagrin of reactionists, it has drawn from under the feet of industry the national ground on which it stood."[12]

The debates of the late nineteenth and early twentieth centuries focused on what socialism should do in concrete political situations—make compromises with other parties in order to change politics and eventually enter politics, or wait for the revolution. The largest European socialist movement, the German SPD, officially took up a Marxian party program in 1891, but its platform became more strained as it grew larger and more influential. It presented itself in a mystifying way as a revolutionary but not a revolution-making party. In practice, its members and supporters were deeply rooted in ordinary life. A majority of members were not even classical industrial workers.[13]

In Marx's famous critique of the SPD's founding program of 1875, the *Critique of the Gotha Program,* Marx explained his belief that the existence of a national working class was simply a transitional feature of the shift from capitalism to socialism. He believed that the party should have distanced itself more emphatically from the nationalism of Lassalle, whose party was being merged into the new SPD. "Lassalle, in opposition to the Communist Manifesto and to all earlier socialism, conceived the workers' movement from the narrowest national standpoint," Marx argued. That was an absurdity: "It is altogether self-evident that, to be able to fight at all, the working class must organize itself at home as a class and that its own country is the immediate arena of its struggle—insofar as its class struggle is national, not in substance, but, as the Communist Manifesto says, 'in form.' But the 'framework of the present-day national state,' for instance, the German Empire, is itself, in its turn, economically 'within the framework' of the world market, politically 'within the framework' of the system of states." The new movement should embrace with enthusiasm the conservatives' accusation of being "rascals without a fatherland" (*vaterlandslose Gesellen*). As Marx described it, "Bismarck's *Norddeutsche* [newspaper] was absolutely right when it announced, to the satisfaction of its master, that the German Workers' party had sworn off internationalism in the new program."[14]

The *Critique* is one of only a few places where Marx addresses the question of the transition to socialism. "In a higher phase of communist society, after the enslaving subordination of the individual to the division of labor, and therewith also the antithesis between mental and physical labor, has vanished; after labor has become not only a means of life but life's prime want; after the productive forces have also increased with the all-around development of the individual, and all the springs of co-operative wealth flow more abundantly—only then can the narrow horizon of bourgeois right be crossed in its entirety and society inscribe on its banners: From each according to his ability, to each according to his needs!"[15] But the blueprint is famously vague: how should cooperative wealth actually be organized?

Some German socialists in particular thought of an increasingly organized structure of business—large firms, linked to each other through cartels and trusts, and often controlled by banks—that they believed could solve the transition problem. The most striking of these accounts came from Rudolf Hilferding, who developed in *Finanzkapital* a theory of increasing organization. Capitalism was becoming not only more concentrated but also more stable. That meant that the final overthrow would come from a political collapse, not from an economic crisis or crises (which Hilferding thought were becoming milder). The scene of action thus needed to be transplanted to the political arena. By the 1920s, when he had become the SPD's key economic thinker (and on two occasions minister of finance), he concluded that "organized capitalism" could be easily controlled by a political process.[16] He was one of—if not *the*—most important intermediaries between the Marxist tradition of thinking about the circumstances of the transition from capitalism to socialism and the social democratic practice of managing a redistributive state.

Socialists had always struggled to come to terms with national political communities. That should not really be surprising, since socialism's theories were evolved essentially before the modern nation-state in its mid-nineteenth-century form (with Germany, Italy, and Japan as the models of new national politics). These new nation-states were, moreover, inherently aggressive and revisionist: channeling internal tensions into foreign policy and military endeavors helped defuse the potential for social protest.

By the early twentieth century, the question of pacifism—resistance to war and militarism—was deeply polarizing the socialist movement. The largest European movement, the German SPD, was hopelessly divided. By 1907, the party's revered leader, the journalist August Bebel, used the opportunity of a parliamentary debate on the military budget to declare that the party supported a militia principle for national defense. A young socialist deputy, Gustav Noske, explained, too, that the party was conditioned by "our acceptance of the principle of nationality," and that it "was our damned duty and obligation . . . to ensure that the German people is not pushed against the wall by any other people."[17] That speech provoked a ferocious backlash from the party's left wing. By the outbreak of war in 1914, the vast majority of SPD deputies, as well as (probably) party members and voters, supported the German war effort, not least because the government could present it as a progressive mobilization against a backward tsarist autocracy, against the knout. Socialists were rapidly drawn into the management of the war effort, and became an integral part of the national community.

Socialists thus had to reimagine themselves realistically in the national setting, and shed their intoxicating dreams of international transformation. They had two possible strategies: one had to do with managing production; the other was about redistributing resources. As those strategies were put into practice during the twentieth century, they were inevitably analyzed and compared—as national solutions.

A Planned Alternative

The First World War gave a definitive answer to what a socialist order could be, both in character and in practical terms. During this era, socialists were drawn to government. The administration first of efforts to acquire raw materials, and then more generally to engage in industrial production and impose rationing, all could be described as "war socialism." That experiment, which was highly successful in increasing armaments production extraordinarily quickly, convinced Lenin that socialism really was possible. But the response to military demand was a relatively simple kind of production, in which planners could decide which weapon or product was most likely to be effective, and then divert resources to its production (and away from non-necessary activities).

By the end of the First World War, after the collapse of the German Empire, a revolutionary upheaval, and a precarious transition to democracy, Walther Rathenau (the heir to a vast industrial empire and the chief wartime planner), along with his chief collaborator Wichard von Moellendorff, started to build a new society. Moellendorff explained, "Up to now the principle ruled in Germany: free in all economic affairs, bound down in all thinking; the purpose of a communal economy (*Gemeinwirtschaft*) is to reverse that."[18] He developed a worldview built on national self-sufficiency and "autarkic self-determination."[19] In Germany that course was soon undone, not least because opponents of extensive nationalization made the argument that such an approach would make it easy for the western Allies to seize German state property in order to extract reparations. Some still believed that Germany could benefit from some sort of new economic order, and might be able to demonstrate "intellectual leadership."[20] But in the Soviet Union, the idea of planning remained an inspiration.

Planned production looked initially less like a suitable way of managing complex demands in peacetime. Even in the Soviet Union, production was initially put back in the hands of artisans and small business owners with the New Economic Policy (NEP) of the 1920s. In the uncertain political system, there was little new investment, and theorists began to argue for a state-led surge in investment. In practice, the end of NEP, and the major collectivization and industrialization drive of the late 1920s and early 1930s, re-created the social psychology of war, this time a war identified as being against the figure of the rich peasant, or rural entrepreneur, the kulak.

The plan departed more and more from rationality as it was taken over by politics and by the ideology of conflict. Consumers complained that they had money but could not buy anything. Vladimir Sorokin's novel *The Queue* gave a devastating account of the loss of time entailed by the most characteristic method of socialist allocation.[21] The most authoritative guide to Stalinist planning, the monumental work of Eugene Zaleski, concluded that "the existence of such a central national plan, coherent and perfect, to be subdivided and implemented at all levels, is only a *myth*."[22] In a similar vein, the Polish socialist economist Oskar Lange concluded that "planning becomes fictitious. What actually is observed is an elemental development."[23] That was Stalin's view also. In 1921, he had written in a letter to Lenin how professors lacked "healthy skepticism," and urged Lenin to put planning in the hands of "men of live politics, ready to act on the principle of 'report fulfillment.' "[24] But in all that struggle, and while proclaiming the virtues of "socialism in one country" as the rest of the world failed to have a proletarian revolution, Stalin saw the importance of the

Soviet experiment as a way of galvanizing a worldwide movement. Socialism still had its strongly internationalist element. Stalin even claimed that "the successes of the five-year plan are mobilising the revolutionary forces of the working class of all countries against capitalism—*such is the indisputable fact.*"[25]

In the 1930s, a theoretical debate was undertaken with the Polish economist and diplomat Oskar Lange on the one side and the Austrian economist and political philosopher Friedrich Hayek on the other. Lange envisaged a world in which a mathematical model could simulate the outcome of market responses to prices. He even stated a surprising rehabilitation of Marxian economics. He started by observing, "This superiority of Marxian economics seems strange, indeed, in view of the fact that it works with concepts which are long since outdated and which ignore the whole development of economic theory since the time of Ricardo."[26] Lange turned the Hilferding argument on its head: in his view, the cartelized and trustified oligopolistic system of capitalism did a poor job of transmitting the coordinating signals that an economy needed to operate. Thus "the trial and error procedure would, or at least could, work much better in a socialist economy than it does in a competitive market. For the Central Planning Board has a much wider knowledge of what is going on in the whole economic system than any private entrepreneur can ever have, and, consequently, may be able to reach the right equilibrium prices by a much shorter series of successive trials than a competitive market actually does."[27]

Hayek's responses emphasized the sheer quantity and complexity of information that would continually need to be processed and calculated in order to make a planned mathematical system respond in a way analogous to a market operation: "Almost every change of any single price would make changes of hundreds of other prices necessary and most of these other changes would by no means be proportional but would be affected by the different degrees of elasticity of demand, by the possibilities of substitution and other changes in the method of production."[28]

Lange's explanations of the problems of practical socialism were telling. The problems were obvious, but in his eyes they were simply technical, resulting from an inadequate and improvised bureaucratic structure. There was not sufficient expertise or *technocracy*. He complained that "the real danger of socialism is that of a bureaucratization of economic life, and not the impossibility of coping with the problem of allocation of resources."[29] In the Second World War, however, the mobilization of politics and society for planning looked as if it was creating a new reality.

Given expertise, the problems were surmountable. The Indian nationalist leader and prime minister Jawaharlal Nehru saw a convergence in the promise of scientific expertise: "Planning and development have become a sort of mathematical problem which may be worked out scientifically. . . . It is extraordinary how both Soviet and American experts agree on this. If a Russian planner comes here, studies our projects and advises us, it is really extraordinary how his conclusions are in agreement with those of, say, an American expert. . . . The moment the scientist or technologist comes to the scene, be he Russian or American, the conclusions are the same for the simple reason that planning and development today are almost a matter of mathematics."[30]

Each development of computing power correspondingly drove a new iteration of the socialist calculation debate.[31] By the 1960s, Lange was observing: "Were I to rewrite my essay ['On the Economic Theory of Socialism'] today my task would be much simpler. My answer to Hayek and [Hayek's early mentor Lionel] Robbins would be: so what's the trouble? Let us put the simultaneous equations on an electronic computer and we shall obtain the solution in less than a second. The market process with its cumbersome tâtonnements [trials and errors] appears old-fashioned. Indeed, it may be considered as a computing device of the pre-electronic age."[32] Gordon Moore's law of the doubling of computing power every two years, first formulated in 1965, seemed to suggest a new path to the realization of socialism.

The discussion was swept away in 1989, but only temporarily. Advances in information technology meant that an enormous amount of decentralized data could be centrally evaluated and subjected to some overarching planning criteria. That was the goal of China's social credit system, announced in 2014 with the goal of establishing a "high-trust society" where individuals and organizations would follow the law because of a complex system of rewards and punishments. It would be a system that no longer required the bureaucratism and arbitrariness that Lange deplored—it could be entirely internally consistent.

The Social Democratic Route

Social democracy also worked in a national setting, to establish a democratic path to the control of the means of production. The main emphasis was not on the control or planning of production, but rather on the redistribution of resources through taxation. The mechanism that had originally constituted the core of the military state—the financing of armies—was now dedicated to the preservation of domestic social stability. Military analogies were sometimes explicitly invoked, as in Lyndon Johnson's War on Poverty. States, which once had had a primarily military purpose, now spent more on transfer payments: by the middle of the 1980s, Sweden was spending one-third of its GNP on social expenditures.[33]

Sweden became a model for how social democracy would work in the interwar years, and after 1945 the Social Democratic Party maintained a decade-long hold on power. It relied on building a movement that could appeal to farmers and white-collar workers as well as the traditional working class, which on its own would never have been large enough to provide the basis for political majorities. Above all, the party generated a vision of the nation as an extended home, or people's home (*folkhemmet*). Hjalmar Branting, a journalist usually viewed as "the father of Swedish socialism," and who was prime minister from 1920 to 1925, explained in his speech as he received the Nobel Peace Prize in 1921: "The sort of internationalism which rejects the sovereignty of a nation within its own borders and which aims ultimately at its complete obliteration in favor of a cosmopolitan unity, has never been other than a caricature of the true international spirit."[34] He quoted the great French socialist leader Jean Jaurès: "When the workers curse their native country, they are, in reality, cursing the social maladjustments which plague it, and this apparent condemnation is only an expression of the yearning for the new nation." Branting concluded: "It is precisely this deeply rooted feeling for the importance of the nation that later becomes the basis and starting point for true internationalism, for a humanity built not of stateless atoms but of sovereign nations in a free union."

National sentiment alone was not enough. The movement promised a transformation, with a preventive social policy that would remove the underlying causes of social problems. The great theorists of this philosophy of a transformative social policy came from the husband-and-wife team of Gunnar and Alva Myrdal, most strikingly in their book on "the population crisis" in 1934. (Perhaps characteristically, he—but not she—received the Nobel Prize for Economics, in 1974, the same year as Friedrich Hayek, whose theories he deplored.) The goal was "a real quantitative increase in the living and development prospects of the rising generation," with "at the same time, a shifting of the costs and responsibilities from the individual family providers to the whole nation."[35]

The Swedish model did not involve large-scale state ownership. Gustav Möller, the Swedish politician generally recognized as the father of the welfare state, saw a socialist society as one where "complete democracy rules and economic exploitation does not exist." But he was extremely skeptical of state ownership or control of business: "There is much truth in our opponents' observation that state management is not as economically advantageous as private management. That is above all because of the bureaucratization within state enterprises."[36] The social democratic impulse was to ameliorate, not catastrophize. Anthony Crosland, the major intellect behind the British Labour Party's attempt to reinvent itself as a social democracy in the second half of the twentieth century, believed that Britain was no longer capitalist. He wrote that "no one would argue that in the contemporary Welfare State the dominant ideology was one of self-help or aggressive individualism." Labor militancy and class conflict were declining. As Crosland put it, quoting the great nineteenth-century prophet Engels, "the masses have got damned lethargic after such prosperity." He then added his own interpretation: "But, unlike him, not everybody would consider this a bad thing."[37]

The improving impulse produced a dilemma, most clearly set out in the midst of the conflictual politics of the Weimar Republic in Germany. Fritz Tarnow, a parliamentarian and trade union organizer (in the woodworkers' union), was a major proponent of the idea of economic democracy in the 1920s; he also advocated a purchasing power theory that might lead to an economic rebalancing. His keynote address at the June 1931 SPD party congress, "Capitalist Economic Anarchy and the Working Class," was delivered near the depth of the Great Depression. He had a striking metaphor: "We are standing at the sickbed of capitalism not only as diagnosticians, but—how should I put it—as a doctor who wants to heal? Or as a cheerful heir, who cannot wait to inherit and would like to help on the process a little? . . . This double role as doctor and heir is a damned difficult part." The communist visual artist and propagandist John Heart-field responded with a brilliant photomontage of a tiger: "Of course we will break the teeth of the tiger of capitalism, but only after we have fed him back to health."[38]

Could that concept be widened beyond the confines of the nation? The discussion of the need to preserve international peace might suggest such an impulse. The theoretician Rudolf Breitscheid placed in the 1925 Heidelberg Program a reference to European economic unity, "a unity which has become necessary for economic reasons, and is in favor of the foundation of the United States of Europe, which would bring about the solidarity of the interests of the people of the world."[39] But an emotional identification with a particular territory was always pointing in a different direction.

After the Second World War, the SPD was reconstituted on Lassallian principles by the heroic figure of Kurt Schumacher. He had suffered under the Nazis, and his body bore the obvious imprint of barbaric torture. He had an impressive claim to represent the real or true country. "For the SPD there is no fictitious fatherland of labor. For us Social Democrats there is the German homeland which we wish to hold together as a governmental, national and economic whole."[40] Other socialist parties developed in the same direction. The British philosopher Alasdair MacIntyre wrote scathingly about how "the British Left is unhappy about foreigners, partly because they theorise."[41]

Some aspects of the social democratic model were undermined by globalization in the late twentieth century. High rates of corporate tax might drive businesses away, so small social democracies in particular reduced their rates of corporate taxation while maintaining very high levels of personal tax. If they were quite small, like Ireland, they could even gamble on a different and more radical model, in which low rates of taxation overall would stimulate economic activity in general, as well as encourage large multinational corporations to headquarter there.

There is a broader reason that social democracy seemed to lose its legitimacy. Social democracy in its heyday depended on experts, and especially on social scientific knowledge. In a sense that development was the logical outcome of Marx's insistence on the scientific character of socialism; it was a true doctrine because it reflected the best scientific data and interpretation. The foremost analyst of the north European model, Francis Sejersted, concluded his analysis of the Scandinavian vision: "The social scientists, with economists in the lead, colonized politics, and rational discourse predominated. But nothing lasts forever."[42] In other countries, there had been a similar trajectory. In the United Kingdom, for instance, in the decades following the Second World War, something approaching a consensus on social and economic issues had developed between the two major parties: a reformism, based on the principles of economic management as set out by Keynes. It was termed *Butskellism* after the Labour leader Hugh Gaitskell and the leading Conservative social thinker R. A. ("Rab") Butler. Crosland argued that socialism was less about planning than about raising general living standards. Planning had "a lower priority than a decade ago," while "higher personal consumption must form part of any statement of the socialist goal on fundamental egalitarian grounds." The mindset of the approach is neatly encapsulated in the economist Roy Harrod's rather hagiographical biography of Keynes: "Happy is the land where a wise man could wield power, simply because he is wise, although he has no support from any political group or from any financial or trade-union interest."[43]

The Dilemmas of Socialism

Socialism and capitalism are conjoined twins, fated to always pull in different directions, but also hopelessly dependent on each other. Socialism had to believe in the eradication of capitalism, but if that ever happened, socialism would lose its raison d'être, becoming simply a version of technocratic management. If socialists emphasized the revolutionary alternative, and a transformation of property relations, their claim would fade if capitalism disappeared, but also if capitalism were too resilient and too adaptive. If socialists emphasized the social democratic mode, however, with its convergence and management of the economy through fiscal redistribution, reliance on market operations would mean that this mode would somewhat resemble capitalism.

It is not surprising that the major twentieth-century theoreticians of the economics of socialism had deeply tragic personal lives. They were buffeted not only by events, but also by ideas. Hilferding spent the last years of his life fleeing from the Nazis. At the end, sitting in the public library of Arles in Provence, he started to work on a long essay titled "The Historic Problem," calling for a revival of religious and ethical thought. It began with an explicit rejection of the Marxist economic determinism that he had previously espoused: "Force determines the outcome. The relationship is not that economics determines the content, aim, and result of force; the outcome of the decision made through force for its part determines economics."[44] After his arrest by the authorities of Vichy France in February 1941, he was handed over to the Germans and died in a Gestapo prison cell in Paris.

Eugene Varga had been an economic adviser to Stalin, and wrote the economic reports for the congresses of the Comintern between 1921 and 1935. He was the major theoretician of the relationship between socialist (or Soviet) and capitalist (or western) economics. In 1946 he published *The Economic Transformation of Capitalism at the End of the Second World War*, in which he argued that the capitalist system was more inherently stable than had been hitherto believed. This led to the closure of the institute that he headed. On April 27, 1949, Varga, following a polemic that lasted for nearly three years, finally recanted. In confessing his mistakes, he wrote that they "form an entire chain of mistakes of a reformist trend which naturally also means mistakes of a cosmopolitan trend because they beautify capitalism." He linked errors that he had committed more than three years before the most recent controversy to a purge of "homeless cosmopolitans." And with a platitudinous "better late than never," he promised to write a new book, correcting the "falsehood." This recantation followed by a little more than a month his letter to the editors of *Pravda* on March 15, 1949, in which he attacked the "organs of black reaction" for accusing him of being "a man of Western orientation" and "denying the possibility of a crisis of overproduction."[45] He then moved to Hungary, where he supported the hardline Stalinist regime of Mátyás Rákosi. After the 1956 revolution and the overthrow of Rákosi, he again looked like a fish out of water because his predictions of the imminent end of capitalism clashed with the Hungarian János Kádár's concept of a reformist socialism.

Hilferding and Varga were victims of the tragic conflict, fought out differently in different national contexts, between socialist theories of a planned society and the politics of radicalized nationalism and national specificity: a politics that even in post-1945 central Europe penetrated deeply into the operationalization of socialism. The leading figures who tried in the late twentieth century to translate a new socialism into practice are also tragic, though in an entirely different way. In each of the four large western European countries, the fortune of socialism was linked to the trajectory of a fallible leader.

Tony Blair in the United Kingdom tried to remake a "New Labour" that would embrace large elements of a market-oriented vision (his opponents thought of him as "neoliberal": more on this later). It was a brilliantly successful act of political transformation. Before he became prime minister, commentators concluded that "Blair is the first Labour leader who barely pretends to be a socialist."[46] But his leadership faltered in the wake of his unconditional support for George W. Bush's 2003 Iraq war, and for the false claims on which the justification for war had been constructed. The author Colin MacCabe spoke for many Labourites in denouncing Blair's betrayal and his "love affair with money."[47] When he left the prime ministership, he embarked on a high-earning career as a speaker and lobbyist.

Gerhard Schröder, as chancellor of Germany, successfully resisted being drawn into the US foreign-policy embrace. He too was accused of being a neoliberal, for championing labor market reforms (known as the Hartz agenda) that were aimed at strengthening Germany's competitive situation, and which in retrospect were credited as being highly successful. But that initiative cost him some popularity. After being narrowly defeated in an election, he moved closer into the orbits of both German manufacturing (especially the automobile industry) and Russia's Vladimir Putin. He became known as much for his Brioni suits as for his vision of politics. In 2017 he became chair of the Russian energy corporation Rosneft. In Russia, the word *Schroederization* became a term of art for the corruption of a political elite.

For Italy's last leader of the Italian Socialist Party (PSI), Bettino Craxi, the evidence of corruption was much more obvious. He had been prime minister for a comparatively long time in the 1980s, but fell in the wake of the generalized corruption scandals that also destroyed the Communist Party and the Christian Democrats. In 1994 he fled Italy to live in exile in Tunis, where he died in 2000.

The discrediting of the French socialist leader François Mitterrand, who had taken his French Socialist Party into the political center in 1983 after a two-year experiment with a much more radical economic platform, came not so much from current policy debates but rather from revelations about the past, exposed after his two-term presidency had ended. The journalist Pierre Péan produced a book of revelations about Mitterrand's work as a young civil servant in the wartime Vichy regime, and about his continued friendship with figures such as the Vichy police chief René Bousquet.[48]

Social democracy, which had collectively taken such a large gamble on the nation-state, was bound for crisis. Yet paradoxically, the Soviet planning model, which looked as if it had failed in the 1980s, seemed as if it might be rescued by information technology. In the 1980s, I wrote that when the chips were down, communism lost its byte. Now it looks as if socialism "with Chinese characteristics" (*Zhongguo tese shehuizhuyi*) is being rescued by a spurt of internationalist capitalist innovation. Socialism again has bytes.

3

Democracy, the Nation-State, and Nationalism

The world is mostly organized into nation-states, and most rich modern states are democracies, that is, they are ruled by governments subject to popular elections held at regular intervals. Surprisingly, fewer and fewer people—politicians, analysts, citizens—are happy with this state of affairs.[1] Public health challenges like the coronavirus, too, easily give the (often illusory) impression that a resolute autocrat, who is really in command, might do a better job than a divided, quarrelsome, and meddlesome democracy.

The modern conception of a nation-state arose in the nineteenth century, at the same time as ideas about capitalism and socialism. The concepts are related to each other, simply by the logic of the circumstances that originally produced them. The great economist Joseph Schumpeter noted that "historically, the modern democracy rose along with capitalism, and in causal connection with it."[2] The purpose of the nation-state was alternatively to manage capitalism, or to prepare the transition to socialism. Indeed, the link between economics and nation-building was made very clear in the German terms for economics, either *Nationalökonomie,* or, in the Germanization of these Latin and Greek roots, *Volkswirtschaft.* At a very early stage, the *Volkswirtschaft* was defined in opposition to the world economy, or *Weltwirtschaft* (although some English-language commentators translate *Weltwirtschaft* as globalization, a little anachronistically).[3]

Even before the Global Financial Crisis of 2007–2008, and well before the coronavirus crisis, many observers worried that democracy was in trouble, that there was a "democratic recession," and that anti-democratic populists were eroding the stability of the political order. In one very powerful interpretation by Dani Rodrik, the democratic weakness was linked to the triumph of globalization, because globalization had eroded the capacity of democratic governments to make key policy choices to improve the lives of their citizens.[4] Capitalism also strains democracy, because it pushes distributional conflict. It has long been established that clashes over economics tear democracies apart. Globalization simply added new layers of conflict between the winners of globalization—a cosmopolitan or mobile elite—and the losers who were less educated and less mobile. Schumpeter saw this point very clearly, and tried to explain what he regarded as an outlier, the unique Swiss success at democracy, by remarking that "there is so little to quarrel about in a world of peasants which, excepting hotels and banks, contains no great capitalist industry."[5]

The millennium now looks as if it was a turning point, the high point of the democratic tide. In Warsaw, the capital of the country widely regarded as the driving force in dissolving communism, a gathering of more than a hundred countries in June 2000 proudly styled itself the Community of Democracies. Participants endorsed the Warsaw Declaration, which committed their governments to uphold democratic principles and practices. The meeting sought to enhance cooperation among participating governments through several avenues, including an informal caucus at the UN General Assembly to share information and support democracy-related issues. The US State Department reported on how "at the international level, the global spread of democracy was affirmed in both governmental and nongovernmental arenas."[6] The think-tank Freedom House in 2000 classified 120 countries as democracies. By 2019 it was noting that the world was in the thirteenth year of a retreat from freedom.[7] Democracy in a national setting looked as if it was incapable of producing political stability. The relationship with the nation-state was strained, perhaps broken.

Definitions

Democracy has a strong normative definition—presented most clearly by Abraham Lincoln in the middle of a civil war that was also about the meaning of democracy. It is "government of the people, by the people, for the people," and it would push, as Lincoln presented it in the Gettysburg Address, "a new birth of freedom." At dramatic moments of remaking government—and democracy—such thoughts are often expressed. They reappeared after the First World War, when old empires broke up and were replaced by nation-states. They were celebrated in President Woodrow Wilson's programmatic statements. They came again after 1989, as the Soviet Empire in eastern Europe and then in the Soviet Union collapsed. But they are very old, and may have been expressed with the most clarity in the famous funeral oration of Pericles:

> Our form of government does not enter into rivalry with the institutions of others. Our government does not copy our neighbors', but is an example to them. It is true that we are called a democracy, for the administration is in the hands of the many and not of the few. But while there exists equal justice to all and alike in their private disputes, the claim of excellence is also recognized; and when a citizen is in any way distinguished, he is preferred to the public service, not as a matter of privilege, but as the reward of merit. Neither is poverty an obstacle, but a man may benefit his country whatever the obscurity of his condition. There is no exclusiveness in our public life, and in our private business we are not suspicious of one another, nor angry with our neighbor if he does what he likes. . . . Our city is thrown open to the world, though, and we never expel a foreigner and prevent him from seeing or learning anything of which the secret if revealed to an enemy might profit him. We rely not upon management or trickery, but upon our own hearts and hands.[8]

The Athenian model, or that of the early Swiss cantons, relied on vast popular assemblies. That sort of open discussion, as celebrated by Thucydides, may always have been illusory. In the aftermath of the American and French Revolutions, ancient Greek ideals were re-created in a new way, but they required imagined communities of citizens, rather than actual meetings, and—except in the most radical phases of the French Revolution—no direct democracy. The nation was now recast as what Benedict Anderson called an imagined community. The greatest exponent of the new theory was Ernest Renan, who in 1882 in a lecture at the Sorbonne distinguished his concept of a nation from the German model, which depended on language and ancestry: "A nation is a soul, a spiritual principle. Two features, which to speak truly are really one, make up this soul, this spiritual principle. One is in the past, the other in the present. One is the common possession of a rich legacy of memories; the other is a current consent, the desire to live together, and the will to continue to assert undivided the inheritance that has been received from the past."[9] He thus came to the famous conclusion that a nation was a daily plebiscite. In fact, social scientists and historians trying to identify what made that plebiscite a positive affirmation of a democracy pointed to a broad institutional base: transport systems that brought the country together, a common education, and a common army that—as one interpretation had it—turned "peasants into Frenchmen."[10] Democracy still depended on an ideal of community.

At the beginning of the nineteenth century, the discussion of how to bind individuals into a collective had been addressed mostly in terms of an education or formation that would change individuals into citizens. The debate was linguistically most interesting in the German case, where a great deal of the theorizing developed, because the word for citizen, *Bürger,* is also the noun for the equivalent of the French *bourgeois.* In particular, the Humboldt brothers in Prussia developed a theory of the creation of a "moral person and a good citizen," whose moral sensibilities would be "refined" through education.[11] The word *Bildung* indeed means both education and formation or molding.

The operational view of democracy emphasized, by contrast with what political scientists regarded as a naïve normative version, that democracy was simply a process of selecting elites. "Democracy does not mean and cannot mean that the people actually rule in any obvious sense of the terms 'people' and 'rule.' "[12] At best democracy could be viewed as an effective control mechanism creating a transparent path of accountability.

The most acute participants in the democratic revolutions pointed this out very clearly. After 1918, in the chaotic aftermath of Germany's military defeat when every radical political option was being fought on the streets, the sociologist Max Weber set out a practical view of how democracy would work. He was working and speaking in Munich, where a monarchy was followed by a brief-lived Bolshevik republic and then a right-wing nationalist regime. Weber was also one of the framers of the Weimar constitution, and realized how choices would be made by administrative structures, bureaucracies, and professional experts. "Both immediate democracy and government by notables are technically inadequate, on the one hand in organizations beyond a certain limit of size, constituting more than a few thousand full-fledged members, or on the other hand, where functions are involved which require technical training or continuity of policy. If, in such a case, permanent technical officials are appointed alongside of shifting heads, actual power will normally tend to fall into the hands of the former, who do the real work, while the latter remain essentially dilettantes."[13]

Czech dissident Václav Havel was much more of an idealist than Weber. Havel thought that the parties that might arise to select government personnel did not matter; instead the quality of the people selected was more fundamental. "People who live in the post-totalitarian system know only too well that the question of whether one or several political parties are in power, and how these parties define and label themselves, is of far less importance than the question of whether or not it is possible to live like a human being."[14]

Both the normative and the operational definitions require an assessment of how the social ties that constitute a nation might be created. During the nineteenth century, an original vision that construed democracy as a step toward freedom and self-realization was quickly replaced by something quite different. What was supposed to hold the nation together, and make democracy work, was not a change in consciousness leading to the creation of citizens, but economic linkages and economic growth.

"A Pure Business Affair"

The nation-state owed its practical beginnings in the nineteenth century to the promise that it could deliver economic growth.[15] What changed in the mid-nineteenth century, and what destroyed that idealistic vision? Nation-building in practice (as opposed to in theory or in philosophy) emerged out of crude power politics. That was especially true in Germany and Italy, the two countries whose unification in the 1860s and 1870s set a new paradigm for the nation-state and its character. Rather than offering an alternative to the traditional balance of power between states, it depended on manipulating that balance using intricate diplomatic maneuvering, pretense, and deception. In addition, the new states that emerged relied on calculations from old states that had definitively not been nations—the kingdoms of Savoy (Piedmont) and Prussia. The new states' very existence represented the success of Piedmontese and Prussian negotiators—and of armies—rather than of liberal majorities. Democracy would get in the way. The Piedmontese politician Count Camillo Cavour repeatedly emphasized that "the competition of a democratic party would compromise the cause of Italian independence." But the shape and character of the state could in turn shape the character of popular or democratic politics. In Germany, Prussian minister-president Otto von Bismarck introduced a universal adult male franchise, even as voting in the state of Prussia remained weighted according to one's ownership of property.

The great theoretician of *Realpolitik,* and the coiner of the term, was a German journalist and a veteran of the pan-European revolutionary wave of 1848, August Ludwig von Rochau. Freedom, Rochau wrote, was not to be achieved through political change, but only through the acquisition of property. Whatever progress had been made in the direction of national unity was a consequence of human self-seeking. A Fatherland was no longer a question of patriotic dreams; "for Germans, unity is basically a pure business affair" (*eine reine Geschäftssache*).[16]

This doctrine amounted to an economic determinism of the type that became commonplace to German thinkers after the middle of the century. The most enduring expression of such determinism was of course Karl Marx's *Das Kapital,* the first volume of which was published in 1867. It was perhaps a less original work than we are usually tempted to suppose, for it echoed and distilled many of the views circulating in contemporary Germany. It sought to demonstrate the necessity of events. In *Das Kapital,* Marx abandoned a Hegelian tradition that he had played an important part in forming during the 1840s, and that had allowed greater room for individual actions and initiatives. The work is a monument to the natural or ineluctable or iron laws of social action. "It is not a question of the higher or lower degree of development of the social antagonisms that result from the natural laws of capitalist production. It is a question of those laws themselves, of those tendencies working with iron necessity towards inevitable results."[17]

German and Italian businessmen, thinkers, as well as politicians saw a need to catch up with the model of preeminence and power offered by

Great Britain. But Britain had some rather unique advantages: above all, it had security at a relatively cheap price because of its island location. For the small and comparatively dynamic ancien-régime states that lay on the old historic Rhineland and Alpine trade route from the North Sea to the Mediterranean, such as the Netherlands, but also Tuscany, Venezia, or Baden, fortification was not nearly so easy. Defense was too expensive, and territorial expansion would produce additional costs that could not be covered from additional revenue. Unconventionally shaped states had a greater incentive to change the status quo: consider Prussia, an odd amalgam of low-quality agricultural land and some rich manufacturing territories in the west of Germany, in the Rhine corridor; or Piemonte, a prosperous and heavily French-influenced territorial state linked to a large and poor Mediterranean island. These two states were already dealing with huge contradictions, between rich and poor, between manufacturers and farmers, between Protestants and Catholics. An expansion might be a way of reducing or relativizing these differences by setting them in a larger context.

Bismarck's story can be read as an example of how popularized economic determinism came to dominate the intellectual horizons of nineteenth-century Germans. Bismarck, it hardly needs to be said, did not set out to apply Marx's political and economic philosophy any more than he believed that he was implementing the elements of *Realpolitik* as formulated by Rochau. He did, however, share many of their assumptions. To begin with, the nineteenth century was, he thought, the age of "material interests," in which the old theories of the ancien régime were redundant—whether legitimism or conservatism, devised as defenses of the ancien régime; or liberalism, conceived as an onslaught on the old order. In this world, individuals were the prisoners of broader movements. They could not alter the inexorable march of historical determination. In 1869, the most powerful man in Germany wrote meekly: "I am not so presumptuous as to believe that such as we make history. My work is to observe the currents and steer my ship in them as best I can. I cannot direct the currents, still less conjure them up."[18]

If individuals had to swim with the tide of destiny, so did nations. National destinies were, if anything, more determined than those of individuals. External events—such as economic change or foreign political

development—mattered much more than the longings of romantic nationalism. These belonged to invention: there was nothing special about
territorial and national identities, or about the "swindle of nationalities,"
as Bismarck termed it. In human affairs, all was subject to perpetual change.
As an illustration of this fluidity, Bismarck thought of the connection
between Prussian and German identities. Were not both simply a matter
of temporizing with external exigencies? Of bowing before an implacable
God of history and destiny? In 1869, Bismarck wrote to Albrecht von
Roon, the Prussian war minister, a sternly upright man whose sympathies
lay with an older and specifically Prussian brand of conservatism. It was
only two years after both of these men, because of the rapidity of political
change and largely as a result of Bismarck's own strategy and actions, had
become part of the North German Confederation. Only one year later,
both were to become subjects of a new German Empire. "You will have
to admit that both we and His Majesty are born *North Germans,* while
around one hundred and seventy years ago our ancestors cheerfully allowed
themselves—for the sake of higher interests—to exchange the glorious
name of *Brandenburgers* for the then rather extinct title of *Prussians,*
without really being Prussians."[19]

Identity changed as a result of clashes and wars. Second, then, the developments of the 1860s were also the outcome of vast and bitter civil wars.
We should place the unification of Italy and Germany alongside the drama
of the much bloodier but also highly divisive American Civil War. In each
case, a more industrialized north defeated a rural—and perhaps more
romantic—south. Perhaps only in the German case has that division been
successfully overcome even in the twenty-first century. At first, the outcome
of the clash of arms was a matter of chance and skill. But the longer the
conflict was maintained, the greater the chances of victory for the side that
could mobilize industrial capacity and taxable resources. Indeed it was the
budgetary aftermath of the North Italian War of 1859 for the Habsburg
Empire and the near bankruptcy of the monarchy that gave Prussia the
chance to reassert itself in German politics.

Third, in the 1860s war and business shifted the emphasis away from a
romantic longing for unity toward a practical emphasis on the benefits of
unity. By the 1860s Germany's most famous businessman, Alfred Krupp,
was seeing the clear parallel between his business development and the

emergence of the German state. In the aftermath of German unification, he made the explicit comparison: "Achieving something depends solely on the will. If a state in the course of one year absorbs and rules many states, then we too will also be able to introduce and manage a dozen new industrial creations. . . . My achievement will stand and fall with Prussia's greatness and military supremacy." By 1871, when the king of Prussia became the German emperor, Krupp had become the symbol of the new Germany, which was built on technical achievement as well as military success. His interpretation of the crushing Prussian victory at the battle of Sedan was clear: "We are now living in the age of steel. Railways, Germany's greatness, France's ruin, are in the steel age, the bronze age is over. Steel has finished being the material of war, it now has a milder destiny, it should be used for the first monument of victory, for monuments of great deeds and great men, as the expression of external and domestic peace, it should ring in church bells, be used for ornaments and commercial purposes, and in coinage."[20]

This attitude had its counterpart in Italy. Patriotism could generate business opportunities. The great Florentine liberal Bettino Ricasoli came to the conclusion that Tuscany was simply financially unviable on its own. In the United States, the Civil War was what Charles and Mary Beard famously called a "second American Revolution," one that made "vast changes in the arrangement of classes, in the accumulation and distribution of wealth, in the course of industrial development, and in the Constitution inherited from the Fathers."[21] Initially, Abraham Lincoln had preferred a straightforward business transaction, in which southern slave owners would be compensated from the federal budget for the loss of property rights involved in emancipation; later he came to see the war as a divinely enforced property transaction. God "gives to both North and South this terrible war . . . until all the wealth piled by the bond-man's two hundred and fifty years of unrequited toil shall be sunk, and until every drop of blood drawn by the lash, shall be paid by another drawn with the sword."[22]

After the unconventional Italian and German state had triumphed, when Cavour and Bismarck stood supreme, the people had to deal with the clear but problematic legacy of how unity had been thought about and fought over. As the politician, artist, and novelist Massimo d'Azeglio famously put it, Italy was made: now it was time to make Italians ("L'Italia è fatta, ora restano da fare gli italiani"). There was a demand for a developmental strategy that would create the sinews of a new state. But the security dilemma that had produced unification had lingering effects: that is, the shift in the age-old continental Austro-French balance that had its origins in the rivalry of Habsburg and Valois meant that the new developmental strategy tended to have a heavy military orientation. The German approach made the house of Krupp the iconic German enterprise of Imperial Germany, and the apparent success of the German model pushed the kingdom of Italy to a developmentalism that in the 1880s focused on building up a new mass-manufacture steel plant, the Società Alti Forni, Fonderie e Acciaierie di Terni, in the improbable location of the Umbrian town of Terni. The plant was intended to become a central Italian equivalent of the German Krupp works, with Terni a replica of Essen. Later, at the end of the twentieth century, ThyssenKrupp would buy the Terni works.

The strong focus on economic success made vulnerable those countries whose national identity had been built around the promise of economic uplift. When growth would falter—especially in the aftermath of a problematic or unsuccessful war—the stage was set for a dramatic backlash.

Lessons from the Weimar Republic

Interwar Europe has become the exemplary case of the failure of democracy. The collapse of the first Italian democracy in the early 1920s with the rise of Mussolini and fascism, and then a decade later the creation of a Nazi government under Adolf Hitler, are frequently interpreted as warnings for democratic practice everywhere. The massive success of the recent, spectacular German television series *Babylon Berlin* is just one contemporary example of how the history of this period has been a testing ground for theories about the weakness of democracy: set in the era of the Weimar Republic, the show offers obvious parallels to the world of the twenty-first century, with its violence, fake news, and the intervention of other states.

Start with the fact that economic shocks—for example, inflationary spirals, depressions, and banking crises—are challenges to all governments, everywhere and always. Weimar Germany started its existence in an inflation that became a hyper-inflation: the inflation was born not just out of the costs of the lost war and the Allied requirement of high reparations payments, but also out of a calculation by the German elites that a move to a balanced budget would produce unemployment and social radicalization, and would thus threaten the political order. By the end of the hyperinflation experience, Germany was close to political collapse, with a communist government in Saxony, a Nazi putsch in Bavaria, and a separatist movement in the Rhineland. The republic recovered, largely because the promise of stability attracted a large inflow of foreign funds. When that inflow ceased, during the Great Depression, Germany was vulnerable again, and a new and even more destructive wave of political radicalization set in.

Economic insecurity and hardship persuade people that any regime must be better than the current one. This is an obvious lesson not just from the Weimar years, but also from a large body of research on the economic logic of democracy.

A second lesson concerns the type of democracy. Weimar was designed to have as representative a system as possible, with proportional representation. Every sixty thousand votes resulted in a seat in parliament. A common verdict is that under extreme economic conditions, proportional representation can make matters worse. In the initial constitutional debates, Friedrich Naumann, the liberal leader, had warned that "proportional representation and democracy are mutually exclusive."[23] But the other makers of the constitution rejected that argument. When a country's politics are fragmented, proportional representation is more likely to deliver an incoherent electoral majority, one comprising groups on the far left and the far right that want to reject "the system," but agree on little else.

Taken together, these two lessons constitute the conventional wisdom among political scientists about the Weimar experience. Too often, though, each lesson is considered in isolation, leading to a dangerous sense of complacency. The first argument lulls people into thinking that only an extreme economic crisis can threaten the political system; the second leads people to assume—incorrectly—that systems of non-proportional representation are inherently more robust.

To preempt complacency, it helps to consider eight further lessons from the Weimar era.

1. *Referenda are dangerous, especially when they are rarely used and the electorate has little experience with them.* In the Weimar Republic, the

National Socialists had virtually disappeared by 1929. But that year, the party was able to reestablish itself by campaigning in a fiercely fought referendum over post–First World War reparations. A referendum or a plebiscite is problematic in that it offers what seems to be a simple choice, without a clear explanation of possible consequences. The 1929 referendum is a good example: it involved an adjustment of the reparations plan that would reduce the annual amount but require paying until 1988. The choice seemed to be between imposing what looked like an impossible burden on the grandchildren of the voting generation and allowing the country to obtain access to foreign capital that would allow Germany to grow, and consequently to pay off the reparations eventually.

Modern referenda also often present questions to voters in overly simple ways: for instance, a referendum in Greece in 2015 about accepting a harsh adjustment program looked intolerable to the majority of Greeks, but lacked any discussion of how voting yes might be necessary for remaining in the currency union, which a vast majority of Greeks also wanted. Or consider the 2016 UK Brexit referendum, where it was difficult for voters to know the range of options that might be available in the event of a "no" vote on European union membership. There may be a way around the problem: if referenda are regularly run, and become routine, as in Switzerland, a greater sense develops of the trade-offs involved in a choice. But when they are rare events on an emotionally salient issue, the scope for destructive choice is great.

2. *It is risky to dissolve parliaments when doing so is not required by established law.* Even a vote that creates the basis for new elections can be interpreted as an admission that democracy has failed. In September 1930, Reichstag elections in Germany were held halfway through a parliamentary term because of a failure to agree on a tax program: that vote gave the Nazis their original electoral breakthrough. In July 1932, in another premature vote, the Nazis won the largest share of the vote (37 percent) in a free but constitutionally unnecessary election.

3. *Constitutions don't necessarily protect the system.* The Weimar constitution, designed by some of the day's most insightful and ethical experts (including Max Weber), was nearly perfect. But when unanticipated events—such as foreign-policy dramas or domestic unrest—are inter-

preted as emergencies requiring an extra-legal framework, constitutional protections can erode rapidly. And the enemies of democracy can foment such events. In the aftermath of the Weimar era's hyperinflation, and right through the Depression, tax and other fiscal packages were passed not by parliamentary majorities but through the emergency power clauses of the constitution. That has been a common course in other countries as well: France responded to the 1930s financial depression with emergency decrees, and used its emergency powers in an *état d'urgence* to respond in 2015 to terrorist attacks and in 2020 to the coronavirus crisis. Hungary's Viktor Orbán, too, used the coronavirus emergency as justification for a far-reaching grab for power, which included the use of prison sentences for journalists.

4. *Business lobbyists can play a baleful behind-the-scenes role in undermining agreements between parliamentary factions.* Germany in the 1920s was more and more in the grip of special, secret deals made by business-interest associations and trade unions—deals that included decisions about which firms could be rescued from the Great Depression. Consequently, it looked as if big banks or giant industrial conglomerates like Vereinigte Stahlwerke were being kept alive while small and medium-sized enterprises went under. That story of selective lobbying has characterized modern emergencies as well, including the Global Financial Crisis and the coronavirus pandemic.

5. *A political culture in which leaders demonize their opponents erodes democracy.* In the Weimar Republic, that pattern began before the Nazis became a significant force. In 1922, Foreign Minister Walther Rathenau was assassinated after having been subjected to an intense, often anti-Semitic campaign of hatred from the nationalist right. Soon thereafter, Chancellor Joseph Wirth, a center-left Catholic, turned to the right-wing parties in parliament and said, "Democracy—yes, but not the kind of democracy that bangs on the table and says: We are now in power!" He concluded his admonition by declaring that "the enemy is on the right"—a statement that ended up fanning the flames of tribalism even more.[24] That type of tribalist rhetoric has been characteristic of post-Trump and post-Brexit politics, too. Attacks on the press as "fake news," the "failing *New York Times*," and demeaning epithets for opponents ("Shifty Adam Schiff," Biden as "sleepy Joe" or "low IQ," "Crazy Bernie Sanders"),

were in part designed to get the other side to respond in similar terms. They did: Sanders hit back with, "What's crazy is that we have a president who is a racist, a sexist, a xenophobe and a fraud." Alexandria Ocasio-Cortez builds her profile by repeatedly calling Trump a "racist." The effect is to deepen polarization, creating a climate in which agreement on other issues becomes harder or impossible. That makes voters less confident in democracy, and more inclined to trust the new autocrats.

6. *The president's family can be dangerous because of its access to power.* In Weimar, the aged field marshal Paul von Hindenburg was elected president in 1925, and reelected in 1932. But by the early 1930s, after several small strokes, he was suffering from dementia, and his weak and incapable son, Oskar, controlled all access to him. The result was that he ended up signing whatever agreements were presented to him. The Hindenburg government also worked to silence opposition: old documents from the First World War, when the leader of the previous semi-democratic government, Chancellor Heinrich Brüning, had been a young captain and criticized the junior Hindenburg, were brought out to discredit the chancellor during the Depression. A similar approach was used more recently against "President Javanka" (President Trump's daughter Ivanka and son-in law Jared Kushner), by both right- and left-wing critics, including Ann Coulter and Steve Bannon on the one side, and Maureen Dowd and Jonathan Swan on the other, who described Ivanka as "dumb as a brick" and Jared as "another pampered scion in the Oval, propped up by his daddy for half his life, accustomed to winging it and swaggering around."[25]

7. *An insurgent group does not need to have an overall majority to control politics, even in a system of proportional representation.* The largest share of the vote that the Nazis ever captured was 37 percent, in July 1932; in another election held that November, their support had fallen to 33 percent. Unfortunately, that decline led other parties to underestimate the Nazis, and to regard them as a possible coalition partner. In 2015 Poland's PiS (law and justice) Party came into power with a meager 37.6 percent of the vote; by the 2019 elections it had increased that support to 43.9 percent.

8. *Incumbents can fight off challenges for some time by buying off a discontented populace, but this strategy won't work forever.* In the Weimar era,

the German state provided generous municipal housing, local government services, agricultural and industrial subsidies, and a large civil service; but it financed those outlays with debt. To be sure, the Weimar Republic initially appeared to have a miracle economy. It was only later that German politics soured, as the government sought foreign support. Other countries found it hard to believe the government's warnings that, without speedy assistance, a political catastrophe would ensue. And it would have been harder still to convince their own electorates to bail out Germany.

It is often assumed that countries with majoritarian electoral systems like those in the United States or the United Kingdom are more resilient than countries with systems of proportional representation. After all, America and Britain's democracies are older, with more deeply entrenched cultures of political civility. But it is essential to recognize that those traditions have been eroded over a long period of time, and all but destroyed in the post-Brexit, post-Trump environment. The tumultuous transition after the Trump presidency, the questioning of the outcome of an election, the coup attempt against the Capitol, in the end appeared as impressive testimony to the inherent strength of American constitutionalism, but the major fissures remained.

There are also economic vulnerabilities. For example, the extent to which a country's economy depends on foreign savings ("other people's money") may be politically irrelevant for long periods—until a crisis hits. With the large countries that have had the most dramatic experience of populist administrations, the United States and the United Kingdom also running large current account deficits in the foreseeable future, a reckoning could be in order, especially if isolationist nationalism among American and British voters produces disenchantment among their foreign creditors.

Restoring Democracy after the Second World War

Rebuilding democracy in a European context after the Second World War replayed many of the discussions of nineteenth-century nation-state formation. How should leaders go about creating an identity for the nascent political organization? Was there a cultural inheritance, or could a particular kind of economic dynamic shape a new entity that would be viable and competitive in a world of Great Powers?

Old-style nationalism looked outdated after 1945. It had been a major cause of the dynamic that drove Europe to war and destruction. Democracy was revived in the context of the nation-state, but with constraints. These included not only internal procedural restraints, such as constitutional courts and the delegation of government activities to institutions with specific mandates, such as central banks which were required to produce a stable monetary policy, but also an international institutional framework. The institutions of European integration—above all the European Economic Community that would develop into the European Union—can be thought of as a support frame designed to let an exhausted elderly Europe walk democratically again. Or like training wheels on the bicycle of the young nation-states, so that they could more gradually and securely gain the confidence to ride democratically again.

There is an academic industry devoted to showing how European developments are not the outcome of what the economic historian Alan Milward termed the "European saints"— Monnet, Schuman, Spaak, Adenauer, De Gasperi—"men who held fast to their faith in European unity and through the righteousness of their beliefs and the single-mindedness of their actions overcame the doubting faithlessness of the world around them." Instead, as Milward and the political scientist Andrew Moravcsik eloquently demonstrate, the process resulted from the outcome of national strategies for the management of bread and butter issues, notably the social protection of the agricultural sector, which was initially politically important.[26] The history of modern Europe may include stars and saints, but the institutions we recognize today built their legitimacy through compensating the farming constituency, which at that time appeared to suffer the most from globalization.

The saints were quite aware of the processes and the calculations that actually drive politics. Jean Monnet formulated this view in the often-cited insight that European history is driven by crises. In his *Memoirs*, he provides an eloquent account of the characteristic frenetic all-night discussions to establish the European Coal and Steel Community, the antecedent of the European Economic Community and hence of the European Union.

Leaving the French Foreign Ministry on the Quai d'Orsay after a long night of negotiation, with the sun rising, Monnet spoke to a French official:

"Now we have a few hours to test and a few months to succeed.
  After that—"
  "After that," said Fontaine, smiling, "we shall face great difficulties, and we shall use them to make further progress.
  That's it, isn't it?"
  "It is indeed," I said. "You've understood what Europe is all about."[27]

The problem is that this method is not very appealing to people outside the limited circle who enjoy the logic of late-night discussions sustained by cold Belgian sandwiches—the *demos* neither likes nor understands the process. Havel castigated the European policy elite for "the erroneous belief that the great European task before us is a purely technical, a purely administrative, or a purely systemic matter, and that all we need to do is come up with ingenious structures, new institutions, and new legal norms and regulations."[28] Instead, any serious political figure has to talk a different language—the language of the saints—while performing a different sort of operation, the calculation of the clods. The exercise induces a political schizophrenia, one that is evident in the most far-ranging exercise in European integration since the 1950s: the making in the 1990s of a European monetary union.

The politicians of the 1990s spoke in the language of Monnet and Adenauer—and in effect of Hugo and Churchill—about avoiding European war. Monnet had been proud to record the dialogue of two young soldiers on a French beach in the early 1950s, when one said, "With the Schuman Plan, one thing is certain: We shall no longer have to go to war."[29] Helmut Kohl understood this language perfectly. For him, the greatest moments were those of Franco-German reconciliation, most strikingly when he held the hand of President François Mitterrand while visiting Verdun, the site of a horrifically bloody siege during the war. It reflected a deep psychological, familiar impulse: he had lost his elder brother in the Second World War, and his mother's brother had been killed in the First World War. Kohl's most recent biographer, Hans Peter Schwarz, rightly emphasizes the centrality of his promise to his mother that there should not—ever—be another European war.[30]

In the early 1990s, as Havel was analyzing the problems of the vision that drove central Europeans after the collapse of communism, the language of the saints reached a crescendo. The problem was that there was no technical preparation, no administrative capacity to take the steps needed to ensure that there would never be a war: no one in the European defense ministries, for instance, was willing to contemplate setting up a single European army; no one in the foreign ministries thought of a single external policy and indeed—as Havel lamented—the official European response to the disintegration of Yugoslavia was tragically confused and its effects destructive. Yet there was a well-established mechanism for negotiating international monetary and currency issues.

The problem is that hitching the European ideal to money creates a series of poisonous identifications: that Europe is all about money and material advantage; and that money can be an alternative language of community, one that is more convenient because using it is a way of sloughing off responsibilities for the past. It sets up Europe for a fall at the moment when finance explodes and the value of money becomes questionable. As the distinguished economic commentator Martin Wolf put it, "in creating the Euro, the Europeans took their project beyond the practical into something more important to people: the fate of their money."[31]

For both France and Germany, the countries that have historically been at the core of the process of European integration, the management of money has been central to a certain vision of identity. De Gaulle was warned by an international civil servant as he stepped into the ruins of Fourth Republic politics: "No country can gain international esteem if it has not a good currency. That the French franc has not been a strong currency has been very damaging to French prestige in recent years. The French are a hard-working and saving people. If they have monetary stability they can stand a great deal of political instability."[32] For Germany, historical memory depicted the destruction of monetary stability that followed the First World War as the beginning of the decline of morality, democracy, and a liberal political order.

The European drama of the past thirty years has been a reprise of the nineteenth-century European experience with nation-building. That should not be surprising. The political language used in both periods has as a common origin the failed revolutions of 1848, with their ensuing turn to the politics of interests that were always seen as national, and could not be fully tied to a universal or normative justification concerned with the realization of rights.

Hegemony

Unlike many of the terms considered in this book, *hegemon* appears to have a clear, self-evident definition, but even in this case, looks can be deceiving. For thousands of years, Alexander of Macedon, or Alexander the Great, was the embodiment of the idea of power. The Greek word *hegemon* means leader or commander. But it was also used to describe the position of a dominant state in an association or league of states, the Hellenic League organized by Philip II of Macedon. It was loosely managed by a governing body of delegates, sometimes compared to the League of Nations or the United Nations, called the *synedrion;* in addition, there was a narrower council or executive board, the *proëdroi,* with five members chosen by lot. The leader of the league (or hegemon) was unambiguously Macedon and its ruler, Philip II, and then his son Alexander the Great. Alexander attacked Thebes in 335 BCE on the grounds that it had violated the rules of the league, gave the synedrion the authority to pass judgment on the city, then implemented the decision of the council. But as his power grew, Alexander frequently violated the rules of the league.[1] (Alexander was so famous for wielding great power that madmen in European bedlam hospitals believed themselves to be Alexander, or perhaps Julius Caesar. Only after 1800 did the psychic attention of madmen shift to Napoleon as an identification figure. Perhaps significantly, few madmen today imagine that they are Donald Trump.)

International relations scholars work differently: instead of going forward from Alexander's time, they extrapolate backward from the twentieth-century United States. The term *hegemon* has become a standard feature of international relations literature, and it is invariably used to describe the United States, with its unparalleled post-1945 ascendency in industry and finance, as well as in military and political power, and the long, drawn-out debate—which started in the 1970s—about relative decline and a changing world order. The distinguished political scientist Robert Keohane provided probably the clearest and cleanest functional definition of a hegemon, as a country willing and able to pay the cost of maintaining the system, even in the face of defection.[2] The hegemon must not only be strong: it must be both willing and able to carry the financial burden of others. "To be considered hegemonic in the world political economy . . . a country must have access to crucial raw materials, control major sources of capital, maintain a large market for imports, and hold comparative advantages in goods with high value added, yielding relatively high wages and profits."[3] That description mostly fits the experience of the United States since the mid-twentieth century, but it may not apply to the earlier nineteenth-century hegemon, Great Britain, which was relatively well supplied with coal as a raw material but not many other raw materials, and hence was quite dependent on a foreign trade that it needed to try to dominate by financial means. Some historians draw connecting lines between this sort of domination, which was racialized as part of colonial rule, and the increasing brutality of domestic policing operations in the United States.[4] Increasingly, too, this link has been made in foreign discussions of the US position. Korean demonstrators, for example, concerned that their country pays too much for American defense, have adapted the slogan of the American Black Lives Matter campaign to "US imperialism means 'I can't breathe.' "[5]

This modern analysis certainly does not apply to previous countries that exercised for some time a political hegemony. Habsburg Spain in the sixteenth and seventeenth centuries, for example, controlled much of the world but couldn't "maintain the system" by stamping out what its rulers and their clerical advisers thought was heresy in the Netherlands and Germany. Louis XIV's, and Napoleon's, France were each massively dominant but did not exert economic or financial hegemony. Of course, the worlds of early modern Spain and France were not at all stable, whereas in the nineteenth and the late twentieth centuries it did look as if a "system" was operating. China for thousands of years was the richest country in the world, with massive economic superiority, but it never really considered transforming that advantage into a territorial expansion of its rule. The lesson of Chinese history is distinctly anti-hegemonic.

But the use of *hegemony* is not confined to international relations discussions. In his *Prison Notebooks,* the Italian Marxist Antonio Gramsci discusses how "the realization of a hegemonic apparatus, in so far as it creates a new ideological terrain, determines a reform of consciousness and of methods of knowledge: it is a fact of knowledge, a philosophical fact."[6] Just as we can think of capital in multiple forms, we ought to think of hegemony as capable of being exercised in subtle or non-direct ways. And culture is the most obvious arena for that kind of quest for dominance. Here too, a term is stretched in a way that sometimes threatens to make it so universal that it is practically hard to detect a precise meaning. The concept is vulnerable to what a leading historian, Perry Anderson, calls the "discursive idealism severing signification from any stable connexion with referents."[7]

How States Dominate Each Other

States had related to each other in ways that were understood systematically. In the course of the sixteenth century, looking at the complex relationships of the multiple states in Italy, the Duchy of Milan, the papal states, the Kingdom of Naples, the Republic of Florence (later the Grand Duchy of Tuscany when it became autocratic), as well as many smaller units, and their propensity to call on much stronger outside powers, such as the King of France, the Holy Roman Emperor (in the German-speaking lands), or the King of Spain, astute observers started to conceptualize the relationship as a balance of power. The humanist politician and diplomat Francesco Barbaro is often considered the first of these, but in fact the fullest account is in the work of the historian (and friend of Machiavelli) Francesco Guicciardini, in his discussion of the impact of the 1494 French invasion of Italy.[8] The story of balancing remained powerful in the nineteenth-century understanding: Britain tried to create a balance of power by constructing alliances against Napoleon's France, and then, after 1815, by building stronger states to surround and contain France. At the time of the major rethinking of concepts in the wake of the 1848 revolutions, German analysts started to apply the term *hegemony* to the relation of German states with each other. In particular, liberals developed the idea that "only Prussian hegemony can save Germany," because Prussia stood for "progress."[9]

During the nineteenth century, something quite new was added to this structure of relationships. States began to use the new international logic of capitalism to construct an international hegemony that depended on something other than simple military might. Britain was for a long time the central power in the consideration of this dynamic, because of the dynamism and wealth created by its leadership in an initial wave of industrialization. Capitalism, and the language of capitalism, looked as if they were English (indeed, in continental Europe, *Manchesterism* was often used as a synonym for the new-style capitalism). Capitalism was also a way in which Britain could increase its dominance or hegemony. In the twentieth century, the Soviet Union tried the mirror image: hegemony through socialism.

The turning point came in 1870–1871, as the Franco-Prussian War altered the balance of power in Europe, by creating a powerful and newly unified Germany, and by weakening France. Before 1870, Paris had been, with London, the center of global finance. Walter Bagehot's classic and still influential 1873 study of finance, *Lombard Street*, describes the novelty during this era of the City of London, "the greatest combination of economical power and economical delicacy that the world has ever seen." He presented the development as a very recent phenomenon, deriving from the aftermath of the Franco-Prussian War. "Concentration of money in banks, though not the sole cause, is the principal cause which has made the Money Market of England so exceedingly rich, so much beyond that of other countries. . . . Not only does this unconscious 'organisation of capital,' to use a continental phrase, make the English specially quick in comparison with their neighbours on the continent at seizing on novel mercantile opportunities, but it makes them likely also to retain any trade on which they have once regularly fastened."[10] The power was the result of the complexity of the system that assessed risks across the world and allocated financial flows accordingly. Power here can be conceived of as influence through the web of dependent relationships that were created: most notably, other governments needed access to London markets if they were to be able to finance their debt (and hence their capacity for military power projection). But that power was, as Bagehot put it, also vulnerable ("delicate") in the sense that it could easily be disrupted by panics in which confidence collapsed. Innovations in financial systems, then, were essential for making this power more robust.

At first, a physical infrastructure provided the basis for the financial links that would lead to a gigantic expansion of commerce. The initial contacts between buyer and seller, the bills of exchange, and insurance depended on the transoceanic cable, first laid in 1866, and on increased use of the steamship.[11] At the beginning of the twentieth century, a further innovation, wireless telegraphy, meant that cargoes could be reallocated while they were still in transit at sea.[12] In addition, most of the world's marine insurance—even for commerce not undertaken in British ships or to British ports—was underwritten by Lloyd's of London. As in the case of trade finance, there were gigantic network effects: a very deep financial market was required in order to absorb potentially large losses. But the network intersected at a single node, with the result that the City of London controlled the world's interactions.

Hegemony based around a model of global social organization created some immediate tensions. In the first place, the nineteenth-century system appeared to give all kinds of advantages to Britain: British merchants and banks profited from the commercial transactions, and the British navy could inform itself about the strategic resource vulnerabilities of its competitors.[13] Second, what would happen when capitalism was challenged? Capitalism, especially on the British model, looked like a vulnerability. Ignacy Daszyński, who later became prime minister of the Second Polish Republic's first government, told the Austrian parliament in 1897: "We don't stand in the sign of Manchesterism any longer. . . . Self-help is a caricature in a police state."[14]

Major rivals—the United States or Germany—might have to evolve alternative models, new forms of social organization. In Germany, that was a much more planned or étatist variety of capitalism; in the United States it was one dominated by very large corporations that became an organized proxy for American power.

The leading American theorist of international relations in the early twentieth century, Alfred Mahan, saw the point very clearly. There was something very odd about British power: "The power of Great Britain was not that of predominance, strictly so called. She never had the military strength, as for a time Philip II, Louis XIV, and Napoleon had, to make her successfully aggressive against a continent determined on resistance. Her predominance was that of a determinative factor, resembling a third party in politics; of a make-weight, which casts the balance from one side to the other." England's "expansion and aggression," Mahan said, "turned not towards Europe, but towards the world outside."[15] Germany, by contrast, was pushing ahead because of an organizational transformation: "There is found now in Germany great preponderance of power, not only military but in organization of every kind."[16]

After the First World War, the dilemmas of the prewar world appeared in their full starkness. The United Kingdom could continue to exercise only some domination, after the heavy cost of the war, by using an international institution, the League of Nations, as a vehicle for hegemony. For other countries—including the United States and France—the League looked suspicious precisely because it was being harnessed in this way. After Woodrow Wilson's original enthusiasm, the United States turned away from the League when Congress refused to ratify the covenant that had established it.

The backlash against internationalism prompted the formulation of a new doctrine of international relations, often called *realism*. It was articulated most eloquently by a British diplomat, E. H. Carr, who had served on the British delegation to the 1919 Paris Peace Conference, then went on to work in the British embassy in Riga. The two facts of his era that struck Carr with the greatest force were the collapse of conventional laissez-faire economics with the Great Depression, and the failure of institutionalized liberal internationalism in the shape of Woodrow Wilson's covenant and the League of Nations. These two facts were, in Carr's view, intricately associated and connected with each other. In particular, the economic catastrophe of the Great Depression had molded politics in a new way, one that showed the bankruptcy of traditional liberalism in both the economic sphere (laissez-faire) and in politics. He saw an urgent need to move beyond the discredited theories of the world before 1914, having reached the conclusion that "the assumptions of nineteenth century liberalism are in fact untenable."[17]

The tendency of modern industry was toward the concentration of production and ownership, because the factory system required large amounts of capital, and because economies of scale produced inevitable advantages for the owners of large sums of capital and of large industrial enterprises. Large enterprises in most countries enhanced their power through cartels, which usually depended on some measure of trade protection (because they would otherwise be undercut and undermined by foreign competitors). Cartels and trusts influenced states, and political power became the tool of economic interests. The law of economic concentration, or of increased polarization, looked very much like Marx's nineteenth-century prediction of increased immiseration, with a pauperized proletariat facing highly concentrated industrial ownership.

Carr's originality lay in the way he translated into a theory of international relations this rather familiar notion of an iron law in which economic power became more concentrated. Carr saw a parallel in that, in his view, the capitalist process of production as well as the international system rested ultimately not on a law based on precepts of morality but on brute force. Such observations seemed appropriate to make in the context of the interwar world. The liberal trading regime of the nineteenth century had been briefly restored in the 1920s, but then collapsed, apparently irredeemably, with the Great Depression. States strove for national self-sufficiency, or autarky, and the result increased the importance of power in the international economy. "In modern conditions the artificial promotion of some degree of autarky is a necessary condition of orderly social existence. Autarky is, however, not only a social necessity, but an instrument of political power." Trade wars and economic struggles became a locus for power politics. Indeed, in the 1930s Carr saw a substitution of the economic weapon for military weapons.[18]

Since in Carr's view interstate relations are fundamentally about power, the law of concentration applied with the same inexorable logic as it had in the domain of economics. Big units would have an inevitable advantage over smaller states. In the world that Carr observed, "there is a clearly marked trend towards integration and the formation of ever larger political and economic units."[19] Thus he shared the economist John Maynard Keynes's contempt for the allegedly artificial new and small states created in the 1919 Paris peace treaties, in part out of the attempt to apply the doctrine of national self-determination. He predicted the inevitable accumulation of power by the big states, and in particular those states that had been left out of the making of Versailles and the other Paris treaties, namely Germany and Soviet Russia.

The application of the theory that the world was moving to power blocs based on the big states led directly to the most notoriously problematic part of Carr's first edition of his most interesting theoretical work, *The Twenty Years' Crisis,* that is, the defense of the rationale behind the 1938 Munich agreement. There, four big powers, Britain, France, Germany, and Italy, had produced a solution to the Czechoslovak "question" (without consulting the Czechs). Carr thought that Munich "corresponded both to a change in the European equilibrium of forces and to accepted canons of international morality."[20]

Like leaders of the western powers, who mobilized opinion by talking about democracy, Carr saw the revisionist powers of the 1930s as having their own, legitimating story, which seemed to him equally valid (or equally invalid) as those presented by any other state. The language of human rights for him was nothing more than a rhetorical weapon, which could be and was used as effectively by the new states, which tried to present the liberation of the proletariat as a universal cause, or the defense of the rights of German-speaking ethnic minorities in central European states as an equally general issue. There existed no valid external criteria for ascertaining whether an action was legitimate or not, for in each case, the rhetoric was nothing more than a fig leaf for the exercise of power. The new powers, Hitler, Mussolini, and Stalin, who more explicitly emphasized power, were in Carr's view actually being more honest.

Politicians who did not, or pretended not to, see the necessity of the new dynamic were necessarily either obtuse or dishonest, and Carr shared fully Keynes's dismal view of the dangers of Woodrow Wilson's idealism. The book indeed goes well beyond Keynes's famous polemic of 1919 and includes a perverse attempt to show the fundamental similarity between the crusading idealisms of Wilson and of Adolf Hitler.[21] International relations were thus necessarily and permanently conflictual, and experiments such as the League of Nations (or later the United Nations) were doomed to failure. As Carr put it, "It seems no longer possible to create an apparent harmony of interests at the expense of somebody else. The conflict can no longer be spirited away."[22]

Carr's resulting doctrine was unappealing even at the time, though it must have struck a powerful chord with many who reacted against what they saw as shallow moralistic posturing, and though it seemed also to reflect the new realities of the age of Stalin and Hitler.

Benign Hegemony

A benign twist to the discussion of hegemony came from an American economist, Charles Kindleberger. In a famous analysis of the Great Depression, Kindleberger argued that it arose out of a failure of world leadership. Great Britain had been the hegemonic power of the nineteenth century, but its creditor status had been severely eroded by the cost of fighting the First World War. The United States had emerged as the world's largest creditor, but it had a double vulnerability. Its financial system was unstable and prone to panics. Its political system was immature and prone to populism and nativism.

In the Depression, according to Kindleberger, the United States should have provided a market open to foreign goods. Instead, the Smoot-Hawley Tariff closed off American markets and provoked other countries into a spiral of retaliatory measures. US financial institutions should have continued to lend to distressed borrowers, in order to prevent a spiral in which the unavailability of finance forced price reductions and intensified the process of world deflation. Instead, the US banks, which were widely blamed for the international lending in the boom that had preceded the bust, became so intimidated by the ferocious political criticism that they were weakened and the flow of American credit stopped.

After the Second World War, as a leading figure in developing the Marshall Plan, Kindleberger set about applying these lessons, advocating that the United States should keep its markets and its flow of funds open to support other countries. That became the model for late twentieth-century American-style hegemony as presented by international relations theory.

But there is a problem with Kindleberger's argument that Kindleberger himself, a very kind and well-meaning man, could never see. He did not like the use of the term *hegemony*, explaining, "I prefer to think of it as responsibility. Hegemony may, however, be more realistic as well as more cynical."[23] The difficulty is that the world is never really very grateful to the country that saved it. Being a hero, a rescuer, or a hegemon is fundamentally a thankless task, and the global leader has never been loved by the rest of the world, even when it pays quite substantial amounts. The suspicion is often greatest from near neighbors—consider Canada, Mexico, or Cuba. In Europe, as the memory of the Second World War receded, a substantial anti-Americanism built up. American politicians, too, became tired of paying for European defense, even during the Cold War. After the Cold War, the critique exploded.

Despite these obstacles, the United States gradually and very imperfectly built up trust through multilateral institutions, in particular by engaging Europe through a defense alliance, as well as by providing assistance through institutions such as the Organization for European Economic Cooperation (OEEC), and later the Organisation for Economic Co-operation and Development (OECD) and the International Monetary Fund (IMF). But Europeans too did surprisingly well at reconciling with their neighbors after the Second World War, in part because the obviously malign conditions of Nazi rule made it more necessary to talk about the past in terms of moral categories than in terms of power politics.

Can the Benign Model Be Replicated?

What alternatives are there to US hegemony? Discussion of this question began in earnest after the 2003 Iraq war, intensified after the Global Financial Crisis of 2007–2008 appeared to damage American capitalism, and reached a fever pitch after the election of Donald Trump as president and his adoption of an erratic and conflictual unilateralism. The old multilateral mechanisms for international policy coordination, which reflected a fundamentally American view of the world, are being torn apart. But for all the worry about twenty-first-century America, it was never clear what the alternative might be.

Those who looked backward generally saw a new role or responsibility for Europe. But Europe was aging demographically, and growing less quickly than the United States or than the dynamic emerging markets. And Europe was embroiled in its own discussion of whether Germany was hegemonic in Europe.

The discussion of the German role in Europe had taken on a new dimension after German unification in 1990. Before 1990, four large countries, France, Germany, Italy, and the United Kingdom, had almost identical populations and economic outputs. The addition of almost 17 million East Germans to the Federal Republic in 1990 upset this demographic balance of Europe, pushing commentators to worry about a "Fourth Reich," with a new Germany applying what its leading philosopher, Jürgen Habermas, called DM[Deutsche Mark]-Nationalism. The claim to hegemony looked even stronger when the European Monetary Union was constructed along lines suggested by German intellectual references and interests, and when the euro replaced the Deutsche Mark. In the European debt crisis, and after the coronavirus crisis, there was an acute awareness that being a hegemon would involve paying a heavy price.

Most Germans responded with the claim that "we are not Europe's hegemon, as the US was in the case of NATO."[24] The political scientists Simon Bulmer and William Paterson describe a "leadership avoidance complex."[25] There are historical, but also practical, reasons for German restraint when it comes to leadership. Modern Germany has been molded by the legacy of the Nazi dictatorship and of the industrialized mass murder of Jews. Auschwitz is the reference point of modern political debate. The openness of Germans to addressing their history has made cooperation and integration possible—and is a striking contrast to, say, the unapologetic stance of Japan's Shinzō Abe toward China and Korea, whose populations were the victims of Japanese aggression in the mid-twentieth century. But exactly that openness by Germany would seem to rule out a straightforward bid for power, at least as power is conventionally seen.

There are also much more practical explanations for why Germany on its own cannot lead on a global level. It is too small in comparison to the United States or China. Its aging population is a source of vulnerability, as is the heavy dependence of the German economy on the automobile industry at a moment of very rapid technical change and of concerns about carbon dioxide emissions and global warming. So Germany needs to work with others—with France in Europe, and with China on a global level. Much of the discussion about cooperation is framed by contemplation of how Germany, and Europe, can shape the economic process of globalization.

The Trump election also changed the terms of the debate. At times, the German media have called on Germany to replace the United States, and to fill the void left after Trump's inauguration in January 2017.[26] The *New York Times* responded to the election with an article under the headline, "As Obama Exits World Stage, Angela Merkel May Be the Liberal West's Last Defender."[27] By 2017, Angela Merkel was explaining: "We have to know that we must fight for our future on our own, for our destiny as Europeans."[28] Obama himself seems to have thought along these lines, and visited Merkel in late 2016 to convince her of her centrality in rescuing multilateralism during the Trump administration. But it was clear that Germany could not achieve that goal alone. The clearest statement by the German chancellor was in her budget speech on November 23, 2016, when she emphasized that increasing globalization increased the need to act collectively, and that Germany could not on its own "fight the whole problem of worldwide hunger, solve the issue of 65 million refugees, or change political order everywhere in the sense that we would like." But she added that Germany should try to shape globalization in light of its experience with the social market economy in a multilateral setting, and should not "withdraw." In particular, "the G20 was the attempt to shape globalization in a human way and to provide for a sensible financial and economic order with the largest and most important economic powers of the world."[29] German leaders too have started to make a case that Germany can promote globalization in the absence of a fully engaged United States (due to its large size, the US economy is inevitably—and has been—less open to the world).[30]

On some occasions, German leaders have seemed to think that they could form a new alliance with China to rescue multilateralism. China and Germany are increasingly aligned on climate change issues, whereas President Trump's emphasis on coal appeared obstructive and destructive. There is also a clear Chinese-German alliance building on resistance to trade protectionism. Chinese president Xi Jinping has been particularly forceful, stating:

> From the historical perspective, economic globalization resulted from growing social productivity, and is a natural outcome of scientific and technological progress, not something created by any individuals or

any countries. Economic globalization has powered global growth and facilitated movement of goods and capital, advances in science, technology and civilization, and interactions among peoples.[31]

Another possible collective alternative leadership grouping would be the BRICs, an acronym originally coined by the economist Jim O'Neill of Goldman Sachs in 2001 to encompass the new, very large, and rapidly growing emerging markets of Brazil, Russia, India, and China (the group was expanded in 2010 to include South Africa, and called BRICS). In June 2009, while responding to the Global Financial Crisis, Russia convened a BRICs summit: the event became annual, and was turned after two years into a BRICS affair. But there were major tensions as well as similarities among the nations, over democracy, and over economic power.

Increasingly, it looked as if China was searching for a different way to reorient the world's power structures. By contrast with the American engagement in multilateralism, or the European search for reconciliation through a plethora of common institutions, power politics is much more a part of the Asian legacy of the twentieth century. A significant transition occurred in the 2010s. Mao Zedong had repeatedly emphasized that China would "never seek hegemony," and Deng Xiaoping contrasted his country with the United States and the Soviet Union that did aspire to hegemony: "A superpower is an imperialist country which everywhere subjects other countries to its aggression, interference, control, subversion or plunder and strives for world hegemony."[32]

Hu Jintao (president from 2003 to 2013) had continued an approach articulated by Deng in the 1980s: "Hide capabilities and bide time" (*Tao guang yang hui*). That strategy, however, had always been predicated on an assessment of the international balance of power. Xi Jinping after becoming party general secretary in 2012, by contrast, moved the focus to "national rejuvenation." From 2013, Xi promoted as the "project of the century" the Belt and Road Initiative, sometimes referred to as a "new Silk Road" (after the term used by nineteenth-century Germans to describe the commercial spine of premodern Eurasia). The aim has been to connect nearly seventy countries and three continents through rail lines, pipelines, highways, ports, and other infrastructure. Together, these projects are meant to crisscross Eurasia and link China to Europe and Africa through an overland "belt" and an overseas "road."

The project seemed on one level to be an opportunity for Asian and African countries to find resources for development that would be free of the kind of governance-related controls and environmental concerns imposed by the multilateral development institutions in Washington, as well as a chance for peripheral European countries smarting with resentment about German dominance to assert their autonomy. At another level, critics began to think of it as creating debt and dependency traps, and as being not that different from previous British or American grabs for hegemony. The real challenge for China's leaders will be to develop a coherent view of the world that does not scare its neighbors—and others. China is triply vulnerable. Its relatively underdeveloped and only partially protected financial sector is crisis prone. The large Belt and Road infrastructure initiative has created a new problem: dependence in the areas opened up by the new Chinese communications thrust. Finally, there is a worry about democratic control; and it is the lack of democracy that has been at the heart of anti-globalization critiques of multilateralism in rich countries.

The Chinese dilemma today is not unlike the American one of the mid-twentieth century. How can a new superpower maintain and extend its power in a world that plays by commercial rules? Its effectiveness as a concentration of power, its sustainability as a state, its ability to satisfy domestic claims: all depend on an open world economy. There are high costs if other states try to close themselves off, and openness cannot be achieved simply at gunpoint.

The United States tried to educate the rest of the world about the principles of progress and prosperity through the work of powerful foundations. Generations of European policymakers as well as academics were galvanized by the Carnegie, Ford, or Rockefeller Foundations. American popular culture made room for a protest whose effects could be contained and taken into the mainstream. Bob Dylan made the American way of life acceptable even to those who were repelled by naked military or economic power. China is certainly taking some pages from the American book. Consider that China Radio International in Kenya has increased its daily output at the same time as Radio Free Europe / Radio Liberty (not to mention the BBC World Service) has been the victim of budget cuts.

But it is hard to see China pushing, and the rest of the world accepting, a Lenovo foundation or the singing of Zhou Bichang as a way of warding off the resentments that the new type of globalization engenders. China will need to look for another path. Yesterday's globalization was thought of as Americanization, the imposition of mindless consumerism; today's globalization may be thought of as Chinafication, the spread of low-wage production.

Anti-Hegemonic Pressures

The challenges to hegemony as conventionally understood come not only from the new geography of economic power, but also from new information technologies that are changing the ways in which power is discussed and thought about. One of the striking features of recent years is the way in which new technologies have prompted a return to very old thinking: to the love of stories that drew our ancestors together around the hearth or the campfire.

Of course we turn to the past when we're worried about the future. The more uncertain we are about what will come, the more we cling to what has been. And the less we know about the future, the more convinced we are that we really understand and believe what we once were. Colossal forces—above all in the world of information technology and artificial intelligence—are shaping a revolutionary transformation in almost every aspect of human life. The result is a deep uncertainty.

The tyranny of the past over contemporary life has two principal pillars, both of which are anchored deeply in human psychology. These mental posts, which relate to elemental human experience, are so firmly fixed that they cannot simply be eradicated. First, the most comfortable place we all ever were was our mother's womb. Everything after that is exposed, uncertain, insecure. No wonder that we are nostalgic and crave a level of security that we can never again attain. Appropriately we howl when we come into the world. Therapy sessions try to reenact that primal scream, so that we can break out of the prison. Or we can be much more restrained about our nostalgia: in Japan, which is grappling with the shock of the new after Emperor Akhito's 2019 abdication, one can buy canned air "from a previous era."

A second fundamental drive, almost as powerful, is the way that the human mind is hardwired to be receptive to stories. An old Hassidic saying quoted by Kafka explains that "God created man in order to tell stories." A new feature of academic analysis over recent years is simply the extent of discussion of and reflection on the human addiction to narratives—an idea that has recently been given a grounding in the dynamics of human evolution. The narrative form is satisfying, according to contemporary neuroscience, because we have evolved to assess other people's minds and motives in order to act persuasively in group settings, say, to better coordinate the hunt for food. As a result, only that sort of explanation is satisfying psychologically. The downside is that in today's more complex social universe, narrative may be completely misleading because it can far too easily seem to explain causation. Because the explanations superficially but erroneously produced by narrative are so intuitively graspable, they prevent a deeper understanding of what may cause social and political phenomena. In consequence, the narrative addiction frustrates attempts to produce reasonable solutions to the dilemmas thrown up by our modern group behavior.

It has by now become a cliché of business and politico chitchat to say that we need a new narrative. Economists are now shifting to the analysis of "narrative economics."[33] Others refer to the "subjectivist turn." We can demonstrate how wishful thinking generates contagion, and how ideas about the world shape the world.[34] But the supremacy of narrative can also mean the justification for tall stories, for the "fake it till you make it" approach of Elizabeth Holmes (of the Theranos fraud) or the pretend German heiress Anna Sorokin (aka Anna Delvey), the Russian truck driver's daughter who fooled New York high society.[35]

Narratives in fact often stand in the way of concrete and effective solutions. The most compelling and comprehensive ones are so fundamental that they lock us in a mental prison. To see this effect today, consider Russia, where many powerful recent narratives have been generated. Since Russian society is so evidently engaged in an experiment of establishing social meaning as a basis for a new social organization, it is easy to conclude that Russia has become the world's influencer, or, in European terms, that the new movement of ideas is from east to west. Everything is malleable. The economist and regime critic Irina Khakamada formulated the new process in an illuminating way: "In the west a politician is not a god, but hired by society to serve the state. But here it is quite the opposite. Politicians hire society to satisfy their permanently growing demands."[36]

Hybrid warfare, an approach to conflict in which the conventionally sharp distinction between war and peace is removed, has been pioneered by Russia with the principal objective of messing with narratives. A mantra of the influential television station RT is that "there is no such thing as objective reporting."[37] Words like *freedom* and *democracy* were turned into meaningless terms, so that people who used them would feel ridiculous. RT has been called by its fans "anti-hegemonic," and it made a major success of covering the Occupy Wall Street movement. Russia has been trying to practice what the historian Timothy Snyder calls "relative power" and "strategic relativism" by weakening the other side, or making it look foolish.[38] Some of the attacks have looked like simple updates of old intelligence and subversion strategies: in the Second World War, for instance, German propagandists such as William Joyce, known as "Lord Haw-Haw" because of his hallmark mocking guffaw, inserted their comments into BBC broadcasts to say "that's a lie." The technique is simple to update. In April 2015, for instance, the French television network TV5Monde suddenly began to broadcast ISIS slogans, and its Facebook page started to post warnings: "Soldiers of France, stay away from the Islamic State! You have the chance to save your families, take advantage of it," read one message. Another proclaimed: "The CyberCaliphate continues its cyberjihad against the enemies of Islamic State."[39]

Vladimir Putin laid out Russia's vision in a series of programmatic speeches addressed to foreign audiences. The two most striking were delivered at the Security Conference in Munich in February 2007, on the eve of the Global Financial Crisis, and at Sochi on the Black Sea coast in 2014, after the invasion of Crimea. At Munich, Putin laid out Russia's strategy as a defense of the principles of democracy, freedom, openness, and international law, against a unipolar United States–dominated world order that was systematically breaking all of those principles. At Munich he told his audience that the American order "certainly has nothing in common with democracy. Because, as you know, democracy is the power of the majority in light of the interests and opinions of the minority. Incidentally, Russia—we—are constantly being taught about democracy. But for some reason those who teach us do not want to learn themselves. I consider that the unipolar model is not only unacceptable but also impossible in today's world." He turned in the question session to nongovernmental organizations (NGOs) that he believed were subverting democracy: "Secret financing. Hidden from society. Where is the democracy here? Can you tell me? No! You can't tell me and you never will be able to. Because there is no democracy here, there is simply one state exerting influence on another."[40]

At Sochi, he made the mass media the focus of the discussion about meaning in narratives:

We have entered a period of differing interpretations and deliberate silences in world politics. International law has been forced to retreat over and over by the onslaught of legal nihilism. Objectivity and justice have been sacrificed on the altar of political expediency. Arbitrary interpretations and biased assessments have replaced legal norms. At the same time, total control of the global mass media has made it possible when desired to portray white as black and black as white. In a situation where you had domination by one country and its allies, or its satellites rather, the search for global solutions often turned into an attempt to impose their own universal recipes. The "unstable construction" of American power "has opened the road wide for inflated national pride, manipulating public opinion and letting the strong bully and suppress the weak.[41]

A secondary strategy is to tell obvious lies. Many commentators have pointed out that the obviousness of the lie is a fundamental part of the message: it shows that the speaker is active, powerful, and capable of changing or bending reality by reconfiguring the narrative. The key executor of the strategy, since adopted in grandiloquent fashion by Donald Trump, is Vladimir Putin. He explained after the occupation of the Crimea that the "green men" were not connected with Russia. On April 17, 2014, he went on to assert: "There are no Russian units in eastern Ukraine—no special services, no tactical advisers. All this is being done by the local residents." Edward Snowden, the National Security Agency contractor who had released thousands of US intelligence documents, including details of American surveillance, to WikiLeaks, then asked, via video link, does Russia spy on its citizens the way the United States does? Putin could then reply: "Thank God, our special services are strictly controlled by the state and society, and their activity is regulated by law."[42]

The WikiLeaks information, and the discussion of Russian influence in the US elections or the UK Brexit referendum, were explained away as important demonstrations of how opinion was shaped. Putin explained: "There's nothing in Russia's interest here; the hysteria has been created only to distract the American people from the main point of what was revealed by hackers. And the main point is that public opinion was manipulated. But no one talks about this. Is it really important who did this? What is inside this information—that is what is important."[43] If any kind of manipulation is possible, nothing is true. And on that basis, no set of rules and no social order is possible. All of this is a recipe for chaos and destruction, one that will be employed always and only by those on the margin: it is a tool of the weak, and it is anti-hegemonic. But one of its most powerful weapons is to make the assertion that any order is hegemonic.

The Global Financial Crisis demonstrated the fragility of American power, and the anti-hegemonic discourse turned against the United States. The European debt crisis that followed almost immediately destroyed the claim that Europe had a superior model, leading to a powerful attack on German hegemony. The coronavirus crisis, barely more than ten years later, did the same for the claim that the new world order would be led by China. The fact that the virus originated in China, as well as the extensive discussion of how the ruling Chinese Communist Party had covered up the initial evidence of the outbreak, silenced and penalized whistleblowers, and pushed an aggressive disinformation (Russian-style) campaign, led to a backlash against China, not just in the United States and Europe, but across the world.

The dehegemonization process, in generating a sense of national decline and humiliation, produces a more militant nationalism, which is evoked to explain the loss of hegemony, and to provide a psychic compensation. That is the case with the support behind Trump's America First campaign, and behind the German right-wing populism of the Alternative für Deutschland. The same momentum is building in Xi Jinping's increasingly nationalist China. Some Chinese commentators are seeing, in response to the coronavirus crisis and the nationalist movement, parallels in the century of humiliation that produced the Boxer Rebellion. A new aggressive diplomacy points out foreign failures. "Wolf warrior" diplomats claim that France deliberately abandoned its elderly population to a lonely coronavirus death. There are anxieties that the Belt and Road Initiative is simply preparation for Chinese military and political domination: in April 2020, for example, Chinese internet rumors started that Kazakhstan had applied to be part of China. Veteran observer Zi Zhongyun, an eighty-nine-year-old longtime historian at the Chinese Academy of Social Sciences, cautioned: "The authorities may have staunched the damage for the moment, but the long-term influence of this kind of 'patriotism,' one that directly undermines the national interest, is hard to counter. In fact, it is a canker that will continue to metastasise." She then came to the remarkable conclusion that "at the moment the trend isn't de-globalisation as much as global de-Sinicisation."[44] Hegemony has been overcome by anti-hegemony. And madmen have largely stopped presenting themselves as Alexander or Napoleon.

5

Multilateralism

with Marzenna James

Both multilateralism and the turn to geopolitics are characteristic twentieth-century phenomena that have endured into our own century. From its beginnings, multilateralism has concealed peculiarities and flaws that have led to greater vulnerability. This chapter examines the origins of multilateralism; the next shows how and why it was dismissed and eroded.

The modern term *multilateralism* first appeared during the Second World War in the discussion of trade relations for the postwar world. It offered what seemed the obvious antidote to the disastrous beggar-thy-neighbor policies that had contributed to and then intensified the Great Depression. At the time, the Great Depression was interpreted as a major cause of the deterioration of international relations and a breeder of aggression and war. The trade element of multilateralism was intrinsically connected to the broader issue of securing international peace. The linkage appeared self-evident to contemporaries. In 1945, the economist Jacob Viner stated bluntly, "There should be no need, in view of the experience of the interwar years, to belabor here the argument for multilateralism as the true basis for commercial policy."[1] Multilateralism in the modern era of globalization thus began with a trade agenda, but that association always constituted its central weakness—in fact, the first threats and challenges to multilateralism emerged in discussions of commercial issues.

States are members of international organizations, and they should be expected to defend not only their rights but also their interests. Multilateralism structurally resembles the framework for commercial negotiation, whereby one country will make deals that give it advantages but will also often accept some adverse outcome as part of an overall package. Indeed, the French term *globaliser* means to bundle issues and implicitly to accept trade-offs of this kind. The outcome is like democracy in a national context—not everyone is pleased, and the losers may thunder against pernicious multilateralism much like those disillusioned with the outcome of democracy will rail against it.

Multilateralism draws all members of an international order into a complex bargaining process. Every side makes trade-offs, offering concessions in one domain in order to obtain gains in another. In the 1980s, the United States agreed to continue to let Japanese cars in, with self-imposed limits ("voluntary export restraints"), if Japan would liberalize its financial system enough to allow US financial institutions to operate from Tokyo. The exercise of coordination can be defined as doing what you would not otherwise do from the point of view of immediate self-interest. But that will only happen if there is a prospect of future gains. It is thus vital that all countries are bound into the system, and that they are committed not to walk away if they feel for the moment that their interests are being sacrificed. If there is a real possibility of exit, many of the promises— motivated by the hope of future gain—will be undone. This feature explains why some interpreters believe that any multilateral system needs a strong sheriff (hegemon) in place.[2] A working international order cannot afford to be here today but gone tomorrow.

During the wartime preparations for a postwar future, the concept of multilateralism was quickly extended from commerce to security. The key principles of the new approach to international relations are spelled out in the Charter of the United Nations. Signed in September 1945, the new foundational document went substantially beyond the 1919 Covenant of the League of Nations, which had simply insisted on a basis in international law, without specifying how new agreements could be forged. The covenant had begun by laying out the novel rationale: "In order to promote international co-operation and to achieve international peace and security, by the acceptance of obligations not to resort to war, by the prescription of open, just and honourable relations between nations, by the firm establishment of the understandings of international law as the actual rule of conduct among Governments, and by the maintenance of justice and a scrupulous respect for all treaty obligations in the dealings of organised peoples with one another." By contrast, the United Nations explained its basis for international order: "To develop friendly relations among nations based on respect for the principle of equal rights and self-determination of peoples, and to take other appropriate measures to strengthen universal peace."

The United Nations system, including the Bretton Woods institutions, the World Bank, and the International Monetary Fund, was not completely new, and large parts of the vision were already included in the Covenant of the League of Nations, whose "Economic and Financial Organisation" also anticipated the International Monetary Fund.[3] But the League was never complete, in that it did not encompass the whole world, whereas both the United Nations and the Bretton Woods institutions were originally intended to be genuinely global.

The twentieth century was shaped by the differences between the two peace settlements: the 1919 Covenant of the League of Nations, forged during the Paris conference, and the United Nations system, which arose through a series of meetings to establish international organizations, culminating in the San Francisco conference of forty-six countries meeting from April to June 1945. The conference started before the end of the European war and concluded before the termination of the Pacific war. It included no peace terms, and in fact legally the treaty ending the Second World War only came in 1990 with the Two Plus Four Agreement establishing German unity (the two were West and East Germany, as the successor states to the German Reich which had launched war in 1939, and the four were France, the Soviet Union, the United Kingdom, and the United States). By contrast, the 1919 Paris conference and the series of treaties it produced (Versailles for Germany, Saint-Germain for Austria, Neuilly for Bulgaria, Trianon for Hungary, and Sèvres for the Ottoman Empire) stood for humiliation. They were enduring sores for the countries they reordered, except in the case of the Treaty of Sèvres, which sparked the Turkish War of Independence and the creation of a new Turkish state that set about revising its own frontiers. The 1945 settlement was about institutions rather than territorial settlement, which was arranged in a different way—with more traditional meetings of the major powers, notably the Big Three, the Soviet Union, the United Kingdom, and the United

States (which met in Potsdam in a reprisal of the role of the 1919 Big Three, that is, France, the United Kingdom, and the United States).

A system of Great Power solutions, sometimes also called a *concert* after the 1815 Vienna settlement, is not at all the equivalent of multilateralism. It is sometimes tempting to think that the Big Three (or the Big Some Other Number) can work out a solution for everyone else's problems—but that is quite different from a general mechanism that facilitates every country's participation in the preserving of peace and prosperity. An arrangement of Great Powers is a challenge to multilateralism, rather than a completion of a principle of recognizing the equality of all state voices. The move back away from real institutionalized multilateralism began in the 1970s, when the oil shocks challenged the political status quo and shook the international economy. Five large industrial countries developed a regular summit meeting process starting in 1975, when the first such "Group of Five" (G5) meeting was held at the French chateau of Rambouillet. The summit had been preceded by regular informal meetings of the finance ministers of those countries, France, Germany, Japan, the United Kingdom, and the United States. Italy and Canada were later added to make a G7.

This western club, however, looked particularly inappropriate as a form of governance after the end of the Cold War. In an effort to be more inclusive, Russia was added to the political meetings in 1997, making the G8; after the annexation of Crimea in 2014, it was excluded again. A larger and more representative group, the G20, included big newcomers: Brazil, China, India, South Africa, and Turkey starting in 2008. It looked as if the hour of the emerging markets had come, as they were pulled into the concert, rather than being drawn into a revived multilateralism. At the first G20 summit meeting, Brazil's Luiz Lula da Silva lectured the big countries about their poor governance: "We are not asking for assistance; we are not asking for you to give us funds. What we want you to do is to fix your own economies. The best thing you can do for us is to return to growth. . . . We are talking about the G20 because the G8 doesn't have any more reason to exist. In other words, the emerging economies have to be taken into consideration in today's globalised world."[4] President Hu Jintao of China demanded a "new international financial order that is fair, just, inclusive and orderly." France's President Nicolas Sarkozy, in advance of the meeting, called for the summit to "re-found capitalism."[5]

When first initiated, this updated concert system looked as if it produced results that were more effective than those of a complex and dysfunctional multilateralism. Solutions to specific problems at the initial meetings of these groups proved innovative and important. The 1975 Rambouillet summit coordinated a peaceful response to the oil crisis, for example, at a moment when many political leaders in western countries were calling for military action. And the April 2009 London G20 summit was a high-water mark of international coordination. But the meetings rapidly deteriorated into regular opportunities for unproductive posturing and demonstrative bickering.

In multilateralism, too, the bargains struck do not simply reflect an amalgamation or simple arithmetic reconciliation of member countries' interests. For a long period, the United Nations was stymied because the Soviet Union simply used its veto power in Security Council votes. The group was also incomplete in that the People's Republic of China was excluded until 1971, when a group of twenty-three countries, led by Albania, introduced a motion in the General Assembly to recognize the People's Republic (communist China) as the only legitimate representative of the Chinese people, on the grounds that "reality" should "not be changed to suit the myth of a so called Republic of China, fabricated out of a portion of Chinese territory."[6] The US suggestion of a dual representation that would also involve Chiang Kai-shek's Republic of China (Taiwan) was rejected. After this, the US delegation repeatedly spoke of the need to combine "realism" and justice in respect to the membership of international organizations. The Bretton Woods institutions, the International Monetary Fund, and the World Bank were much more central in the Cold War precisely because (contrary to the intentions of the 1944 Bretton Woods conference) the Soviet Union never joined. China was a member, but until 1980 the seat was held by Taiwan, not the People's Republic. Only after the collapse of the Soviet Union did the Russian Federation join the International Monetary Fund, in 1992.

Idealism versus Realism

At the inaugural session of the 1944 Bretton Woods conference, in which forty-four countries (members of the wartime coalition, the United Nations) were represented, US Treasury Secretary Henry Morgenthau set out the philosophy of international cooperation with great clarity. He declared: "I hope that this Conference will focus its attention upon two elementary economic axioms. The first of these is this: that prosperity has no fixed limits. It is not a finite substance to be diminished by division. On the contrary, the more of it that other nations enjoy, the more each nation will have for itself. . . . The second axiom is a corollary of the first. Prosperity, like peace, is indivisible. We cannot afford to have it scattered here or there among the fortunate or to enjoy it at the expense of others. Poverty, wherever it exists, is menacing to us all and undermines the well-being of each of us. It can no more be localized than war, but spreads and saps the economic strength of all the more-favored areas of the earth."[7]

Behind the lofty ideals, however, were also—very obviously—the security and economic interests of one dominant country that was not inclined to compromise much on its vision of the future. It was a very American settlement. Only one of the other forty-three countries really mattered in the negotiations: the United Kingdom. There was thus a high measure of bilateralism rather than multilateralism about the outcome. The operation worked in large part because the US administration saw an international treaty as locking into place its domestic agenda, preserving the legacy of the New Deal. The principle of the obligation to introduce currency convertibility, limits on discriminatory trading practices, and increased access to each other's markets had been inserted into Anglo-American relations as article 7 of the March 1941 Lend-Lease Agreement, which was generally known as "the Consideration." The original draft of the State Department specified that the two countries would commit themselves to "promote mutually advantageous economic relations between them and the betterment of world-wide economic relations; they shall provide against discrimination in either the United States of America or the United Kingdom against the importation of any product originating in the other country." The measure appeared in Washington as a sledgehammer to break the carapace of British Imperial Preference, a system of tariffs and trade agreements between parts of the British Empire. (The same language had been used in clause 4 of the Atlantic Charter, drawn up in shipboard meetings during Winston Churchill's first visit to President Roosevelt.) The governments committed themselves "to further the enjoyment by all States, great or small, victor or vanquished, of access, on equal terms, to the trade and to the raw materials of the world." The strategy of Secretary of State Cordell Hull, a convinced free trader, for limiting protectionist impulses rested on two pillars. First was the need to limit congressional or parliamentary politics.

The origins of this pillar arose from the Smoot-Hawley Tariff and the disasters of Depression-era trade policies. As political scientist Elmer Schattschneider showed, the 1930 Smoot-Hawley Tariff had changed its nature in the course of congressional debate, as individual parliamentarians added on measures to protect local interests. The logic of this argument is analogous to the collective-action mechanism suggested by political scientist Mancur Olson: an accumulation of small interests will lead to a suboptimal outcome, because each small interest will see major gains in a protectionist measure, and the collective is happy to accept this since the overall cost of each add-on measure is relatively trivial. Olson's suggestion is that only an overarching articulation of a general interest can solve the collective action problem: in terms of concrete politics, this meant strengthening the executive and the presidency at the expense of the legislature. This was exactly the course that Cordell Hull followed with the Reciprocal Trade Agreements Act of 1934, legislation that allowed the president to conclude bilateral trade treaties.[8]

The second logic behind Hull's strategy lay in the perception that it is safer to anchor liberal arrangements in a legal or constitutional form, and in this way also remove them from party and parliamentary politics. Anchoring the open economy in international treaties would be a way of tying political hands, or—in today's political science terminology—embedding the liberal international order.[9] In this way, an international order might create permanent constitutional guarantees for the preferences of the United States as a whole (but not necessarily of individual Americans or individual parliamentarians).

The uncompromising attitude of the United States brought the inescapable conclusion even to opponents and skeptics (such as the British economist and key architect of the Bretton Woods order, John Maynard Keynes) that trade liberalization would not be subject to discussion or bargaining—that the US intention was to impose free trade on other countries to ensure ready markets for its manufactured goods, while maintaining some domestic protections for itself. Keynes, then, was eager to move ahead with an international trade organization to ensure that the United States was also constrained. But after the conclusion of the war, when countries started haggling about the exemptions they desired from such an international trade organization, the US Congress indeed revolted, and the proposed institution collapsed. As a result, the initial Bretton Woods gathering simply made concrete what preexisting diplomacy had already established: because of the consensus that trade should not be debated, the initial conference dealt instead with currency stabilization.

American negotiators themselves were quite aware of their negotiating advantage, and knew that they should use it. As Morgenthau told Assistant Secretary Harry Dexter White, the principal US negotiator for the Bretton Woods settlement, "Now the advantage is ours here, and I personally think we should take it." White replied: "If the advantage were theirs, they would take it."[10] The most obvious reflection of the advantage was the centrality of the US currency in the international monetary system, a position that the dollar retained even after the fixed-exchange-rate regime broke down in 1971. The US negotiators had always insisted on the preeminence of the dollar, and in the middle of the Bretton Woods negotiations, in the context of an apparently trivial discussion concerning when countries should make their initial payments into the new International Monetary Fund, they pushed for a formula that put the dollar at the center: par values could be expressed in terms of either gold or the US dollar (and since few countries had substantial gold reserves, no one was likely to take the gold option). The fixation on the dollar produced a fundamental flaw, not simply within the Bretton Woods settlement, but also in the financial world that succeeded it: a flaw that was exposed when the fixed-exchange-rate regime broke down in the early 1970s.

Could a multilateral and peaceful order be self-sustaining and self-correcting? Keynes did not believe in what might be called the *globalization paradigm:* the theory, elaborated already by Montesquieu and celebrated by Richard Cobden and John Bright, as well as by Norman Angell, that commerce and commercial interconnectedness would by themselves bring international peace and order. That was why a profound reordering of the international currency regime was needed. In 1919, disgusted by the settlement after the First World War, he had written:

Bankers are used to this system, and believe it to be a necessary part of the permanent order of society. They are disposed to believe, therefore, by analogy with it, that a comparable system between Governments, on a far vaster and definitely oppressive scale, represented by no real assets, and less closely associated with the property system, is natural and reasonable and in conformity with human nature. I doubt this view of the world. Even capitalism at home, which engages many local sympathies, which plays a real part in the daily process of production, and upon the security of which the present organisation of society largely depends, is not very safe.[11]

The Bretton Woods scheme required worldwide agreement on the control of capital movements, which was presented as a "permanent feature" of the postwar system.[12] The union would work closely not only with an agency dedicated to stabilizing prices (in order "to control the Trade Cycle"), but also with a supranational peace-keeping agency ("charged with the duty of preserving the peace and maintaining international order"). The British draft concluded that the proposal was "capable of arousing enthusiasm because it makes a beginning at the future economic ordering of the world between nations and the 'winning of the peace,' and might help to create the conditions and the atmosphere in which much else would be made easier."[13]

Keynes had been asked by the British government to prepare a counter-scheme to Nazi economics minister Walther Funk's remarkable (but deeply insincere) plan for European prosperity of 1940. He rejected decisively a return to 1920s internationalism as a pattern for postwar relations. In his proposals, Keynes spoke of "the craving for social and personal security" after the war.[14] But there were as yet few details on how an international economy might be managed to promote such security. Very different types of economies needed to be integrated in the common vision: economies that, like the United Kingdom and United States, would rely on Keynesian macroeconomic demand management; as well as those following the Soviet model, with central planning, including of external trade. The Soviet delegation was a part of Bretton Woods, and some of the more obscure wording of the agreement is the result of the need to take into account Soviet peculiarities.

Every country had to be free to shape a domestic agenda that would meet domestic priorities, while connecting with the international economy in ways that were reconciled with peace and broad international objectives. There were three possibilities for achieving these goals:

1. States might simply decide that international harmony was in their self-interest. The experience of the 1930s, however, did not seem encouraging.
2. An international juridical framework might be established to arbitrate in cases where national and international economic objectives clashed.
3. An entirely automatic mechanism might point states in the direction of peace and prosperity without a complex and lengthy bureaucratic or juridical process.

Discussions of the postwar order swung between acceptance of the second and third of these choices, and ended up including elements of both. Automatism was attractive because it was apolitical, but worrisome because it might not always fit with widely perceived needs. It was agreed that an element of discretion was needed, which might best be provided through the creation of an institution with legal powers established by treaty. The resulting compromise is the foundation of the Bretton Woods achievement. Keynes's scheme proposed an international bank, which he called the Clearing Union, with a new unit of account that would be the basis for the issue of a new international currency.

A new currency that was not a national currency was the key element of Keynes's vision: it would free the international monetary system from the convoluted international diplomacy conducted by national central banks fixed on the gold standard, which had been so destructive in the interwar years. The proposed currency's name, bancor, indicates the way in which the new money was conceived as an artificially created replacement for gold, which should gradually be expelled from the civilized conduct of international economics. Gold might be sold by central banks to the new international bank for bancor, but would not be bought. The "barbarous relics" of the past were cast off, as was the old and painful adjustment mechanism for countries that spent too much abroad (or ran current account deficits) or that spent too little (had current account surpluses). Keynes's critique was that during the 1920s those countries that had payment surpluses had not expanded quickly enough to avoid the threat of inadequate demand and hence economic depression.

The object of the Clearing Union's activities would be to avoid balance-of-payments imbalances through the creation of a body of rules and practices relating to debtors' overdrafts on the bank and creditors' positive balances. Quotas were created for each country in the union: half of the average of imports and exports over the past five years. These quotas determined the limits up to which debtors could borrow (at interest rates that rose with the quantity of their debts). For their part, creditors had to transfer to the union surpluses above their quota, and pay charges to the union if their balances rose above a quarter of their quota. The Keynes scheme created a nearly perfect symmetry: it was to be as unpleasant and as costly to hold credit balances as to be a debtor. The result would be to prevent policies such as those followed by the United States and France in the later 1920s: instead, the rules of the Clearing Union would drive such creditor states to expand.[15] In subsequent drafts of his proposal, Keynes wrestled with "the most difficult question": "to determine . . . how much to decide by rule and how much to leave to discretion."[16]

An abstract and impersonal operation would give the most scope for the operation of markets, and for the preservation of national sovereignty. The most extreme version of a rule-bound system, however, the gold standard, had led to deflation and depression. Successive British drafts of the agreement, passed among Keynes, the British Treasury, and the Bank of England, gradually increased the discretionary element in what had originally been a neat and simple automatic process. Monetary authorities preferred (often they still do) "to operate by vague requests backed by vague sanctions, rather than by publishing definite rules."[17] By the fourth draft of the agreement, the balance had shifted toward discretion. The governing board of the international bank might set conditions under which countries would be allowed to increase their debit balances, including by surrendering their gold reserve, ceding control over capital transactions, and devaluing their currency. But even after rules of conduct were replaced with policy consultations, there still existed a symmetry between the constraints on debtors and those on creditors. If a credit balance exceeded half the quota, the country would still be required to "discuss with the Governing Board (but still retain the ultimate decision in its own hands)" an expansion of domestic credit and demand, an exchange-rate revaluation, an increase in wages, tariff reductions, or international loans for the development of backward countries. The United States would gradually intervene in the negotiations to avoid being forced into expansionary policies simply by virtue of its debtor position. This was possible because international capital movements would largely be controlled.

Members' widespread agreement in the initial bargaining positions made the outcome easier. Keynes wrote of his proposals that they "lay no claim to originality. They are an attempt to reduce to practical shape certain general ideas belonging to the contemporary climate of economic opinion, which have been given publicity in recent months by writers of several different nationalities. It is difficult to see how any plan can be successful which does not use these general ideas, which are born of the spirit of the age."[18] That was a broadly accurate assessment of Bretton Woods. There was some discomfort over the role of the dollar—including by Keynes—but it was abundantly obvious that, with Germany and Japan bombed and ruined, the world's trade, for the foreseeable future, would depend on dollars.

Trade Pacts, Growth, and Manufacturing

The Bretton Woods agreement looked as if it was predicated on a transition to an open international trading system, under the supervision of another institution, the International Trade Organization. But that institution never materialized: in December 1945, the United States invited the wartime allies to launch a multilateral agreement for the reciprocal reduction of tariffs on trade in goods, and by 1948 there was an agreement on a founding document (the Havana Charter) that was signed by fifty-six countries. The promise was considerable, but it was not realized. The US Congress repeatedly rejected the document, and it was never submitted to the Senate. Instead, a provisional institution, the General Agreement on Tariffs and Trade (GATT) became the forum for rounds of negotiation on the removal of trade quotas and the reduction of tariffs.

The negotiating system created something of an optical illusion. Trade does not usually balance between pairs of countries. For instance, in the initial postwar expansion, European producers would sell simple machinery and engineering equipment to South America, which would sell rubber and coffee to North America, which would sell more sophisticated equipment to the Europeans. Or the balancing could take place through the sale of services: as Europe developed, it needed less sophisticated US machinery, but American forces were stationed in Europe and the United States bought services for them. Or the balancing could be in the form of investment flows: US-based multinational companies started to buy companies or properties in other countries. But the trade negotiations in the GATT system started bilaterally and reached agreements that were then multilateralized through the application of Most Favored Nation (MFN) clauses, where a signatory of an MFN agreement would get the same trade concession that had been agreed to bilaterally. Thus the thinking was always about particular goods that were the subject of controversy: for instance, in the 1960s Europeans in the "chicken war" put restrictions on the import of US chicken, which led the United States to retaliate with higher duties on light trucks from Europe, which were thus effectively excluded from the US market.

Trade overall became the motor of economic growth: it drove a rapid recovery in western Europe that stood in marked contrast to the dismal performance of the interwar years, then catalyzed hope for a global development strategy. Article 18 of the original GATT charter allowed developing countries to limit concessions on import duties, and to provide subsidies, if such steps would allow the introduction of new industries to raise living standards, while article 37 committed industrial countries to reduce or eliminate barriers to the products of less developed countries. But the European countries could not agree on steps to implement these promises, and in 1965 the agreement was reworked to allow exceptions in agriculture, steel, and textiles—the products most likely to come from poorer countries. Textiles too were restricted under various schemes that were eventually unified under the 1974 Multi Fiber Agreement, which came to an end only in 2005.

The last multilateral round of trade negotiations, the Doha round, started in 2001 (after the GATT had been replaced in 1994 by the World Trade Organization). Doha promised to extend the principle of multilateralism to include an emphasis on development: developing countries should, according to the initial declaration, "secure a share in the growth of world trade commensurate with the needs of their economic development. In this context, enhanced market access, balanced rules, and well targeted, sustainably financed technical assistance and capacity-building programmes have important roles to play."[19] Negotiations had become much more complex, in part simply due to the number of countries involved. The GATT originally had twenty-three members. The World Trade Organization (WTO), by contrast, was established by 123 countries, and by 2001 the organization became practically global when China joined as the 143rd member (Russia became the 156th member in 2012). In retrospect, Chinese membership appears as the watershed in the story of the WTO, when new members decided that trade multilateralism was not working for them, and the old members believed that they were being taken advantage of by the new members. The Doha round was particularly stymied by a dispute over the inclusion of environmental measures that divided large emerging markets from the industrial world: the late-arriving countries feared that the rich, established members were using environmental concerns as a pretext to impose extra costs so as to hinder and slow down potential new rivals.

The increased complexity of trade negotiations also resulted from domestic politics. As the trade regime was established, lobbying grew more sophisticated, and interest groups more numerous.

Trade expanded, consistently, at faster rates than industrial production. The average world tariff rate (calculated with a weighted mean) had increased in the early 1990s and stood at 9.7 percent in 1994; by 2010 it was half that, at 4.3 percent (the United States was at 2.81 percent and the European Union at 2.84 percent).[20] In the most recent phase, the drive to expand trade came more from bilateral negotiations rather than from the general framework. In 2002, the US Congress passed the Trade Act, which included presidential authority for trade promotion, and in 2004 the United States concluded deals with Australia and Morocco, and later with a range of Central American countries. But then Congress started to block agreements, and only in 2011 did the United States conclude trade deals with South Korea, Colombia, and Panama. In 2006 the European Union formulated a new trade strategy that relied on bilateral negotiations in order to "proceed faster and further in promoting openness and integration."[21]

At the beginning of 2018, the Trump administration launched a dramatically new approach, described in a report by the US trade representative that was published at the beginning of 2018: "As a general matter, we believe that these goals can be best accomplished by focusing on bilateral negotiations rather than multilateral negotiations—and by renegotiating and revising trade agreements when our goals are not being met."[22] The chair of the President's Council of Economic Advisers, Kevin Hassett, claimed that China had "misbehaved" as a member of the World Trade Organization, and that the organization had "failed" the United States.[23] The US trade representative's office documented how "in the 16 years before China joined the WTO—from 1984 to 2000—US industrial production grew by almost 71 percent. In the period from 2000 to 2016, US industrial production grew by less than 9 percent."[24] But even the bilateral agreements came in for criticism: "From 2011 (the last full year before the US-Korea FTA went into effect) to 2016, the total value of US goods exported to South Korea fell by $1.2 billion. Meanwhile, US imports of goods from South Korea grew by more than $13 billion."[25]

The political change of 2016 meant that *multilateralism* became a dirty word in the country that originally had insisted on it. From the beginning, however, representative institutions—including the US Congress—had treated the idea with considerable skepticism. And after that, trade wars— touted by Donald Trump as "good, and easy to win"—came with a substantial economic cost (in addition to a wider political fallout). By 2019, farmers had been hit by retaliatory measures, and some 300,000 manufacturing jobs and 0.3 percent of GDP had been lost, before the obviously much more severe impact of the pandemic.[26]

The Primacy of the Dollar

Bretton Woods was explicitly oriented around the US dollar. This became a source of complaint, first from other countries that worried the dollar orientation allowed the United States to finance deficits—arising from its imports, its military spending overseas, and its acquisitions of foreign companies—and to impose inflation on the world. French finance minister Valéry Giscard d'Estaing called this the "exorbitant privilege." Then it was the turn of the United States to express resentment at the system's constraints, because it was uniquely trapped: it was the only country that could not alter the value of its currency against the standard (the dollar), and derive an export stimulus by devaluing. In the end it was the United States that destroyed the dollar-based fixed-exchange-rate order in 1971. The "non-system" that replaced it, which relied on large financial flows, was if anything even more dollar-oriented than the system that lasted from the 1940s to the early 1970s. The first postwar era had substantially limited international movements of capital.

In the late 1960s, as the Bretton Woods system was disintegrating, the economist Robert Mundell made three predictions: that the Soviet Union would fall apart, that Europe would have a single currency, and that the dollar would remain the leading international currency and the center of the international monetary system.[27] Since the prediction was followed quickly by August 1971 and the collapse of the par value system, with the depreciation of the dollar, all of these predictions looked quite wild. But until now they have been accurate.

There were some attempts to devise a multilateral alternative to dependence on the US dollar. In the 1960s an extensive debate about the adequacy of dollar-denominated reserves led to an initiative to create a new international currency, the IMF's strangely named special drawing right (SDR). But because the United States insisted on so many restrictions (it could only be used by the official sector, governments, and central banks), it could never become a rival currency. In the late 1970s, in an extended phase of dollar weakness and skepticism about the position of the United States, the IMF tried to devise a "substitution account," in which countries would be allowed to convert their dollar holdings into SDRs, which would thus get an extended role. The scheme failed to take off because it proved impossible to work out who would compensate the "account" in the case of a depreciating dollar. The dollar remained not only king, but also the central problem of the international monetary order.

The feeling of entrapment remained. In what is now usually called "Bretton Woods II," many emerging markets, especially in Asia, pegged their currencies to the dollar.[28] By far the most conspicuous participator in this new version of the old regime was China, which firmly fixed its currency to the US dollar until 2005. Intervention to maintain what looked to the United States like an undervalued exchange rate required a large buildup of dollar reserves. Critics in the United States believed that China and other countries that were running large surpluses were manipulating the exchange rate to benefit their own exporters. In addition, the buildup of dollar assets and the dependence on the US dollar as the ultimate safe asset encouraged unproductive investments in the United States, in ways that many believe fueled the property and mortgage (especially subprime mortgage) bubble that burst in 2007. Matthew Klein and Michael Pettis have argued in their book *Trade Wars Are Class Wars* that during this period, exorbitant privilege turned into an exorbitant sacrifice. As Americans took on more debt, they bought more abroad, which led to deindustrialization and greater inequality in the United States. American consumers preferred to buy goods made abroad at the expense of American manufacturers, and employment in US manufacturing shrank.[29]

The dollar stayed as the central international currency even after the 2008 Global Financial Crisis, which only heightened the demand for a safe asset. Indeed, one immediate reaction to the freezing of the interbank market in the crisis was the demand for dollar liquidity by banks all over the world that had funded themselves through short-term borrowing on the US money market. The immediate result was emergency lending supplied by central banks in those major industrial countries that had access to swap lines at the Federal Reserve. A limited number of countries with emerging markets deemed essential to Washington also negotiated swap lines: Brazil, Mexico, South Korea, and Singapore. The exclusion of India from that list produced considerable bitterness. In the subsequent decade, the use of the dollar as an official reserve currency fell slightly—although it remained by far the largest share, at about two-thirds in 2019, but the dollar's share of the currency in which debt securities were denominated rose from 48 percent in 2008 to 64 percent at the end of 2018.[30] Official flows of reserves in the years after the financial crisis pushed up the value of the dollar: without those large official purchases, there would have been a net outflow driven by private sector flows.

Trade and currency relations are closely associated with each other, even if they are sometimes treated as separate issues to be handled by quite different negotiating teams—in the United States, the Department of Commerce and the Treasury; in the European Union, the Commission and the European Central Bank. Historically, one way of defusing pressures to engage in damaging trade protectionism has been to try to depreciate the currency. In 1970, for example, the US Congress almost passed the Mills bill, which would have imposed quotas on shoes and textiles. President

Richard Nixon responded in August 1971 by proposing a currency move: the end of the old gold convertibility at thirty-five dollars an ounce (along with a temporary import surcharge while the currency depreciation affected purchasing behavior). A similar dynamic occurred during the mid-1980s. When the dollar soared, and Americans complained increasingly about unfair trade practices, especially in Japan, US Treasury Secretary James Baker presented currency initiatives at the Plaza meeting in New York as an alternative to congressionally imposed measures to restrict imports. And in the 2000s, increased worries about Chinese imports were linked to a concern about the undervaluation of the Chinese currency and the over-valuation of the dollar, especially when the dollar surged in value during the early stages of the Global Financial Crisis.

There was always a risk that the instrumentalization of the dollar for political ends, as a weapon of statecraft, would backfire. Financial sanctions were highly effective in their original version as directed against a small and isolated country like North Korea; the more their use is extended against Iran or Russia, or employed as threats against Chinese companies, the more counterproductive they are. They push Russia and China, but also Europe, quickly to develop alternative mechanisms for payment and settlement. Juan Zarate, who as assistant secretary to the US Treasury in the 2000s was responsible for combating financial crime and terrorist financing, wrote a book in 2013 in which he warned against the extension of the sanctions regime and the long-run threat that such an extension would pose to US influence and power.[31]

The dollar's long-standing centrality was prompted by the demand for a deep and liquid safe asset, and that centrality will only disappear when alternative safe assets emerge, backed in some cases by non-state providers. The alternatives touted—the euro or the renminbi—never looked like convincing successors to dollar hegemony. But the dollar's long reign over the international financial system constitutes a fundamental contradiction of the principle of multilateralism. It depends on the United States being both economically stable and culturally and financially open. It also produces in the United States a demand for some end to a system that is felt to be entrapping Americans. In this regard, Nixon's move in 1971 and Trump's insistence on America First are responses to a world order that appears to make the American people poorer and generally worse off and in this way contributes to what Trump memorably termed "American carnage."

The process of disintegration and dissolution affects other aspects of postwar multilateralism. Already before 2016, the World Trade Organization was struggling, and the Doha round of negotiations was incomplete, but the Trump administration delivered a coup de grâce by refusing to nominate judges to the crucial mechanism for arbitrating disputes, the Appellate Body. The Trump administration's withdrawal from the Paris Climate Agreement despite the increasingly urgent danger posed by global warming, and from the World Health Organization at the height of the COVID-19 pandemic, further underscored that the old multilateralism was dead.

Is there any hope of emerging from the resulting trap? In trying to destroy multilateralism, the United States is self-lacerating. Internal conflicts are deliberately exacerbated. And as the dysfunctionalities of the United States are revealed, and US competence and state effectiveness come under greater scrutiny, the more urgent the search for currency alternatives becomes. Keynes's original concerns of 1945 are more pertinent than ever. Does that new order require a new sort of global organization, a genuine multilateralism?

In the same way that the Versailles Treaty produced a negative mythology, in which all the bad and unstable elements of interwar politics were attributed to the peace treaty rather than to the war's destruction, Bretton Woods took on a positive mythology. According to that version, an act of enlightened creative internationalism removed obstacles to aligning the interests of multiple nation-states and of economic agents, providing a new synthesis of state and market. Bretton Woods was the intellectual sugar, covering and masking the bitter taste of the pill of realpolitik dollar hegemony. But it also provided a sugar coating for the unpleasant taste of internationalism in the domestic context of American politics. In the post-1970s debate, which continues today, two issues were conflated: the question of why there has not been another Bretton Woods; and the perception that the world economy is in a mess, and that an international market order (or capitalism) has not been properly restored. The conflation leads to the continual demand for another Bretton Woods, and, indeed, for another Keynes, or another United States in its 1944 embodiment as a power standing for liberal international principles. In other words, it continually regenerates the myth of Bretton Woods, or of how benign multilateralism once rescued the world. That demand will persist as long as the problem that Keynes failed to solve at Bretton Woods remains: how to construct a safe asset that can be the basis of a monetary order and is not a national currency.

6

The Frightening German *Politik* Terms

with Marzenna James

Geopolitics and *multilateralism* have the same kind of relationship as *socialism* and *capitalism:* people who like the one term and use it to analyze the world around them generally think of the other as alternatively meaningless, corrupt, or dangerous. Geopolitics for its adherents becomes a way to explain why multilateralism cannot possibly work. Talking about geopolitics in any big international or multilateral institution generally produces wrinkled brows and twitching noses. For their part, geopoliticians often treat multilateralists as self-interested or limited people who cannot see the reality of the big picture. Geopoliticians in particular pride themselves on thinking on a vast scale, as well as on cutting out what they think of as cheap moralizing. The magnitude of the vision, in their view, dispenses with the need for pettifogging restraint and hesitation. The visionaries also like to emphasize their hard-headedness, and tend to use *reality* frequently, as in *geopolitical realities.*

Weltpolitik

The impulse for thinking big began very pleasantly and agreeably. In the *Sattelzeit* of the French Revolutionary and Napoleonic wars, a new conception of politics emerged, most aggressively and assertively in Germany. After Napoleon's armies had humiliated the ancient and inefficient German states on the battlefield, there was no real German state left. With the old order dissolved, Germans could dream about endless political possibilities.

And they thought big, letting their imaginations take over. A striking essay in the *Allgemeine Literatur Zeitung* in 1814 began with the assertion that "in the new age, politics has become the most free of arts and sciences." The author then developed a concept of *Weltpolitik,* a phrase that came to haunt German history and German policymakers. "Thus, from the commonality of perceptions, the thought or idea emerges, and from the common elements of these, a general idea arises. In politics one must move from the individual objects and their relations to what is common in the state, and then in the world, if one wants to be protected from dreams and ecstatic raptures, and to draw general thoughts from living sources. That is what Aristotle did, and after him, everyone who was concerned about science."[1]

Weltpolitik was about universal connectivity. It was a concept that reached its early apogee in Georg Wilhelm Friedrich Hegel's idea of the *Weltgeist,* or world spirit. It gripped the elderly Johann Wolfgang von Goethe, who discoursed with Eckermann about Asian influence and *Weltliteratur.* It haunted the composer Richard Wagner, whose most imaginative and innovative work, the operatic drama *Tristan und Isolde,* was about bringing Asian tonality and spirituality into communion with the legacy of a broken Christian tradition.[2]

Realpolitik

Somehow in this process of mentally trying to unite the world, something went badly wrong. The new conflictual turn was the consequence of a globalization shock, the Europe-wide hunger and discontent and then the social revolutions of 1848. The outstanding theorist of the new philosophy was August Ludwig von Rochau, who is now almost entirely forgotten, but whose main book's title, *Realpolitik,* still rings in our ears. Rochau was a liberal journalist who had participated in the revolutionary movements of 1848, and then, after the defeat, learned the lesson that the revolutions had failed because they were too preachy, and too much driven by ideas. Ideas are divisive. If instead people and states would think about interests, they could negotiate and achieve peaceful and beneficial outcomes. According to Rochau, 1848 and philosophical idealism had failed because the Frankfurt Assembly had had no army and no realistic concept of foreign policy. A united Germany could be formed only on the basis of the possibilities offered by the European state system. But above all, the correct policy depended on its conformity with the "spirit of the age." Rochau was obsessed with the idea of a zeitgeist. "A policy contrary to the *Zeitgeist* carried on as a systematic policy and over a long period of time is not simply incapable of execution, it is also unthinkable." This meant for Rochau that political institutions and assemblies could work only if they were properly representative—or, as he put it, if they were "the correct expression of social forces."[3]

In 1869 Rochau published a second volume of the *Realpolitik,* after the Prussian victory over Austria at Königgrätz, and after the formation of the North German Confederation around Bismarck's Prussia in 1867 had apparently vindicated Rochau's original arguments of 1853. *Realpolitik* as a concept could clearly be applied to Bismarck's disregard for almost all the traditional conservative principles—in particular for the theory of legitimacy—and to his rapid formation and then destruction of foreign political alliances. In the 1869 version, Rochau's admiration for power politics appears without any moral fig leaf: "The test of political power is the struggle. . . . The highest judgement in all cases of power against power is war."[4]

The new version of *Realpolitik* also depicted with a new and brutal candor the basis of Prussia's might. Freedom, Rochau wrote, was not to be achieved through political change but only through the acquisition of property. Whatever progress had been made in the direction of national unity was a consequence of human self-seeking. The original volume of *Realpolitik* had begun with the assertion that "the state arises and consists according to a law of nature, which humans follow consciously or unconsciously. Man is a political animal according to an ancient wisdom, while the well-known law of the modern age is that the state comes from God: these sentences mean the same thing." National unity—which Rochau saw as an overriding political goal—would be produced "not by a principle, an idea or a contract . . . , but through a superior force which swallows the others."[5] That phrasing anticipated the famous declaration of Bismarck just under a decade later that "the great questions of the day will not be settled by means of speeches and majority decisions but by iron and blood."[6]

The new philosophy of realism, born out of 1848, took up an older tradition, one most associated with the Florentine public servant, historian, and thinker Niccolò Machiavelli. There is indeed a powerful case for thinking of Rochauism or *Realpolitik* as simply extended Machiavellianism, applied to the nineteenth-century condition.

The invocation of Machiavellianism in a time of convulsion is still very popular as a diagnosis; it is much less often offered up as an explicit strategy. French president Emmanuel Macron wrote his master's thesis on Machiavelli, and drew on the Florentine for tips on how to modernize his country's ailing economy. Central bankers and journalists turned to Machiavelli in the midst of the European debt crisis of the 2010s to help them understand European Central Bank president Mario Draghi's policy approach. And an influential Moscow think tank called Niccolo M. took the concept in a radical direction while advising the Kremlin on unconventional policies, offensive military communication technologies, and hybrid warfare.

But Machiavelli is generally poorly understood, and the term *Machiavellian* is often used as a blanket denunciation (like *fascism* or *neoliberalism*). That usage seems to have developed very quickly. Shakespeare's Richard of Gloucester (the future Richard III, the playwright's most thoroughly evil villain) promises to "set the murderous Machiavel to school." The reference is anachronistic—the scene Shakespeare is describing took place in 1464, five years before the birth of Niccolò di Bernardo dei Machiavelli—but the thought behind it is simple. Machiavelli laid out an advice manual on how rulers should be duplicitous, deceptive, and untransparent.

The most notorious chapter of Machiavelli's *Prince,* chapter 18, explains the circumstances in which it is permissible—even desirable—for rulers to break promises, and appears to argue that the most successful rulers think "little about keeping faith" and know "how cunningly to manipulate men's minds." The chapter has been widely interpreted to mean that leaders should lie as often as possible. Machiavelli's message, however, was more complex. With an expert analysis of the wider implications of deception and "spinning" the truth, he demonstrates, through a range of examples, that manipulation can work only if the ruler convincingly pretends *not* to be engaging in it. Thus the deception and the cover-up must be ever more complex and multilayered. In fact, Machiavelli explains clearly how leaders must cultivate a reputation for being dependable and sincere. The prince needed the appearance of consistency, and had to project the virtues that would underpin that image: only that would create a solid foundation for effective policies. "To those seeing and hearing him, the ruler should appear to be all mercy, all faithfulness, all integrity, all humanity and all religion. And there is nothing more necessary than to seem to possess this last quality." In other words, politicians should never seem—much less say—that they do not believe in anything.

That lesson can also be applied in a modern setting, and thinkers from Rochau to the Italian Marxist Antonio Gramsci have self-consciously looked for a modern prince. Democratic politics and modern policymaking are based on promises. Political parties and candidates use promises to woo voters, and then to win support for policies. People will not respond to implausible pledges, especially if the politicians making them seem unreliable. There is a deep longing for consistency. How might that be attained? The modern Machiavellians find an answer in the apparently obvious facts of geography and location.

Machtpolitik

Realpolitik was subject to constant redefinitions. *Machtpolitik,* or power politics, was a way of thinking about its application in the complicated politics of the European continent, which provided an expanded form of the complex, ever-shifting configurations and alliances of the Italian peninsula at the end of the fifteenth century. Otto von Bismarck, who was appointed minister-president of Prussia in a near revolutionary situation in 1862, became the touchstone of the new power politics. In a famous exchange of correspondence with two conservative thinkers, the brothers Gerlach, Bismarck argued that the only duty of a Prussian civil servant and diplomat was to advance the interests of his monarch: it was a matter of indifference what form of government existed in other states, and France was France whether it had a king, a republic, or an emperor.

The application of such principles was not just a feature of delicate experiments in the balance of power. It also applied as states expanded their interventions in economic policy, and in the negotiation of commercial arrangements that would not only benefit particular interest groups, but might also affect national strength and the capacity to project power. Mid-nineteenth-century Germans and their successors readily saw the connection. *Machtpolitik* was indispensable for commercial policy. Only social democratic illusionists, the economist Gustav Schmoller wrote, would deny the role of state power in making favorable commercial policy. As long as there was a state, it would try to shape and form economic relations.[7]

In imperial Germany, *Weltpolitik* (politics on a world scale) became a political slogan under Kaiser Wilhelm II as he tried to set a new course to modernize or update Bismarckianism. The main applier of the policy was Bernhard von Bülow, Bismarck's successor as German chancellor from 1900 to 1909. The principal inspiration of the new vision was the reflection that Bismarck's view had been too limited to Europe's geography, and that a broader perspective was needed if Germany were to contain France, marginalize Russia, and compete with Britain. As foreign secretary, Bülow had launched the new era when he told the Reichstag: "in one word: We wish to throw no one into the shade, but we also want our own place in the sun."[8] Bülow was regarded with great suspicion by the éminence grise of Bismarckian foreign-policy thinking, Friedrich von Holstein, who noted: "Bülow at all times is uncritically suspicious of everybody, but apart from that he is a very amiable and easy superior. In his youth he read but didn't digest Machiavelli; the teachings of this professor of intrigue often lead him astray and lessen his reliability in his relations with others."[9] Bülow himself wrote to his principal protector, the sinister Philipp Eulenburg: "Politics is business in human flesh."[10]

Geopolitik

In the aftermath of the First World War and the failure of *Weltpolitik,* a new term was needed in the German tradition. It was supplied by Karl Haushofer, an officer and strategic theorist at the Munich Military Academy who had been deeply influenced by a relatively brief spell as a military attaché in Tokyo (1908–1910). The word *Geopolitik,* which Haushofer took up with relish, had been coined by a Swedish politician, Johan Rudolf Kjellén, above all in his 1900 book *Introduction to Swedish Geography.* Kjellén later developed the theory that European history was driven by the contest for three river basins: the Rhine, the Danube, and the Vistula. *Geopolitik* is a classically ambiguous or nebulous term, with both innocent and dangerous uses. For some, it conveys a vague sense of continents and big geographical spaces; for others, it is about a claim that reality consists of endless conflict and struggle, in which space matters more than ideas, maps more than chaps. Haushofer started the conflation and the view of geopolitics as a story of a bitter struggle, a contest of haves and have-nots, in a zero-sum game. He believed that it was his mission to create a new political science, "the science of the political life form in a natural living space." Geopolitics was the doctrine of the "earth-connectedness of political processes." As such, it "would and must become the conscience of the state."[11] The view that geography matters could be contrasted with what was portrayed as a naïve version of globalism, that the world was flat and that globalization made distance disappear, in an "end of geography" that paralleled an "end of history." Haushofer started the conflation of geography with conflict and the view of geopolitics as a story of a bitter struggle, a contest of haves and have-nots, in a zero-sum game.

Haushofer considered his major influences to be the German geographer Friedrich Ratzel, whose work centered around the concept of space (*Raum*) and who introduced the concept *Lebensraum* or living space, and the English geographer (and director of the London School of Economics) Halford Mackinder. Mackinder was fascinated by the way that the railroad had opened up vast continental interiors, making possible a new sort of integration and power politics. Globalization of the past had been seaborne, driven by Arab, Venetian, Portuguese, Spanish, Dutch, and English sailors; globalization in the future would depend on vast armies in continental spaces. He was, like many followers of the Tory imperialist politician Joseph Chamberlain, obsessed by British decline.[12] In 1904, he expounded a theory about the "heartland," in "The Geographical Pivot of History," a lecture given to the British Geographical Society. In his lecture, Mackinder explained the need to "seek a formula which shall express certain aspects, at any rate, of geographical causation in universal history." He thought of himself as describing a completely new era of globalization, in which "every explosion of social forces, instead of being dissipated in a surrounding circuit of unknown space and barbaric chaos, will be sharply re-echoed from the far side of the globe, and weak elements in the political and economic organism of the world will be shattered in consequence." But he also laid down a distinction, which became very influential in both Germany and Russia, between the different ideologies and structures of maritime and land powers, although he—unlike the German and Russian successors—saw Rome as a sea power and the Greeks as a Slavic land power.

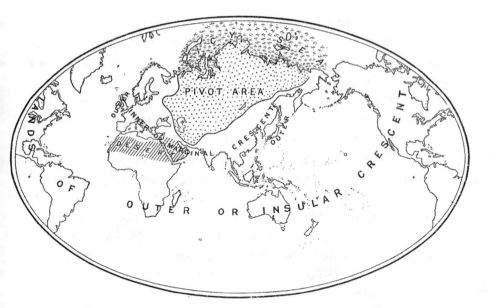

Figure 2. Halford Mackinder's vision of world power: "The Natural Seats of Power" map. *Source:* H. J. Mackinder, "The Geographical Pivot of History," *Geographical Journal* 23, no. 4 (1904): 435.

As he explained, "It is probably one of the most striking coincidences of history that the seaward and the landward expansion of Europe should, in a sense, continue the ancient opposition between Roman and Greek."[13] The critical impulse, to which Mackinder gave the label "pivot area," came from the center of the Eurasian landmass (see Figure 2).

Haushofer was fascinated by Asian politics and used his Tokyo experience to write a doctoral thesis: "Dai Nihon: Betrachtungen über Groß-Japans Wehrkraft, Weltstellung und Zukunft" (Reflections on greater Japan's military strength, world position, and future). Oddly it looked as if the countries on the "outer crescent" identified by Mackinder knew better how to use or apply power than the continental countries, which needed still to learn geopolitics. Specifically, Haushofer was convinced that Germany should imitate Japan and Japan's pursuit of clashes with its neighbors, China and Russia. Haushofer wanted to "direct Central Europe's gaze to the strengthening and rejuvenation that Japan owes to the storm of steel" produced by war.[14]

Haushofer lived on a farm beautifully situated on rolling hills near a Bavarian lake. It had been bought by Georg Ludwig Mayer-Doss, a cigar manufacturer in Mannheim, and a Catholic convert from Judaism, as a present for Haushofer on his marriage to Mayer-Doss's talented daughter, Martha Mechtild. (Mayer had long ago married the glamorous daughter of a Bavarian aristocrat and leading disciple of the philosopher of pessimism Arthur Schopenhauer, Adam Ludwig von Doss.) The marriage thus brought Haushofer a farm, money, and an aristocratic pedigree. Martha developed as a major figure in feminist organizations, and she used her facility with foreign languages, including Japanese, to help her husband's work—Haushofer, though fascinated by Japan, could not fluently read or communicate in the language. Throughout his life, Haushofer was passionately devoted to Martha, even as he needled her with anti-Semitic outbursts and boorish statements about masculine superiority.

After the end of the First World War, Haushofer thought that there was a need for a vast public reeducation to "awaken the sleeping geopolitical instinct" that British and Japanese people already possessed. He believed that the lack of this instinct was leading to "decomposition" in Upper Silesia, on "the dissolving Rhine front," a trend that would be followed by "dissolution" on the Vistula and Danubian fronts as well.[15] One of Haushofer's students, Rudolf Hess, brought Haushofer's view of *Geopolitik* to the attention of Adolf Hitler, who found the concept useful and congruent with his amoral view of international relations, and made the critical term *Lebensraum* a central part of a new political program. Haushofer's most intense contact with Hitler was probably during Hitler's very loose confinement in Landsberg prison after the failure of the 1923 Beer Hall putsch. Haushofer was there regularly visiting Rudolf Hess, to whom the Nazi leader was dictating his biographical manifesto *Mein Kampf*.

Particularly in Britain and the United States, Haushofer was frequently regarded as the central influence on Hitler. Immediately after the 1939 Nazi-Soviet pact, the British *New Statesman and Nation* explained that the Russo-German agreement had "little to do with the official 'ideology' of the Nazi programme, the rantings against 'Bolshevik subhumanity' or the romantic vision of a trek of German colonists on the medieval model to win a new 'Lebensraum' in the Ukraine. They are hard and realistic and to a considerable extent they have been stolen from the intellectual arsenal of British Imperialism," that is, from Mackinder.[16] On the other side of the Atlantic, similar interpretations emerged of what was seen as the "super-brain of Nazism": "Major General Professor Dr. Karl Haushofer and his Geo-Political Institute in Munich with its 1000 scientists, technicians and spies are almost unknown to the public, even in the Reich. But their ideas, their charts, maps, statistics, information and plans have dictated Hitler's moves from the very beginning. . . . It was Haushofer who taught the hysterical, planless agitator in a Munich jail to think in terms of continents and empires. Haushofer virtually dictated the famous Chapter XVI of *Mein Kampf* which outlines the foreign policy Hitler has since followed to the letter."[17] At Nuremberg, US chief of counsel Sidney S. Alderman, writing a memorandum for the American prosecutor, Supreme Court Justice Robert H. Jackson, wrote that "Haushofer was Hitler's intellectual god-father. It was Haushofer, rather than Hess, who wrote *Mein Kampf* and who furnished the backbone for the Nazi bible and what we call the common criminal plan. Geo-politics was not merely academic theory. It was a driving, dynamic plan for the conquest of the heartland of Eurasia and for domination of the world by the conquest of that heartland."[18] Jackson, however, appears not to have been convinced, and a few weeks later released Haushofer from internment. The background to Jackson's surprising decision was the intervention of Edmund Walsh, a Jesuit scholar of international relations, geopolitician, and founder of Georgetown University's School of Foreign Service. Haushofer quickly saw Colonel Walsh as his benign and powerful "mentor," and succeeded in convincing him that *Mein Kampf* was just one of "many ephemeral agitational publications" that had nothing to do with geopolitics.[19] Haushofer's timing was fortuitous: the concept of geopolitics had begun to fascinate many US thinkers.

Walsh was not an obvious candidate to be a geopolitician: as a Jesuit, he had always insisted on the strong necessity of morality in foreign relations. But by the end of the Second World War, he believed that "with the annihilation of the German *Geopolitik,* a new form [of] geopolitics is asserting itself in Eastern and Central Europe," and the Soviets were "succeeding brilliantly in acquiring domination of Mackinder's heartland." Geopolitics was turning into a new rationale for dominance: "Unless you can back up your ideals and your hopes by something more than mere words, then the steam-roller goes on and on and on."[20]

Haushofer also had a substantial following in the Soviet Union. The most prominent disciple was Karl Radek, secretary of the Comintern, who later became a critic of Stalin, but in the 1930s maintained contacts with German diplomats that his friends attempted to justify as an anticipation of the geopolitically necessary Stalin-Hitler pact of August 1939.[21] Radek also was involved in an initiative to translate Haushofer's work into Russian. There was a wider interest: a Russian geopolitical journal flourished in the 1920s. The 1929 *Great Soviet Encyclopedia* included an interesting article by the Hungarian cartographer and Soviet intelligence official Alexander Radó on "Geopolitics," which it explained as a largely German phenomenon, one intensified by the experience of German defeat and revolution in 1918–1919: "The rapid growth over the past decade of the 'geopolitical direction,' which has left the bounds of the geographic studies and has adopted a specific political character, is closely linked to the turn in the political fate of Germany, which took place as a result of the imperial war. . . . Geopolitics ideologically sharpened and distinguished itself as a distinct academic system only thanks to the ideological upheavals linked to the imperialist war and revolution in Germany."[22]

Geopolitics and Political Turbulence

Geopolitics indeed became attractive as a mode of analysis for dealing with political turbulence. The Yale political scientist Nicolas Spykman, one of the founders of the American school of geopolitics, wrote in the *American Political Science Review* in 1938 (before the Munich Agreement): "Size, shape, location, topography, and climate posit conditions from which there is no escape, however skilled the Foreign Office, and however resourceful the General Staff. . . . the present configuration of Czechoslovakia invites the loss of her western wedge of territory; Syria and Iraq will continue to be the crossroads between East and West. . . . With these facts foreign policy must reckon. It can deal with them skillfully or ineptly; it can modify them; but it cannot ignore them. For geography does not argue. It simply is."[23] That view was strikingly echoed by the isolationist "America First" aviator Charles Lindbergh, immediately after the outbreak of the European war in 1939, when he told a large radio audience that "one need only glance at a map to see where our true frontiers lie."[24]

This way of discussing international relations was commonplace for a substantial number of German foreign-policy thinkers in the aftermath of the First World War. They distrusted all ideas, including liberal internationalism, believing them to be cynical camouflage for the pursuit of British or American hegemony. Many of these figures fled from Hitler's Germany. The historian John Bew in a neat turn of phrase describes many post-1945 Americans' suspicion of "an unwelcome import from the dark heart of *Mitteleuropa* that went against the grain of more noble Anglo-American traditions."[25] The critics of realists were quick to draw the lines of influence to the sinister politics of interwar Germany. Thus the Harvard political scientist Carl Friedrich, also an émigré, accused the diplomat and strategist George Kennan of proliferating an "American version of German Realpolitik."[26] Many Americans found geopolitics appealing because it allowed them to think of their country as innocent. Due to the country's position on Mackinder's "insular crescent" and its relative lack of immediate neighbors, the United States seemed better positioned to project non-threatening power across Eurasia, the Middle East, and Africa.[27]

There was always a fundamental ambiguity in the geopolitical vision. Some thought it deeply destructive, with Mackinder's biographer Brian Blouet explaining that "the history of geopolitics is a history of bad ideas—sometimes mad ideas—that have led countries to wars and recessions."[28] Others insist that the geopolitical essays had "little practical value."[29] The mad, bad science could be a rationale for overthrowing a political order, because it was deemed as senseless, or for trying to preserve that order. In a memorandum written in the closing days of the European conflict in 1945, George Kennan wrote from the US embassy in Moscow a document that formulated the key concepts of the future doctrine of containment, and which drew very clearly on theories of the heartland and the permanent contestation between peoples:

> Behind Russia's stubborn expansion lies only the age-old sense of
> insecurity of a sedentary people reared on an exposed plain in the
> neighborhood of fierce nomadic peoples. Will this urge, now become
> a permanent feature of Russian psychology, provide the basis for a
> successful expansion of Russia into new areas of east and west? And
> if initially successful, will it know where to stop? Will it not be

inexorably carried forward, by its very nature, in a struggle to reach the whole—to attain complete mastery of the shores of the Atlantic and the Pacific? There is every reason to believe that in the newly-acquired areas the Russians will continue to put politics before economics, cost what it may. They will not hesitate to ruin the productivity of entire branches of economic life, if by doing so they can reduce to helplessness and dependence elements which might otherwise oppose their power. The resulting decline in living standards will appear to them, in many cases, a well deserved corrective to the smug Philistinism of the peoples involved; and they will be astonished and disgusted at the unwillingness of these peoples to accept a standard of living as low as that of the Soviet peoples. But no one in Moscow believes that the western world, once confronted with the life-size wolf of Soviet displeasure standing at the door and threatening to blow the house in, would be able to stand firm. And it is on this disbelief that Soviet global policy is based.[30]

Built into the foundations of geopolitics was a concern that Russia was the dynamic force at the center of the heartland. One month after the outbreak of the Second World War, Winston Churchill described one of the new "important things" of the war as "the assertion of the power of Russia. Russia has pursued a cold policy of self-interest. . . . I cannot forecast to you the action of Russia. It is a riddle wrapped in mystery inside an enigma; but perhaps there is a key. That key is Russian national interest. It cannot be in accordance with the interest or safety of Russia that Germany should plant itself upon the shores of the Black Sea, or that it should overrun the Balkan states and subjugate the Slavonic peoples of Southeastern Europe. That would be contrary to the historic life interests of Russia."[31]

The problem that Kennan subsequently wrestled with, and which was never adequately resolved, was the relationship between the analysis and the policy prescription: in particular, did the conclusion that another country was mentally gripped by a geopolitical vision constitute a reason for trying to block or contain it, or rather a motivation for understanding it and condoning the action of its leaders? Kennan with intellectual brilliance exemplified both sides of this dilemma: he was the toughest and most hard-minded exponent of containment in the 1940s and 1950s, and in the 1990s was one of the most critical voices against the eastern expansion of the western treaty organization NATO to include the central European states formerly under Soviet influence. By the late 1990s he had become a Cassandra: "I think the Russians will gradually react quite adversely and it will affect their policies. I think it is a tragic mistake. There was no reason for this whatsoever. No one was threatening anybody else. This expansion would make the Founding Fathers of this country turn over in their graves. We have signed up to protect a whole series of countries, even though we have neither the resources nor the intention to do so in any serious way. [NATO expansion] was simply a light-hearted action by a Senate that has no real interest in foreign affairs."[32]

The most influential of the German émigré thinkers about *Realpolitik*, Hans Morgenthau, was always cautious—for obvious reasons—about stressing the German lineage of his version of realism. He defensively wrote that he had also emphasized the "negative connotations" of the nation-state and power; but he also compared contemporary Washington, DC's "dearth of men who are capable of thinking in political terms" with the "brilliant and successful moves" of Cavour and Bismarck, mid-nineteenth-century builders of new political societies.[33] Morgenthau came to be a critic of the US engagement globally, and especially in Southeast Asia. In his view, it was a moral mistake to pin policy to a moral message rather than to think of the "real" features of power politics.

Many thinkers in this tradition of realist geopolitics became skeptical of the official Cold War mindset, in which typically a mildly reformist domestic agenda was coupled with hardline anti-communist and anti-Soviet foreign policy. They thought instead that the Soviet Union was nothing more than a version of nineteenth-century Russia, pursuing its own understandable and inherently legitimate interests. Communism was simply a cynical mask, used in a way not that different from the British use of liberal internationalism in the interwar period, or the eloquent US deployment of an updated version of that vision after the Second World War.

Those who believed in realist geopolitics prided themselves in being cleverer and more realistic than their woolly headed opponents. They also consistently complained that an establishment in policymaking, academia, and think-tank journalism was marginalizing them. Morgenthau thought the United States was in the grip of an "obsolescent philosophy of foreign affairs," one that depended on a legalistic-moralistic position that needed to be revised or discarded in the real world.[34] His intellectual heir, John Mearsheimer of Chicago, believed that liberalism was bound to fail, and with heavy costs. Liberals, the realists argued, did acknowledge that there were differences of opinion, and that a state was needed to keep the peace. "But there is no world state to keep countries at bay when they have profound disagreements. The structure of the international system is anarchic, not hierarchic, which means that liberalism applied to international politics cannot work. Countries thus have little choice but to act according to balance-of-power logic if they are to survive."[35] There is no universal culture.[36] Hence the kind of thinking that originally drove early nineteenth-century Germans to think of *Weltpolitik* in the first place is delusional. Ignoring geopolitics will lead to disaster: the best case that Mearsheimer thought he could present was the way the United States had made Russia an enemy by trying to draw its neighbors (in particular Ukraine) into a supposedly universal strategy.[37] Mackinder's heartland was back: Ukraine and Russia became the flashpoint for the geopolitical conception of the challenges that were defining the twenty-first century.

The geopoliticians characteristically complained that they were being marginalized by a foreign-policy establishment that spanned both political parties. Of all American presidents before 2016, only Richard Nixon looked remotely sympathetic to this mindset: the wooing of China was Nixon's master stroke to force the Soviet Union to practice détente and peaceful coexistence. The others—the Bushes, Carter, Clinton, Ford, Kennedy, Johnson, Obama, even Reagan—looked as if they had bought into the idea of the world as a dangerous place, with the United States as exemplar and policeman, an idea that would inevitably end in destruction, death, demoralization (and drained dollars). Donald Trump looked highly attractive to this group, because he obviously did not care about ideas and propagated more simply or crudely than any other president the slogan of "America First."

The flaw of this group was a peculiarity that was inherent in the thought structure built around the brutal German terminology from 1848. Geopoliticians were obsessed with the state, with its strength or weakness. States were all that mattered. But states in practice are subject to all manner of pressures, adapting well in some circumstances but failing miserably in others.

Conflict and war were built into the thinking on geopolitics, but it was also clear in the nuclear age that war between major countries was unlikely or even, as some claimed, impossible. A consequence was that the zero-sum aspect of geopolitics was recast at *geoeconomics*. Countries would still compete, but not by war; rather by other means. Edward Luttwak, a political scientist who cast himself as a purveyor of grand strategy, provided one of the clearest definitions of the new approach: a game "played by countries that have already ruled out any warfare at all among themselves." He also wanted to explain that the worldview was pushed by bureaucrats and technocrats: "Only by invoking geo-economic imperatives can they claim authority over mere businessmen and the citizenry at large."[38] The French analyst Pascal Loriot added the thought that geoeconomics could be less attached to geography than geopolitics, in that it also operated in a "virtual" space.[39] The concept was eventually reduced to the trivial by Mike Pompeo, Trump's longest-serving secretary of state, as "hanging out with your buddies at a cool cocktail party."[40]

Geopolitics had a powerful attraction in Russia, the focus of Mackinder's 1904 pivot. Like it had in 1920s Germany, the doctrine flourished in the wake of the disintegration of a powerful old empire, pushed by the perception that disintegration would mean political humiliation imposed by the outside world. There was then a renaissance of geopolitics in 1990s Russia, in the aftermath of the collapse of the Soviet Union, which Vladimir Putin famously styled in his 2005 State of the Nation address "the greatest geopolitical catastrophe of the century." Putin argued that there was a spiral of decay triggered by the collapse of the Soviet empire: "The epidemic of collapse has spilled over to Russia itself."[41] The man who prompted the revival was the Russian political analyst Alexander Dugin, who later explained the origins of his interpretation: "in the 1980s–'90s I encountered the status of geopolitics as a discipline in the international expert community. I discovered geopolitics by way of Karl Haushofer and the works of the Conservative Revolution and I thought that geopolitics is a kind of politically incorrect doctrine which is greatly explanatory and of great use to us, to Russia. In my eyes, I thought that geopolitics has the status of something past, something prohibited, something politically incorrect—and I liked that."[42]

Dugin bears more than a casual resemblance to his mentor Karl Haus-hofer. In the same way as more commentators outside Germany held Haushofer to be the strategic mastermind of Hitlerism, it is much more common in the West than in Russia to attribute to Dugin Vladimir Putin's espousal of the obviously geopolitical Eurasian project.[43] Dugin talks about creating a Eurasian empire and a new fascist international (a mirror image of the old Russian-centered idea of a Communist International) that en-compasses Europe; Putin often seems more interested in re-creating a Russian empire and sphere of influence and in weakening the European Union and the United States. When the United States imposed sanctions on key figures in Russia in 2015, it included Dugin on the list. Putin him-self consistently downplays the connection of Dugin to the Russian gov-ernment. But it may well be useful to Putin to have at hand even more radical figures in order to appear reasonable, calculated, and statesmanlike in his methodology and approach to international relations.[44]

Geopolitics became central to international discussions after the 2007–2008 Global Financial Crisis, and it appeared to link the two legacy themes from the Cold War: the role of the United States, and the Soviet legacy for Russia. Geopolitics, as in post-1919 Germany, looked like an appealing way of explaining a newly chaotic world to the confused. The evident hard-headedness of the philosophy increased its attraction.

Putin was always interested in using peripheral conflicts to boost his power, and owed his initial rise to the Chechen war. But in 2005 Putin appeared to be still committed to globalization, claiming that "Russia is extremely interested in a major inflow of private, including foreign, invest-ment. This is our strategic choice and strategic approach." In October 2011, he announced the launch of a new "many-tiered, multi-speed inte-gration process in the post-Soviet space."[45]

Ukraine became the center of a tussle. At stake were contrasting views of how the world could and should be ordered—or how the inner crescent struggled over the heartland. The developments of the 2010s follow the script of Mackinder and Haushofer. Since 2009 Ukraine had been part of a largely unremarked and unremarkable Eastern Partnership Program with the European Union and had worked on an EU–Ukraine Association Agreement that included a Deep and Comprehensive Free Trade Area (DCFTA) agreement. This kind of security relationship with the European

Union was not nearly as threatening to Russia as, say, American discussion of possibly extending NATO membership to Georgia. But after a wave of revolutionary changes during the Arab Spring (from December 2010) and then unrest in Russia from 2011 to 2013, Russia was looking to apply its own version of containment. It determined that Ukraine was the place to draw the line, and it exerted massive pressure on Ukraine to end its process of westernization. Ukrainian president Viktor Yanukovych was scheduled to sign the trade treaty at the EU summit taking place in Vilnius on November 28–29, 2013.[46] When he pulled away, he was reproached by German chancellor Angela Merkel and other European leaders. Yanukovych explained the situation in terms of a geopolitical context by evoking a picture of Ukraine supposedly caught in the middle of a competition for power between the European Union and Russia.

In response to the DCFTA decision, hundreds of thousands of protesters took to the streets, demanding closer integration with the European Union (giving rise to the term *Euromaidan,* or Revolution of Dignity, to denote the 2013–2014 protests that swept Ukraine). Brutal *Berkut* special police units were deployed to suppress the crowds.[47] Police snipers killed more than one hundred demonstrators but still failed to break the Euromaidan Revolution in the capital city Kiev. Yanukovych, who had remained adamant that he would not reconsider his decision to scupper the EU-Ukraine trade treaty, hastily packed and left for Russia with his interior minister in late February 2014.[48] From the Russian perspective, it looked like an illegal coup had occurred, and Russian units moved into Crimea and into the border regions in eastern Ukraine. President Putin signed a formal treaty that pronounced Crimea a part of the Russian Federation, and the Russian parliament, the upper Duma, ratified the forced territorial acquisition within three days, without consulting the Ukrainians. This step destroyed Ukraine's chance of membership in the European Union, by creating an apparently insoluble border problem.

How does it feel to be a small country near the middle of the heartland? The Ukrainian government accused Russia of secretly sending thousands of troops and weapons across the border as well as recruiting, funding, training, and mobilizing Ukrainians in a battle to overthrow the government. Ukrainian media portray the Russian government as supplying mercenaries, enlisting them from among Russian nationalists and sympathizers around the world. Ukrainian politicians see Russia implementing a global strategy for political control with a long pedigree, dating back to tsarist as well as Soviet imperialism. Speaking on the occasion of the seventy-fifth anniversary of the founding of the United Nations, Ukrainian ambassador to the United Nations Sergiy Kyslytsya characterized the Russian strategy in terms of a clear contrast: Russian "coercion" as opposed to the "diversity and free choice" in western institutions. Kyslytsya discussed Russia's "neo-imperialistic ambitions" in the context of a power strategy "combining totalitarian ideology with the goals and principles of the UN Charter. . . . Such attitude to this Organization in 75 years has only been defiantly and cynically improved by some states while declaring adherence to the principles of the Charter."[49] The struggle from this perspective was about regional clashes and local interests and organizations.

By contrast, geopolitics was at the heart of the Russian government's interpretation. From that perspective, the conflict had originated with a push from the United States and the European Union. According to Putin, the transatlantic community had for a long time meddled in Ukrainian elections in "a mockery of the constitution. And now they have thrown in an organized and well-equipped army of militants."[50] Vasily Nebenzia, Russia's ambassador to the United Nations, claimed that it was the European Union that had "triggered and detonated the so-called 'Maidan Revolution' in Kiev and led to still ravaging civil conflict in Ukraine."[51] It was the Ukrainian government that had broken international law: it had illegally ousted President Yanukovych, discriminated against minorities, and provoked Russian speakers in eastern Ukraine to take up arms. Putin explained how "nationalists, neo-Nazis, Russophobes and anti-Semites executed this conflict. They continue to set the tone in Ukraine."[52] The transatlantic community "act as they please: here and there, they use force against sovereign states." Regarding institutional cooperation, he commented, "To make this aggression look legitimate, they force the necessary resolutions from international organisations." Indeed, "they have lied to us many times, made decisions behind our backs, placed us before an accomplished fact." He gave as examples the wars in Yugoslavia; furthermore, "they hit Afghanistan, Iraq, and frankly violated the UN Security Council resolution on Libya, . . . controlled 'color revolutions,' . . . the infamous policy of containment, led in the 18th, 19th, and 20th centuries, continues today. They are constantly trying to sweep us into a corner."[53]

The Russian perspective on the Ukraine Crisis depends on two assumptions: that the world is brutally unipolar with the United States as the main cause of international developments; and that this unipolarity has a devastating effect on weaker states. The effect of this worldview makes political domination of small states by Russia look legitimate. Putin's Presidential Address to the Nation in response to the 2020 coronavirus crisis included a brief reference to the two fundamental assumptions of Russia's view of international relations. It consisted of just two sentences: "The globalisation and integration processes are going through a difficult test, and leading countries are making their choice in favour of technological and industrial independence. Because they understand that in this situation, in matters of security and development, they can only rely on themselves—on the human, workforce, and scientific potential of their countries."[54] The two sentences conveyed the essence of the Russian notion of international relations: international politics is a constant, brutal power struggle by Great Powers. It can take many forms, but fundamentally nothing ever changes. In the face of the pandemic, big (or "real") countries do not show solidarity, but rather turn to self-sufficiency and autarky. The word "only" signals the most radical strain of geopolitical thinking about the world.

The Kennan paradox of the relationship between analysis and policy response remained: did the analysis require strict containment or a softer, more understanding approach? The dilemma was personified by the veteran foreign-policy strategist Henry Kissinger, US national security adviser and then secretary of state from 1969 to 1977. In his 2014 book *World Order*, he called for dialogue among nation-states, based on the assumption that in international politics there are no universally accepted rules, only alternative views. Kissinger wrote: "In the world of geopolitics, the order established and proclaimed as universal by the Western countries stands at a turning point. Its nostrums are understood globally but there is no consensus about their application; indeed, concepts such as democracy, human rights, and international law are given such divergent interpretations that warring parties regularly invoke them against each other as battle cries. The system's rules have been promulgated but have proved ineffective absent active enforcement."[55] He recognized a separate Russian conception of international politics that might explain or even justify the annexation of Crimea. Europe and the United States had not appreciated that, for Russia, "Ukraine can never be just a foreign country." Kissinger reserved his harshest criticism for the Ukrainian leaders. "Ukraine has been independent for only 23 years; it had previously been under some kind of foreign rule since the 14th century. Not surprisingly, its leaders have not learned the art of compromise, even less of historical perspective."[56] As for Ukraine's economic integration with the European Union, Kissinger sees this process not in the context of the chance to replicate the success of peace and prosperity among the European Union's longtime members, but in the context of the talks "culminating in the demonstrations in Kiev." In his view, "All these, and their impact, should have been the subject of a dialogue with Russia."[57]

The geopolitical vision has no room for civil society. It treats masses of population as irrational drivers rather than reasoning persons. It does not pay much attention to procedures or how decisions are made. Legalism is treated with contempt. So geopolitical thinkers and makers find it hard to understand entities that do not work in that rather brutal way. For them, constitutionalism as embodied in the United States or in the post-1945 European order looks strange.

The European Union conceptually was the antithesis of *Geopolitik* (and all the other terrible German terms): it was born out of a reaction against hyper-power and its ideologies. Before the global crisis, it was common to think of Europe as the embodiment of soft power, while the United States was hard power. The two sides of the Atlantic looked like Venus and Mars.[58] The European integration project was designed in part to limit what individual countries could do; that is, it tied them down. The historian Alan Milward liked to call the 1950s drive "the rescue of the European nation-state," but that description only works if we think of a self-limiting type of integration that prevents the member countries from dreaming too big, that is, from dreaming of *Machtpolitik*.[59]

When geopolitics seemed to grip the world, it was inevitable that some version would also influence European thinking. The European Union looks multilateral, but only two large countries could claim to be old-fashioned power states. France has a nuclear capacity, and persistently jealously guarded its prerogative to sit as a permanent member of the UN Security Council. Germany has a degree of financial and economic power, and occasionally commentators drew an analogy between Germany's currency and France's *force de frappe* (defensive nuclear strike force). But focusing on the Big Two consistently eroded the European Union's principles, and it is not surprising that the European Union was also tempted by the geopolitical mindset. The third large member of the European Union, Italy, in particular, persistently chafed under both German and French directives, on the economy, on immigration, on mobility. A Big Any Number—in this case a Big Two—indeed undermines the principles of multilateralism. Thus it was natural to think of ways in which the European Union could itself become a major player, and so defuse the explosive potential inherent in looking for leadership from France or Germany.

The German politician Ursula von der Leyen took up the idea of geopolitics even before she started her term as president of the European Commission in 2019. She wanted to distinguish a "geopolitical Commission" from a "political Commission" that had in the past been accused of interfering excessively in the internal affairs of EU member states. Europeans should manage the world, rather than each other. The argument that large member countries like France, Germany, or Italy could not on their own be influential in global politics appeared attractive. In a globalized world, many Europeans thought that Europe needed a voice. Josep Borrell, the European Union's high representative of the European Union or de facto foreign minister, gave programmatic statements about the problems of multilateralism and openness, and how "we must relearn the language of power and conceive of Europe as a top-tier geostrategic actor."[60]

But was geopolitics the best way of letting that European voice sound? *Weltpolitik* began as a search for a commonality of perceptions at a time when old imperial systems were disintegrating and political and social realities were quickly shifting; it ended in a view of geopolitics that suggested that no such commonality was really achievable. The first version could provide an embracing basis for a new and universal vision; the second fosters division. To geopoliticize is to invite a constant engagement with the psychodrama of the heartland.

7

Debt

Debt is unique among the terms examined in this book, because the concept of debt does not have either an inventor or an obvious beginning. But it has become increasingly central to the language of globalization. There is no end of debt in sight—however much analysts complain about the consequences of the buildup of government, corporate, and personal debt all over the world, and even as activists demand a biblical cancellation of debt, that is, a jubilee. Jubilees are also characterized as carnivalesque assertions of unrule, or a return to a benign state of nature. Shakespeare's populist rebel Jack Cade explains: "Is not this a lamentable thing, that of the skin of an innocent lamb should be made parchment, that parchment, being scribbl'd o'er, should undo a man?"[1]

Debt creates the obligations that tie the global economy together. Scholars—archaeologists, historians—agree that debt is considerably older than money or coins.[2] Clay cuneiform tablets in Mesopotamia, for example, record Sumerian debt contracts measured in units of grain or animals (sheep) over five thousand years ago, around 7500–3350 BCE.

The fact of debt is old, but so too is the dilemma of how to understand its consequences for relationships between people. Debt came to be a central feature in the development of both civil society and the concept of responsibility. It is at the heart of the moral economy.

The evolution of debt was central to a theory of ethics. All Plato's virtues—temperance, prudence, courage, and justice—can be either developed internally or are based on external influences; often they derive from the combination of inborn proclivities toward teaching and practice, and develop in individuals over the course of entire lifetimes.[3] Courage, which was later often redescribed as the virtue of fortitude, involved meeting obligations, and not running away from them. Debts help to socialize us. They are one aspect that constitutes the key to human personhood, in that they provide a recognition that we are bound by our past actions, and thus have a continuous identity as a person. On that basis, promises occur between persons: you know who I am and can rely on me, even if circumstances change. Without that trust, there is endless suspicion.

Debts can also very obviously be highly oppressive, creating chains of obligation and, in many premodern societies, bondage and debt peonage. It thus deprived people of their humanity. That is because circumstances obviously do change: there are accidents, climatic and health catastrophes, and other circumstances that make it impossible to repay. Many religions, including Judaism, Christianity, and Islam, consequently evolved prohibitions against lending on interest, or usury. Islam indeed still maintains notional restrictions, and the application of Islamic law leads to the inclusion of an equity or risk-sharing element in financial instruments. Some analysts in consequence suggest that Islamic law provides a more adequate basis for a modern economy, in that it excludes debt instruments. Yet there is little evidence that Islamic law actually changes much of Muslims' financial behavior.[4] In Judaism and Christianity the foundational texts of the prohibition of lending at interest are Deuteronomy 23:19: "Thou shalt not lend upon usury to thy brother; usury of money, usury of victuals, usury of any thing that is lent upon usury"; and Leviticus 25:35–37: "And if thy brother be waxen poor, and fallen in decay with thee; then thou shalt relieve him: yea, though he be a stranger, or a sojourner; that he may live with thee. Thou shalt not give him thy money upon usury, nor lend him thy victuals for increase."

There appeared to be an easy way to bridge the gap between debt as something that fosters responsibility, civility, and order, and debt as a source of individual distress and disorder: make debt the affair of governments. That was the view of classical antiquity, and it has a parallel in the modern view, which sees governments as creating a particular secure or stable asset.

State Debt

In Greek city-states, the public treasury, secured in grand temples, held what were notionally loans of citizens that could be used for emergencies. These did not usually pay any interest. If the citizens lost because the loans were not repaid, they had simply made a sacrifice for a greater good. The loans in this way represented one idea of civic community. The link of state debt and religion was clearly expressed in the form of the building, which much later (especially in the eighteenth and early nineteenth centuries) provided a model for bank buildings.

Monarchs and absolute rulers, by contrast, would attempt to raise the same kind of credit—the distinction between that and taxation was not always clear. But there was little prospect of being repaid, and the lenders became smarter about concealing their wealth from royal agents (in effect tax collectors). So monarchs would borrow, paying interest, from merchants in other territories, and frequently impose partial or complete defaults. There was no knowing in advance precisely what challenge—usually military—the monarch might take up. And there was obviously no way to be certain that the king would make repayments according to the original contract. These defaults could not be too complete, because otherwise the king's reputation and his ability to take on more debt would be limited. But there was an arbitrariness about the process, which created uncertainty, and that translated into higher interest rates. Getting better terms for debt was a central spur to the process of creating political accountability, and even democracy.

In Genoa, a lending strategy developed that became widely admired as a model for how to foster collective responsibility. Citizens lent money to the city through a corporation, the Casa di San Giorgio (Bank of Saint George), which was founded in 1408 in order to consolidate the various debts of the republic of Genoa. Machiavelli in the *Istorie fiorentine* wrote that the Casa represented the principles of liberty, civil life, and justice.[5] The Scottish adventurer William Paterson used the Genoese example as a model for his plan for reordering English finance through what became the Bank of England: "And there being no Country in Christendom where Property hath been more sacred and secure for some Ages past, notwithstanding all our Revolutions, than in England, it must needs follow, that nothing less than a Conquest, wherein all Property, Justice, and Right must fail, can any way affect this Foundation: And in such case this would be but in common with every thing else."[6] The bank was organized much like the Genoese model: the shareowners of the bank lent to the English government, and their investment looked secure because they were politically influential enough to dominate the parliament and thus ensure that there would be always sufficient taxes collected to service the debt. The establishment of the Bank of England formed the centerpiece of the "English financial revolution," which by dramatically reducing the cost of English borrowing increased the government's capacity to pay for military, especially naval, infrastructure and services. It was thus central to the projection of power, and to the creation of a British Empire.[7]

There were other imitators. The first US treasury secretary, Alexander Hamilton, was deeply influenced by the British example, and studied the case of the Bank of England in detail. When he proposed in 1790 that the federal government assume the debts of individual states (debts they had incurred from the Revolutionary War), he saw the compromise needed to take on these very different debt burdens as creating a new polity. Debt would become, he wrote, "the strong cement of our union."[8]

Napoleon, too, founded Banque de France on the same principle as the Bank of England. The sanctity of sovereign debt had a particular, and lasting, importance for France: the French Revolution was widely interpreted as having arisen out of King Louis XVI's unwillingness to engage in the kind of debt default or restructuring that had periodically characterized the ancien régime in France (and early modern European monarchies more generally). The high debt burden arising out of the Seven Years' War and then from the War of the American Revolution could readily have been cancelled, but instead Louis called the Estates General to find a way of raising revenue. The parliamentarians then used the property of the crown and of the church (*biens nationaux*) as a security for national debt, and for fighting their own military campaigns against the domestic and foreign enemies of the Revolution.

Much more recently, after the emergence of the European or Eurozone debt crisis in 2010, Hamilton and his views on debt resurfaced. Should there be some measure of debt mutualization? The United States pushed Europe very heavily in this direction as a way of making Europe financially more stable. Treasury Secretary Tim Geithner gave German finance minister

Wolfgang Schäuble, a major resister against the idea of a common European debt, a copy of Ron Chernow's Hamilton biography. After the coronavirus crisis hit, Schäuble's successor, Olaf Scholz, took up the language of the "Hamiltonian moment."

Debt on the part of the state depends on a complex network of promises and engagements. It gives the state the resources to perform its central functions—defense, the administration of law and justice—and engenders loyalty from the beneficiaries of state-provided security. That is why the choice of being Hamiltonian is so difficult: it may build new bonds, but it also presupposes some initial common sentiment. People in the past believed that they were committed to die for the fatherland, but it is too much of a mental and emotional stretch to die for debt mutualization.

And then there was the problem of states promising too much. What would happen if the state could not pay, and all the paper chits were worthless? Public order would be threatened. That experience confronted France twice in the course of the eighteenth century: first when the Scotsman John Law tried to set up a project based very much on the Bank of England model to consolidate the royal debts at the end of the spectacularly costly (and for France disastrous) War of Spanish Succession; and second with the financial experimentation of the French Revolution, when assignats, secured on the *biens nationaux,* were over-issued. In 1720, Law's scheme gave rise to a host of pamphlets and caricatures, in which it is the devil who creates the money that deceives. In many of the popular versions, the devil shits money: the delusion created by unbacked money is the devil's excrement.

Some of the refugees who fled from revolutionary France ended up in the small German court city of Weimar. Stories told about the assignats inspired the insertion of a monetary episode into the old German tale of Doktor Faustus. In the second part of Goethe's version, the devil, Mephistopheles, accompanies Johannes Faust to the court of a medieval emperor, in the middle of an economic downturn when the fields are fallow and industry idle. Mephisto says that paper money can be issued against precious metals in the ground, and that there is no need even to dig out the gold. All that matters is trust. The result, paper money, immediately breeds confidence and sets everyone back to work. The emperor's officials report back delightedly: "The Chancellor told me, 'Give everyone a high festive pleasure, make the welfare of the people, with just a few strokes of your pen.' " Faust responds: "Wise men will, when they have studied it, place infinite trust in what is infinite."[9]

The episode, in Goethe's telling, is still full of resonance in the twenty-first century, when no one alive has a clear memory of the hyperinflation of Germany in the early 1920s. In the midst of struggles over the European debt crisis, in September 2012, the head of the German central bank, Jens Weidmann, took time out for a literary excursion: "In the Second Part of Faust, the state can get rid of its debt to begin with. At the same time, private consumer demand rises sharply, fuelling an upswing. In due course, however, all this activity degenerates into inflation, destroying the monetary system because the money rapidly loses its value. . . . If a central bank can potentially create unlimited money from nothing, how can it ensure that money is sufficiently scarce to retain its value? Yes, this temptation certainly exists, and many in monetary history have succumbed to it."[10]

The message is not meant just for capitalists. One of the most memorable rewritings of the Faust episode appears in Mikhail Bulgakov's striking satire of Stalinism, *The Master and Margarita*. In the twelfth chapter, the devil appears in the Moscow Variety Theater and performs black magic: one of his acts is to create banknotes that rain down on the audience. Outside the theater, however, they turn into worthless scraps of paper. The devil in Bulgakov's fiction insists that the notes are "real money"—*chervonets*—a word that refers to the new Soviet currency issued in the 1920s that claimed to be the equivalent of tsarist gold coins (*chervonets* means "red," for red gold).

There are two responses to the concern about the abuse of monetary magic. One is to be permanently frightened by the prospect of an inflation that will wipe away not only the value of debt, but also the basis of every contract. The other is to hope that some benevolent outsider—someone who is not the devil—will take over or assume the debt. When the state is taken over by evil or self-interested personalities, it is destroyed; whereas if the state jumps in as a benevolent outsider, it appears as the rescuer, the savior.

Individual Debt

Looking for the rescuer is quite appealing because it corresponds to the historical trajectory of debt for most of the nineteenth and twentieth centuries. In the mostly stable currency world of nineteenth-century

Europe, the absolute security of state debt marked a striking contrast with the uncertainties and vicissitudes that plagued individuals. On an individual level, over-indebtedness is always possible, not just because of spendthrift behavior, but also because of the vagaries of an individual's life, including illness, loss of occupation, and death. Nineteenth-century writers were obsessed with indebtedness. Honoré de Balzac describes the power of his most compelling and enigmatic figure Vautrin. In Madame Vauquer's boardinghouse, Vautrin can extend his influence as a creditor: "He had several times lent money to Mme. Vauquer, or to the boarders; but, somehow, those whom he obliged felt that they would sooner face death than fail to repay him; a certain resolute look, sometimes seen on his face, inspired fear of him, for all his appearance of easy good-nature." The novel *Père Goriot* revolves around the dynamic of debt. The old man has as his maxim: "Money is life. Money is all powerful." His daughter, Delphine de Nucingen, who marries a prominent banker, explains: "I spent the money my poor father gave me, and then I ran into debt. . . . When I had to confess my debts to him, debts that every young woman runs up, for jewelry and trifles of various kinds, I suffered tortures. . . . Money counts for something only when feeling is dead."[11]

Charles Dickens, whose father had been imprisoned in the Marshalsea debtors' prison in Southwark in 1824 because of a relatively small sum owed to a baker, gave a striking account of life in the prison in several of his novels, most extensively in *Little Dorrit*. The debtors, as he saw it, had suffered from the overcomplexity and intransparency of life: "The affairs of this debtor were perplexed by a partnership, of which he knew no more than that he had invested money in it; by legal matters of assignment and settlement, conveyance here and conveyance there, suspicion of unlawful preference of creditors in this direction, and of mysterious spiriting away of property in that; and as nobody on the face of the earth could be more incapable of explaining any single item in the heap of confusion than the debtor himself, nothing comprehensible could be made of his case. To question him in detail, and endeavour to reconcile his answers; to closet him with accountants and sharp practitioners, learned in the wiles of insolvency and bankruptcy; was only to put the case out at compound interest and incomprehensibility. The irresolute fingers fluttered more and more ineffectually about the trembling lip on every such occasion, and the sharpest practitioners gave him up as a hopeless job."[12] Nineteenth-century literature is full of similar accounts of individuals who are destroyed because of their inability to handle their financial affairs.

Such financial tragedy doubtless continued to exist in the twentieth century, but it becomes much less central or obsessive as a literary theme. The answer to individual precariousness was insurance, especially state-provided social and sickness insurance. Bismarck's Germany and Scandinavian Europe were pioneers in the late nineteenth century, but by the early twentieth century social reformers and policy makers everywhere wanted to learn from that example. Such legislation ensured that there was no need to resort to the loan shark. In the twentieth century, concern with the devastating consequences of private over-indebtedness—which effectively excludes individuals from society—drove an increase in consumer protection legislation (against the unscrupulous selling of loans). It also generated a demand for macroeconomic stabilization, in order to eliminate the business-cycle fluctuations that drove the dynamic of over-indebtedness.

The enhanced security created by well-intended policies only set off a further process, however. Financial predators could use the new security to tempt consumers into new purchases and higher debt. Particularly in societies that prided themselves as being the most advanced, or most financialized, notably the United States and the United Kingdom, private debt exploded. Sometimes it was viewed as a compensation for the stagnation of lower incomes at the end of the twentieth century, or as a mechanism to stave off discontent. To be sustainable, debt needs to be a moderate burden: but financial markets do not like moderation, and instead swing between euphoria and revulsion. In the revulsion phase, credit dries up. The feelings of revulsion that arise in the world of private contracts spill over into the political area also, and debt becomes moralized.

"There is an almost religious presumption of guilt among the borrowers," the Harvard economist Benjamin Friedman told a group of international economists at the Bank for International Settlements.[13] He quoted the historian Henry Roseveare, "An ethic transmuted into a cult, this ideal of economical and therefore virtuous government passed from the hands of prigs like Pitt into those of high priests like Gladstone. It became a religion of financial orthodoxy whose Trinity was Free Trade, Balanced Budgets and the Gold Standard, whose Original Sin was the National Debt. It seems no accident that 'Conversion' and 'Redemption' should be the operations most closely associated with the Debt's reduction."[14] The British politician and economist Stuart Holland wrote about the peculiarity of the German language: "German for debt—*Schuld*—meaning guilt. In stressing this in his *Genealogy of Morals,* Nietzsche also observed that there was a tendency in Germany among strong creditors to demand penitence from weak debtors for their debt-guilt and to punish them if they did not seek redemption." The future Greek finance minister Yanis Varoufakis reposted and endorsed this interpretation, adding, "Back in the bleak era of the Black Death most Europeans believed that the plague was caused by sinful living and would be exorcised through self flagellation."[15] But in fact, sin is associated with the word for debt in many European languages, not just German. The phrase "Forgive us our debts, as we forgive our debtors," with its ambivalence, occurs in the Lord's Prayer in Latin, and consequently in languages that have a Latin root: *dimitte nobis debita nostra sicut et nos dimittimus debitoribus nostris.* And in the parable of the Unmerciful Servant, Jesus tells the story of a man who ruthlessly demands money from his own debtors, but then is treated much more harshly by an even more powerful man to whom he is a debtor. "Then his lord, after that he had called him, said unto him, O thou wicked servant, I forgave thee all that debt, because thou desiredst me. Shouldest not thou also have had compassion on thy fellow servant, even as I had pity on thee? And his lord was wroth, and delivered him to the tormentors, till he should pay all that was due unto him."[16]

In the globalized world, debt spilled over across frontiers. Problems became apparent when shocks hit: the Global Financial Crisis of 2007–2008, when the interbank market froze and debtors everywhere no longer had access to funding; or when the sudden, severe impact of the coronavirus pandemic killed demand. Before 2020, global supply chains stretched across the world for all kinds of products: from complex engineering designs to clothing and textiles. When the arrival of the pandemic suddenly kept shoppers home, the big retailers that dominated the cheap fashion industry simply stopped paying their bills—including for goods already in transit, waiting in ports, and even already delivered. They could do that because they were powerful.[17] In general, corporate debt looks as if it is privileged, with special tax treatment, in ways that are quite difficult to justify logically or rationally.[18]

Corporate Debt

One of the peculiarities of the period of hyper-financialization and globalization of the past thirty years has been the explosion of corporate debt. A similar increase occurred in the previous era of globalization before the First World War, especially in the United States: there, just as one century later, the surge in corporate debt fueled a mergers and acquisitions boom that led to the formation of gigantic enterprises. The trajectory of the US economy for much of the twentieth century was determined by the corporate mergers of the first decade of the twentieth century, which created giants such as US Steel and Standard Oil.

The mergers boom followed from a strange case of unintended consequences: in this case from a move in the 1890s that was driven by populist mistrust of big business and by the campaign against the trusts. The move relied on the tax deductibility of corporate debt. In theoretical financial analysis, a key theorem is the well-known Modigliani and Miller (MM) analysis, in which decisions related to a company's balance-sheet size and relative equity and debt can be modeled separately, and the value of a firm is not affected by its capital structure, that is, by how it finances its growth.[19] But in fact, the choice between equity and debt financing is often driven by tax considerations.[20]

The story of the privileging of corporate debt in the United States starts with a tariff reform. President Grover Cleveland was a Democrat who had come to office with a promise to reverse the high tariffs on imports of "the necessaries of life." In his State of the Union address in 1893, he suggested, in addition to tariff reform, levying "a small tax upon incomes derived from certain corporate investments" to replace revenues lost as part of tariff reform. There should be a "more just and equitable system of Federal taxation." This was near the height of the campaign of the populists, who forcefully articulated the view "that corporate bodies are the natural enemies of the people."[21]

The 1894 Wilson-Gorman Tariff Act lowered trade barriers that had protected Northern industry and established a 2 percent corporate tax rate on net income. Congress also amended the tax code in 1894 by including a corporate interest tax deduction. Advocates of the new package argued that this would lead to a weakening of the powerful business leaders who held large concentrations of equity. There was also a geographic element to the redistribution that Congress envisaged, to the South from the North.[22] A possible explanation for this exemption is that taxing government, municipal, and mortgage bonds would have put a burden on Southerners as well as Northerners.[23] The North was outraged. Senator Henry Cabot Lodge (a Republican from Massachusetts) argued that Wilson's tariff was "full of protection administered as preference chiefly to Southern interests, and in this way threw overboard all the principles which the Democratic party had been advocating."[24] Critics argued that it was an imposition of a (Southern) Sugar Trust as an alternative to the Northern trusts.

Section 28 of the Wilson-Gorman Tariff Act also enacted the first peacetime personal income tax, but the Supreme Court struck it down one year later in *Pollock v. Farmers' Loan & Trust Co.* As a consequence, debt still had a tax benefit, but the income tax that was originally part of the package was dropped, and would become possible only after the 1913 passage of the Sixteenth Amendment. This meant that debt instruments, in which "the vast proportion" of the wealthy's assets were invested, faced a reduced tax bill while poor equity holders were still taxed.[25] It was of course obvious that the rich bondholders would be massive winners, but "other priorities—including the protection of leveraged domestic industries and concerns about the constitutionality of targeting bondholders—took precedence."[26]

The interest exemption incentivized industrial concentration. That is, the law disproportionately benefited companies that were already dominant in their industry because mature and stable companies generally carry larger debt burdens.[27] In a new discussion in 1909, when the idea of an income tax was revisited, there was an extensive discussion of how the tax system favored large owners of corporations, who had substantial bonded debt. The *New York Times* reported: "The division here, it is understood, is somewhat geographical, the Eastern Senators being as a general thing opposed to taxing any money connected with bonds, while the Westerners are said to be in favor of finding a way to tax such fortunes as that of Andrew Carnegie, which consists almost entirely of bond holdings."[28]

In 1913 and 1916, the cap on corporate interest deductions was raised to the value of the capital stock plus one-half the amount of outstanding debt. The cap was not lifted entirely until 1918, when it was removed temporarily to equalize the effects of the World War I excess profits tax.[29] But that

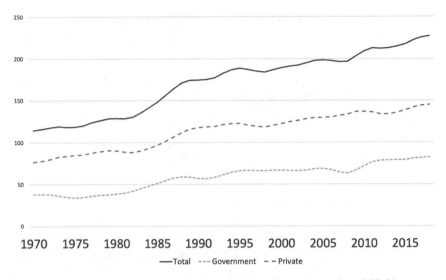

Figure 3. Global debt as percentage of world gross domestic product (GDP).
Source: M. Ayhan Kose, Peter Nagle, Franziska Ohnsorge, and Naotaka Sugawara, *Global Waves of Debt: Causes and Consequences* (Washington, DC: World Bank, 2019), p. 6.

exemption lasted, amazingly, until 2017, when it was ended by the Trump tax reform (the Tax Cuts and Jobs Act), which also lowered the corporate tax rate from 35 to 21 percent.

Corporate debt, when it explodes, becomes a public policy problem. Countries do not want to let large businesses, or large numbers of small businesses, fail. Financial institutions represent a particular vulnerability, in that their extinction might threaten economic life as a whole. And larger corporations are often very effective at lobbying. The consequence is that governments, faced by severe shocks, take on large amounts of corporate debt in the aftermath of rescue operations: after the Global Financial Crisis, for example, or again after the COVID-19 shock. In an emergency, then, a great deal of corporate debt becomes indistinguishable from state debt.

Corporate debt (along with individual private debt) increased rapidly in the early 2000s, constituting a particular problem of advanced countries and making for a vulnerability in the Global Financial Crisis. But since 2008, debt in emerging market countries, especially China, has exploded (see Figure 3).

In other words, at a time when the United States was trying to rein in its addiction to corporate debt, that path was being adopted with celebratory urgency by China as an anti-crisis measure. In 2008, credit to the non-financial sector amounted to 72.5 percent of GDP in the United States and 93.9 percent in China; by 2018 the Chinese level, 149.1 percent, was double that of the United States, which was at 74.4 percent.[30] Along with the torch of international economic leadership, the United States had passed on the torch of debt, with all of its burdens.

International Borrowing

Sovereign debt creates civil society when it is domestic debt, and when there are clear governance mechanisms. Could international debt have the same educative influence on international civil society? Unfortunately, quite often it has an opposite effect: debt in the context of international relations becomes explosive rather than stabilizing.

The international capital market always looked quite different than the domestic market, and seemed to encourage irresponsibility and default. In 1776, the Enlightenment philosopher Nicolas de Caritat, Marquis de Condorcet, wrote that interest in "the general happiness of the society ceases almost absolutely for the owner of money, who, by a banking operation, within an instant becomes English, Dutch, or Russian."[31] The German conservative Romantic writer Adam Müller wrote in 1809 that "society expands and intensifies. By a letter, by a bill of exchange, by a bar of silver, the London merchant reaches out his hand across the oceans to his correspondent in Madras, and helps him to wage the great war against the earth."[32] If the merchant—and often his government—was waging war, it was obvious who was the enemy. Debt was used to establish dependence; it was a tool of subjugation, intended to extract resources and impose imperialism.

Yet, in a seeming paradox, debt was also an instrument used by movements that sought to liberate themselves from empire. The American Revolution was financed in part by states (the thirteen colonies) borrowing abroad, on foreign (mostly Dutch) capital markets, as well as by patriots who subscribed to debt certificates. In the 1820s, the newly established Latin American states started to build their infrastructure by issuing debt, mostly on the London market: there were issues from Buenos Aires, Brazil, Central America, Colombia, Chile, Guadalajara, Mexico, Peru, and even from fictional states such as "Poyais." The enthusiasm or mania for this debt was followed quickly by a wave of defaults, and by 1827 all the bonds were in default. It would take a long time for the countries to restore their credibility; they gained large-scale access to the European capital markets only much later, in the very different circumstances of the 1870s and 1880s (and that mania too was followed by a wave of defaults).[33]

It was not just states liberating themselves from the Spanish Empire: Greece financed its war of independence in that way, with bonds issued in London in 1824–1825, and then again after independence was achieved— though the bonds quickly needed a restructuring that brought in a creditors' committee that put Britain, France, and Russia in control of government revenues.[34] Debt was needed to pay for the political and military effort required to overcome imperialism, and the practice of debt plunged the newly independent states into a new subjection: independence became dependence.

In the nineteenth century, countries could be sucked into the orbit of the Great Powers because of the potency of financial markets. Egypt, the Ottoman Empire, Russia, and China were all "opened up" by such credit operations. In non-democratic imperial systems, the imperial security umbrella, coupled with the extension of legal principles from the metropol, functioned in a similar way and reassured investors that the country was capable of sustaining greater debt levels. The effect has been attributed to imperial order, but it is hard to determine whether it is due more to the effects of good policy, imposed as a result of reform-minded administrators, or to the power of the empire to compel repayment.[35] In the aftermath of some crises, the imperial system simply expanded to swallow up bankrupt debtor entities: well-known examples are Egypt in 1875, or Newfoundland in 1933. But even very big and powerful political units sought financial shelter via cooperation with financially stronger powers. In an extreme example in early 1915, the Russian government suggested a fiscal and political union with France and the United Kingdom to allow it continued access to credit markets.[36]

Confucius's *Analects* had by contrast stated that "the Ruler does not compete for profits with the people." But the new international debt regime was the consequence of large-scale financial penalties imposed by foreign powers in the wake of military defeat: the kind of financial exactions that paralleled the siphoning off of profits by the East India Company after the British victory in the Battle of Plassey. There was the indemnity that Japan inflicted after the first Sino-Japanese war, and then the indemnity after the Boxer Rebellion, when foreign armies seized Beijing. In both cases, the customs revenues were the basis for paying the annuities to the eight foreign powers that had invaded China and that, as a result of the financial settlement and the role of the Customs Service, had an interest in the preservation of the Qing dynasty.

For the borrowers, diplomatic and political calculations played a central role. The Ottoman Empire was a major part of the European power system. A default in 1875 brought major upheaval. The debt was restructured in 1878 following the Russo-Turkish war, with a debt administration imposed by the creditors (*Administration de la dette publique ottomane*) that solicited customs and tobacco revenues directly. In this particular setting, sovereign bankruptcy was relatively easy to manage because the international political system accepted and even encouraged intrusion into the sovereignty of the debtor country. The inability to service debt was interpreted by more powerful countries as a symptom of a broader failure of a state.

The problem behind a high level of external debt is that the creditors are not represented in any parliament, and the political representatives of debtor classes (or those who have to pay taxes in order to service debt) may well have a powerful incentive to default. The substitute for domestic political credibility for the international market lay in some sort of strong diplomatic commitment, in which a security agreement underpins the financial and economic relationship. The strongest form of such association was empire, where countries that were the subject of imperial rule were not expected to vote about external debt but were perfectly aware that the metropol could impose harsh sanctions in the case of non-compliance. Some other forms of political imposition looked similar, and could be described as "informal empire."

Other rival states learned from the Ottomans that survival as a Great Power depended on a strengthening of not just military, but also economic, fundamentals. The story of how diplomatic commitments enhance credibility is especially evident in the well-known case of Imperial Russia, which was a non-democracy or autocracy that locked into international security commitments. The Russian autocracy too sought foreign money, but it mixed military and administrative demands with an increased interest in economic development. In the 1890s, an innovative finance minister, Count Sergei Witte, viewed foreign money as a way of overcoming economic backwardness, while persuading the conservatives around the tsar that economic development was a necessity for Russia's standing as a Great Power.[37]

The beginning of the diplomatic rapprochement of Russia with France in 1891 was accompanied by a French bond issue, which the supporters of the new diplomacy celebrated as a "financial plebiscite." The Witte boom was the outcome of a long period of rapprochement with the international financial order, and would have been unthinkable without a painful period of preparing Russia's entry into the gold standard (under Witte's predecessor, Ivan Vyshnegradsky). On the face of it, the Russian experience could be read as a case of the gold standard acting as a "good housekeeping seal of approval," since it limited the possibility of adopting the Argentine approach of the 1880s, which involved government operations in both paper and gold.

In the Russian case, the official sector clearly influenced the capacity of the private sector to borrow. Sub-sovereign debt—such as loans to the City of Moscow—were an alternative route to obtain finance when sovereign lending was subject to political conditions and limits. But foreign investors had even greater hopes in the capacity of the state to enforce their interests. The Russian central bank, instituted as part of Russia's joining the gold standard, was seen as the "Red Cross of the bourse," ready to intervene if bond or stock prices fell and new foreign investors might be warned off.[38] Russia survived a sharp contraction in 1900–1901, as well as a political crisis with war and revolution in 1905, with no default. It raised new money immediately after the revolution of 1905. By 1914, almost half of Russia's 1.73 million ruble government debt was held abroad; four-fifths was in French hands, with the United Kingdom holding 14 percent. The diplomatic, military, and financial calculations were intricately tied together, and skillfully used by Russia as a way of locking in the creditors politically and economically.[39]

It was the aftermath of the First World War that provided the most dramatic object lesson in the poison that came with international debt.

John Maynard Keynes had already in 1919 in *The Economic Consequences of the Peace* delivered a prophetic warning of the complexities that would arise from the combination of reparations claims and debt. Postwar Germany struggled with the reparations settlement, but also concealed the extent of both its domestic and international debt levels. Unlike in the United States and United Kingdom, there was an enormous opacity surrounding German debt operations. In particular, no one could really calculate the true amount of German debt (since much of the reparation claim was admitted by everyone to be a pure fiction). It was unclear which debt would be prioritized in the event of a crunch.

The European side of the Great Depression followed from that debt complexity, and from quite deliberate German policy choices. The revised reparation plan of 1924 (Dawes Plan) set off a flood of capital movements into Germany, with both long-term bond issues (and to some extent equity sales), as well as shorter-term bank credits, which were often initially granted by American banks and securities houses that hoped eventually to get into the issue business. The inflow of private credit was supposed to raise German industrial capacity, so that the country could meet the reparation liabilities. The buildup of German debt also raised the possibility that, at some time in the future, the private creditors could be played off against the official (reparations) creditors. In particular, the eventual logic would involve the political economy of the major new creditor country, the United States. Since the United States held war debt owed by France and the United Kingdom, and since France would be willing to reduce its reparations claim only if its war-debt liabilities were also lowered, pressure from American private creditors might lead the US government to decide that a general lowering of war debts and reparations might be needed for the good of the world. This calculation always relied on the problematic assumption that a relatively small number of private bond-holders (the number usually given is 600,000) and some influential East Coast banks would be powerful enough to push the US government to inflict a loss on the general community of taxpayers. Did Germans really think that they could move US politics in this way? Perhaps, but if so they were hopelessly naïve. At the Lausanne Conference in 1932, during the pain and tragedy of the Great Depression, the United States would act behind the scenes to entice French negotiators effectively to abandon their reparations claim.

But no one in Washington, in the lead-up to a highly contested and polarized presidential election in November 1932, would agree to cancel war debts; and indeed the issue was left hanging so that in December 1932 France defaulted on its debt—a situation that produced sanctimonious outrage in the US Congress.

Most German economists believed that the infusion of American capital that accompanied the Dawes Plan was a beneficent influence. As the economist Adolf Weber put it in 1929: "The binding through chains of our interests with the interests of foreigners, in particular America, compelled our enemies to moderation, which was in the interest of the capital that worked for us."[40]

The worry was that the mechanism to protect the transfer of debt-service payments that had been laid down under the 1924 Dawes Plan, with the agent-general for reparations acting as a kind of buffer or protector, was replaced by a 1929 provision under the Young Plan, whereby Germany could suspend a part of the annuity that had been designated as conditional or postponable (two-thirds of the annuity), but only for a period of ten years.[41] The apparent seniority of the commercial debt that had existed as a result of the Dawes provisions thus disappeared: indeed an explicit goal of the Young Plan was to make political reparations as similar to and inseparable from commercial debt as possible. As the eventual formulation in the Young Committee report put it: "If Germany were to be given a definite task to perform on her own responsibility, and if the committee were to substitute for many of the features of the Dawes plan machinery of a nonpolitical character in the realm of general finance, it was clearly necessary to elaborate a system for handling the annuities in a way which so far as it led to their commercialization would remove them from the sphere of inter-governmental relations."[42]

In 1932 an effective cancellation of reparations debt occurred at the international conference at Lausanne: did that make Germany more stable? On the contrary, freed of the constraints imposed by the need to make the reparation payments, Germany could embark on a much more aggressively revanchist foreign policy.

In the 1930s, in response to the Great Depression, a wave of defaults occurred in the Latin American and central European countries of Brazil, Chile, Colombia, Costa Rica, El Salvador, Guatemala, Peru, and Uruguay, and Austria, Bulgaria, Germany, Greece, Hungary, Poland, Romania, and Yugoslavia.[43] By contrast, in the economic upheavals of the 1980s, in a situation widely discussed as a "debt crisis," there were surprisingly few defaults. The only substantial defaults in the Latin American debt crisis of the 1980s were Peru and Brazil, and Brazil's default crisis lasted for only a brief period in 1987. The contrast with the Great Depression produced a wave of reflection on why countries try to avoid default, and there are obvious answers: debtors do not want to be cut off from future borrowing, while creditors have increased regulatory incentives to "extend and pretend," that is, to offer new credit in order not to run into default.[44]

International debt may create incentives for countries to build up debt and then play their creditors off against each other. This would be a reprise of the bad old politics of domestic debt, when medieval and early modern monarchs tantalized their creditors with particular offers and special advantages or privileges over others. In a modern setting, the sum total of debt in a domestic context is clearly laid out, in order to give debt holders a sense of the overall amount of their claims. But foreign debt is often bewilderingly obscure, creditors lack information, and the question of whether they will be repaid becomes a guessing game.

Can international debt become more like domestic debt? Only with the establishment of clear rules—including codes about publicizing the amounts of debt, so that the extent of governments' commitments are fully transparent—as well as a mechanism for arbitrating the seniority of different claimants. There have been attempts to move in this direction, moves that are often accompanied by an initial reduction of debt for cases of high levels of indebtedness. In the early 2000s, some senior figures at the IMF proposed a process like bankruptcy court, one that would provide "a predictable, orderly, and rapid process for restructuring the debts of sovereigns that are implementing appropriate policies." This proposal, however, never won the approval of the US government and its representatives, and consequently faded.[45] Instead, in 2005, at the meeting of the G8, an initiative was suggested whereby the claims of three multilateral institutions—the IMF, the International Development Association of the World Bank, and the African Development Fund—would be cancelled for countries that agreed to reforms under the Heavily Indebted Poor Countries Initiative.

For many countries, the coronavirus crisis raises the question of debt sustainability even more brutally than did the Global Financial Crisis of 2007–2008. When the pandemic hit, almost a hundred countries went to the IMF for emergency funding from a newly created rapid financing instrument. As a result of the earlier financial collapse, however, and of the measures taken to counter it, countries went into the new crisis with much higher levels of debt. There were also many cases in which different claimants looked as if they might be played off against each other. Particularly after the outbreak of the Global Financial Crisis, China had engaged in a large-scale lending exercise, often on very different conditions than those of multilateral development banks. A recent study found "hidden debts," with 50 percent of China's lending to developing countries not reported to the IMF or World Bank.[46]

In the early and mid-2000s, the complex interlinkage of what Niall Ferguson and Moritz Schularick dubbed "Chimerica" looked as if it was a stabilizing force, but one with a latent instability.[47] China provided cheap goods to US consumers, who went into debt; and Chinese savers and the Chinese government bought up US Treasury debt, providing further liquidity to finance the US spending spree. The mechanism of the linkage looked quite stable, because the United States wanted to continue to borrow and binge, while China, in accumulating US debt, knew that it could not liquidate that debt without collapsing its value. So both sides were locked in. After the 2007–2008 Global Financial Crisis, China gradually ran down its surpluses, and Chinese-state debt managers tried slowly to diversify their foreign assets. But the mechanism could not survive the slide of China and the United States into more confrontation and a new Cold War–style crisis in 2020, when accusations about the source of the coronavirus pandemic exacerbated already escalating trade and political tensions. As US politicians started discussing imposing reparations on China for having supposedly launched the virus and misled the world about its origins, the obvious route to reparation looked as if it might be a selective default on foreign-held American debt—a return to the logic of Germany in the Great Depression. The United States could clearly argue that in a catastrophe it was better to disappoint the Chinese investor, principally the communist-led state, than to impose more sacrifices on the American taxpayer.

Debt and its complex politics represent a powerful force that progressively erodes contemporary globalization. Or, to go back to the Hamiltonian metaphor, instead of being a strong cement for a union, it has become a high-charge explosive.

There are once again proposals to channel debt through international institutions in order to systematize it and make it credible again. The coronavirus pandemic had an outsize impact on poor countries dependent on capital inflows (which came to an abrupt stop with the outbreak) and on exports of commodities and goods such as textiles, for which demand temporarily collapsed. Over a hundred countries went to the IMF and explained that they required international financial support. The G20 as an immediate response agreed to a temporary halt to bilateral loan repayments from a group of seventy-six of the poorest countries. One proposal then suggested that multilateral institutions such as the World Bank create a central credit facility, allowing those countries requesting temporary relief to deposit their stayed interest payments to official and private creditors for use in emergency funding to fight the pandemic.[48] International institutions are supposed to take the poison out of debt relations in a way analogous to the classical era's sanctification of debt through the state.

The situation in which both sides think that they are locked in looks like a variant of the famous Master and Slave dialectic in Hegel's *Phenomenology of Spirit*. Both sides are trapped. The Slave is not recognized as fully human, or as an equal by the Master, and is not free. The Master is free, but does not find that he is recognized as a human by the Slave. He is constantly worried by the fragility of the relationship, and the fact that the Slave is building up an alternative universe of values in which the Master is not represented.

The dynamics of debt when combined with the forces of globalization produce a trap. Another way of seeing it is through the 1969 hit song by Mark James and Elvis Presley about the trap created by suspicion in a relationship: "We can't build our dreams on suspicious minds." Humans are always suspicious, especially when they think of foreigners. Debt is the way that dreams of solidarity are changed into nightmares.

8

Technocracy

Globalization is often linked to the idea of *technocracy,* rule by unelected and self-selecting "experts." Technocrats have particular skills, or expert knowledge, that set them apart from politicians, who are generalists. There is often also an implication in the term *technocracy* that politicians will evade unpleasant choices, whereas technocrats are in a better position to depict in a clearsighted way the long-term developments, and what—often painful—decisions or sacrifices need to be made in the present. Technocrats seem to come into their own in exceptional times, when a new approach is required to solve unprecedented challenges. There is always a problem, though, in that technocrats typically observe small-scale or micro phenomena, and these need to be aggregated in order to be comprehensible or to provide a plan for action. The weak point always lies in the attempt to draw macro conclusions from a precise observation and analysis of micro phenomena.

Technocracy as a term was born in and out of the First World War. The California engineer William H. Smyth introduced the word in 1919 to describe "the rule of the people made effective through the agency of their servants, the scientists and engineers." He started out with some contemptuous observations on democracy ("In the rough, Democracy is the rule of the mob, the rule of the masses, the rule of the majority—the rule of un-intelligence. But even so, it is better than any form of governmental control based upon self-interest—not excepting Benevolent Autocracy.") He went on to explain what he considered a new principle of organization:

"This we did by organizing and coordinating the Scientific Knowledge, the Technical Talent, and the Practical Skill of the entire Community: focused them in the National Government, and applied this Unified National Force to the accomplishment of a Unified National Purpose. For this unique experiment in rationalized Industrial Democracy I have coined the term 'Technocracy.' " He continues: "Dog-eat-dog. Until appropriate economic institutions and instrumentalities are available, humanly effective Industrial Democracy must remain an unrealizable ideal, a theory unattainable as a work-a-day principle of Social Life, and for the efficient distribution of the products of toil, upon which human life rests."[1] A "National Council should be the apex of the Nation's Industrial Management."[2]

The expressions with which Smyth launched the new term were eccentric, but he was in reality simply describing how the belligerents had organized their operations during the First World War. The French minister of commerce, Étienne Clémentel, was a characteristic representative of the new type: he collected staff outside the usual legal experts of the French bureaucracy, often from the École Centrale des Arts et Manufactures, a technical training school, and had a preference for engineers. He wanted to rationalize and centralize administration, and regarded that as a primarily technical task. There was a need to end business as usual, to "overturn the watertight compartments that serve to separate the government, parliament, the administration, commerce, and industry. The war forced us to collaborate."[3] Clémentel worked above all very closely with an engineer named Louis Loucheur from the École Polytechnique, who became the undersecretary for armaments and war manufactures, as well as a central figure in pushing the new vision of rule by experts.

Interest in technocracy as a solution to organizational problems increased during the Second World War. The main focus of that new development was the United States, whose new approach to science and scientific knowledge underpinned the spectacular strength and international dominance of the US economy in the postwar period. The Manhattan Project—which developed the atomic bomb—had a research budget that was larger in 1944 and 1945 than that of the entire Department of Defense. It introduced a new vision of "big science." The Office of Scientific Research and Development (OSRD), a US federal agency headed by Vannevar Bush and responsible for" wartime military research and development, laid a basis for public-private cooperation. Bush's 1945 report, *Science: The Endless Frontier*, set out a bold vision: "Science, by itself, provides no panacea for individual, social, and economic ills. It can be effective in the national welfare only as a member of a team, whether the conditions be peace or war. But without scientific progress no amount of achievement in other directions can insure our health, prosperity, and security as a nation in the modern world." The report laid out in a stunning way—one that later generated some pushback from practitioners—how "basic research is the pacemaker of technological progress."[4]

The question remained of how to translate the innovations of basic research into applied technology. Just after the war, the mathematician and scientist Warren Weaver, director of the Division of Natural Sciences at the Rockefeller Foundation, set out a vision of the future, writing how "physical scientists, with the mathematicians often in the vanguard, developed powerful techniques of probability theory and of statistical mechanics to deal with what may be called problems of disorganized complexity. . . . The great advances that science can and must achieve in the next fifty years will be largely contributed to by voluntary mixed teams, somewhat similar to the operations analysis groups of war days, their activities made effective by the use of large, flexible, and highspeed computing machines."[5] A technical revolution was needed to coordinate all the individual inputs.

James Burnham, a professor of philosophy who for some time in the 1930s was a Trotskyist, and then followed an intellectual trajectory that eventually brought him to conservatism, reflected in a 1941 wartime book on the downfall of capitalism, which he believed would be replaced in a "managerial revolution" (the title of his book, a bestseller). In his view, "capitalist ideologies and slogans have largely lost their power to appeal to the masses," in part due to the inability of capitalism "any longer to exploit and develop the backward areas successfully."[6] It looked to Burnham as though the managerial revolution was, unfortunately, already under way in both the Soviet Union and Nazi Germany, and that the new logic—whereby the capitalist property system would be demolished, and a sort of socialism or collectivism would take its place—was driving a transcendence of the nation-state, and hence European integration.

Military Technocrats

When societies go to war, they need technocrats. When the term *technocracy* emerged, it was inherently linked with learning lessons from a dramatic military mobilization. The first technocrats were in fact soldiers. Their work involved not only organizing the movement and provisioning of large numbers of people, but also making projections about the future with an assessment of probabilities, while being aware that there would be continual change and shocks. The great military theorist Carl von Clause-witz thought of war as an extension of politics by other means, but one that required a great deal more coordination: "Military activity in general is served by an enormous amount of expertise and skills, all of which are needed to place a well-equipped force in the field. They coalesce into a few great results before they attain their final purpose in war, like streams combining to form rivers before they flow into the sea."[7] He explained further: "Everything looks simple; the knowledge required does not look remarkable, the strategic options are so obvious that by comparison the simplest problem of higher mathematics has an impressive scientific dignity. Once war has actually been seen the difficulties become clear; but it is still extremely hard to describe the unseen, all-pervading element that brings about this change of perspective. . . . The military machine . . . is basically very simple and very easy to manage. But we should bear in mind that none of its components is of one piece: each part is composed of indi-viduals, every one of whom retains his potential of friction."[8] Managing the mess or fog of war to implement the overall vision involves overcom-ing what Clausewitz termed "friction." It involved not just common sense but also applying some sort of scientific or mathematical principle: "Many intelligence reports in war are contradictory; even more are false, and most are uncertain. What one can reasonably ask of an officer is that he should possess a standard of judgment, which he can gain only from knowledge of men and affairs and from common sense. He should be guided by the laws of probability."[9]

The relationship between the technocrat and the overall political author-ity is a central question—indeed it is *the* central question—of technocracy. Who controls the technocrats in the army? Smyth tried to present tech-nocrats in a humble way as the servants of the people, but they in fact often turn into masters, controlling everything from an ivory tower. The problem of control is illustrated in the case of an influential misreading of Clausewitz. He is often reported as claiming that Napoleon was the God of War. This is a misinterpretation, but an interesting one, of what Clausewitz wrote in *On War*. There was indeed in his account a "Kriegsgott selbst," the "god of war in person," who confronted and defeated the Prussian and Austrian armies in 1806; Clausewitz was contrasting the wars of Frederick the Great in the mid-eighteenth century with the war of the early nineteenth century. As he puts it, "Careful study of history shows where the difference between these cases lies. In the eighteenth century, in the days of the Silesian campaigns, war was still an affair for governments alone, and the people's role was simply that of an instrument. At the onset of the nineteenth century, peoples themselves were in the scale on either side. The generals opposing Frederick the Great were acting on instructions—which implied that caution was one of their distinguishing characteristics. But now the opponent of the Austrians and Prussians was—to put it bluntly—the God of War himself."[10] The context makes it obvious that Clausewitz was not thinking so much of the French leader as of the fact of a popular mobilization. Napoleon needed to guide that god of war.[11]

It was clear—and it became even clearer as the industrialization of the nineteenth century brought bigger and better equipped armies—that the people were not generally in control. The First World War produced a debate about *militarism*—what happened when generals have too much control. According to one popular theory, German militarism had caused the war: civilians like the German chancellor, Theobald von Bethman Hollweg, had been sidelined, and the military had relied too much on its own inflexible plans. The mobilization preparations were conducted on the basis of an intuitive scheme for dealing with a two-front war developed by General Schlieffen, who had retired in 1906 and died in January 1913. It required modification very rapidly in August 1914 as the German high command was taken aback by the speed of Russian mobilization on the eastern front, in East Prussia. In 1915, Princeton University president John Grier Hibben asked: "What is militarism? It is the madness of a nation. Militarism is not created by the army, but the nature and scope of the army is determined by the policy of the nation. Militarism is essentially a theory of the state. Where militarism exists the government is a part of the army, instead of the army being a part of the government. . . . Its ethic is the maxim that the end justifies the means."[12] In fact, every country recognized that it needed more than a little military expertise. Thus, for instance, the British Labour Party statesman Arthur Henderson, driver of the League of Nations disarmament conferences and eventual recipient of the Nobel Peace Prize, argued: "We mean by 'Prussian Militarism' an organised effort towards world domination by an illegitimate application of immoralised military power. We do not suggest that every form of militarism or use of force is wrong."[13]

In fact, when things go really wrong, there is in many countries a demand that the military take control. Military modernization followed coups against ineffectual traditional leaders. Armies, in particular their mid-level officers (characteristically colonels), turned "an instrument of repression in its own interests or that of kings into the vanguard of nationalism and social reform."[14] The great model for that sort of movement was Marshall Mustafa Kemal Atatürk's 1919 seizure of power in the Republic of Turkey (later legitimated by an election); other examples include Colonel Gamal Abdel Nasser's overthrow of the Egyptian monarchy in 1952, and Colonel Muammar Mohammed Abu Minyar Gaddafi's coup against the Libyan monarchy in 1969.[15] Nasser and Gaddafi remained popularly known as "Colonel."

The military has been involved in regime change more recently as well. In February 1981, when the Polish communist leadership ran into a dead end in the face of the Solidarność labor movement, the minister of defense, General Wojciech Jaruzelski, became prime minister and later imposed martial law in a bid both to stem the opposition and to push through a reform. In the coronavirus crisis of 2020, the role of the military increased in Indonesia and the Philippines. General Prayuth Chan-o-cha in Thailand declared a state of emergency and created a crisis response team mostly composed of senior military officers, with no medical experts. Even in the United States, at the most chaotic moments of the Trump presidency, there were stories about a plan by the military to take control in the event of some irresponsible action.[16] In rich industrial countries, generally no one thinks of military coups, but they do think about rule by "experts" or "grown-ups" when politics become confused.

Economists

The prototype for a new sort of expert thinking came from engineers. To some, the Great Depression seemed to require a military-style mobilization. During the Depression, engineering largely lost its attraction as a career—there was not very much being built, and some young engineers turned their attention to economics, which was being called on to resolve quite practical, logistical questions of coordination. In an entertaining history of his profession, the Harvard economist Greg Mankiw wrote: "God put macroeconomists on earth not to propose and test elegant theories but to solve practical problems. The problems He gave us, moreover, were not modest in dimension."[17]

It was in answering the Great Depression that economists emerged as the most significant social scientists for policymaking. The model was provided by the British economist John Maynard Keynes, but Keynes's major and transformational work of the 1930s, *The General Theory of Employment Interest and Money*, was precisely what it said it was, an elegant and rhetorically persuasive book about the possibilities of bad (less than full employment) equilibria. It was not really a manual: that came later, and only really with a new war. The war gave the impetus to the sense that concrete coordination policies needed to be implemented—and quickly. The statistical framework was provided above all by Richard Stone, the statistician Colin Clark, and James Meade, who developed national income accounting primarily as a way of managing the economy in the Second World War, so as to avoid the mistakes of the First World War.

After the war ended, the same models that were used to mobilize for war were used to make decisions about the allocation of investment in postwar reconstruction, since they too required large-scale analysis of data. Charles Kindleberger reported: "The first work ever done that I know about in economics on computers used the Pentagon's computers at night for the Marshall Plan."[18]

As the pressing needs of wartime mobilization and postwar reconstruction faded, new worries arose. By the 1970s, the Keynesian framework seemed to be in deep trouble. There was more inflation—commentators began to speak about the Great Inflation—but it was also combined with rising levels of unemployment after the oil price shock of 1973–1974.

Inflation and the mismanagement of the dollar appeared to put the international position of the United States into question: Europeans accused US economic policymakers of using their hegemony over the currency to impose on them the costs of American wars and American welfare problems. In their article "After Keynesian Macroeconomics," Thomas Sargent and Robert Lucas (who would both be awarded the Nobel Prize in Economics) wrote, "For policy, the central fact is that Keynesian policy recommendations have no sounder basis, in a scientific sense, than recommendations of non-Keynesian economists or, for that matter, noneconomists."[19]

Another framework arrived that seemed to explain the failures of Keynesianism and at the same time offer an answer to the major policy dilemma of the time: how to tackle inflation. Milton Friedman's formulation of monetarism picked up an old tradition that went back to Irving Fisher but especially the interwar Chicago economists. Friedman's new insight depended on a massive empirical investigation, conducted with Anna Schwartz and published in the *Monetary History of the United States*. There he showed how remarkably stable over a long period of time was the "money multiplier," the ratio of the percentage change in income to the percentage change in the money stock: in the United States this figure had been around two. The reserve base fixed by the central bank determined the money stock (via the "money multiplier"), which in turn determined nominal income (via the velocity of money). The ratio between currency and deposits was also quite stable over long periods of time.[20]

The Friedman approach, however, did not provide a practical framework for monetary policymaking in any major country, with the possible exception of Switzerland (which did have the world's best anti-inflation track record). In Germany, another country with a low inflation record, the powerful central bank introduced in the mid-1970s a monetary target, but saw the announcement of a target not as a real policy constraint but rather as an effective way of guiding expectations, and in particular the wage-bargaining behavior of employers and trade unions. The United Kingdom, for its part, had a vigorous debate about the use of monetarism as a policy tool in the early 1980s, but from 1983 on, it gradually retreated from the use of monetary targets. And the highly influential Fed chair Paul Volcker once said, "we must develop a co-ordinated set of policies designed to attack inflation from a number of directions rather than placing the entire burden on monetary policy. . . . I believe it is imperative to keep the goal of budgetary balance in the forefront of our thinking about spending and revenue decisions."[21]

Instead, dynamic stochastic general equilibrium (DSGE) models were used to generate a wide range of scenarios of responses to monetary policy changes, with the central feature being an economy that was consistently "shocked" by market changes. The models made the idea of market shocks a more or less continual feature of market economies, but in their original formulation did not include any room for financial shocks—which proved in 2007–2008 to be a great vulnerability. A torrent of criticism of these models' limited applicability ensued.[22] Looking back, one of the pioneers of New Keynesian modeling argued that a "stated aim was to discard Keynesian theorizing and replace it with market-clearing models that could be convincingly brought to the data and then used for policy analysis. By that standard, the movement failed." In particular, "real business cycle theories omitted any role of monetary policy, unanticipated or otherwise, in explaining economic fluctuations. The emphasis switched to the role of random shocks to technology and the intertemporal substitution in consumption and leisure that these shocks induced."[23]

In terms of policy, the new paradigm relied on a simple assumption, shared by almost all mainstream economists: monetary stability would automatically produce financial stability. In 2003, a famous paper that launched the term "the Great Moderation" emphasized—in addition to the role played by monetary policy—the part played by "good luck," or smaller international macroeconomic shocks.[24] The practitioners assumed a clear relationship between financial and monetary stability. One of the classic arguments for greater attention to monetary stability is that it reduces unpredictability and financial shocks. Schwartz suggested that "if inflation and price instability prevail, so will financial instability." The argument was that monetary uncertainty would mask or distort prices, and thus lead to an inefficient allocation of resources. This approach was even termed the "Schwartz hypothesis" and derived some measure of support from empirical testing.[25] Bank of England governor Eddie George suggested something similar even before Schwartz had really formulated the position, when he claimed that "the line that leads from monetary policy to the health of the financial system is pretty clear."[26] But recent experience seems to challenge this view. In the United Kingdom during the 1950s and 1960s, for instance, there was a substantial fluctuation in inflation performance, but great financial stability. As inflation performance improved after the 1980s, financial instability came back globally. Some commentators then suggested that monetary stability might produce a false sense of confidence that would lead to excessive risk-taking. Before 2007 this was a minority view, largely associated with the Bank for International Settlements, but after the Global Financial Crisis it looked almost self-evident.[27]

The Global Financial Crisis led to a widespread view that mainstream economics had failed, and needed to be reconstructed or reinvented. An iconic moment came in November 2008, soon after the failure of Lehman Brothers, when the Queen of England visited the London School of Economics to open the New Academic Building, and asked, "Why did nobody notice it?" Professor Luis Garicano, director of research at the London School of Economics' management department, replied with a classic exposition of the dangers of groupthink: "At every stage, someone was relying on somebody else and everyone thought they were doing the right thing."[28] Dissident economists of the past—especially Hyman Minsky, who had developed an approach that put financial instability at the center, and Charles Kindleberger, who had popularized the Minsky hypothesis and applied it in the context of international economic relations—now received much more recognition.

The 2008 story also shook confidence in economists as experts. A key part of the debate in the United Kingdom about possibly leaving the European Union, or Brexit, was about the failure of economists. This led voters to doubt the reliability and evenhandedness of economic forecasts (by experts from the Treasury, the Bank of England, or the International Monetary Fund) that Brexit would cause a severe economic shock.

More generally, in the aftermath of the Global Financial Crisis, economists as talking heads were pitted against each other. If many economists were hostile to Brexit, a few could still be found who were sympathetic. There were economists on both sides of debates about the euro crisis. And a few economists thought that parts of Donald Trump's agenda might bring economic growth: tax cuts would promote business investment, the threat and partial implementation of protectionism would bring American jobs back, and so on. Most economists were skeptical, but until early 2020 the strong growth of the US economy seemed to be proving them wrong. They could only warn about high debt burdens from sustained fiscal deficits that might at some stage in the future be a problem. The obvious politicization of economic debate had further discredited the role of economists.

Technocratic Governments

Governments' use of experts to deal with a national emergency—often an economic one—have a long history. During the postwar period, Italy in particular frequently called on officials from the Banca d'Italia to assume governmental positions at critical moments. Right at the beginning of Italy's postwar history, in 1947–1948, the economist and governor of the central bank Luigi Einaudi took over the position of finance minister and deputy prime minister, without leaving the central bank; in 1948 he was elected president of the Republic. In the 1990s, the major conventional center-right and center-left parties disintegrated in a series of corruption scandals, and in 1993 another governor, Carlo Azeglio Ciampi, became prime minister.

At the height of the euro debt crisis, in November 2011, the governments of Greece and Italy collapsed almost simultaneously. In Greece, the socialist government of George Papandreou fell apart after it proposed a referendum on the austerity program imposed as part of the international rescue package. A new cabinet of experts under the former vice-president of the European Central Bank, Lucas Papademos, was formed with the goal of implementing a new austerity program before parliamentary elections, pushing through unpopular measures such as opening closed professions, adjusting the minimum wage, and eliminating one month's additional salary customarily paid to employees. In Italy, the bitterly divided Berlusconi government was also replaced by a "technocratic" cabinet under the economist Mario Monti, the former commissioner for competition policy in the European Commission. The parallel moves in Greece and Italy were interpreted as anti-democratic coups by populists, including Berlusconi, who remade his agenda in a new populist orientation. As Alexis Tsipras, leader of the increasingly popular far-left party Syriza (an abbreviation for the Greek words for "coalition of the radical left"), put it: "This development amounts to a merciless distortion of popular sovereignty. The choice of Mr Papademos is a guarantee that the same policies that have destroyed us will be continued with greater force and consequence."[29] Neither Papademos nor Monti lasted long in government, and Monti signally failed when he tried to build his own political party. But the sense that traditional party politics had been unsuccessful remained, and it continued to be hard for parties that saw themselves as readily accountable to voters to make painful decisions.

Experts and Climate Change

Other kinds of technical experts went through the same cycle of presenting advice that then became contested and mired in controversy. Thinking about the environment also depended on the accurate identification and then the analysis of long-run trends, and produced a new range of expertise. Economists reflected on the way in which carbon energy had replaced human and animal power, and had pushed a transformation of the economy—of wages, living conditions, and life expectancy. In the nineteenth century, the focus was largely on coal, which had been the foundation of Britain's transformative industrial revolution; in the twentieth century and after, the concern was oil, which had raised new geopolitical problems.

Few politicians had any background in the natural sciences, though it is striking that the two long-term leaders of advanced industrial countries who had done postgraduate work in the natural sciences were both female: Margaret Thatcher and Angela Merkel. Thatcher was the first major political leader to address the challenge of climate change, in a 1988 speech to the Royal Society, where she was deeply disappointed that there were no TV cameras and no media coverage, but still laid out the threat: "the increase in the greenhouse gases—carbon dioxide, methane, and chlorofluorocarbons—which has led some to fear that we are creating a global heat trap which could lead to climatic instability. We are told that a warming effect of 1°C per decade would greatly exceed the capacity of our natural habitat to cope. Such warming could cause accelerated melting of glacial ice and a consequent increase in the sea level of several feet over the next century."[30] And in 2011, German chancellor Angela Merkel, in the immediate aftermath of the reactor catastrophe of Fukushima, announced the speeding up of Germany's phase-out of nuclear power, and called for a "new architecture" for energy: "As the first big industrialized nation, we can achieve such a transformation toward efficient and renewable energies, with all the opportunities that brings for exports, developing new technologies and jobs."[31] But by and large, scientific influence has been episodic, and has occurred behind the scenes rather than at the center of political debate.

In his 1865 book *Coal Question,* Stanley Jevons, the father of modern mathematical and marginalist economics, began with a celebration of the black commodity, before turning to an anxiety about the future of Britain. He wrote: "Day by day it becomes more evident that the Coal we happily possess in excellent quality and abundance is the mainspring of modern material civilization. . . . Coal in truth stands not beside but entirely above all other commodities. It is the material energy of the country—the universal aid—the factor in everything we do. With coal almost any feat is possible or easy; without it we are thrown back into the laborious poverty of early times." At that time, at the beginning of the new phase of globalization, coal was largely limited to Britain, or perhaps more generally to English-speaking countries. "Of a total produce of 136½ millions of tons, 103 millions are produced by nations of British origin and language, and 80 millions are produced in Great Britain itself." But Jevons envisioned coal, as a tool and technology, potentially spreading around the world, in an act of globalization or global sharing: "The alternatives before us are simple. Our empire and race already comprise one-fifth of the world's population; and by our plantation of new states, by our guardianship of the seas, by our penetrating commerce, by the example of our just laws and firm constitution, and above all by the dissemination of our new arts, we stimulate the progress of mankind in a degree not to be measured. If we lavishly and boldly push forward in the creation and distribution of our riches, it is hard to over-estimate the pitch of beneficial influence to which we may attain in the present. But the maintenance of such a position is physically impossible. We have to make the momentous choice between brief greatness and longer continued mediocrity."[32]

Almost immediately after coal transformed the world, thinkers mentally conditioned by the principle of exhaustibility concluded that the new material too would reach limits. The most famous expression of this resource pessimism came from the physicist William Thomson, Lord Kelvin, who believed that "The sub-terranean coal-stores of the world are becoming exhausted surely, and the price of coal is upward bound—upward bound on the whole, though no doubt it will have its ups and downs in the future as it has had in the last, and as must be the case in respect to every marketable commodity. . . . Therefore it is more probable that windmills or windmotors in some form will again be in the ascendant."[33] Chinese commentators joined in this chorus. As the diplomat Xue Fucheng wrote in his diaries from the early 1890s: "If precious materials are rare it is because China was the earliest to extract them, we have extracted them and used them to the limit. . . . Recently those who envy the foreign machines have become the majority and the trend will be difficult to suppress for long. Mining will necessarily proliferate. After another four or five thousand years, when we have exhausted our mines, then the foreign mines will also be spent. After that time, what will happen to our mineral products? In this matter one cannot but be worried for the earth."[34]

Into the late twentieth century, the major problem continued to be seen as the exhaustion of fossil-fuel supplies. That was, for instance, the major conclusion of the 1972 Club of Rome report, *The Limits of Growth*, which created an international sensation with 30 million copies sold. Other pollution costs of energy dependence were also discussed—in particular, the depletion of ozone in the atmosphere.

The answer to the twin challenges of exhaustion and pollution was thought to be coordination. In a landmark issue of *Scientific American* on "Managing Planet Earth," in 1989, the issue was framed this way: a "requirement for adaptive planetary management is the construction of mechanisms at the national and international level to coordinate managerial activities. The need for formal international agreements in this area has been highlighted by the Montreal Protocol on Substances that Deplete the Ozone Layer and discussion of a possible international law of the atmosphere."[35]

The late 1980s produced a brief euphoria about the possibility of coordination. In 1988 the UN Framework Convention on Climate Change was established. The Montreal accord, signed in 1987, may have generated the impression that international agreement was easy, in that a schedule was set up to phase out the production of ozone-depleting chlorofluoro-carbons. The task was relatively simple, and indeed profitable, because a readily available alternative existed (hydrofluorocarbons), though this alternative would turn out to be a powerful greenhouse gas with a strong effect on global warming. At the time the Montreal process seemed like the path to the future, and UN Secretary-General Kofi Annan called it "perhaps the single most successful international agreement to date."[36]

The *Scientific American* article gave some sense of the limits of the possibility for cooperation. The author, William C. Clark, scraped around to find some example of positive progress toward cooperation. His examples were all non-American. "In the Soviet Union, issues of ecological deterioration became a central point of debate in the first Congress of People's Deputies. In Kenya, an innovative project sponsored by the African Academy of Sciences has begun to explore and articulate alternative possibilities for the continent's development in the 21st century. In West Germany, a high-level commission representing all political parties and the scientific community evolved a consensual *Vorsorge*, or prevention, principle to guide the nation's environmental policies. In Sweden, a national best-seller and focal point for political debate emerged when the environmental scientist and artist Gunnar Brusewitz collaborated in 'painting the future' of Swedish landscapes under alternative paths of development."[37] It is true that environmental degradation became a major theme of Soviet discussion, above all on the part of a critical intelligentsia, and especially in the wake of the Chernobyl nuclear accident of 1986; but in fact the environmental challenge was completely incapable of resolution in the Soviet system. Many African states revolted against attempts to impose environmental or ecological conditions in foreign aid programs and in the next decades turned to China precisely because it offered a model of growth in which the environment was sacrificed to achieve faster economic development. It is striking that none of the examples of the national coordination given generated an effective blueprint for how to achieve "global management."

At this stage another issue came to the fore: environmental impacts on the planet as a whole. Initial discussion of the effects of carbon dioxide (CO_2) came about as a chance result of attempts to provide global meteorological calculations. The climatologist Syukuro ("Suki") Manabe had in the 1960s come across the global warming effect of CO_2 emissions as he tried to reduce the complexity of a three-dimensional climate model—which could not be handled by the computing power at the time—to one dimension, of gases going in and out. The resulting General Circulation Model was presented in the *Journal of Atmospheric Science* in 1967: thus the problem was identified before it became a global challenge. It was only in the years after the establishment of the UN Framework Convention that the world's CO_2 output exploded, because of the fast development of so-called merging economies. Since 2000, the largest increase in energy consumption has come from coal, at a rate of growth double that of petroleum and three times that of natural gas.[38]

The aftermath of the Global Financial Crisis intensified the debate about climate change. A key part of the appeal of Donald Trump was that he promised to increase US carbon energy production (from shale oil and gas) and consequently make the United States less dependent on imports. Russia's Vladimir Putin had from the beginning embarked on a bold gamble: not to diversify the Russian economy, but to rely on the abundance of natural resources, above all carbon energy. The export of that energy, often on long-term contracts and at prices that looked as if they might be below world market prices, looked like a way of binding other countries—in the former Soviet Union territories, but also in Europe—to Russian policy interests. Russia was thus highly dependent on a high oil price, and worried about attempts to limit carbon emissions.

Putin at a press conference at the end of 2019 explained that "nobody knows the origins of global climate change." Instead, he opined, "We know that in the history of our Earth there have been periods of warming and cooling and it could depend on processes in the universe. A small angle in the axis in the rotation of the Earth or its orbit around the Sun could push the planet into serious climate changes."[39] At the beginning of 2020, Trump told the World Economic Forum in Davos that the world should not listen to "prophets of doom" such as the climate activist Greta Thunberg, or "alarmists" who wanted to "control every aspect of our lives." In the past he had discussed climate change as "mythical," "nonexistent," or "an expensive hoax," although, rather inconsistently, he had also in 2009 signed a newspaper advertisement calling attention to "the catastrophic and irreversible consequences for humanity and our planet" of climate change. In 2012, he went further, arguing that the issue had been "created by and for the Chinese in order to make US manufacturing non-competitive."[40]

In the United Kingdom, the pro-Brexit former Conservative politician Nigel Lawson argued that global temperatures had not been rising and attacked the climate focus of Al Gore: "It's the same old clap-trap. He's the sort of bloke who goes around saying the end of the world is nigh."[41] Anne Widdecombe, a former Conservative MP standing for the United Kingdom Independence Party (UKIP), in a 2014 column for the *Daily Express*, described Lawson's book as the "best refutation of the doom mongers."[42] The German Alternative für Deutschland started as a rather wonkish party led by economics professors professing to be pro-European but hostile to the euro; after 2015 it turned itself into a populist anti-immigration party; and from 2017, as the migration issue started to fade, it became an anti-ecology and anti-Green movement, warning against "degenerate fear-mongering" by environmentalists who wanted to turn Europe into "a deindustrialized settlement covered in wind turbines." It capitalized on the fear of many German motorists that their diesel cars, previously pushed by government tax incentives, would be worthless.[43] In the Netherlands, Thierry Baudet of the populist-nationalist Forum for Democracy also made warnings against "climate change hysteria" a key part of his platform.[44] And in France, Marine Le Pen's National Rally Party (RN) campaigned against wind energy and denounced the United Nations framework convention on climate change as a "communist project."[45]

Epidemiologists and the Coronavirus Pandemic

The coronavirus crisis shed a harsh light on a new group of experts: epidemiologists (and public health specialists in general). Their advice was crucial to making decisions about whether and how much of the economy should be shuttered.

The origins of the British response to the crisis lay in its response to a 2001 epidemic of foot-and-mouth disease, when the United Kingdom had used academic epidemiologists from Imperial College London, Cambridge University, and the University of Edinburgh to produce real-time models as a basis for policy decisions, and established the Scientific

Advisory Group for Emergencies (SAGE), whose membership remained secret from the public. The advice given about foot-and-mouth was later heavily criticized as having led to unnecessary culling of animals, because the original model suggested that animals were infectious before they showed signs of disease.[46]

The UK coronavirus response was at first spectacularly erratic and inconsistent. On March 12, 2020, Prime Minister Boris Johnson announced that the United Kingdom would not limit large gatherings or close schools because "the scientific advice is that this could do more harm than good at this time." The government's chief science adviser, Patrick Vallance, spoke of a containment plan based on herd immunity, under which some 60 percent of the population would have to contract the virus. Just a few days later, there was a change of approach, made on the basis of a report of March 16, 2020, from a team of epidemiologists at Imperial College, London under Neil Ferguson, whose reputation had been largely established in the foot-and-mouth crisis. It warned that without preventive measures, COVID-19 could kill 510,000 people, but even with the government's then preferred strategy of "mitigation," there would be a quarter of a million deaths, and the National Health Service would be impossibly burdened. The model underlying the report's grim conclusions had been fed with data from the rapidly escalating pandemic in Italy.[47] A rival report from Oxford University reached very different conclusions, arguing (in what was almost certainly an exaggeration) that up to half the UK population might already have been affected, and that the government was thus well on its way to establishing herd immunity.[48]

In Sweden, meanwhile, the scientific response led by Anders Tegnell suggested that no full-scale lockdown was needed. This approach immediately produced a higher level of fatalities than in other Scandinavian countries that had adopted more restrictive policies, but also not the level of mortality suggested by the Ferguson study in the United Kingdom.

The models depended on ad hoc and unsupported assumptions about how populations would practice social distancing, assumptions that would not be consistently met. At an early stage in the crisis, the man who became the public face of science in the US response to the crisis, Anthony Fauci, director of the National Institute of Allergy and Infectious Diseases, explained: "I know my modeling colleagues are going to not be happy with me, but models are as good as the assumptions you put into them. And as we get more data, then you put it in and that might change."[49] Sure enough, the diversity of epidemiological models and their conflicting results prompted a striking backlash by the scientific community. A review of the major models concluded that "the language of these papers suggests a degree of certainty that is simply not justified. Even if the parameter values are representative of a wide range of cases within the context of the given model, none of these authors attempts to quantify uncertainty about the validity of their broader modeling choices."[50]

Epidemiology was not the only expertise needed during this worldwide crisis. The shutdowns themselves demanded calculations about their effects, including on human mental health, food insecurity, homelessness, and causes of death beyond coronavirus infection. To take just one example, it became easy to argue that some of the measures intended to bolster incomes during an emergency period were making matters worse by encouraging employers to shed staff, and thus aggravating a longer-term economic and social problem of inequality and marginalization.

A New Sort of Technocrat

By the beginning of the twenty-first century, the link between technocrats and war had been reframed, as the boundaries between conventional war and other sorts of influence became blurred. The practitioners of a new *hybrid war* called themselves technologists, and the concept of *political technology* emerged after the collapse of the Soviet Union, often using techniques of opinion manipulation that had been developed by the Soviet security apparatus. The 1996 election in the Russian Federation, won unexpectedly by Boris Yeltsin, was a watershed, and the 1999 arrangement to preserve Yeltsin's regime with a transition to Vladimir Putin may have marked a high point, according to Andrew Wilson, one of the main analysts of the phenomenon. Wilson quotes one of the technologists, Sergey Markov, as stating that "all political technologies abolish the difference between the true and the not-true." There were political lessons to be learned from advertising and consumer capitalism: "People believe they buy certain goods because they make the decision, but it's not true. Public opinion is made more and more by computers, which have no opinion of their own. They totally depend on what disk is inserted."[51]

This sort of approach spread rapidly beyond Russia. Elections could be won by targeting the right audiences with selective messages designed to nudge them. Both sides in any campaign thought that the other was using more sophisticated techniques, and the outcome was ascribed not to the power or coherence or attraction of an argument, but to how micro-arguments had been matched to their best audience. The major figures who won elections were no longer the political figureheads, but the controllers of information. The result was sometimes called *guru-ism*. Barack Obama, for example, is credited with mobilizing a *youthquake* in 2008 when his young and enthusiastic campaigners successfully targeted particular voting groups and helped him win the US presidency. By 2012, after a bad setback in the midterm elections, the campaign was depending on the analysis of big data for finding and motivating new groups of potential voters.[52] The chief analytics officer on Barack Obama's 2012 election campaign, and the founder of Civis Analytics in 2013 (with financial support from Google) was Dan Wagner, a mathematician in his early twenties. Wagner used Facebook groups of "friends" to identify some 15 million "persuadable voters" in the swing states.[53]

In 2015, David Cameron's Conservatives in Britain won with the assistance of Jim Messina, who had been a significant force behind the design of the 2012 Obama campaign, "the most data-driven campaign ever." The successful strategy involved persuading voters that a vote for the Liberal Democrats would be a vote for Labour, and that Labour and the Scottish National Party were likely to break up the country. In the 2016 Brexit referendum, Dominic Cummings believed that the result was due to the operations director of Vote Leave, Victoria Woodcock, who devised a "canvassing software" named after her: "Vics" or Voter Intention Collection System.[54] Zac Moffatt, Mitt Romney's former digital director who founded the company Targeted Victory, explained: "Software is eating politics."[55]

These experiences set the stage for the 2016, and the 2020, presidential campaigns. Any kind of influence—Russian, for instance—was imaginable. And for the foreign influencers, even stories about influence were helpful, because they would delegitimize the political process still further.

The Revolt against Experts

It is easy to see why periodic revolts against technocrats and experts take place. These leaders make decisions on the basis of prognoses that are problematic, uncertain, and often, after the passage of time—or sometimes quickly—shown to be flawed. Putting together micro analyses in a context that also generates a macro vision is an exercise in vulnerability because of the number of simplifying assumptions that are required. In addition, technocrats as a group have deliberately cut themselves off from the very human environment that gave them meaning. In 1960 in the scientific journal *Astronautics,* Manfred Clynes and Nathan Kline coined the term *cyborg,* from "cybernetic organism," writing that they "thought it would be good to have a new concept, a concept of persons who can free themselves from the constraints of the environment to the extent that they wished."[56] But a cyborg is not human.

The attempts to reassert the human are emotionally appealing. Albert Camus's postwar novel *La Peste* (The plague) in part used the plague in the Algerian city of Oran as a way of depicting the evil—and the dilemmas—created by the Nazi occupation of France. But the novel provides a much more general statement. "Our citizens work hard, but solely with the object of getting rich. Their chief interest is in commerce, and their chief aim in life is, as they call it, 'doing business.' . . . It will be said, no doubt, that these habits are not peculiar to our town; really all our contemporaries are much the same.' " Dr Bernard Rieux, the narrator of the work, "was thinking it has no importance whether such things have or have not a meaning; all we need consider is the answer given to men's hope." Rieux, a doctor who does not believe in any grand ideas, does not offer a general scheme for helping people or changing the world. He just wants to help—and to be human.

The philosopher Alasdair MacIntyre in *After Virtue* sets out a polemic against the world of technocrats applying special knowledge, a world in which "government itself becomes a hierarchy of bureaucratic managers, and the major justification advanced for the intervention of government in society is the contention that government has resources of competence which most citizens do not possess." He then calls that claim to authority a "moral fiction."[57] It may be a moral fiction, but it is a fiction created by a society that believes that techniques or specialized knowledge are important to guiding social organization. The drive to create and use techniques generally arises out of a specific challenge—the classic one is military conflict. But technocrats generate discontent when societies can no longer muster the sense of purpose that led them to cede at least some of their power over to experts, and when the different tribes of technocrats fall out with each other.

9

Populism

Populism has become a ubiquitous term that has lost almost all definitional clarity. It is often linked to the globalization discussion, in that populists are the anti-globalists, or to use the terminology of the British journalist David Goodhart, the rooted "somewheres" who are opposed to the mobile "anywheres."[1] Populists think of themselves as tied to a particular population: that means that there needs to be a clear separation between "our people" and everyone else. The populist imagination has thus always had a clear enemy: the globalists, or the global elite, or any cross-national movement. It is characteristically anti-capitalist, anti-socialist, anti-clerical (or at least anti-Catholic), and in the twenty-first century, anti-Islamist. The resistance of populists to mobility is not just a question of geographic location, and of resistance to movement from one place to another; there is also an element in populism that is directed against movement over time, and that is anxious or hostile about change. But anti-mobility is not generally the way in which populism as a phenomenon is defined.

Populism is in fact usually a vague term of abuse, and analysts have struggled to provide a clearer account. The two most frequent definitions by political scientists involve, first, the assertion that populists claim to be the sole representatives of a real "people," opposed to an "elite," and second, that populists make all kinds of promises that are unrealistic and undeliverable. Neither definition really helps very much. Nobody is going to win elections by telling voters that they stand for an elite. Any broad political movement tries to present itself as not being a sectional or partial interest, and as having the interests of a whole population at heart. To take an obvious example, socialists or Social Democrats could not hope to gain power if they presented themselves as a particularly working-class party, even though they might often assert that the working class was the "real people." Thus social democratic political movements successfully (like the Christian Democrats) remade themselves as people's parties. But that orientation toward the working class doesn't make them populist, except in a way that is conceptually useless. And making untenable promises—well, come on, that's what almost every politician will and probably should do. It's the task of a free press and of a public sphere to discuss the promises and if necessary show why they can't be fulfilled. (Though the success of a policy does not always depend on the intentions and the integrity of its promoters: bad policies can fail because of bad luck and bad conditions, and bad policies can turn out to be surprisingly effective.)

A third angle of many definitions of populism presents its advocates as inherently authoritarian, even though they might claim to represent the people.[2] The leadership will decide what is good for the people, rather than leaving that outcome to a genuine process of popular debate and discussion. Populists avoid scrutiny or challenge. Donald Trump likes to talk about "my people," and Boris Johnson's stock phrase is "We are delivering the people's government." Again, most politicians—not just populist politicians—will often argue that they know best, and political leaders often hide what they are doing. Total political transparency would be an illusion. But it is certainly true that populists in power—Viktor Orbán, Jarosław Kaczyński, Donald Trump—stifle judicial processes that would prevent the arbitrary exercise of their power. Elections are manipulated, the press is intimidated, and journalists are beaten up or killed. Chance emergencies, such as the coronavirus pandemic, give them opportunities to exert power beyond traditional limits. Donald Trump declared, "The federal government has absolute power. It has the power. As to whether or not I'll use that power, we'll see."[3] Or: "When somebody's the president of the United States, the authority is total. And that is the way it's gonna be. It's total. And the governors know that."[4] Prayuth Chan-o-cha, the autocratic prime minister of Thailand, explained that "right now it is health over liberty"; Orbán used the coronavirus as a chance to introduce rule by decree, a move that Erdoğan in Turkey had made in 2016, after a failed coup.[5]

A more realistic, and useful, approach would involve thinking of the spread of the label populism and the claim to be populist as simple, obvious signs of a deep malaise. The populists and their advocates can of course be cited endlessly on this: they like pointing out what's wrong with the establishment. They are the first to claim that "something's rotten in the state of Denmark." The Fox News talk show host Tucker Carlson rightly claimed that "you don't get populist politics unless your institutions are failing. Because satisfied people don't resort to populist politics."[6] So the flaring up of populism is a sign of dysfunction and dissatisfaction. Just to be clear—Hamlet wasn't a populist, although Shakespeare includes a reference by Claudius to "the great love the general gender bear him, Who, dipping all his faults in their affection, Would, like the spring that turneth wood to stone, Convert his gyves to grace."[7]

True Democracy

Populism is often proud of being unreflective, instinctual, and anti-intellectual, and it claims to be based on "real experience" rather than technocrats' abstract knowledge and claim to authority. The radical populists of interwar Europe, but especially those in the German Nazi movement, referred to "das gesunde Volksempfinden," the healthy gut response of the people. That language has resurfaced. An Austrian parliamentarian of the far right FPK (Freedom Party in Carinthia), for instance, called the insistence on a government debt brake (an automatic limitation of public sector indebtedness) a violation of the people's healthy feelings—and then provoked a counterblast by commentators who pointed out that the phrase was Nazi language.[8] The populists know that "Folks are dumb where I come from, they ain't had any learning."[9] They were and are also contemptuous (and perhaps in some cases rightly so) of those who look down and patronize them from the ivory tower. They dislike experts. Donald Trump's catastrophically distracting and unscientific phrase in confronting the coronavirus is unfortunately characteristic: "I'm not a doctor, but I have common sense."[10]

A part of this anti-intellectual case is the defense of traditions, in the absence of any clear conviction of why or how traditions should matter.

Vladimir Putin is often effective in sounding this sort of note: "I am not trying to insult anyone because we have been condemned for our alleged homophobia. But we have no problem with LGBT persons. God forbid, let them live as they wish. But some things do appear excessive to us. They claim now that children can play five or six gender roles. Let everyone be happy, we have no problem with that. But this must not be allowed to overshadow the culture, traditions and traditional family values of millions of people making up the core population."[11]

Populist leaders claim, too, that they are more democratic than the establishment. This theme takes up an old discussion from the nineteenth century, in which the true people, from the *pays réel* or real country, exposed the fictions of constitutional definitions because many were excluded from the franchise in the legal country, *pays légal*. A recent iteration is the claim that a new *illiberal democracy* has emerged. The term was first developed by a critic, Fareed Zakaria, but then widely embraced by the illiberal democrats themselves (Mussolini in interwar Italy had similarly appreciated the term *totalitarianism* that was originally deployed by socialist critics).[12] Zakaria in 1997 described a spectrum, "from modest offenders like Argentina to near-tyrannies like Kazakhstan and Belarus, with countries like Romania and Bangladesh in between. Along much of the spectrum, elections are rarely as free and fair as in the West today, but they do reflect the reality of popular participation in politics and support for those elected."[13] By the 2010s the examples were much less on the "modest" range of the spectrum. Dani Rodrik has examined this shift, reflecting on "why illiberal democracies are on the rise."[14]

The canonical self-portrayal of modern populist illiberalism was the speech delivered in 2014 by Hungary's Viktor Orbán to a summer camp mostly for young nationalist Hungarians provocatively staged in the Romanian town Băile Tuşnad, once part of the Hungarian empire and briefly seized back by Hungary in the Second World War. One striking and characteristic part of the speech is the message that corruption of values comes from outside influences that try to poison the healthy spirit of the country, but also that the country needs to reform itself in order to defend its vision and impose it more generally: "I can announce the good news that we won the elections. . . . the strength of American 'soft power' is deteriorating, because liberal values today incorporate corruption, sex and violence, and with this liberal values discredit America and American modernization. . . . In order to be able to do this [make our community competitive] in 2010, and especially these days, we needed to courageously state a sentence, a sentence that, similar to the ones enumerated here, was considered to be a sacrilege in the liberal world order. We needed to state that a democracy is not necessarily liberal. Just because something is not liberal, it still can be a democracy."[15] Vladimir Putin sounded a similar note, blasting western liberal democracy for opening "a direct path to degradation and primitivism, resulting in a profound demographic and moral crisis." He told the *Financial Times* in an interview in 2019: "Every crime must have its punishment. The liberal idea has become obsolete. It has come into conflict with the interests of the overwhelming majority of the population."[16]

The populist model, which is typically claimed to be exportable, at first perhaps to neighboring countries, is often primarily intended for domestic consumption: the "people" need to feel good about themselves. In 2018, after winning a presidential election on the heels of a constitutional reform that led Freedom House to reclassify Turkey as "not free," Recep Tayyip Erdoğan boasted that "Turkey has given a lesson in democracy to the entire world."[17]

Erdoğan's recent speeches show how far he has moved, but he has always demonstrated a desire to think of democracy in terms different than those of the American tradition of proceduralism. In 2003, at the beginning of his rule (as prime minister), he had this to say to a Harvard University audience about democracy in the Middle East: "The advanced levels which the democratic world has attained at the end of lengthy processes may have created the perception in the region that democracy is a distant concept; this perception can be addressed. Specific institutions and rules help construct a democracy. However, democracy cannot be defined as the existence of parliaments and elections alone. In fact, describing democracy solely in mechanistic terms can be misleading. What should be targeted is a concept of organic, and not just mechanic, democracy that preserves the rule of law, separation of powers, and that is participatory and pluralistic. In my own private terminology, I refer to this as 'deep democracy.' In other words, the bar should be maintained at the level of a pluralistic and participatory democracy."[18]

In practice, populists in power engage multiple techniques to ensure that they remain in power—from intimidation or suppression of the media, more generalized harassment, the internment or assassination of opponents, legal and constitutional changes, or the suspension of elections. Soon after he came to power in 1999, Putin started to use the term "managed democracy." Vladimir Korsunsky, editor of the independent political website Graniru.org, calls Russia a "staged democracy." Erdoğan once notoriously described democracy as a "tram . . . it goes as far as we want it to go, and then we get off."[19]

The political philosopher Jan Werner Müller is the foremost exponent of the interpretation that populists can be best understood as asserting an exclusive claim to represent the people, while at the same time delegitimating any other kind of representation. That is the separation, the sharp line that is being drawn. It is at its clearest when Erdoğan says: "We are the people. Who are you?" Or "the recent elections have clearly shown that the people are the most powerful judge in differentiating good from bad and right from wrong. The people possess *compos mentis;* the Turkish people do not need guardians or custodians. The era in which some saw themselves as guardian or custodian, and believed that 'the people cannot know, cannot understand or cannot decide' has been closed for ever."[20] This understanding has been repeatedly formulated in the modern era: the conflict is between the people and those who claim to speak for them.

The Origins of Populism

The term *populism* came to be widely used in the United States in the nineteenth century. It described a farmers' revolt against both East Coast elites and industrial workers, as well as a demand for a more accommodative monetary and economic policy, and for trade protection. It aimed at the "misgovernment" of "the plutocrats, the aristocrats, and all the other rats."[21] Richard Hofstadter used the 1895 manifesto of the People's Party—the populist movement—as a key piece of evidence of his depiction of the "paranoid style" in American politics: "As early as 1865–66 a conspiracy was entered into between the gold gamblers of Europe and America. . . . For nearly thirty years these conspirators have kept the people quarreling over less important matters while they have pursued with unrelenting zeal their one central purpose. . . . Every device of treachery, every resource of statecraft, and every artifice known to the secret cabals of the international gold ring are being used to deal a blow to the prosperity of the people and the financial and commercial independence of the country."[22] In 1896, the populist program stated that "the influence of European money-changers has been more potent in shaping legislation than the voice of the American people." The Democratic Party in 1896 made an alliance with the populists and put forward William Jennings Bryan as its anti-gold presidential candidate, arguing that the depression of 1873 had been a consequence of the restoration of the gold standard, "without the knowledge or approval of the American people," producing "the enrichment of the money-lending lass at home and abroad." The campaign against money men was often given a strong anti-Semitic element.[23] Hofstadter concluded that the populists had a picture of the world that rendered them "credulous and vulnerable."

The political representatives of populism sometimes tried to put their case more cogently and less conspiratorially. William Vincent Allen, of Nebraska, in a lengthy Senate speech, condemned "studied policy on the part of the Republican party to transfer power from the people into the hand of the few," adding, "Every reform throughout all the ages of the world came from beneath and not from the top." His party was not— he thought—one of cranks and extremists, "not a socialistic party in the modern sense of the term," and not "wild-eyed, long-haired inflationists," but instead merely advocates of "honest money."[24] Many modern analysts of populism have been much more sympathetic than Hofstadter, describing the nineteenth-century adherents as early advocates of a communal life based on solidarity and a healthy political localism.[25]

The claim that populists are irresponsible is a staple of the political science literature: they exist because they overpromise to an alienated part of the population, and then use bluster, suppression of thought, or even violence to mask their failure when in power. In relation to modern debates about globalization, the term first came to be widely used to distinguish a particular style of Latin American politics that had first been seen in the 1930s, but developed powerfully in the second half of the twentieth century. In contrast to leftists or Marxists who espoused structuralist interpretations of the world economy, which they then proposed to change or overthrow, the populists promised a simple national fix. This version sounded leftist—or at least redistributionist—but it was not seriously thought out, and it usually ended up hurting the cause more than helping it. As one influential formulation had it, it was an "approach to economics that emphasizes growth and income redistribution and deemphasizes the risks of inflation and deficit finance, external constraints, and the reaction of economic agents to aggressive nonmarket policies." The government of populists, however, would produce an economic collapse, which eventually delegitimated the movement: "Pervasive shortages, extreme acceleration of inflation, and an obvious foreign exchange gap lead to capital flight and demonetization of the economy. The budget deficit deteriorates violently because of a steep decline in tax collection and increasing subsidy costs."[26] The basic story was not dissimilar to the kind of fraudulent overpromising described centuries ago by Shakespeare in Jack Cade's revolt in *Henry VI, Part 2:* "There shall be in England seven halfpenny loaves sold for a penny: the three-hooped pot shall have ten hoops, and I will make it felony to drink small beer: all the realm shall be in common; and in Cheapside shall my palfrey go to grass: and when I am king, as king I will be, . . . there shall be no money."[27] This is clearly deceptive. As the Shakespeare scholar Stephen Greenblatt concludes, "Populism may look like an embrace of the have-nots, but in reality it is a form of cynical exploitation."[28]

Populism Updated

European populism in the early twenty-first century similarly involved an attack on economic orthodoxy and on what it characterized as "austerity." In a right-wing variant, it also emphasized national tradition, and opposed both supranationalism, above all in the form of the European Union, and migration. It blamed emigration for the brain drain that was afflicting eastern and southern Europe, and immigration, especially Islamic immigration, for undermining Christianity and traditional European culture. Socioeconomic populism was fueled by the Global Financial Crisis, but since 2012 has receded. Meanwhile a cultural populism has continued to advance.

The Global Financial Crisis of 2007–2008 prompted a growth of populism in many rich industrial countries, one fueled by distrust of "experts" and "globalists." New political figures emerged claiming to speak to the immediate concerns of the people. According to them, the interests of a global elite were at odds with a people who were less mobile. Institutions such as the European Commission, the European Central Bank, and the IMF became a major target of attacks in the two European countries where populism took over the government: Hungary, with its right-wing populists; and Greece, with its coalition of left-wing and right-wing populists. Both countries had been involved in substantial IMF initiatives created to deal with irresponsible programs that had predated the populist movements. In Hungary (and in Poland), a large number of people were experiencing financial difficulty because of foreign currency mortgages (often in Swiss francs) sold by big international banking groups: with currency depreciation in the wake of the financial crisis, the service and amortization charges had risen dramatically and made the mortgages unaffordable. In this context, an anti-bank platform directed at trying to seize profits from foreign banks had a powerful appeal. In Greece, foreign banks had lent money and bought Greek government bonds; but then, in the crisis, the large French and German banks had sold much of their holdings, and contributed to the problem of government debt becoming impossibly expensive to fund. Populists across the continent demanded economic measures that would produce an immediate benefit, without "austerity" measures. They also pushed back against the IMF's approach to economic data as a guide to policy formulation, by using highly politicized judicial measures to threaten national officials who might follow that approach.

Left-wing populists make very similar claims when they see supranational institutions as a core part of a general "neoliberal project" that has eroded local and national autonomy and favored big financial groups.

In practice, identifying what is and is not populist is a hard exercise. In Greece, for instance, the most severely affected eurozone crisis country, the center-right New Democracy—which had been in government until the eve of the crisis, when it was pushed out by elections in October 2009—fiercely criticized the austerity programs negotiated by the center-left Panhellenic Socialist Movement (PASOK) in 2010 and 2011, and sounded "populist" to north European politicians. After it took power in 2012, it shifted to a more moderate position, accepted a new program, and then in late 2014 started to move a little away from orthodoxy. The government provoked a political crisis leading to new elections that it knew it would lose, and a "populist" party of the left, Syriza, formed a government that for a few months was based on out-and-out confrontation with the "troika"—that is, the European Commission, the European Central Bank, and the IMF. It called a referendum that turned down the troika program, but then accepted an even harsher program and gradually transformed itself into a quite mainstream center-left movement that attracted much sympathy from northern European policymakers.

The problem with the view that experts had the right solutions was that those experts were often unclear about how their solutions should be translated into political practice. As Jean-Claude Juncker, president of the European Commission, explained, "Politicians are vote maximisers. . . . For the politician, the Euro can render vote-maximising more difficult, as a smooth and frictionless participation in the monetary union sometimes entails that difficult decisions have to be undertaken or that unpopular reforms have to be initiated."[29] Even more memorably: "We all know what to do, we just don't know how to get re-elected after we've done it." There was never any effective advice on how to deal with the arguments of the populists.

It was also not clear that populist governments were destined to repeat the 1980s and 1990s cycle of policy experimentation followed by failure, as had happened in Latin America. Policies that were deemed by their critics to be populist appeared to bring results that ranged from reasonable recovery in Portugal to quite strong growth in Romania or Hungary. The link between structural reform and growth capacity was weakened because of the international anti-crisis policies that kept interest rates low and prompted a search for higher yield and higher risk. It became easier to run large deficits, and consequently easier for populist governments to make good on promises to pay out more to their supporters. The international risk factors decreased as the severity of international crisis receded, and the costs of populism appeared to be lowered. In this environment, there was less room for "technocratic" solutions.

One of the striking features of the European debt crisis is that populist parties in power did indeed erode and evade previous fiscal limits, but the policies were successful for longer than just the short time frame of what Rudi Dornbusch and Sebastian Edwards have termed a cycle of *macroeconomic populism*. There is no sense that markets are punishing right-wing populists in central Europe (Hungary and Poland); and Portugal, with its left-wing populist government and a substantial recovery, is often (and in an exaggerated fashion) hailed as a miracle case.

The increased longevity of fiscal populism is a reflection of the consequences of a low-interest-rate regime throughout the world: monetary conditions are closely correlated, and US policy has a considerable influence. Cheap borrowing means that those countries running greater fiscal deficits are effectively getting a free lunch.

Populism in the Time of Coronavirus

The coronavirus changed the dynamics of the debate about populism and experts yet again. Some sorts of experts—in particular, doctors who did not claim to know too much about the broad epidemiological development—appeared as heroes.

The virus lent itself to blame games. At some points, Trump insistently called it the China virus; his secretary of state, Mike Pompeo, broke up a G7 meeting because he insisted on calling it the Wuhan virus. In China, accounts circulated of how the virus had been introduced to Wuhan by the US military, and when reinfections occurred in China, they were interpreted as having come from Chinese people returning from abroad. In Europe, disputes flared up around whether Germany was blocking supplies of medical equipment to Italy.

A number of health and mortality indicators were used during the crisis to assess the effectiveness of public policy responses around the world. Some "populist" governments in smaller European countries performed relatively well. Others—Bolsonaro's in Brazil, or Trump's in the United States—did spectacularly badly. The crisis raised the prestige of medical and other expertise, and made populist know-nothings look foolish. Thus in Italy, the center of the early European outbreak, the former Italian prime minister Matteo Renzi called on his successor, Giuseppe Conte, to abandon "the path of populism."[30]

The political scientist Margaret Canovan has tried to apply political philosopher Michael Oakeshott's distinction between the politics of skepticism and the politics of faith to the analysis of populism.[31] A more recent and bleaker recasting is historian Timothy Snyder's distinction between the "politics of inevitability," with politicians explaining that they have no alternative but to follow a present course of austerity, global integration, and so on, with a mythologized "politics of eternity," in which a nation is stuck in an eternally recurring cycle of suffering and victimhood. In his view, the idea of permanent victimhood—often due to subjugation to an (evil) empire—is more and more a driver of political processes. The Irish columnist Fintan O'Toole, for his part, has brilliantly demonstrated how envy of other oppressed peoples drove English nationalists to revolt against the European Union in Brexit.[32] But perhaps the most vivid description of populism is captured in a much-mythologized scene in the ceremonial hall of the University of Salamanca in 1936. There the nationalist General Millán Astray confronted the elderly poet and professor Miguel de Una-muno with the dramatic slogan "¡Abajo la inteligencia! ¡Viva la muerte!" (Down with intelligence! Long live death!) We'll never really know whether Unamuno replied with the striking defense of the intellect that was put in his mouth by historian Hugh Thomas, but it's rewarding to imagine just the same: "This is the temple of intelligence, and I am its high priest. You are profaning its sacred domain. You will win, because you have enough brute force. But you will not convince. In order to convince it is necessary to persuade, and to persuade you will need something that you lack: reason and right in the struggle."[33]

10

Globalism

Among the many powerful words that Walter Lippmann coined or popularized was *globalism*—*globalization* came only much later. *Globalist* conjures up a unique vision of evil: the demented ranting ideologue grasping for universal power. The most powerful image in the mid-twentieth century of the dictator—and of his illusions—was the globe standing in an oversized office. Hitler put a globe in his grandiose Chancellery in Berlin and in his mountain retreat in Berchtesgaden to make a point about a new politics that would transcend Europe. Charlie Chaplin seized the idea and made it into a central theme for the film *The Great Dictator*. It is a stunning image—of ridicule (see Figure 4). And when the former Republican US presidential candidate and advocate of "One World" internationalism, Wendell Wilkie, embarked on a tour of the world, the first feature that struck his attention was Stalin's big globe. Having a globe, being a globalist, was a sign of ambition: but in projecting their own vision of globalism, figures like Wilkie made themselves politically vulnerable. No one likes a globalist.

Globalism became one of Donald Trump's favorite terms of abuse, and it is one guaranteed to strike a chord with his domestic political base. At the United Nations in September 2019, he stated that globalism had "exerted a religious pall over past leaders causing them to ignore their own national interests." He held out an alternative: "The future does not belong to the globalists. The future belongs to patriots." There was then a defense of patriotism: "The true good of the nation can only be pursued by those

Figure 4. Charlie Chaplin as Adenoid Hynkel in *The Great Dictator* (1940).
Reproduced by permission of Chaplin Office: *The Great Dictator,* Copyright
© Roy Export S.A.S.

who love it, by citizens who are rooted in its history, who are nourished by its culture, committed to its values, attached to its people."[1] He wasn't speaking to the international politicians and international bureaucrats who were listening uncomfortably to the president of the United States, but rather to himself and his audience outside New York.

At first, the use of the terminology appears peculiar. After all, wasn't Trump an international businessman who went across the world doing "deals," promoting his brands, and boasting about the range of his contacts? As he put it: "Made a lot of money in China. I deal with Europe, I deal with Asia, I deal with China all the time."[2] Nothing except perhaps Coca-Cola could be more of an American global brand than Trump.

The highly ideological UN speech, crafted by the White House ideologue Stephen Miller, seems to have caught Trump's imagination, and he repeatedly returned to the theme. At a rally in Houston, he would go on to claim that "radical Democrats want to turn back the clock" in order to restore the "rule of corrupt, power-hungry globalists." He then gave a definition: "You know what a globalist is, right? You know what a globalist is? A globalist is a person that wants the globe to do well, frankly, not caring about our country so much. And you know what? We can't have that."[3]

There is always an identification of an enemy attached to the concept of globalist. Some critics have suggested that the use of the term "globalist," like its near equivalent "cosmopolitan," was a cryptic way of making an anti-Semitic appeal.[4] Trump used the term to ridicule his first chair of the National Economic Council, Gary Cohn, for his dissent over Trump's apparent approval of a white supremacist and neo-Nazi rally in Charlottesville. Cohn, who is Jewish, had told the *Financial Times,* unambiguously the newspaper of the global elite, that the administration "can and must do better" to condemn hate groups.[5]

The link between attacks on globalists and attacks on Jews comes out of the environment that originally produced the term. In the aftermath of the Great Depression, with racist and ethnic nationalism flourishing, and capitalism discredited, Jews were attacked as the agents of both an international capitalism and an international socialism. In a striking speech to workers in the Berlin Siemens factory, on November 10, 1933, Hitler did not use the word "Jew" once. But he did talk of a "small rootless international clique," "people who are at home nowhere and everywhere, who do not have a soil on which they have grown up, but who live in Berlin today, in Brussels tomorrow, Paris the day after that, and then again in Prague or Vienna or London, and who feel at home everywhere and nowhere." Someone in the audience then shouted, "the Jews."[6]

The origins of the modern American usage lay in a fierce debate before and during the Second World War about isolationism. For the First World War, Woodrow Wilson had first campaigned against American involvement in the European conflict, then was drawn in after the Germans declared that they would target Americans with unconditional submarine warfare. After the war ended, he tried to devise a peace settlement that reflected what he thought of as American ideals. But Congress rejected the Covenant and its apparatus—notably the League of Nations. The United States remained detached from the big issues of European diplomacy, and was not represented officially at the major conferences on reparations and war debts. Instead, private citizens—major industrialists—became involved in what was sometimes called "dollar diplomacy."

During the 1930s, isolationism continued to be a significant political theme. Charles Lindbergh pushed an "America First" movement. Franklin Roosevelt, who was increasingly concerned with the fascist threat, realized that American involvement in the Second World War would be controversial. The Japanese attack on Pearl Harbor and the subsequent declaration of war on the United States by Nazi Germany made the wartime alliance politically possible, but the worry about foreign entanglements remained. As the end of the war approached, it was clear that the United States would need to remake the world again.

An unlikely figure introduced the idea of globalism to the American discussion. Ernst Jäckh, an émigré German scholar at Columbia University, used the word to describe "Hitlerism" in a book titled *The War for Man's Soul*. The German leader "reaches out for the sun itself. He has set out to conquer the world to make the globe a German possession! He aims at more than military or economic and political conquest. He has embarked on a 'holy war' as the God-sent leader of a 'chosen people' bred not for imperialism but for globalism—his world without end." Later Jäckh defines Nazi ideology as aiming at not only continental hegemony, but also global intellectual and political dominance.[7]

Jäckh was a very German intellectual. He had emerged before the First World War as an affable cultivator of the political elite, someone who propagated the projection of German power on a world stage, especially in the Middle East. He had been in the circle of the progressive but very imperialist liberal Friedrich Naumann, the advocate of a Mitteleuropa concept. After the war, Jäckh founded a new political science and foreign-policy institute and thinktank, the Hochschule für Politik. He prided himself on having been on good terms with every German chancellor since the days of the German Empire. He never revealed to his American audience quite how desperately he tried to cultivate relations with Adolf Hitler after January 1933. After the appointment of Hitler as chancellor, Jäckh energetically sought engagement with the Nazi movement.[8]

Jäckh was translating for the American world some peculiarly German concerns. The grasping for world power would be familiar to Germans from the Wagnerian tales that Hitler loved. At the outset of the *Ring of the Nibelung,* one of the Rhinemaidens reveals the secret of the river and teases the dwarf Alberich with the promise of world power:

> Der Welt Erbe gewänne zu eigen,
> wer aus dem Rheingold schüfe den Ring,
> der masslose Macht ihm verlieh'.

> (Whoever creates a Ring from the Rhine's gold would derive
> from it endless power and assume for himself the entire
> inheritance of the world.)

Alberich, who seizes the gold of the Rhine, makes himself into the world's first globalist.

The critique that Jäckh presented was so powerful because it was not just Hitler or fascism that posed a global threat, but also communism. In this way, a word out of the vocabulary of a very nationalist German migrated into American discourse. In fact, the new concept of a threat from globalists would build the intellectual bridge between the Second World War and the Cold War. Lenin inherited internationalism from nineteenth-century Marxism. In their *Communist Manifesto,* Karl Marx and Friedrich Engels had observed how "national differences and antagonisms between peoples are daily vanishing more and more," and promised that "the supremacy of the proletariat will cause them to vanish still faster." The theory of Marxism envisioned revolution as a worldwide event, not confined to Russia alone. Lenin saw a global revolution as making possible the achievement of the Bolsheviks' aims in Russia. He said over and over again that without revolutionary movements in other countries, a final Soviet victory would be hopeless: "Our salvation from these difficulties is an all-European revolution."[9] This doctrine lay behind the establishment of the Third International, or Comintern. Globalism could then be used to describe Soviet goals.

The discussion of globalism and global responsibilities appeared elsewhere in the Second World War, which after all was a truly global war in the sense that the First World War had not been. How globalist or universal should the United States become? The United States embarked on a global mission to re-create international order, but that endeavor could be interpreted as imperial overreach, or as making American producers vulnerable. The conservative journalist Clare Boothe Luce, in her first speech to Congress after her election as a Republican representative for Connecticut, attacked Vice President Henry Wallace's suggestion that American airports might be opened up after the end of the war: "He does a great deal of global thinking, but much of what Mr. Wallace calls his global thinking is, no matter how you slice it, still globaloney."[10]

The critique also came as a reaction against Wendell Wilkie's best-seller *One World,* an appeal for the re-creation of "a new society of independent nations, free alike from the economic injustices of the West and the political malpractices of the East."[11] Luce had once campaigned for Wilkie, a passionate believer in Wilsonian internationalism and the unsuccessful Republican presidential candidate in the 1940 election. Wilkie argued that Americans should transcend their "narrow nationalism" but also avoid "international imperialism." On a tour around the world, he had announced in the capital of Nationalist China, Chongqing, that the Second World War must be an anti-imperial war. He told his radio audience that the end of the war would also "mean an end to the empire of nations over other nations."[12]

So *globalism* became a term of ridicule and disdain, even and especially for those who saw the desirability of a greater American role in the world, or American leadership. A 1943 exhibition featuring work by Mark Rothko had a catalog that presented the theme as an overcoming of American isolationism: "it is time for us to accept cultural values on a truly global plane." Many of the viewers were unpersuaded. *New York Times* art critic Edward Alden Jewell's reflection on the exhibit had as its heading "'Globalism' Pops into View," and concluded, "so far Globalism seems to guarantee a rather bleak and cheerless future."[13] *Globalism* became a distinctly hostile term.

Walter Lippmann, who championed Wilkie's plea that Americans should learn to understand "the shrunken world in which they live," was the intellectual who definitively turned the tables on globalism.[14] Once upon a time he had been a visionary who pushed Wilson and Wilsonianism. No longer. He now wanted to appeal to a policy based on interest, limited ends and means, not ideology. But he saw this pragmatism or realism as being at odds with "an overwhelming disposition to regard the choices before us not as relative but as absolute. We are disposed to think that the issue is either this or that, either all or nothing, either isolationism or globalism, either total peace or total war, either one world or no world, either disarmament or absolute weapons, either pious resolutions or atomic bombs, either disarmament or military supremacy, either nonintervention or a crusade, either democracy or tyranny, either the abolition of war or preventive war, either appeasement or unconditional surrender, either non-resistance or a strategy of annihilation."[15] After that, globalism came to be referred to as Walter Lippmann's phrase.

Hans Morgenthau, another refugee scholar like Jäckh, had wrestled with the idea of the political as a way of trying to explain the circumstances in which states could resolve conflicts without resorting to force. He had a brief encounter with Carl Schmitt, who believed politics are constituted by the polarity of friend and enemy, in the final years of the Weimar Republic, and later claimed that Schmitt had seemed to possess a "demonic" quality. Morgenthau's own approach is usually described as "realism." Like Jäckh, he saw the Second World War as the product of a Nazi "claim to universality," and blamed Woodrow Wilson for promoting a "crusade" that would "make the world safe for democracy." Nazism was a response to that climate, articulating a "new moral code that would replace the vicious creed of bolshevism and the decadent morality of democracy and impose itself upon the world."[16] That was a message of dangerous universality. Morgenthau took up the Lippmann theme and in the 1960s turned it into a critique of American engagement in Vietnam. Both isolationism and globalism were perversions in which the usual political process of negotiating difference was ruled out: "Isolationism is a kind of introverted globalism, and globalism is a kind of isolationism turned inside out."[17]

Morgenthau used as a central concept for his analysis the notion that ideas—or as he put it, ideologies—were ambiguous. The one that struck him as most laden with ambiguity was anti-imperialism. "The most widely practiced disguise and justification of imperialism has . . . always been the ideology of anti-imperialism."[18] Nazism presented itself as opposed to traditional French and British imperialism. Communism declared imperialism to be the enemy of the international working class. Both implied a new form of imperial thinking.

The only way out of this world of ambiguous terms was to look for a deep foundation, and a transcendental logic. Both domestic and international politics should be guided by moral codes. This was also a theme of

Lippmann's writing: in particular, Lippmann's most deeply felt and passionately argued book, *Power Politics,* attempted to revive the natural law
tradition of thinking about a universal moral law that transcended individual national interpretations. Oddly, Lippmann's philosophy in the 1950s
was almost entirely ignored. It was only when it was reformulated in the
context of Vietnam in the 1960s that it produced a national debate. In
1967, Lippmann denounced the "uncivilized, unchivalrous, inhumane role
of the US." When his critics called him neo-isolationist, he replied, "Neo-
isolationism is the direct product of foolish globalism."[19] Morgenthau
reflected that "morality is not just another branch of human activity, coordinate to the substantive branches, such as politics and economics. Quite
to the contrary, it is superimposed upon them . . . delineating the legitimate
sphere of a particular branch of action altogether."[20] He also tried to link
the successful pursuit of national interest to alignment with a higher or
transcendent order:

> In order to be worthy of our lasting sympathy, a nation must pur-
> sue its interests for the sake of a transcendent purpose that gives
> meaning to the day-by-day operations of its foreign policy. The em-
> pires of the Huns and Mongols, eminently successful in political
> and military terms, mean nothing to us, but ancient Greece, Rome,
> and Israel do. We remember Greece, Rome, and Israel . . . because
> they were not just political organizations whose purpose was lim-
> ited to their survival and physical growth but civilizations, unique
> realizations of human potentialities that we have in common with
> them.[21]

This school was able to lay the foundation for a powerful moral critique
of Vietnam. For Morgenthau, "It is this marriage between Wilsonian
globalism and the belief in the paramountcy of American power that characterizes the third postwar period of American foreign policy."[22]

Wayne Morse and Ernest Gruening, the two Democratic senators who were
the only dissenters in the Gulf of Tonkin resolution that set the United States
on the road to full engagement in Vietnam, used Lippmann's term *globalism*
as part of their indictment of American foreign policy; indeed, Stephen Am-
brose called his critical book on the subject *Rise to Globalism.*[23] Meanwhile,
the relatively small group of high-profile scholars opposed to globalism, in-

cluding J. William Fulbright, Eugene J. McCarthy, and Arthur M. Schlesinger, occasionally redefined their policy desideratum as *limitationism*.[24]

After Vietnam, however, *globalism* faded as a term in political debate. When the impetus to reorder the world was revived in the 1990s as internationalist liberal interventionism, it rapidly provoked a reassertion of the same objections raised by Lippmann and Morgenthau. The critical point of reference for figures such as Andrew Bacevich was however more Reinhold Niebuhr, with a specifically Christian interpretation of a moral realism. Bacevich spoke of four lessons that he wanted to draw from Niebuhr: the "'persistent sin' of American exceptionalism, the ultimate indecipherability of history, the false allure of simple foreign policy solutions, and the need to appreciate the limits of American power."[25] At this point, Bacevich had dropped the terms *globalist* and *globalism*. That was because there was a much more obvious addition to the vocabulary. He could now recast the exceptionalist endeavor as "a grand project of political-economic convergence and integration commonly referred to as globalization." But *globalization* was still nothing more than "a euphemism for soft, or informal, empire." In his enthusiasm for globalization, President Bill Clinton had, Bacevich says, "exacerbated the contradictions of American history."[26] In 2018, Bacevich returned to the older term, *globalism,* but only to denounce "utopian globalism," and to describe the possibility of a foreign policy "that promises to achieve of the aim of the original America First movement: to ensure the safety and well-being of the United States without engaging in needless wars." That involved saving the idea from the Trump reality, or recasting "a slogan burdened with an ugly history—including the taint of anti-Semitism—into a concrete program of enlightened action."[27]

Bacevich drew on the work of R. R. Reno, editor of the conservative Catholic periodical *First Things,* who described "utopian globalism" as an ideology that "disenfranchises the vast majority and empowers a technocratic elite."[28] Yet both liberals and conservatives had almost universally embraced globalization and technical change.[29] Reno argued that "globalism" was the best way of describing a post-1989 "metaphysical dream": "Like all dreams, it is impressionistic. But the outlines are well known at this point. The free flow of capital, goods, and labor brings universal prosperity. A global technological revolution relieves man's estate. A scientific, pragmatic consensus puts the old ideological quarrels behind us, allowing for consensus-driven problem solving. The emerging human rights regime guarantees human dignity."[30] He concluded that "Mr. Trump's stark juxtaposition of globalism and Americanism is crude and hyperbolic, but necessarily so."[31]

Globalism had by then also emerged as a term used by radical-right conspiracy theorists, where it tipped into meaningless hyperbole. It appeared frequently in Breitbart News, and in the journalistic alt-right empire of Alex Jones's InfoWars. Jones spoke of a "global digital panopticon control system," controlled by corporate and political elites, that generated "the total form of slavery."[32] Jones explained that "I just want you to know Bill Clinton, Hillary Clinton, the globalists, Michael Moore, Lord [Jacob] Rothschild, the Rockefellers, all of them: Listen up. You hate everybody because you hate yourself. You're filth. You're garbage. So you want us to all exterminate ourselves and depopulate? I got an idea. How about you slit your own throat or jam some ice picks in your own eyes? How about you hang yourself tonight? Because if you want us to die, I say you need to die first. I curse you."[33] In another widely publicized presentation, the Canadian White Identitarian Lauren Southern explained that globalism was about an elite that generated "corporate welfare" at the expense of everyone else, but might have originated with naïve people who "read too much Immanuel Kant."[34] But when she tweeted that "today's imperialism is known as globalism," she was in fact picking up the meaning that had evolved as a critique of post-1945 US foreign policy.[35] The usage is international: the Romanian left-populist leader Liviu Dragnea, for instance, regularly denounces globalists who operate a "parallel state" (the equivalent of Trump's "deep state").

The revival of the term *globalism* as a rejection of excessive or unlimited internationalism and interventionism could have been a reflection of deep, long-held frustrations concerning American foreign policy. But in Trump's vision, it was entirely detached from the concept of moral order that gave the only possible grounding of the critique.

11

Globalization and Its Neologisms

Globalization was not coined by Walter Lippmann, but it did facilitate the return of Lippmann's concern about globalism as a new variety of imperialism. As a term, *globalization* first swept the world in the 1990s and reached its initial highpoint of popularity in 2000 and 2001, amid worldwide protests against the process of globalization. The term became a focus for mobilization everywhere, but especially in France. In 2001, for instance, *Le Monde* contained more than 3,500 references to *mondialisation,* the French equivalent. But then use of the word steadily fell—more than 80 percent by 2006. Since the outbreak of the Global Financial Crisis in 2007, the word's usage in major global newspapers such as the *New York Times* and the *Financial Times* fell still further, until being revived in 2016 (see Figure 5). That is, *globalization* was conceptually on its way out, but then came back into widespread use, buoyed by a new sense of urgency and a new critical discourse in the aftermath of the Brexit referendum and the Trump election, which appeared to herald a new anti-globalization mood. By the time of the coronavirus crisis, President Trump's trade adviser, Peter Navarro, was saying: "We wouldn't be having this problem if we had the domestic production of essential medicines, medical supplies like masks and medical equipment like ventilators. . . . If we made it here, we wouldn't be faced with this. That was the original sin."[1]

A brief history of *globalization* will help to explain why the concept seems so ambivalent and malleable. Before 1972, the year that the *Oxford English Dictionary* identifies *globalization* as first being used in its current sense,

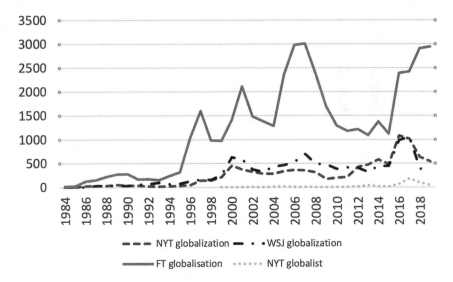

Figure 5. Newspaper references to *globalization* and *globalist*. Note the most recent surge, around the time of the 2016 US presidential election and Brexit referendum vote. Calculated from Factiva, documenting references in the *New York Times, Wall Street Journal,* and *Financial Times.*

and into the 1970s, it was a diplomatic term conveying the linkage between disparate policy areas (for example, in negotiating simultaneously on financial and security matters). In France, in particular, *globaliser* and *globalisation* were regularly used in this way, especially in the 1970s, as the economic and security framework of the world seemed to be shaking. The links between the 1973 Yom Kippur War and the oil price shocks that sent the industrial world into a state of both high inflation and recession pointed out the need for a very generalized policy debate about global interconnections.

The *Oxford English Dictionary* etymology ignores the non-English origins of the term, which lie in the inventive linguistic terminology of continental European student radicalism. In 1970, the radical left-wing Italian underground periodical *Sinistra Proletaria* carried an article entitled "The Process of Globalization of Capitalist Society," which described the then-dominant computing and software corporation IBM as an "organization which presents itself as a totality and controls all its activities towards the goal of profit and 'globalizes' all activity in the productive process." Because IBM, according to the article, produced in fourteen countries and sold in 109, it "contains in itself the globalization (*mondializzazione*) of capitalist imperialism." This obscure left-wing publication, then, is the true first-known reference to globalization in its contemporary sense, and it lays down the association with capitalism and imperialism.

Since then, the term has had ups and downs. It became faddish in the 1990s, almost entirely as a term of abuse. In the late 1990s and early 2000s, anti-globalization demonstrations targeted the World Trade Organization, the International Monetary Fund, the World Economic Forum, and McDonald's. Globalization was seen at this time—as it had been in the late 1960s, by the Italian leftists—as the exploitation of the world's poor by a plutocratic and technocratic elite. The iconic figure of the anti-globalization riots was a sheep farmer from Aveyron in the French Pyrenees who had been raised in California. José Bové achieved fame by dismantling the construction site for a McDonald's restaurant in the small town of Millau, and then began to enunciate the principles of sovereignty—*souverainisme*. The world was poised for a new debate, one between globalization and the nation-state.

Some analysts saw the new language of globality, rather than the facts of increasing global interchange, as the key limit on national politics. Historian Sebastian Conrad described how in the 1990s, "the rhetoric of globalization seemed to undermine the power of the nation-state."[2] The British philosopher John Gray, who had turned from Hayekianism to a critique of neoliberalism, explained that the problem of globalization was that it reduced political choice, which led to "over-diminished expectations."[3]

In the 2000s, the meaning of *globalization* shifted and began to take on a semi-positive note, in large part because it increasingly looked as if the major winners of globalization included many rapidly growing emerging markets. Indeed, China and India, which had previously been described as "under-developed" or "Third World," were becoming incipient global hegemons, while others—Brazil, South Africa, Nigeria—were developing as regional superpowers. As a result of very substantial growth in emerging markets, the level of poverty worldwide sank remarkably. Globalization looked as if it was handing out global opportunities, and nation-states looked rather outmoded. Moreover, many former critics of globalization began to recognize global connectedness as a way of solving global problems such as climate change, economic crisis, and poverty. There was indeed, as R. R. Reno claimed, a new near consensus among liberals and conservatives that globalization was beneficial. Social liberals liked the way that new ideas and a pluralism of values eroded traditional restrictions and old morality. And many conservatives saw globalization as a realization of an economic freedom interpreted as wealth creation.

Historians then started to project globalization backward, to periods when no one would have considered the term. Globalization was at times presented as an almost constant feature of the process of human history—from the spreading of the first human DNA from the descendants of the mitochondrial "Eve," the matrilineal mother of all humans 200,000 years ago in the Kalahari desert. The process is no longer seen only as a story of the capital-market-driven integration of the last two decades of the twentieth century, or even of an "early wave of globalization" in the nineteenth century, when the gold standard and the Atlantic telegram seemed to unite the world. Instead, the wider and deeper historical vision is of a globalization that encompasses all of that experience, as well as the Roman Empire and the Song dynasty— even the globalization of the human species from a common African origin. It is the tale of all humanity.

Clearly, the terms that we use to describe complex political and social phenomena have odd ambiguities. Some concepts designed as criticisms are quickly inverted to become celebratory. By 2011, anti-globalization rhetoric had largely faded, and globalization began to be considered more dispassionately, as a fundamental characteristic of the human story in which disparate geographies and diverse themes are inextricably intertwined. Evidence also surfaced that globalization, while promoting inequality within countries, was reducing poverty overall. In short, globalization lost its polemical bite and, with that loss, its attractions as a concept faded.

The critique of globalization would return after 2014, when it looked as if many aspects of globalization—in trade, in migration, and in finance—were faltering. At this point the critique's focus shifted: the victims of globalization were not so much poor people in poor countries (who had been left largely outside the globalization framework), but rather marginalized people in rich countries. As a result, globalization became enmeshed with the earlier and continuing critique of globalism, and a great deal of populist sand was tipped into the wheels of globalization, causing *slobalization,* a slowing or hindering of globalization.

Economic Beginnings of Globalization

Globalization started as a reflection of the activity of multinational corporations. In its simplest sense, as used by economists, globalization is more generally about the mobility of the factors of production, capital, and labor; about product flows or trade; and about the movement of ideas and techniques. The relationship between all these elements of mobility is often and surprisingly overlooked, but it can help explain important shifts and trends. To take just one example, in the great surge of globalization that occurred during the late nineteenth century, emigrants from Europe drove development in North America, South America, and Australia. They built new settlements, which required infrastructure like railroads, tram systems, and municipal water supplies—as well as capital to fund it all. The flows of labor and capital were synchronized.

When worries surfaced about one type of flow, they would inevitably affect the incentives for the other flows. When trade flows are interrupted, countries that export goods experience unemployment or underemployment. There is increased pressure on individuals from those countries to move across frontiers, and that generates fear among the destination countries about competitive wage pressure, which moves their leaders to restrict migration. So the focus shifts to debates about the movement of people, a focus that can also produce unintended consequences. Restrictive legislation on immigration in the 1920s, in the United States for instance, produced a weakness in construction and the housing market by the late 1920s, and so may have set the stage for the Great Depression. Finally, when countries cannot trade freely, they can find it impossible to generate the resources to service and repay external debt, so they experience debt crises, and capital flows are interrupted. Globalization flows are thus intertwined in ways that are sometimes obvious, but sometimes not.

Many of these global contacts require rules of engagement. How can contracts relating to the trading of goods or capital be enforced? Who provides a legal framework, and an enforcement mechanism? How should migrants and settlers be treated? Modern globalization worked on the basis of a complex system of rules, some generated through negotiated international agreements (such as the Bretton Woods Agreement in 1944, when the World Bank and the IMF were established); some formulated by large and powerful governments and then disseminated more widely (via trade law); some generated through agreements of public regulatory authorities (like the International Organization of Securities Commissions—IOSCO— which creates securities regulations); and some private standard setters (such as IOS, the International Organization for Standards). A key feature of modern globalization is that the domestic regulatory order and the international system are intertwined, in what John Ruggie first termed *embedded liberalism*.[4] Ruggie and other scholars of international relations such as John Ikenberry have used this phrase to describe how after 1945 the United States saw international order as a way of securing the political and economic agenda of the 1930s New Deal, by extending principles of free trade and human welfare beyond national borders.[5]

Globalization as a State of Mind

Globalization is also about a mindset, about how people think of international flows. The conceptual framework is needed if some international order, or some overarching legal framework, is to be created. But once it is in place, the concept of globalization flips from being primarily economic—concerned with the movement of the factors of production— to a cultural or even psychological phenomenon. Globalization is then something quite different from the economists' concept: it is how we deal with the unfamiliar, the stranger, the other. It is about how the inhabitants of a particular part of the world see the rest of humanity. In this context, globalization can feel like something foreign, something from the outside being imposed on a particular region, a particular people.

Probably the European country that has been struggling longest with the legacy of globalization is Italy, where the modern term originated. The Italian story is about recent relative decline, but also about a long-term trajectory of winding down economically. At the end of the Middle Ages, northern Italian cities had the highest income in the world. Italy was a center of skilled craft production, with luxury goods that commanded a global market. The closing of the eastern Mediterranean by the Ottoman Empire in the sixteenth century, however, coincided with the opening up of alternative trade routes, around the Cape of Good Hope, and then even from New Spain (Mexico) across the Pacific to China. Italy fell back relative to other countries, while other parts of Europe—the Netherlands and then England—developed superiority in manufacturing. Skilled workers emigrated from Italy and took its secrets—silk production, or Murano's glass-blowing—elsewhere.

Globalization angst is driven in part by the problems of once-rich areas, once-leading sectors, once-dynamic producers as they are confronted by competition. The original winners resent that others are imitating and excelling. And for all those who participate in the global marketplace, there can be anxiety that parts of the local culture are being lost. An essential part of the globalization story, then, is concerned with making comparisons. A recent book, *The Light That Failed,* is devoted to explaining that imitating other models makes everyone, the borrowers but also the lenders, feel uncomfortable. The book's authors, Ivan Krastev and Stephen Holmes, describe the difficulties, the shame, and the hatred created by cultural borrowing. As they put it, "the globalization of communication has made the world a village, but this village is ruled by a dictatorship of global comparisons."[6]

The story of post-Renaissance Italian decline was mirrored in the late twentieth century. After a dynamic period of creativity and growth after the Second World War, it became apparent that Italy had specialized in industries where the basic processes could relatively easily be exported to, and imitated by, other countries. One of the dynamos of Italy's postwar miracle was "white goods"—large consumer durables like refrigerators, washing machines, and dryers that were part of the big consumer boom of the second half of the twentieth century. But these were easily manufactured outside Europe, especially in Asia. That was also true of Italy's historic strengths in high fashion, clothing, and textiles. Italian firms started to move operations to eastern Europe after the end of communism, especially to Romania, where there were few language obstacles because of the common Latinate roots. Skilled Italian workers went on multiyear contracts to China and other Asian countries in order to train foreign workers in traditional Italian skills.

The "Made in Italy" label was still an attraction. There was emigration and imitation; but there was also immigration and an erosion of living standards. Many products were imported in an almost totally finished state, then completed with relatively trivial processes (stitching on buttons or cutting buttonholes) so the result could carry the prized "Made in Italy" tag. And cheap foreign workers were also imported, so that the historic textile town of Prato near Florence became largely Chinese, dominated by migrants from Wenzhou.

In the modern Italian discussion, globalization was often associated with Europeanization. Both terms meant opening markets and facing the consequences of labor mobility. A global product or labor shock thus meant that Italians turned against the European version of multilateralism. Italy's foremost populist, Lega Party leader Matteo Salvini, when offered a panino with one of Italy's most successful exports, Nutella, rejected it brusquely: "And you know why, Signora? Because I found out that Nutella uses Turkish nuts. I prefer to help companies that use Italian products. I prefer to eat Italian and help Italian farmers because they need help."[7] A Lega pamphlet in 2014 explained, "If we do not manage to change the EU and it continues to damage our economy with absurd rules, then we could consider also leaving the EU, something which probably would not be a tragedy."[8]

Globalization is also about changes in taste. National branding is an important part of the packaging of globalization, especially in consumer goods. At the beginning, tastes were assumed to be firmly local. An early journalistic survey of globalization in the 1980s concluded that consumption habits would be very sticky, and so would limit the proliferation of global brands. "Bill Maeyer [chief executive of the Large Domestic Appliances division of the Philips Group] is in no doubt whatever that Asians will continue to eat rice rather than potatoes, and Italians spaghetti. He also suspects that Germans will persist in their penchant for apple strudel, rather than English fruitcake. Howard Kehrl [vice-chair of General Motors] agrees. He forecasts that, though American cars will become increasingly influenced by West German and Italian design, they will continue to have a character all of their own."[9] But in fact the various brands have spilled over national frontiers, contributed to globalization, and so pushed the reaction against it.

When I first visited Japan in the late 1980s, the country was booming and Tokyo was filled with very quaint and particular stores with idiosyncratically Japanese goods. When I revisited the same streets in the early 2000s, the country seemed mired in stagnation, and the shops were identical to those in the equivalent areas of Paris, London, or New York: Prada, Louis Vuitton, Ermenegildo Zegna, Burberry.

While homogenization through borrowing looks shocking, and many people feel it as a loss (I agree with them), the process is not at all new. It was exactly this kind of borrowing that characterized the powerful new nations of the nineteenth century: Germany, Italy, and Japan. Georg Wilhelm Friedrich Hegel in particular identified it as characteristic of what he thought of as "world historical nations." The early pioneer of the revival of the German language, Christian Thomasius, complained in 1687 that "today everything must be French with us: French clothes, French food, French household goods, French language, French morals, French sins, and even French diseases are everywhere the rage."[10] But classical Greece, England, even the United States provided models. Italians looked at Germany after the 1860s as a model of how to achieve national integration. Japan sent out the Iwakura mission in 1871–1873 immediately after the Meiji Restoration to learn from the United States and Europe, then produced a legal code, a university system, a monetary order, an army, and a navy based closely on what Japanese leaders thought to be the best practice. Indeed, they convinced themselves that their victory over China was due to the multiplicity of their European inspirations—French, German, British—while Qing China had only copied Britain. Borrowing took place over very long periods. And it always, eventually, produced a sense of discomfort and alienation.

The Significance of Trade

A great deal of the contemporary discussion about globalization focuses on foreign trade, its effects on living standards and jobs, and the correct policy responses: that is, protection or the promotion of national champions. Trade is the most obvious material manifestation of the strange and abiding legacy of past solutions.

Trade protectionism has been a major element in classic moments of deglobalization, in particular in the waning of the so-called first age of globalization in the late nineteenth century. The dynamic of the pushback in the late nineteenth century is in consequence often regarded as a model for how deglobalization might operate. Before the First World War, protective tariffs were an important way of protecting the losers of globalization. When shipping and transportation costs fell sharply in the third quarter of the nineteenth century and international markets were more closely integrated, European farmers were the most obvious losers, and they were the first to mobilize politically and demand protection, in the form of not only tariffs on food imports, but also favorable railroad freight rates, as well as restrictive veterinary and hygiene requirements for imports.[11] Then, however, industrial pressure groups used the political dynamic to demand similar privileges for their products.[12] Advanced countries (with the notable exception of the United Kingdom) set relatively high rates of industrial protection, the highest being implemented in the United States, while those that were also colonial powers imposed low tariffs on goods manufactured in their own colonial and semi-colonial territories. The idea of compensating losers is still regarded, often on the basis of the historical parallel, as a way of ensuring that globalization will be more sustainable.[13]

The late nineteenth-century example may be problematic as a policy guide for today, however. It is not clear that nineteenth-century trade protection really compensated losers. In Italy and the United States, for example, tariff protection created new losers, because it was fundamentally an industrial north that benefited at the expense of an agricultural and increasingly underdeveloped south.

In the interwar years, protection occurred on a bigger scale that then started clearly to undermine and erode the gains from globalization. For a long time, analysts were convinced by a textbook interpretation of why the Great Depression had occurred. According to this interpretation, the highly protectionist US tariff act of 1930 (the Smoot-Hawley Tariff Act) had driven the world into depression by causing other countries to react to US protectionism, setting off a vicious spiral. Charles Kindleberger popularized the spiral image that was first used by the League of Nations to depict this trade contraction (see Figure 6).[14]

The historical portrayal of Smoot-Hawley as the origin of the Great Depression has, however, largely been revised.[15] Smoot-Hawley was a mistake, with some dramatic implications for specific sectors (for the Japanese silk industry, for instance, and for Swiss watches)—but by the spring of 1931 there were signs of recovery in the United States. In the aftermath of a worldwide contagious financial crisis in 1931, however, the world moved to limit trade not only with higher tariffs but also increasingly through restrictive quotas, which represented a much harsher form of

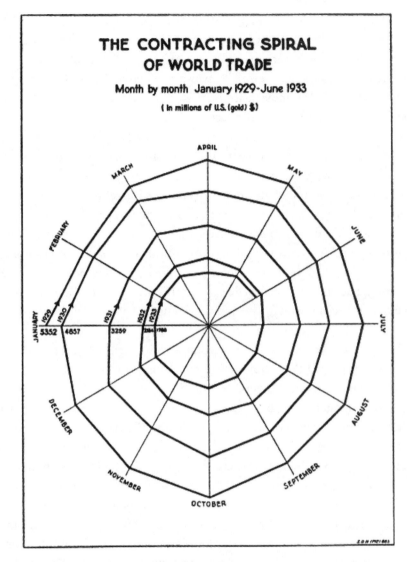

Figure 6. The "Kindleberger spiral" describing the contraction in world trade between January 1929 and June 1933. *Source:* League of Nations, *World Economic Survey, 1932–1933* (Geneva, 1933), p. 8.

restriction. The backlash against trade was then—and has always been—part of a much broader worry about trade and economics.

Nearly eighty years later, international trade suffered dramatically from the Global Financial Crisis, with a collapse between September 2008 and

April 2009 that was sharper than that of the Great Depression. It then recovered.[16] Since 2014, however, world trade has been growing less quickly than world economic activity. This presents a remarkable difference from the great postwar period of trade expansion, when trade consistently grew faster than economic activity. In the past, trade drove economic development, but that is no longer the case.

The faltering growth of world trade may not be due to specific trade measures. It may instead reflect an "on-shoring" of production, where processes that were formerly off-shored to low-wage production centers are brought home and carried out with labor-saving technology (robotization). Producing nearer to consumers, and shortening supply chains, allows quicker and more reactive manufacturing: in some cases (such as clothing and textiles) this makes it easier to respond to rapid shifts in fashion or consumer taste.[17] Not every region is affected equally, however. A great deal of the decline in global trade can be attributed to significant emerging markets, especially China, shortening chains by handling more stages of the production process domestically.

Popular books now describe a "second machine age."[18] But it may be too early to tell whether the relative fall in trade compared with output is a cyclical or a long-term phenomenon.[19] Moreover, while the volume of physical trade is no longer rising as quickly as it once was, data is moving in much larger volumes. Overall cross-border internet traffic increased from 2005 to 2012 by a factor of eighteen.[20] A recent calculation is that data flows in 2014 were worth $2.8 trillion, or 3.6 percent of world GDP.[21] So the shift in trade behavior might also be simply an indicator of increasing dematerialization.

Discussion of long-distance trade has often turned into a denunciation of unnecessary luxuries. Both Aristotle and Aquinas recognized that some products needed to be traded over long distances, but believed that local production was more moral, because foreigners would disrupt civic life. The elder Pliny complained about how Rome was being drained by expensive imports of unneeded luxuries from India, China, and the Arabian peninsula, and Sextus Propertius complained that "proud Rome is brought down by her wealth." Martin Luther polemicized against the luxurious Italian products that were eroding the market for sturdy German homespun goods. The British historian C. V. Wedgwood traced the Thirty Years' War back to a spiritually driven backlash against the excessive materialism of the Renaissance. The American Revolution also began with a sort of anti-globalization revolt, against British taxes but also against the luxury goods (tea) manufactured by the English multinational companies.

Because of the often very intensely localized impact of foreign trade, it is easy to point to job losses in stories about the disruptive impact of trade—then, as now. The Rust Belt of the United States includes some states that not only have deep concerns about deindustrialization, but also are central to the election process because they are narrowly contested. A celebrated study showed that Chinese imports were responsible for about a quarter of American job losses in the 1990s and 2000s.[22] In a similar way, areas of Britain that were shocked by trade with China voted for Brexit, presumably thinking that a post–European Union United Kingdom could handle its trade policies more aggressively (even though many proponents of Brexit insisted that they wanted a more "global Britain").[23] In France, the emotional highpoint of the 2017 presidential election campaign came at a clash between patriots and globalists at a factory in Amiens, where Marine Le Pen had come to promise assistance to workers threatened by job losses when household equipment production moved to Poland. In practice, however, most job losses in traditional manufacturing are the consequence of technical change rather than shifts in trade.

Today, the debate about trade protectionism looks as important as it was in previous eras of deglobalization, but despite fiery rhetoric about trade wars, the implementation of trade protections may well play a lesser role in driving the deglobalization dynamic. Words are likely to be hotter and tougher than the actions. The 2016 US presidential election campaign centered on trade discussions, with former secretary of state Hillary Clinton urging withdrawal from the Trans-Pacific Partnership (TPP) that she had negotiated, and Donald Trump promising 45 percent retaliatory tariffs. The Trump administration included many aggressive trade strategists, from Commerce Secretary Wilbur Ross to the head of the new National Trade Council, Peter Navarro, author of the 2011 book *Death by China*. President Trump himself often expressed a vigorous sympathy for this case and strong criticism of "unfair" trade partners, especially China and Germany. In March 2018, defenders of free trade in the administration were rebuffed, and director of the National Economic Council Gary Cohn resigned, when the president decided to impose tariffs on steel and aluminum, citing national security reasons. Trump also announced via tweet that "trade wars are good, and easy to win."[24] In the longer term, the erosion of the multilateral system may occur through the progressive undermining of the World Trade Organization, as the US administration blocked the appointment of new appellate judges for its arbitration process, and thus prevented the effective working of the organization.

But the actual trade policy of the Trump administration was rather muted in comparison to the ringing sounds of the political rhetoric, and was closer to the American mainstream than many horrified observers believe. Some of the initial moves, including the turn against the Trans-Pacific Partnership and the Transatlantic Trade and Investment Partnership, would have probably occurred even if the Democratic candidate Hillary Clinton had won in 2016. Many postwar US administrations have launched some sort of protective trade initiative, and of course protectionism is deeply woven into the political economy of the United States: in the nineteenth century, Alexander Hamilton made the epochal decision to fund the service of a new federal debt through a customs duty that benefited the manufacturing northern states but antagonized the cotton-exporting South.[25] The initial clashes of the Trump administration came in unlikely areas—and not so much with China, which was rhetorically targeted in the 2016 election campaign. Europe and Canada, for example, rather than China, looked to be the major victims of the proposed steel tariff. Why did Canada become a principal initial antagonist? The lumber, paper, and pulp producers who face Canadian competition are geographically concentrated, and can mount a powerful campaign. The same holds for US washing machine producers who might benefit from the 2017 US tariffs on South Korea. There was another reason that some countries were singled out: the first countries targeted were also weaker or more vulnerable members of the international system, so trade deals with them were attempted first, then the same tactics were applied to try to open the Chinese market to US producers. Threats of trade wars were also used to resolve disputes over migration (with Mexico) and taxation (with France and the European Union). There was a standard model of ratcheting up the language of conflict in order then to celebrate the "greatness" of a modest deal.

The most obvious reason that large-scale trade wars are unlikely to develop quickly in the twenty-first-century environment is that the costs for would-be trade warriors are high. In particular, if the social problem that is being addressed is increased inequality in industrial countries, trade is a remedy rather than a cause. There is substantial evidence that the gains from trade are greatest for poorer consumers.[26] Or put more simply, many poor people in industrial countries are dependent on cheap imports—from clothing to their food.

Second, trade between specialized and clustered providers of niche goods is the hallmark of modern globalization, as opposed to the nineteenth-century version, which was principally an exchange of commodities for manufactured goods. The modern economy is driven as much by cheap information flows as by the ability to move goods cheaply, as the economist Richard Baldwin has recently demonstrated.[27]

Third, substantial job losses have already occurred, and are unlikely to be reversed by changing trade patterns. It is not easy to "protect the losers" anymore, because many of the jobs have already disappeared. For instance, in the steel industry, just 140,000 jobs are left in the United States, compared to 4.7 million steelworkers in China. The right-wing populist Marine Le Pen's unsuccessful 2017 French presidential campaign focused on the loss of textile jobs in northern France. An example of the story of lost jobs was Calais: when in 2005 the EU abolished textile import quotas, there were thirty thousand jobs devoted to making lace for luxury products. Today, there are only a few thousand lace workers, but teenagers all over Europe wear cheap lace products made in Asia or eastern Europe.

The complex global value chains that constitute the modern trading environment may change for other reasons: fashion shifts and just-in-time technology, for example, can make long-distance transport less desirable. Some of the oft-remarked slowing down of global trade after 2012, then, may be due to these effects rather than the bite of a new protectionist sentiment.

The 2020 coronavirus pandemic highlighted a completely different aspect of the problems inherent in trade, value chains, and interconnectedness. It raised an issue that had before arisen only in military conflicts: for security reasons, a country does not want to be dependent on foreign imports. In the initial stages of the coronavirus pandemic, stories, true and occasionally false, circulated about how countries were trying to seize scarce resources. Germany was not allowing medical equipment to be sent to Italian hospitals. The US government diverted to the United States two hundred thousand N95 facemasks en route to Germany as they were being transferred between planes in Thailand. The United States stopped the paper company 3M from sending masks to Canada and Latin America, only to discover that to make the masks, 3M relied on wood pulp produced in western Canada; at the same time, the US government urged 3M to increase its production of masks in factories located in other countries. Americans, too, were shocked to discover that China produced between 80 and 90 percent of antibiotics sold in the United States, as well as 70 percent of the world's supply of Paracetamol, vital in treating fevers, and that the generic antibiotics manufactured in India were also dependent on Chinese intermediary products.

A response—in large countries such as the United States—was to demand that "vital" goods should be made locally. But that is obviously not a realistic proposition for smaller countries, which continue to be dependent not only on their neighbors, but also on distant producers. For them, the crisis demonstrated the need to keep supply and shipping chains reliably administered—perhaps under the supervision of international institutions— to ensure that they were not discriminated against.

Trade in goods covers a shrinking proportion of economic activity. We are more dependent on services. Just as agriculture declined as a source of employment over the past two centuries, so too with increased automation and the application of information technologies, the share of manufacturing employment is likely to shrink until it becomes—like agriculture is today in most rich countries—fundamentally trivial.

The critical issue for the future is services—and who provides them. Services are more heavily protected. They can be internationalized in some cases—paralegal work, many medical services (radiology)—but not in others (tourism and hospitality). That is why the most realistic, and incidentally also the most optimistic, scenarios on how to avoid anti-globalization populist backlashes focus on raising educational levels and improving the quality and provision of a wider array of services. That possibility, however, raises the question of whether the new services demanded will be provided by foreigners.

The changes wrought by the coronavirus may accelerate that development. More medical services, including remote monitoring and diagnosis, will be delivered at a distance, with telemedicine. Many of these remote services were technically possible before the crisis, and some procedures, notably radiology, often took place over long distances, often across national borders. But the pandemic has changed perceptions of the risks posed to both medical practitioners and patients by in-person consultations. Large numbers of people are deciding not to go to doctors' offices or hospitals because they are worried about infection.

Education is being transformed into long-distance learning, with virtual lectures, seminars, and classes being held via Zoom or other internet platforms. Something is obviously lost from the lack of immediate personal experience, but there is also a great deal that is gained. People are connecting across the world. Personally, I find it adds context and understanding to see students and colleagues in their home environments, not just in a bland classroom or conference center. And this kind of education may be much easier to scale up—with the result that it becomes more widely accessible.

The short-term effect of the coronavirus pandemic will be to deglobalize some production. But a global challenge will also produce a global response, and the globalization of services may well intensify.

Global Migration

The history of globalization is also marked by nativist backlashes against migration: they feature prominently in the turn against globalization in the late nineteenth century, but the phenomenon has a much longer history. A manuscript fragment recently identified as being in the hand of William Shakespeare deals with a popular tumult against foreigners, with Londoners "breaking out in hideous violence" when the early sixteenth-century chancellor, Sir Thomas More, intervened to plead for compassion (as well as for obedience to princes who forbade such tumult). To reinforce his argument, Shakespeare's More supposed that the rioters might be punished and expelled; they would then need to look for safety in some foreign city.

Migration directly affects social standing and inequality. Take two extreme examples: letting in only highly skilled professionals might make for greater creativity and innovation, but would also lower the skill premium (the value to employers of hiring someone with that skill) and so challenge the position of an established elite. On the other end of the spectrum, large-scale unskilled immigration depresses wages and makes it cheaper for an elite to buy services (nannies, homecare), and so increases inequality. Clashes about migration thus inherently involve distributional issues. But few like to address those issues directly.

Almost all modern discussion has been focused on low-wage and low-skill immigration, which has an impact on wage levels and working conditions for domestic workers. But the case for resisting downward pressure on wages is rarely framed as a purely material or economic one. For instance, arguments about migration have often conflated the wage effects of low-skill immigration with more general arguments about cultural risk and contamination. In 1882 the US Congress passed the Chinese Exclusion Act, which banned the immigration of Chinese laborers (and required every Chinese person arriving in the United States to have a certificate declaring his or her occupation). The act was regularly renewed, and bills were passed for a more general limitation of migration—bills that until the First World War were regularly vetoed by the president. Around the same time, an 1892 work by the great German sociologist Max Weber examined the immigration of Polish rural workers into Germany, worrying that "the higher culture is not victorious but rather loses in the existential fight with lower cultures."[28]

After the First World War, anti-immigration sentiment increased throughout the world, and produced a legislative response. Two Restriction Acts, in 1921 and 1924, aimed to restrict the country-of-origin and skills mix of US immigrants by setting quotas based on their share of the US population in 1890, before a big surge of eastern and southern European immigration had occurred. Other classic countries of immigration, Canada and Australia as well as South Africa, also introduced lists of "preferred" countries. Limiting migration had a clear effect: it lowered demand for new residential construction in the United States during the 1920s. Over the next decades, migration continued to fall not only as a result of the new legislation, but also as a consequence of declining economic opportunities with the Great Depression.

Unlike declines in trade and finance, there is no evidence that migration slowed following the Global Financial Crisis of 2007–2008. Indeed, migration continued to increase, although at a slightly lower rate during the period 2010–2015 than before (see Figure 7).

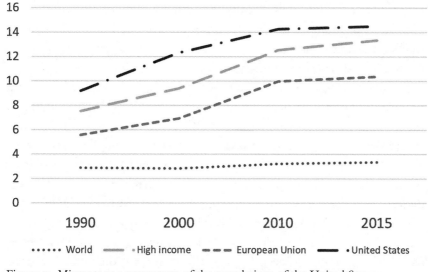

Figure 7. Migrants as a percentage of the populations of the United States, high-income countries, the European Union, and the world. *Source:* World Bank.

A surge of immigration into Europe in 2015, due in part to a large flow of refugees fleeing wars in Syria and Afghanistan, and in part to significant numbers of economic migrants from (non-EU) southeastern Europe, North Africa, and West Africa, put the migration issue at the top of the political agenda. German chancellor Angela Merkel was widely criticized both within and outside Germany for unilaterally letting migrants in, although it is not clear that she had many alternatives. The wish to restrict migration—underlined by criticism of Merkel—played a substantial part in both the 2016 Brexit vote and in the US presidential election. The cultural argument frequently rests on the idea that immigrants are terrorists or criminals, not on a purely economic case.

Observers often note that many of the people who feel most strongly about immigration do not live in areas directly affected by the migrants. Thus, the anxiety about Merkel's 2015 decision is most pronounced in the northern and eastern areas of Germany (in the former Soviet-controlled German Democratic Republic), where few migrants choose to settle. Swiss anti-immigration electoral initiatives gain the greatest support in regions with the least immigration.[29] In the United States, the discussion is intense in the Midwest, far from California, Arizona, Texas, and Florida, which experience the big inflows. Brexit-supporting peripheral Britain, too, has a lower proportion of immigrants than do metropolitan and EU-membership-supporting London. Overall there is little correlation between voting for Brexit and migration history, though there is some evidence that the pro-Brexit vote reflects a rising number of immigrants specifically from the new member countries of eastern and southeastern Europe.[30] An attractive explanation for this phenomenon is that migration intensifies preexisting and primarily cultural class tensions. In this scenario, middle-class inhabitants of dynamic hub cities see migration as beneficial because it ensures a constant stream of low-paid service workers (nannies, waiters, baristas, delivery drivers, and so on) who support a lifestyle that is alien to the lower-income, inland population. But it is not just a question of lifestyle choice: in Europe and North America, key industries such as construction and food preparation (especially meat-processing) rely on immigrant labor.

In the wake of the political discussion, legal immigration has been curtailed in a number of countries. In particular, in the United States and United Kingdom there are initiatives to limit migration by using a skill-based points system (for example, the US Reforming American Immigration for Strong Employment Act, or RAISE). Unlike goods and capital flows, however, illegal migration is very hard or perhaps even impossible to control. In the past, many industrial countries simply instituted periodic amnesties as a way to both regularize the position of illegal immigrants and police them more effectively—a key issue in an age of international or globalized terrorism.[31]

Future migration may be accelerated by push factors: climate change leading to desertification, civil wars or inter-state conflict, and perceptions of disparities between living standards. A permanent "solution" to the migration challenge would involve economic, social, and political stabilization: in other words, a continued attempt to more equitably disperse the benefits of globalization across geographic and cultural boundaries.

When Financial Flows Are Interrupted

Another answer to the question of what starts the backlash phase is that globalization breaks down with financial crises. Finance constitutes the most volatile of the international linkages, and is prone to sudden stops. When this happens, globalization magnifies the problem. One well-known finding from economic history is that the nineteenth-century era of gold-standard integration had more financial flows, but also more banking crises, than the era of limited financial interconnectedness ("financial repression") in the two decades that followed the Second World War. Financial integration in the twentieth century followed a U-shaped trajectory, with substantial cross-border linkages in the earlier part of the century that reemerged in the 1970s and after.[32]

Financial crises—and health crises—are often blamed on the foreigner, and their aftermath generates a new nationalism. This is especially the case after deep financial crises. In addition, regulatory responses to crises can be used for great-power politics. Two historical episodes show these dynamics at work: the US panic of 1907, and the central European financial collapse of 1931.

The panic of October 1907 showed the fast-growing industrial powers (especially Germany and the United States) the desirability of mobilizing financial power. The crash revealed the dangers of relying on the United Kingdom as a preeminent financial center, and encouraged other countries to build up their own financial systems so that they should not be so dependent on Britain, and so vulnerable. The crisis unambiguously originated in the United States, which had already experienced financial stress in late 1906 and a stock market collapse in March 1907. The October panic affected at first the new trust companies, but it was severe enough that the New York banks were forced to restrict depositors from converting their deposits into currency. The consequent demand for cash produced an interest-rate surge that drew in gold imports, but also led to spikes in interest rates elsewhere, with great bank strains in Italy, Sweden, Egypt, and Germany.

The financial operations of the world in the early 1900s were concentrated in Britain, and specifically in the City of London. Since exporters could not have financial agents in every city that imported from them, the world's finance trading was run through London merchant banks. If a Hamburg or New York merchant wanted to buy coffee from Brazil, they would sign a commitment (a bill) to pay in three months' time upon the coffee's arrival in their port; the bill might be drawn on a local bank, or it could be turned into cash by the exporter (or "discounted") at a London bank. A physical infrastructure, the transoceanic cable, provided the basis for the financial links. In addition, most of the world's marine insurance—even for commerce not undertaken in British ships or to British ports—was underwritten by Lloyd's of London. British observers congratulated themselves on their superiority in a world that was increasingly "cosmopolitan" as a result of the "marvellous developments of traffic and telegraphy," as the *Economist* put it. "We have no reason to be ashamed. The collapse of the American system has put our supremacy into relief. . . . London is sensitive but safe."[33]

The 1907 experience convinced some American financiers that New York needed to develop its own commercial trading system that could handle bills in the same way as the London market.[34] The central figure on the technical side in pushing for the development of an American acceptance market was Paul Warburg, the immigrant younger brother of a great (and fourth-generation) Hamburg banker, Max Warburg, who was the personal adviser to Kaiser Wilhelm II. Paul Warburg was a key player in the bankers' discussions on Jekyll Island and then in drawing up the institutional design of the Federal Reserve System. The two banking brothers, Paul and Max Warburg, in fact worked together from both sides of the Atlantic, energetically pushing for German-American institutions that would offer an alternative to the British industrial and financial monopoly. They were convinced that Germany and the United States were growing stronger year by year while British power would erode. The language of Warburg's public appeals made analogies to armies and defense: "Under present conditions in the United States . . . instead of sending an army, we send each soldier to fight alone." His proposed reform would "create a new and most powerful medium of international exchange—a new defense against gold shipments."[35] In the tense debates about the design of a proposed US central bank, Warburg consistently presented the issue in terms of a need to increase American security in the face of substantial vulnerability. As Warburg presented it, the term chosen in the original Aldrich Plan, as well as the eventual name of the new central bank, brought a clear, deliberate, and explicit analogy with military or naval reserves.[36]

The central European credit crisis of 1931 turned the course of the Great Depression. Indeed, it almost certainly would not have been the Great Depression without that collapse: there were indications of a substantial recovery in the United States in the spring. Then an Austrian bank, the Creditanstalt, failed, with contagion effects immediately hitting Hungary and within days also Germany, which was larger and more systemic. The notion that a large bank failure could set off ripple effects that would bring down the world was a historical lesson that informed policy in 2008: Ben Bernanke worried over the weekend of the Lehman Brothers collapse that the United States was having a new Creditanstalt moment.[37]

A banking crisis pushed the world to a much more pronounced form of trade protectionism. With bank credits blocked by standstill agreements and financial flows frozen, deficit countries had to engage in vigorous policy measures to correct their external accounts. The banking crisis was followed by the imposition of exchange control, and then by bilateral trade agreements and clearing arrangements in which countries sought to manage their trade, as well as the financial payments for trade and services, on a bilateral basis. The first of these agreements was between Hungary and Yugoslavia in January 1932; Germany followed with agreements with Hungary and then with other east-central European states.[38] Economists complained: "Tariffs, exchange restrictions, quotas, import prohibitions, barter trade agreements, central trade-clearing arrangements—all the fusty relics of medieval trade regulation, discredited through five hundred years of theory and hard experience, were dragged out of the lumber rooms and hailed as the products of the latest enlightenment."[39] It also appeared that the new arrangements had a political economy of contagion: "Bilateralism, on the contrary, propagates and augments itself. When a particular country finds, for example, that because its trading partners have instituted clearing it is beginning to lose its inflow of free exchange for the purpose of commanding necessary raw materials, it may consider itself constrained to impose clearing upon those countries selling the raw materials. The process thus tends to work in a vicious spiral."[40] There was also a spiral as security concerns made arguments about using trade restrictions to decrease dependence on foreign imports of strategic goods more plausible. Trade multilateralism was destroyed by the fallout from the financial crisis, and prompted a shift to thinking in security terms.

The domestic legislative response to the Great Depression also involved bank regulation: the separation of investment and commercial banking in the 1933 US Glass-Steagall Act was replicated in analogous legislation in Belgium and Italy. The regulation of finance, and enhanced fiscal interest in banking activity, contributed to the reduction of international flows.

Like the Great Depression, the 2007–2008 crisis also set off a renationalization of finance, especially in the aftermath of bank failures. Bank resolution—a process of dissolving a bank rapidly to avoid harm to the system—could only at the outset of the crisis be managed by national authorities (only afterward did Europe move slowly and hesitantly toward a "banking union"), because of the fiscal costs involved. Mervyn King, as governor of the Bank of England, said that "most large complex financial institutions are global—at least in life if not in death." Faced with potentially large future claims, governments pushed initially to tighten regulation, and to impose particularly hard national standards in order to make their banking systems even more secure: the "Swiss finish" in Switzerland, or gold-plating for UK regulations. National regulators in Europe started to treat the national corporations that constituted the legal entities in large transnational banking groups as the appropriate objects for regulation, and in this way restricted exposures across borders: for instance, Deutsche Bank S.p.A. in Italy, Deutsche Bank Sociedad Anónima Española, or Deutsche Bank AG in Germany were all legally separate entities, and no longer seen as part of a Deutsche Bank Group.

Moves to increase bank capitalization in order to make them safer in practice went in the same direction. Since raising new capital in the middle of a financial crisis was hard and initially expensive, an easier route to higher capital ratios lay in selling bank assets, above all bank holdings in non-core areas. There is thus evidence of increased home bias in finance, as banks disposed their holdings in foreign countries, a move also in part pushed by protectionist impulses from their national regulators.[41]

In Europe, government support for banks, combined with an unconventional monetary policy that explicitly targets domestic lending in order to overcome recession, pushed banks to focus on domestic rather than international lending—and to acquire national government bonds.[42] And when after the crash it was revealed that British banks had allegedly made 80 percent of their loans to foreign borrowers, the British government pressed them to reverse their priorities.[43]

It is not clear, though, that this triple push to renationalization of banking was really a worldwide phenomenon. The Bank for International Settlements has argued that banking or financial deglobalization is a European phenomenon rather than a global one. European banks in particular reduced their assets, while other banks were able to raise the capital they needed without this step.[44]

The coronavirus raised a new challenge. As the rhetoric about who was responsible escalated between the United States and China, the threat of a financial war escalated. Republican senator Lindsey Graham, a onetime critic of Donald Trump who then became one of his leading defenders, argued that the United States should retaliate against China for the millions of infections and the tens of thousands of American deaths by selectively defaulting on US debt held by China. This would be a nuclear option, one that would destroy the credibility of the world's most important safe asset, the US dollar. Even the debate about such an option raises the probability that China might preemptively sell its dollar debt—a move that in normal times it would be unlikely to make, because of the fear that doing so would trigger a price collapse. Countries are very emphatically back in the pre-1914 mode of trying to use the financial system to inflict damage on each other. Finance, a longtime tool of influence, is once again becoming a weapon of economic destruction.

Globalization's Effects on Governance

The underlying causes or drivers of deglobalization analyzed so far—psychological responses to foreignness and immediate pragmatic responses to financial crises—are related to each other. The response to financial crisis triggers a much deeper set of political-psychological responses.

When capital moves easily, it looks international and anonymous; but when capital retreats, the borrowers left high and dry become highly sensitive to whose capital, and whose interests, are driving the process. Since 2008, there has been a partial renationalization of finance, driven in particular by regulatory concerns. Along with concerns about residence (that is, migration), the most explosive issues between the United Kingdom and the European Union in the Brexit negotiations concerned financial services, with the result that this whole sector was simply left out of the final agreement. Even before the 2016 Brexit vote, the European Union was sharpening its approach to the doctrine of equivalence, in which institutions regulated in an equivalent regime were permitted to be active in the European Union. The move to lighter regulation in the United States with the revision of the Dodd-Frank framework for financial regulation is also pushing the European Union to exclude what it regards as dangerously or unfairly regulated foreign institutions. Currently, protectionism is much more visible in discussions of services than in talks concerning manufactures (where the interwar globalization backlash had focused).

Capital movements have become part of a zero-sum calculus that appears in other aspects of international relations.[45] Dependence on external capital could be regarded as a source of vulnerability. Access to official rescue resources, such as the Federal Reserve's swap line, is granted with partiality and preference, with some significant emerging markets given access but others (such as India) turned away.

At an early stage in the Global Financial Crisis of 2007–2008, there was an impressive coordination of multilateral international action. Many observers concluded that "the system worked." A book with that title by Daniel Drezner argued that the world economy bounced back because "global economic governance functioned properly to maintain economic openness and build resiliency into the international system."[46] The coordination successes of 2008–2009 seemed to stand in stark contrast to the failed negotiations of the Great Depression, and the disastrous 1933 World Economic Conference. The high points of international cooperation were the G20 summits of 2009 in London and then in Pittsburgh, which led to commitments to global economic coordination, macroeconomic stimulus, and an extension of the IMF's lending capacity in order to contain potentially contagious crises. The various plans worked. The spiral of trade decline (which from September 2008 had looked like the interwar Kindleberger spiral) stopped abruptly in April 2009.

Subsequent summits, however, were much less impressive. Seoul, in November 2010, was overshadowed by a futile attempt by the United States to impose limits on current account surpluses, targeting in particular China and Germany, which resisted. Cannes, in November 2011, was dominated by the unresolved European crisis. Regular statements about the need to resist protectionism looked like boilerplate, and were not accompanied by effective action. And the G20 shunted itself into irrelevance at the 2017 Hamburg summit, which was preceded by the United States announcing its withdrawal from the Paris Agreement on climate change. The dropping of a ritual call for trade liberalization probably made no difference from the policy perspective, and officials could still argue that the process was operating, but the illusion of coordinated action was fading.

The changing character of coordination reflected a shift in the world's economic geography. The Global Financial Crisis appeared to have been much more destructive to the industrial world than to the large emerging markets, and both the United States and Europe engaged in a painful domestic political reflection on the consequences of globalization. But leadership figures prominently in many accounts of how globalization works. Nineteenth-century globalization developed under a largely British set of rules—including court decisions about debt claims. In the second half of the twentieth century, by contrast, the United States was at the center of currency arrangements and the ultimate defender of the multilateral system. While the United States and the United Kingdom were the main architects of the post-1945 order, with its United Nations systems, they now appear to be pioneers in the reverse direction, steering an erratic, inconsistent, and domestically highly contested course away from multilateralism. The Brexit referendum and the election of Donald Trump have brought a new style of politics: one that both turns away from multilateralism and rejects expert or scientific opinion. Donald Trump was the first president openly to address the question of the decline (what in his inauguration address he termed the "carnage") of the United States, which he interpreted as the consequence of unfair foreign competition.

Charles Kindleberger's famous argument about hegemonic stability traced the interwar dysfunction to the inability of the United Kingdom and the unwillingness of the United States to lead in the aftermath of the First World War. It might be thought that the long decline of Britain was in itself not particularly destructive, and it is true that the blasé weariness of declining hegemons was not especially problematic on its own. But without Britain's strong presence, the world lacked an effective police officer, and the competition to replace Britain, as well as the neuroses of rising powers, created systemic dangers. The really high risks came from other countries competing to replace Britain, above all Germany and Japan.

In the twenty-first century, the United States has become the subject of a new leadership crisis. China and Europe—or perhaps more accurately

Germany—now see themselves cast, perhaps reluctantly and hesitantly, as the new defenders of global order. China and Germany are increasingly aligned on climate change issues, whereas President Trump's emphasis on the centrality of coal and other fossil fuels appears obstructive and destructive. There is a clear Chinese-German alliance building to resist trade protectionism, which has been rhetorically dismissed as an exercise in locking oneself in a dark room—a phrase, translated from Chinese, that Chancellor Angela Merkel has described as "very memorable."[47] Chinese president Xi Jinping has been particularly forceful about the need to defend globalization.[48]

Sometimes the international as well as German media have called on Germany to replace the United States, and to fill the void left after January 2017.[49] The clearest recent statement by the German chancellor was in her budget speech on November 23, 2016, in which she emphasized that the intensification of globalization increased the need to act collectively, and that Germany could not on its own "fight the whole problem of worldwide hunger, solve the issue of 65 million refugees, or change political order everywhere in the sense that we would like." But she added that Germany should try to shape globalization in light of its experience with the social market economy in a multilateral setting, and should not "withdraw." In particular, "the G20 was the attempt to shape globalization in a human way and to provide for a sensible financial and economic order with the largest and most important economic powers of the world."[50]

Germany is not well placed to act as a hegemon: it is too small. China is triply vulnerable. Its relatively underdeveloped and partially protected financial sector is crisis prone. The large Belt and Road infrastructure initiative has created a new geopolitical problem of dependence in those areas opened up by the new Chinese communications thrust. Finally, there is a worry about democratic control; and it is the lack of democracy that has been at the heart of anti-globalization critiques of multilateralism in rich countries. After the coronavirus crisis, a radical critique of hegemony set in that has made interpreters see the new setback to globalization as not only deglobalization or de-Americanization, but also a "global de-Sinicisation."[51] Just as the Global Financial Crisis led to disillusion with the United States as the epicenter of the crisis, and soon thereafter the euro crisis had the same consequence for discussions of German hegemony, the coronavirus pandemic has worked against visions of China as a new hegemonic power.

Decisionism

Globalization depends on a complex system of rules, and on the acceptance of judicial decisions and arbitrations made in other countries. Deglobalization, by contrast, is facilitated by a mode of thinking that regards general rules, of the sort required for effective international coordination, as redundant, ineffective, or even harmful. One of the consequences of financial crises is that breaking the rules appears attractive and even necessary as a response to exceptional circumstances. When there is an existential challenge, rules seem cumbersome—like unnecessary limitations on a country's freedom to maneuver during difficult times. Almost everyone likes a temporary waiver of rules in order to avoid catastrophe. There are also political incentives to engaging in activism: no elected official wants to look as if they are standing inactive, bound by complex rules (and even worse by foreign rules).

The 2007–2008 Global Financial Crisis produced a new mindset, in which exceptional measures were considered as a response to any issue, no matter how unexceptional the circumstances. Constitutional safeguards could be dismissed as petty-minded bureaucratic concerns. Former Federal Reserve chair Paul Volcker noted that the Fed had gone to "the very edge of its lawful and implied powers."[52]

But why not go beyond that edge if the general welfare demands it? The answer lies in an old justification for autocracy, where one person can see what is in the public good, and then announces that the autocrat's judgment should be the supreme law, *Salus populi suprema lex esto*. The American lawyer, founder of the Republic, and second president of the United States, John Adams, noted the ambiguity of the concept: "The public good, the *salus populi* is the professed end of all government, the most despotic, as well as the most free."[53]

The push to exceptionalism also follows from the discrediting of traditional political parties in the wake of a financial crisis.[54] Stable party politics in most industrial countries had been built on an alternation of moderate center-right and center-left parties, which embraced the international order (and in the European case, the European order). They competed for the median voter and thus needed to move to political center ground. The globalization backlash, however, fuels nationalist parties on both the right and the left that want to protect a vision of the past—national glory combined with an idea of social welfare that is seen as threatened by internationalism. This vision conjures up exceptional measures and strong leaders.

A powerful leader can and should fix things by himself (it is interesting that none of the new post-crisis leaders are women; they are all "strong men"). Strong men set themselves up to tackle specific pressing problems— the drug trade in the Philippines, terrorism in Russia or Turkey, or the fallout from the financial crisis in Hungary. The selective focus on one "crisis" then generates a mindset in which all other problems also become crises that demand immediate, effective, and unfettered political action.

The doctrine associated with the great German interwar political and legal thinker Carl Schmitt, and sometimes termed *decisionism,* well describes the mentality of the post-crisis response. In decisionism, the primary interest of the political process lies in who can make decisions, and politics is measured and defined by decisions, not processes. In external affairs, this notion corresponds to an increased concern with sovereignty. The concept of sovereignty is reasserted as a political process that cannot be appealed to an external agent. The main weakness of globalization is seen as its simultaneous erosion of sovereignty with an augmentation of governance through international agreements, conventions, and norms. The process through which decisions are made, and whether it is transparent or democratic, is irrelevant.

Decisionism, therefore, is inherently arbitrary. The sovereign "needs" to act forcefully to protect a particular threatened interest. It can target obvious symbols. That was true in the great interwar surge of protectionism, when the United States, via the Smoot-Hawley Tariff, penalized some nationally important goods: Swiss watches and Japanese silk products. There are also current examples of how the targets of protectionism are chosen for maximum publicity. Trump's automobile tariffs against iconic German firms, such as BMW, were designed to make a political splash. Similarly, the European response to the threat of US protectionism has been to specify particular products—such as Bourbon whiskey—that relate to areas that supported Trump electorally. Japan retaliated by hiking duties on frozen American beef.

Decisionism is impatient about conventional bureaucratic processes that might assure fairness and accountability. At the outset of the Trump administration, Stephen Bannon, the chief White House strategist, in an important speech to the Conservative Political Action Conference, defined the key corollaries of what he thought of as the sovereignty revolution: economic nationalism and the "deconstruction of the administrative state."[55] These features of the revolutionary program are linked, and revolutions are fundamentally about rethinking the state's connections with the international order.

To many people, arguments for decisionism look like those for fascism, and, after all, Carl Schmitt was initially an enthusiastic supporter of National Socialism in Germany. *Fascism* has been widely and rather indiscriminately employed in political debate since the 1960s as a term of denunciation. Historians had tended to be critical of its inflationary use, because that distracted from the real crimes of the interwar period. With widespread populism, and especially after the 2016 Trump victory, the term has seemed more relevant. In 2017, in her book *Fascism: A Warning,* Madeleine Albright pointed out how some favorite Trump expressions were taken from Mussolini's vocabulary, including "drenare la palude," or "drain the swamp." In 2018, Yale's Jason Stanley wrote a book entitled *How Fascism Works,* comparing specific policies of the Trump administration (especially the internment of immigrant children) to Nazi practices in the 1930s.[56]

Yet *fascism* has been peculiarly and notoriously difficult to define. Indeed the original fascist party, Mussolini's Italian movement, did not really produce a definition until ten years after the seizure of power. In 1932, Mussolini at last gave a statement of "The Doctrine of Fascism" for the *Enciclopedia Italiana*. In it he stated: "Fascism is a religious conception in which man is seen in his immanent relationship with a superior law and with an objective Will that transcends the particular individual and raises him to conscious membership of a spiritual society." Within a nation, there were classes and interest associations ("syndicates"), but they were subordinated to the state. Mussolini also reflected on democracy, which he rejected in its form of rule by the majority. Instead he argued that fascism was "the purest form of democracy," if democracy was thought of not as the most popular but as the "most powerful" idea "which acts within the nation as the conscience and the will of a few, even of One."[57]

The definition given by Mussolini of democracy is vague, but Trump has been even more vague. Moreover, Trumpism has only partially and feebly set off the spiral of competing radicalization of his followers that characterized the fascist and the Nazi movements, in which adherents outbid each other in "working towards the Führer."[58] That dynamic exploded briefly in the assault on the Capitol on January 6, 2021. The modern fascistoids employ terribly violent language, with often tragic and murderous consequences, but they do not stage invasions and do not really aim at war. The best account of the relation of modern would-be authoritarians like Trump or Viktor Orbán to fascism is the idea that in borrowing some of the theatricality of interwar radicalism, they were "performing fascism."[59]

The link of the revisionist anti-global agenda to domestic politics follows from the technology and the complexity of modern life. Globalization depends not simply on a principle of openness to foreign goods, foreign capital, and migrants—but also on a complex system of regulating all of these flows. None of the movements simply happen by themselves. Foreign goods cannot come in without adhering to safety and product information standards, capital flows are managed by means of controls on bank lending, and migration is subject to many checks and conditions. For smaller and less powerful countries, it is important to keep these regulatory mechanisms in place: a functioning international order is part of their security framework.

For larger countries, the situation is not so simple. The promise held out by populist myth-builders is that getting rid of international entanglements can make life simpler, less regulated, and above all less subject to the dictates of an administrative class. They want no globalization—that is, they prefer *nobalization*. Globalization understood as "embedded liberalism" is under attack because of a reaction against complex rules. Nobalization or disembedded unilateralism, by contrast, derives its rhetorical ammunition for changes in the domestic system from the (frequently mendacious) claim to speak for the good of the people and the principle of national sovereignty. In this way, globalization has become a key weapon in the political arsenal of populism as it continues its struggle against a domestic technocracy.

12

Neoliberalism

Neoliberalism is a catch-all word that has been used to explain more or less everything that has gone wrong with the world over the past half century. The prefix *neo* is indeed used more generally as a warning sign of some political poison: consider the vigorous condemnations of neoconservatism, neokeynesianism, neorealism, and neomarxism.[1] (Perhaps *post* has more positive connotations—as in postmodern, postnational, postcommunist, postconservative, and even posthuman—but that prefix gives the misleading impression that it is easy, or even possible, to just put the past behind you.) The portmanteau label *neoliberalism,* and not the original idea, has now become an obstacle to precise analytical thought. Today the term is used pervasively and promiscuously, often as a go-to term of denunciation. It is used to describe both conservative economists and countercultural bobos, market fundamentalists and anything-goes libertarians. It carries a sense of excessive confidence in the capacity of individuals and of *individualism.*[2] Almost no one today will say that they are a neoliberal.[3] The widespread use of *neoliberal* as a generic term of abuse—especially by those who have been castigated as neoliberals themselves—hinders the rational discussion of problems, and thus damages the prospects for developing effective and coordinated policies to tackle urgent global problems.

Neoliberalism has much to answer for. It was an idea, became a phenomenon, and morphed into an incantation. The original idea of neoliberalism is quite different and distinct from the political and economic phenomena that have been widely described as neoliberalism over the last thirty years. Considering the term's origins, moreover, uncovers a rich previous debate that contains many lessons for the world's current predicaments.

Self-described neoliberalism emerged as a current of thinking early in the twentieth century, in reaction to the great wave of deglobalization that followed the Great Depression. It began in 1938 as a response to a crisis in liberalism and the rise of totalitarian doctrines—as Jurgen Reinhoudt and Serge Audier have shown in their edition of the original Walter Lippmann colloquium, now available in both English and German.[4] This 1938 colloquium was attended by French and American liberals as well as some German emigrés. Discussion focused on maintaining open and competitive markets, restricting disturbances following from financial cycles or financialization, curtailing the destructive consequences of political lobbying, and combating a narrow focus on *homo oeconomicus*. There were quite divergent viewpoints: some looked back to classic nineteenth-century liberalism, while others proposed a new policy regime and new and innovative roles for the state. The purveyors of the original concept of neoliberalism wanted to maintain an open and dynamic but civilized world in the face of increased nationalism, authoritarianism, and radical popular mobilization. The doctrine was a response to a doctrine of exceptionalism and crisis response.

The debates of the last thirty years have some analogies with the dismal mental world of the 1930s. Since the 1980s, a cycle of intense globalization and technical change has produced powerful monopolies driven by network advantages, a destructive financial cycle, a massive extension of special-interest lobbying (in large part to preserve the position of those monopolies), and a widespread impoverishment of the concept of what it is to be human. All these changes are conventionally summed up in the neologism *neoliberalism*, but the label seems bizarre in that it was precisely such phenomena that excited the passion, hostility, critical analysis, and policy prescriptions of the original neoliberals. Joseph Stiglitz recently concluded: "If the 2008 financial crisis failed to make us realize that unfettered markets don't work, the climate crisis certainly should: neoliberalism will literally bring an end to our civilization."[5] But then he came up with a set of policy proposals that revive much of neoliberalism's original impulse to lay out a path for reforming and restoring capitalism.

Analyzing the apparent contradictions of neoliberalism is like dealing with an old-style photographic negative: the contemporary critique has reversed the tone and color of the original. How does the story of its origins fit with a discussion of its highly peculiar trajectory since the 1980s?

A Weaponized Word in Policy Debates

Neoliberalism's current use as a critical term originated especially on the left. It is above all used to condemn fiscal austerity, privatization, and the liberalization of international capital movements. This usage was shaped in particular by discussion of Latin American adjustment programs, notably in General Pinochet's dictatorship in Chile. Then the term was used to describe international policy responses to the 1997–1998 East Asia crisis. The 2007–2008 worldwide financial crisis, and its aftermath in the European debt crisis, globalized the concept.

More broadly, a new consensus is forming that the whole phenomenon of capitalism is flawed and failing. Neoliberalism, the policy regime that had breathed new life into capitalism, is thus now almost universally excoriated. It is "the god that failed."[6] Neoliberalism has become a way of naming a world that is uncomfortable and disruptive, and that people resent because it is incomprehensible and unfathomable.

The deep contempt for neoliberalism has been taken up as well—perhaps even more vigorously and rancorously—by the political right. There was more than a touch of it in Theresa May's 2016 citizens of the world speech: "But today, too many people in positions of power behave as though they have more in common with international elites than with the people down the road, the people they employ, the people they pass in the street. But if you believe you're a citizen of the world, you're a citizen of nowhere. You don't understand what the very word 'citizenship' means."[7] It is central to the widespread attack on cosmopolitan technocrats. May's chief policy adviser, and the main writer of the 2016 speech, Nick Timothy, recently analyzed the

> deep cultural and intellectual bias across the top of British society. It is no conspiracy, but in the civil service, the media, business, courts, quangos and universities, there is a remarkable uniformity

of opinion that has shaped our country and the decisions of our governments for the past few decades. Market forces matter more than institutions. "Modernisation"—whatever that really means— matters more than tradition.[8]

Here tradition looks like a comfort, and neoliberalism can then be recast as the malign force that prevents a simple reversion to a fictionalized past. That sentiment is also part of the new right's revulsion against "woke" business elites, who are regularly depicted as part of a liberal conspiracy to reshape the thinking of consumers. May's successor Boris Johnson pithily commented, "Fuck business." Fox talk show host Tucker Carlson's rant against capitalism is becoming a commonplace in the ideological foundation of Trumpism. He spoke of "mercenaries who feel no long-term obligation to the people they rule" and who "don't even bother to understand our problems."[9]

The mantra has spread to the political center as well. Questioned by the periodical *Le Point*, Bruno Le Maire, the center-right French minister of the economy, criticized capitalism, arguing that it is currently at a dead end. He held capitalism responsible for three global curses: increasing inequalities, environmental problems, and authoritarian regimes.[10] Gordon Brown, who had been seen as the chief architect of a neoliberal-light regulatory practice in the United Kingdom, recently tried to explain how he had always wanted to "swim against the neoliberal tide."[11] Immediately after the financial crisis, the Austrian cybernetics and management expert Fredmund Malik, certainly not an extremist, penned an article for *Die Zeit* with the heading "Der Kapitalismus ist gescheitert."[12] "Capitalism has failed" and "capitalism is doomed" have become mantras of a nervous and uncertain world. Multilateral international institutions, Christian churches, and centrist parties have become convinced that they must distance themselves from a failed model. So have business leaders. An academic industry has devoted itself to tracing the malign ancestry of neoliberal "doctrine" and its perpetuation by secretive bodies such as the Mont Pèlerin Society.[13] That effort has evoked some counter-responses.[14]

The criticism is just as widespread outside the western industrial world. In China, "Xi Jinping Thought" involves rejecting the link between liberal democracy and the market economy and asserting the superiority of "renewed socialism" and "socialism with Chinese characteristics."[15] Vladimir

Putin meanwhile took the opportunity of an interview with the *Financial Times*, often thought of as the voice of the global neoliberal elite, to claim that the liberal idea had "outlived its purpose" and that liberals "cannot simply dictate anything to anyone just like they have been attempting to do over the recent decades."[16]

Even at the International Monetary Fund—which is often presented as a core part of the neoliberal institutional infrastructure—criticism began to be directed against neoliberalism. An article by the deputy director of the research division, Jonathan Ostry, started with the concession that "there is much to cheer in the neoliberal agenda," particularly with regard to trade expansion. But the good news did not extend to two central planks in neoliberalism, capital market liberalization and "fiscal consolidation, sometimes called 'austerity.' " The article explicitly attacked the notion of expansionary fiscal contraction—the idea that in some cases a shrinking of the state would boost private-sector development. And it named as culprits the academic Alberto Alesina and the policymaker Jean-Claude Trichet.[17] The *Financial Times* commented on the piece and interviewed Ostry, who noted that his article did not reflect "mainstream culture" at the IMF and would not have made it into a Fund publication as recently as five years ago. "But cultures are slow moving things."[18] Thus a profound cultural shift is under way.

The historian Julia Ott recently demanded in *Dissent* that "we must identify the perpetrators and perpetuators of neoliberalism and hold them accountable," before adding: "Sometimes, these may be us."[19] What is striking in the discussion is how much emotional energy is devoted to attempting to find the person whose ideas set the world off on this dangerous trajectory, an equivalent of Patient Zero, Gaëtan Dugas in the AIDS epidemic, or the Wuhan seafood market for COVID-19. A search for origins—or a narrative—has become the main way of compensating for the inability to offer helpful policies. Those who have been blamed for putting the world on the bad course include policymakers or academics in the Global Financial Crisis (Trichet, Alesina, or Kenneth Rogoff); the predominantly French policymakers who in the 1980s designed a system for managing globalization (Jacques Delors, Pascal Lamy, Jacques de Larosière, or Trichet, again); thinkers around Geneva who wondered how to use international order to constrain what they held to be irresponsible domestic policies; or Friedrich von Hayek or Milton Friedman, the policy intellectuals who are supposed to have originally inspired Thatcher and Reagan.[20]

The emphasis on personalities is a distraction. In today's world, analysts are often dealing with phenomena that are much older than the concepts themselves; capitalism and globalization are obvious examples. Analysts also revel in the naming and renaming. When it became obvious that a previously central organizing concept (Marxism as an intellectual current, with communism as a political practice) had failed, it was necessary to invent another concept that could be described in similar terms—hence neoliberalism as the god that failed. A famous objection to the conflation of Marxism with the Soviet experience of "real existing socialism" is that Marx had quite a different vision than the people who laid claim to his heritage. Exactly the same analytical point holds about the 1930s intellectuals who devised neoliberalism. I thus turn to the original vision of these progenitors.

Neoliberalism as Prophecy

Liberalism, the language of individual rights, was the dominant form of discourse in the nineteenth century in Europe and those parts of the world that Europeans influenced or to which they exported their ideas. By the beginning of the twentieth century, many liberals were looking for a more expansive concept—sometimes called New Liberalism—with a generous, broadened measure of social rights and consequently of social transfers. In the interwar years, it looked as if liberalism—certainly in its older version—had been discredited along with parliamentarism, representative government, capitalism, and the market economy. In their place came authoritarianism directed toward popular mobilization and foreign-policy aggression, and planning as a tool of economic management. It looked very much like lessons from First World War policies were being applied. Collectives, not individuals, mattered.

The August 1938 meeting of intellectuals in Paris that is usually conceived of as the birthplace of the term *neoliberalism* was a reaction to the new authoritarianism. The "Colloque Walter Lippmann" was convened by the deeply conservative anti-fascist French philosopher Louis Rougier and included not only some old-style classical liberals, such as Ludwig von Mises and Jacques Rueff, but also newer figures who wanted to transcend the nineteenth-century model.[21] The main participants were American, British, or French; the Germans and Austrians who were present were all exiles from Nazi rule. Both groups were inevitably obsessed by the relationship between the problems of capitalism and the breakdown of democracy. Rougier began the meeting by explaining why he thought Walter Lippmann was so important:

> The second merit of Walter Lippmann's book is to have shown that the liberal regime is not only the result of a natural spontaneous order as numerous authors of the Codes of Nature in the eighteenth century proclaimed; but that it is also the result of a legal order that presupposes a legal interventionism of the State. Economic life unfolds in a legal framework that establishes the system of property, of contracts, of patents, of bankruptcy, the status of professional associations and of commercial societies [corporations], money and banking, all things that are not facts of nature as the laws of economic equilibrium are, but rather contingent creations of the legislator.[22]

It is worth pointing out several features of the new worldview that was being debated, precisely because they look both so different from modern caricatures of neoliberalism, and so similar to what some of the critics of modern neoliberalism envisage.

Striving for Open Competition

First, this generation of neoliberal thinkers was acutely and primarily concerned with the principle of competition and with competition policy. At the 1938 colloquium, the German economist Wilhelm Röpke—a staunch anti-Nazi who taught at the Graduate Institute in Geneva and was, strikingly, the only non-Jewish and non-socialist German economist to leave Nazi Germany—began his exposition on the decline of liberalism with a commentary about the impact of technical change on business structure:

> The tendency towards economic concentration and, as a result, towards State control [*étatisation*] of businesses is mainly attributed

to the development of technology and mechanization. Technology develops as fixed capital increases, that is as the general cost increases each day; it is a development that excludes the mechanism on which the philosophy of liberalism has been built.[23]

Alexander Rüstow, another German (and an ex-socialist) who was living in exile in Turkey, blamed state policy and the power of interest groups. He concluded, anticipating Schumpeter's *Capitalism, Socialism, and Democracy,* that

it is not competition that kills competition. It is rather the intellectual and moral weakness of the State that, at first ignorant of and negligent in its duties as policeman of the market, lets competition degenerate, then lets its rights be abused by robber knights [*chevaliers pillards*] to deal the fatal blow to this degenerate competition.[24]

After the Second World War, German neoliberals sometimes seemed to suggest that they had been driven fundamentally by opposition to the evils of National Socialism. Their critics observed that they had also applied their neoliberal analysis of state "weakness" to pre-1933 German democracy and that, in attacking the institutions of the Weimar Republic, they had opened the way for the authoritarian or totalitarian state. The German sociologist Wolfgang Streeck goes much further and sees a parallel between the theorist of decisionism Carl Schmitt—who for some time was very close to the Nazi regime—and the postwar German ordoliberals. The ordoliberals represented an extension of neoliberalism in one direction, and emphatically insisted on the necessity of a prior ordering framework (*ordo*, or "order" in Latin) rather than thinking in a Hayekian way about the spontaneous creation of social and political order. In the Hayekian version of neoliberalism, the depoliticization of the economy is itself an act of politics.[25] There is a deep confusion in Streeck's critique between the neoliberal vision of a "strong" state that is isolated from and not dependent on particular pressure or interest groups, and a state that acts strongly and arbitrarily on behalf of favored interests.

In fact, there was a strong link between the neoliberal analysis of Weimar's flawed democracy and the later dissection of Nazi pathology. The neoliberal critique of cartels and business organizations in the Weimar Republic and of interactions between organized capitalism and organized labor in the form of trade unions suggested that a failure of interventionism had produced a demand for yet more intervention. Ensuring open competition and restricting cartels were thus ways of preventing public authorities from overreaching through micro-interventions.

The debate was not simply cast in terms of an analysis of German peculiarity. The neoliberals' view on the importance of competition and the pernicious character of cartels was also characteristic of a parallel movement on the other side of the Atlantic. This movement found its powerful legislative embodiment in the so-called Second New Deal, which had arisen because of a legal challenge to President Roosevelt's original and more activist vision. The "first" New Deal, and in particular the National Industrial Recovery Act of 1933, looked much more like then-fashionable European corporatism, and its debt to Mussolini's Italy was barely concealed. In 1935, the Supreme Court ruled Title I of the 1933 act unconstitutional. After the war, however, the US military government in Germany and Italy pushed this competitive vision of the New Deal, as it sought to eliminate the corporatist legacy of fascism and Nazism in Europe.

An authentic US tradition, which had originated in anti-trust discussions before the First World War, combined with the inheritance of constitutionalism to shape the mid-twentieth-century American approach. This tradition was represented in particular by the Chicago economist Henry Calvert Simons, whose best-known work was the 1934 essay *A Positive Program for Laissez Faire*. It started with the proposition that "the great enemy of democracy is monopoly in all its forms" and urged the elimination of all forms of monopolistic market power, including the breakup of large oligopolistic corporations and the application of antitrust laws to labor unions.[26]

A 1951 article by Milton Friedman in the Norwegian business periodical *Farmand,* which became a central mouthpiece of the Mont Pèlerin Society, laid out the case very clearly:

> Neo-liberalism would accept the nineteenth century liberal emphasis on the fundamental importance of the individual, but it would substitute for the nineteenth century goal of laissezfaire as a means

to this end, the goal of the competitive order. It would seek to use competition among producers to protect consumers from exploitation, competition among employers to protect workers and owners of property, and competition among consumers to protect the enterprises themselves. The state would police the system, establish conditions favorable to competition and prevent monopoly, provide a stable monetary framework, and relieve acute misery and distress. The citizens would be protected against the state by the existence of a free private market; and against one another by the preservation of competition.[27]

The postwar neoliberals were also concerned about restricting cross-national efforts by lobbying groups to limit competition. Criticizing the planning for Bretton Woods and the Keynes and White plans, Henry Simons commented that they were

> primarily concerned with exchange rates and not with stabilization of the purchasing power of either the dollar or the pound (or of Unitas or Bancor). While properly concerned about nationalistic exchange-control and its consequences for trade, these Reports [the official plans for the postwar world] have little to say about tariffs or about the trade restraints of private monopolies. Indeed, they explicitly accept "commodity agreements." Thus, real, fundamental planning for economic stability and international economic cooperation under less restricted trade seems to have bogged down completely, while international monopoly schemes are burgeoning and thriving all over the place. . . . We recognize at least vaguely the threat to world order and prosperity arising from beggar-my-neighbor policies in international economic relations. We do not recognize, save perhaps during total war, the threat to domestic order and prosperity arising from such policies on the part of functional groups organized to restrain trade or to secure special governmental restraints on their behalf.[28]

Maintaining open international trade and combating special interests were thus simply two sides of the same coin: both were concerned with ensuring that markets transmitted price signals correctly.

Taming Credit Cycles

Second, neoliberalism in its original incarnation was skeptical about finance and credit creation. Simons in particular was critical of bank-driven credit booms and wanted to think of ways of curtailing banking so that it would be socially useful rather than dangerous. He was the author of what became known as the Chicago Plan, under which the banking system's monetary and credit functions would be separated through the requirement of 100 percent reserves of government-issued money against customer deposits. New credits could only be made on the basis of retained earnings, again in the form of government-issued money. The plan would thus prevent any autonomous bank creation of money. It would make credit cycles impossible and eliminate the possibility of bank runs. In the aftermath of the 2008 Global Financial Crisis, the Simons proposals attracted new attention and were again frequently seen as an ideal, though practically unrealizable, way of preventing disruption resulting from financialization.[29]

Friedrich Hayek, as an economist in post-1918 Austria, made a similar critique of bank-based credit cycles in *Prices and Production*. He saw it as one of his goals to "prevent the periodic misdirections of production caused by additional credit," but then added: "We are still very far from the point when either our theoretical knowledge or the education of the general public provide justification for revolutionary reform or hope of carrying such reforms to a successful conclusion."[30]

The theme of bank credit and its dangers was less central to the 1938 Paris colloquium, but it did make an appearance in the contributions of some of the more radical participants. Thus the New Zealander J. B. Condliffe, a former League of Nations official and a trade economist, first complained about the pernicious influence of large financial groups, then explained: "The same is true of the expansion of credit. The fixed interest rates born of the war are unbearable for the masses. They have been imposed by people who have not had to make sacrifices for them and it is consumers who will suffer the consequences of them. It will be necessary to reduce monopolies, re-establish the equality of classes, notably in education."[31] Credit cycles could lead not only to mis-signaling in prices and thus a distortion in the allocation of capital, but also to direct burdens on many people.

Breaking the Link between Politics and Economics

Third, some participants in the discussions of the late 1930s were highly critical of the idea that economic motives alone drive politics. This line of thought was also presented as a diagnosis of what had gone wrong in interwar Germany. German nationalism had become, beginning in the mid-nineteenth century, focused too much on economics and too little on building a genuine national community.[32] *Homo oeconomicus* was not a desirable kind of analysis, but rather a fundamental problem for cultural and political stability.

The obsession with money and money-making—the commercialization of society—was in fact a standard and much talked-about and deprecated part of nineteenth-century life in the classical liberal period. Its supreme chronicler was Honoré de Balzac, above all in his later novels. The character Crevel in *La Cousine Bette* sets out the view of the century:

> Everyone makes the most of their money and plays with it as best they can. You are deceiving yourself, dear angel, if you believe that it is King Louis-Philippe who reigns, and he himself is not at all deceived about it. He knows like all of us that above the Charter there is the holy, the venerated, the solid, the kind, the gracious, the beautiful, the noble, the young, the all-powerful hundred sous coin! Now, my beautiful angel, money requires interest, and he is always busy collecting it![33]

But of course, the critique is even older than this. It is found in a very poignant form in Ecclesiastes (10:19): "money answereth all things."

The Generalization of Rules

Fourth, and perhaps most importantly, neoliberal and ordoliberal thinkers believed that general rules were needed as an antidote to particular measures that favored specified interests. Such rules, they argued, would also be the surest way of defeating the pernicious power of lobbyists, who had poisoned and delegitimated the political process.

The insistence on rules is often associated with Austrian economists, notably Friedrich Hayek, but it is worth noting that the idea of consistent (and time-consistent) rules being superior to discretion appears very early in the Chicago tradition, quite strikingly in a short 1931 book *The Problem of Unemployment* by Paul Douglas and Aaron Director.[34]

Hayek's most popular and influential book, *The Road to Serfdom*, written as a warning to the western Allies in the last phase of the Second World War, accurately identified that the Weimar Republic's interventionist approach, with its origins in wartime planning of *Kriegssozialismus*, created path dependency. The answer to any policy failure or setback was not an abandonment of the policy, but rather a more radical version of it. There was thus a ratcheting effect. Partial controls seemed ineffective, so the Nazis wanted a more extensive and more radically enforced system of control.[35] As Hayek put it:

> Both competition and central direction become poor and inefficient tools if they are incomplete; they are alternative principles used to solve the same problem, and a mixture of the two means that neither will really work and that the result will be worse than if either system had been consistently relied upon.[36]

A widespread response to the great financial crisis of 1931 was the imposition of capital controls, which drew the state further into micromanaging economic activity. Economic planning, as Hayek saw it, was inherently discriminatory: "It cannot tie itself down in advance to general and formal rules which prevent arbitrariness. . . . It must constantly decide questions which cannot be answered by formal principles only, and in making these decisions it must set up distinctions of merit between the needs of different people."[37]

The issue of arbitrariness applies in a particular way to the actual implementation of capital controls. They were instituted in both Austria and Germany starting in 1931—that is, before the onset of political dictatorship (Hitler came to power in January 1933, and in 1934 Austrian conservatives created the *Ständesstaat*). But dictatorship increased the means of enforcing controls. Hayek cites the German liberal Wilhelm Röpke to the effect that "while the last resort of a competitive economy is the bailiff, the ultimate sanction of the planned economy is the hangman."[38] If he had known Hitler's table talk at the time, he actually could have cited the dictator himself: "Inflation does not arise when money enters circulation, but only when the individual demands more money for the same service. Here we must intervene. That is what I had to explain to [economics minister and central bank president Hjalmar] Schacht, that the first cause of the stability of our currency is the concentration camp."[39]

Political decisions about who should benefit from the allocation of foreign exchange became arbitrary, with those developing the closest contacts with the regime benefiting most. The allocation of scarce raw materials was, in fact, the basis of Nazi economic planning, as Hayek recognized: "The controller of the supply of such raw material as petrol or timber, rubber or tin, would be the master of the fate of whole industries and countries."[40] In short, the planning laid the basis for widespread corruption.

Arbitrary too was the decision about who should be investigated for breaches of foreign-exchange regulations. In 1931, the German government imposed taxes and penalties on capital flight (the *Reichsfluchtsteuer*, or emigration tax). They were ineffective and were progressively tightened, with increasing penalties, including a death penalty after 1938. Until the end of 1938, these regulations were not—in their formulation—explicitly discriminatory, and they applied to all Germans. After 1933, however, they were used as an instrument especially against an ethnic minority, Germany's Jewish minority, in accordance with the Nazis' anti-Semitic program. The stereotypes about and behavior of this vulnerable minority reinforced one another. Facing mounting anti-Semitism, the Jewish population tried to move their capital out of many central European countries; as they fell afoul of new legislation to control speculation, they seemed to correspond to the stereotype of the "Jewish" speculator, and anti-Semitic governments then used reports of their actions to fan the flames of hatred. For instance, in Hungary, in the year before the introduction of anti-Semitic legislation in 1938, 112 out of 187 currency offenses were committed by individuals that the Hungarian authorities identified as Jewish.[41]

The administration of economic control was thus a central part of the fundamental and malevolent injustice of central European dictatorships. Awareness of what had gone wrong, not only institutionally and administratively but also intellectually, drove a reordering after 1945. In response to authoritarianism and dictatorship, some decisions were delegated to administrative authorities as a way of relieving the political burden on democracy, and of ensuring that those decisions were carried out competently and with respect for the law. The concepts of "delegation" and "mediated legitimacy" became key constraints on administrations.[42] Probably the best-known instances of such practices occurred in the context of constitutional courts and judicial review, and in establishing independent central banks. The banks' mandates were carefully constructed: the most famous of the laws surrounding the banks' founding, the German Bundesbank law, required the Bundesbank to support the economic policies of the federal government. Many—but not all—elements of neoliberalism were taken into European policy design after 1945, but only in part because of the influence of European neoliberals. More significantly, American planners and the US military, under the influence of the modified or second New Deal, propagated a vision of competition as the fundamental principle of regulation and thus a central feature of policy design during their post-1945 occupation regimes.[43] A key part of the neoliberals' vision was thus realized in the early postwar period, long before the Thatcher and Reagan "revolutions."

Neoliberalism after the Second World War

As democracy was rescued after 1945 in the framework of a liberal order in western Europe, the need for a new elaboration of liberalism seemed to fade, as did the usage of the term *neoliberalism,* which had never achieved much currency or political traction. The original debates and their circumstances were thus largely forgotten.

The word itself was mostly shelved until the late 1980s, when it took off again with the end of communism and the Iron Curtain. At this stage, many pioneers of neoliberalism did not use the term. It does not appear in Milton and Rose Friedman's 1980 popularization, *Free to Choose,* where instead the classic authors—above all Adam Smith—appear as the heroes. Neoliberals such as Walter Eucken or even Henry Simons are not mentioned. By the 1980s, Hayek thought that he should celebrate liberalism, not neoliberalism.[44]

But neoliberalism was resurfacing, in surprising contexts. The term *neoliberal* was being used by those who simply wanted to transcend what they thought of as antiquated traditions in their particular political milieu. In the United States, an influential group of modernizing Democrats called themselves neoliberals as a way to seek support beyond what presidential candidate Walter Mondale could garner from the traditional Democratic base: organized labor. Gary Hart, who almost took the presidential nomination in 1987 before he was derailed by a sex scandal, was part of this group, as were Senator Bill Bradley of New Jersey, Representative Richard A. Gephardt of Missouri, and probably the most powerful intellectual of the group, Senator Paul E. Tsongas of Massachusetts. A survey of American politics in 1985 concluded: "With exceptions, they support environmental protection, health and safety regulation, voting rights and civil rights, reproductive choice and the Equal Rights Amendment."[45] The philosopher Michael Novak commented that neoliberals "have a down-home sense of the way things work and they know that money being put into a sinking industry is either being put there through political favoritism or it is going to be wasted."

Neoliberalism's evolution and expansion as a concept was associated with a spillover of economic thinking into other disciplines, including law, sociology, psychology, and even, in some cases, history. Its central insight, derived from economics, put tradeoffs, externalities, and opportunity cost at the center of a calculus of behavior. The most obviously influential of these cognitive spillovers occurred in law.

In the 1980s, the application of a consumer welfare standard altered policy on competition: according to this argument, bigness did not constitute an abuse of power if it resulted in gains for consumers. This argument had already been at the center of the discussion of trusts in the nineteenth century and then of anti-trust litigation in the early twentieth century. In the most famous case—that of Standard Oil—New York State's initial investigation in 1879 concluded that the trust lowered rather than increased petroleum product prices for consumers.[46] The consumer welfare approach was revived in Chicago by theorists such as the economist Ronald Coase, the pioneer of the transactions approach to the nature of the firm, and above all by the legal scholar Aaron Director, who established the *Journal of Law and Economics* as a way of promoting a new synthesis of the disciplines. The most forthright statement of the case was probably in Robert Bork's *The Antitrust Paradox*.[47]

This intellectual turn undoubtedly had an immediate policy effect in halting the epochal Department of Justice antitrust case against IBM in

1981. That decision is rich in irony: it did not come soon enough to stop IBM from changing its controversial practice of bundling hardware and software for mainframe computers, which was at the heart of the Department of Justice case, when it came to the personal computer (PC). As a result, IBM let a small and almost unknown company develop PC software instead—and Microsoft, once it became a giant, had its own antitrust case dropped. The consumer welfare standard was informed by the microeconomics of networks in the old setting—as, for instance, in the case of Standard Oil, whose extensive network of pipelines entailed a decreasing marginal cost to provide service. This standard did not anticipate the full effects of the information technology revolution, in which decreasing marginal costs shrank to practically zero marginal cost and, in doing so, changed the economics of scale and the extent of monopolization.

The biggest push for a generalized academic adoption of the term neoliberalism in the humanities (and perhaps in some fields of social science) before the collapse of communism came from the massively influential Michel Foucault. In 1979 he gave a set of lectures at the Collège de France on "The Birth of Biopolitics," which were later transcribed from tapes and published posthumously—and much later translated into English.[48] Their central theme is the emergence of neoliberalism, depicted relatively sympathetically in an examination of German thought and of ordoliberalism. Foucault follows with a rather less sympathetic treatment of how, largely through the work of University of Chicago economists Theodore Schultz and Gary Becker, a new concept of personality developed. For this school, "everything for which human beings attempt to realize their ends, from marriage, to crime, to expenditures on children, can be understood 'economically' according to a particular calculation of cost for benefit."[49] The domain of economic theory was thus substantially broadened into an overall account of how human motivation can be shaped and human action and outcomes affected.[50]

Liberalism, in its traditional nineteenth-century sense, clearly delimited the private from the public. That distinction collapsed in times of emergency, when everything seemed to become public. But the differentiation was also strained when the private ceased to exist because it could be constantly altered or manipulated from the outside.

The key issue in analyzing the developments of the late twentieth century has lain for many historians in explaining how a rather peculiar doctrine, propagated by a few obscure think tanks, could become culturally hegemonic—that is, how such an idea could become contagious. Of the University of Chicago gurus, Becker was much more important in pushing the neoliberal orientation than Bork. It seemed that economic thinking had overreached itself and that all aspects of human behavior were now seen through an economic lens—that the economy was all that mattered. Bill Clinton's strategist James Carville captured this sentiment iconically in 1992: "It's the economy, stupid." But wasn't such an approach shallow and stultifying, and at odds with the richness and depth of human personality and motivation? After the collapse of communism in 1989–1991, for instance, freedom was increasingly defended as a road to prosperity and well-being rather than an end in itself—a move that irritated many Soviet-era dissidents, delighted some ex–Soviet bloc citizens, and was caricatured viciously by some Western observers as "bananas for everyone."[51]

The new social order might be understood as a synthesis of the idea of minimal state intervention with an assertion of personal freedom. The progressive commentator Michael Lind has a striking metaphor for how simultaneous campaigns by a college-educated "overclass" had demolished the post-1945 settlement. There was no conspiracy or cabal. As Lind puts it, "the libertarian economist James Buchanan did not meet with the Beat poet Allen Ginsberg halfway between Mont-Pèlerin and Haight-Ashbury in the 1960s to plot a transfer of power in all three realms of politics, economics, and culture."[52] In fact, Foucault himself, who had worked in Hamburg at the end of the 1950s and later taught at Berkeley, might well be considered the most influential intermediary between Californian bohemianism and German political-legal thinking. But doesn't that sort of interpretation overemphasize the role of an individual thinker?

Another interpretation treats the preeminent influence on economic and social behavior as emanating from a completely different academic discipline—behavioral psychology. That starting point is the basis for Shoshana Zuboff's massively influential diagnosis of contemporary capitalism as based on surveillance and manipulation. She sees the behavioralist B. F. Skinner as the critical figure in pushing for an engineering of behavior that would move from prediction to control. Technology could be used incrementally to reduce the scope for privacy—or as he put it, "The problem of privacy may, therefore, eventually be solved by technical advances."[53]

There had long been concern about marketing and behavior modification: indeed, in his 1934 tract, Henry Simons commented with horror how

> the possibility of profitably utilizing resources to manipulate demand is, perhaps, the greatest source of diseconomy under the existing system. If present tendencies continue, we may soon reach a situation where most of our resources are utilized in persuading people to buy one thing rather than another: and only a minor fraction actually employed in creating things to be bought.[54]

The world needed a theory about how sentiment could be changed, and Skinner became the instigator of this new intellectual practice that aimed for control of behavioral outcomes. He is oddly twinned with Hayek, who was castigated for insisting on a spontaneous or uncontrolled social order. When it appeared that the spontaneous could in fact be controlled, neoliberalism would break away from its original moorings.

The Global Financial Crisis and Fears of Capitalism

After 2008, critical discussion of neoliberalism reached a fever pitch. The new zeitgeist seems to have several origins. In part it appears to be a simple reaction to financial destabilization: in the same way that the First World War and its monetary aftermath seemed dislocating and unfair—and generated a ferocious reaction—the Global Financial Crisis engendered a belief that the system was rigged. Rescue mechanisms, too, are at the heart of the controversy. Governments and central banks supported large financial institutions because their collapse would be systemically endangering; in the eyes of many policymakers, there was a risk of repeating the Great Depression. At the same time, it became increasingly obvious that the small-scale losers—homeowners whose mortgages were underwater and employees who had lost their jobs—were not compensated because they were not systemically important.[55] And of course that seemed profoundly unfair.

But the Global Financial Crisis did not stand on its own as a singular event. It occurred precisely at a moment of gigantic technical and social transformation, and responses to it have been filtered through these new realities. On its own, the Global Financial Crisis would not have driven the new critique of capitalism. But when taken together, the aftermath of the financial crisis, the new economics of tech-driven change, and apocalyptic concerns brought about by the urgent need to confront climate and health challenges have generated a political environment in which the conventional process of testing and evaluating policy measures has been discredited as simply a byproduct of a technocratic neoliberal mindset.

Joseph Stiglitz has recently tried to defend what he calls "progressive capitalism," or left market economics, as the only creative and valuable alternative to what he sees as two illusory options that preserve key elements of neoliberalism: left liberalism (neoliberalism with a human face, as in the policy world of Tony Blair, Bill Clinton, and Barack Obama) or revived ethno-nationalism (the policy world of Donald Trump, Viktor Orbán, and Matteo Salvini).[56] But actually what he is arguing for—whether right or wrong—is really just what neoliberalism was originally all about.

Modern neoliberalism got its bad reputation from unleashing what looked like a new financialized capitalism, one celebrated by "market fundamentalists" who liked one-way bets in which they played a market casino and kept the gains when they won, but spread the losses to the corporations they worked for, and above all to taxpayers, when they lost. But the widespread narrative that the economic catastrophe of the 2007–2008 Global Financial Crisis was caused simply by the absence of regulation and control is wrong-headed. Financial behavior rapidly and regularly finds a way of circumventing regulation, and the existence of regulation gives a false impression of security. In that sense, there can never be enough regulation to produce complete stability.

Neither is it true that large international capital flows inevitably create a contagious and generalized crisis, though they may well make for more instability and localized disturbances. A world with no capital flows would also be a world in which there are serious macroeconomic dislocations because of the misallocation of capital. What produced the 2007–2008 crisis was the inadequately regulated interplay of large financial flows with excessively complex corporate bodies that had distorted both internal and external incentive structures. It was those structures that were in need of reform.

In fact, the sketch that Stiglitz has recently provided of an alternative "progressive capitalism" is remarkably similar to central elements in the original concept of neoliberalism. Stiglitz advocates for appropriately balancing markets, states, and civil society; applying science to produce innovation; curtailing monopoly power; and breaking the link between economic and political power. That was exactly the kind of program that the economists and intellectuals assembled in Paris for the 1938 Colloque Walter Lippman had in mind.

Old-School Neoliberalism as a Possible Model

As Stiglitz's programmatic statement suggests, a framework for managing economic processes can still offer a promising, optimistic vision of the future. In the circumstances of the 1930s, this new vision was conceived as an alternative to the planning fetishism of communists (five-year plans) and National Socialists (four-year plans), and above all to the doctrines of political control that both communist and fascist planning necessarily, and enthusiastically, required. In today's world, there is an equally urgent need for a new approach.

The four main features of the 1930s debates identified earlier are all acutely relevant to today's challenges. First, competition is required for continuing innovation, and regulatory action is required on both a national and a supranational level to prevent distortions of competition, including by tax policy. Second, financial booms and credit cycles produce dangerous distortions and require control through a monetary policy that minimizes price distortions, including in asset prices. Third, social identity cannot effectively be built solely on the basis of the promise of economic performance. And fourth, urgent collective tasks can be accomplished most effectively by presenting them as general problems to be solved within a framework of general laws rather than through particular interventions.

Capitalism does not inherently favor authoritarianism, any more than it can simply be held responsible for environmental destruction. It is worth remembering that much of the destruction of the past hundred years followed from central planning, that is, from non-democratic and non-market approaches to regulation. The genius of capitalism in the past—and today—is that it can produce answers to problems that often challenge the simple prescriptions of states, because capitalism offers a way of combining ideas and initiatives from very large numbers of people, penalizing dysfunctional behaviors, and rewarding useful innovation. Today the United States could channel its immense technical resources and abilities into developing ways to bind carbon dioxide or develop non-carbon sources of energy. Such technologies need to be encouraged through appropriate signals and rewards—in other words, through a price mechanism. A recent proposal signed by all former Federal Reserve chairs and twenty-seven Nobel Prize economists put a steadily rising carbon tax at the center of a viable path to environmental sustainability.[57] A more immediate sign of how innovation can work is the number of competing companies producing different types of vaccine in a quick response to the challenge of the coronavirus. But we should not rely on technocrats alone to run or regulate capitalism; we all need to be engaged in the business of making choices and decisions.

The 1938 vision is highly contemporary. Breaking the fashionable link between capitalism, on the one hand, and politics and the state, on the other, was and is still essential. The issues in the 1930s were abuse of corporate power and the sinister involvement of corporations in politics. In Italy and Germany, there was a partial synthesis of private business interests with the politics of fascism. This synthesis depended in part on corruption, and in part on shared ideology. There was also then a debate, analogous to today's, about the socialization of losses and the extension of stimulus or rescue packages. A working market order has to allow risks to be fully borne by those who are taking a bet: there should be no room for private activity or businesses that are too big, too complex, or too strategic to be allowed to fail. Transparent rules and processes are essential in order to limit, control, and punish corruption. It was exactly the separation of the two spheres—of political and economic activity—that made the British economist John Maynard Keynes so eager to assert that tyrannizing over a bank balance was preferable to tyrannizing over fellow citizens.

The issues of enforcing competition in the digital twenty-first century are even more urgent than they were in the mid-twentieth century. The economic effects of networks with zero marginal cost but ever-increasing returns of scale tend inexorably to produce a single, dominant supplier of a complex bundle of services and information—including the transmission of ideas. For this reason, some leading contemporary capitalists actually denounce the principle of competition. The malaise of today is not that we feel like victims of an anonymous market: we feel like victims of large corporations that have too much information about us and are thus too personal, while they themselves are not easily held accountable for mistakes, crimes, or frauds.

Micro-targeting was a central instrument of mid-twentieth-century totalitarianism, and it is also a feature of the untransparent algorithms that underpin contemporary surveillance capitalism. Businesses too, as in the 1930s, are increasingly attempting to use ideas as a way of marketing themselves and of controlling vast and opaque networks driven by emotion as much as interest. Opening up competition thus requires more general access to reliably generated information: in the twenty-first century, equal access to information will become as, or even more, important than equal access to physical resources.

The old-fashioned liberal—as well as the neoliberal—defense of capitalism was about freedom, not prosperity. The most fundamental freedoms involve thought and expression. The prosperity that might ensue was a byproduct, not the essence, of freedom. But asserting the centrality of freedom always raised a practical problem. In the real world, people did not seem to be free and had differing capacities for realizing freedom. In addition, they often did not consider themselves free and had different perceptions of their capacities to be free. Inequality, too, was a constraint on personal development in that it lowered individuals' abilities to actualize a greater potential and to increase their freedom.

Because of these problems, those who wanted to present a concrete program for improving the present moral order regularly framed their analysis by explaining what had gone wrong at some previous time. They sketched a caricature of an old, bad capitalism that would be replaced by a better and more open system. In the mid-twentieth century, many called that bad world Manchesterism, evoking Friedrich Engels's grim accounts of working conditions in the cotton mills or Charles Dickens's loathsome capitalists and utilitarians. Such critics emphasized that they were building a middle road between socialism and that old discredited Manchesterism, and elaborated the concept of a "social market economy." By the beginning of our millennium, the equivalent intellectual operation was to heap opprobrium on a cartoon version of neoliberalism.

Debates over neoliberalism are intrinsically bound up with discussions of globalization. Dani Rodrik highlighted a political trilemma: only two out of the three policy options of global economic integration, the nation-state, and democracy can be chosen. But this analysis is too simple.[58] Rodrik's formulation is based on an analogy with the classical macroeconomic trilemma or impossible trinity of fixed exchange rates, capital mobility, and autonomous monetary policy. But there are never completely free capital movements, there is always a home bias in capital allocation, exchange rates are never completely fixed, and monetary policy anywhere is influenced by monetary policy elsewhere. Rodrik's political economy model faces similar frictions and the choices are not absolute. A nation-state doesn't exist completely on its own, and democracy doesn't mean that people are free to choose absolutely anything that they might imagine. Democracies are ways of exercising choice among alternatives, not among multiple alternative universes. It often appears that if the stakes are too high in democratic decisions, the process is eroded and attacked.

These dilemmas emerge with special drama in cases that involve international debt, either private or public (there is, in practice, little distinction in emergency situations, because the impossible burdens of large amounts of private debt mean that the public sector steps in). A democracy might, for instance, decide that it does not want to repay its debt. That step has implications for future access to markets, and restraints—often through the creation of international order—allow for a more time-consistent strategy. International coordination mechanisms and the infrastructure of multilateralism are motivated precisely by the need to manage this type of tradeoff. They enable nations to work out how to make rational choices that will not have a harmful influence or effect on others.

Most essentially, unlike short-term crisis interventions, such an institutional structure opens up choices that extend longer into the future. It also influences how individuals behave, which in turn shapes group dynamics. For truly effective and binding choices to be possible, people need to be surrounded by real, not just virtual, networks that encourage them to think about long-term consequences. They need true and long-term friends, lovers, relations, and associates, not just Tinder dates who can be left-swiped away or Facebook pals who can be "unfriended." An immense amount of thought and effort is currently being put into developing defenses against trolls and systemic misinformation. The only way of countering that world in the long run is to emphasize what makes us truly human:

not fleeting, instant reactions, but a depth of commitment. Contentment, satisfaction, and dignity are the common goods—the non-priced goods—that we should produce, and they are global goods.

At the end of Keynes's *General Theory,* the great economist warns that those who consider themselves "practical men . . . are usually the slaves of some defunct economist." It is a very well-known quote; indeed, Hayek used it at the inaugural Mont Pèlerin meeting in 1947. One way of ending the servitude described by Keynes is by using the original intellectual DNA of neoliberalism to try to assess accurately what problems the defunct economists were addressing. The original vision of the 1930s neoliberals was a response to crisis and emergency thinking, to calls for exceptional measures. They were living in an era that demanded collective answers, but typical responses to that demand had been highly flawed. They tried to chart a path to longer-term credibility and sustainability based on simple and transparent principles.

As Hayek so wisely warned about overreliance on fuzzy concepts: "The important problems are in large measure obscured by the use of words which imply anthropomorphic or personalised explanations of social institutions."[59] Neoliberalism should not be taken as a personalized explanation of the world of early twenty-first-century institutions. Its original tenets might rather be considered an antidote to the multiple distortions and dystopias that poison the economic, social, and political vocabulary of our age.

13

Crisis

No vocabulary for globalization would be complete without the word *crisis*. It is a fine example of the inflationary diffusion of language, or when terms are used so indiscriminately and often that they lose meaning. Everything that globalization produces is now a crisis. For Reinhart Kosellek, the great historian of concepts, crisis has become "a structural signature of modernity."[1] Crisis, Paul Krugman said twenty years ago, is the price of globalization.[2] He was writing in the wake of the 1997 East Asian financial crisis, but the discussion of the ubiquity of crisis is not confined to finance and economics. The response to globalization can be a financial crisis, but also a political or social crisis, a moral crisis, a psychological crisis, a climate or environmental crisis, or even a medical crisis.

With the coronavirus pandemic in 2020, the term has circled back to its original usage, which was strictly medical. In ancient Greek medicine, and for those who taught it over millennia, a crisis was the point in the course of a disease when the patient either recovered quickly, or declined further and died. The Greek term *krisis* was derived from the word *krino*, to decide: it was a moment of decision, when a critical choice was made. Consider the use of the word in the following article on typhus fever in a European crisis year, 1848, when a bacterium was aggravating the social and economic misery, as well as the political turmoil. Robert Patterson, an Edinburgh physician, wrote of the fever:

The mind was in general tranquil, but, in some few cases, there was a tendency to incoherent talking, especially about the third, fourth, or fifth day, when, not unfrequently, considerable delirium occurred, before the critical evacuation took place. After a period of longer or shorter duration, generally upon the fifth, or from five to seven days, during which time the patient has been lying in a state much the same as described, he begins to experience a gradual remission of his sufferings. The skin becomes by degrees moister, until it is covered with copious perspiration. This diaphoresis is in general critical; sometimes it is ushered in by a severe rigor, while, at other times, it comes on more suddenly. It continues for a time most abundant, bedewing the face and hand with large drops of moisture, and saturating the bed-clothes, after which the patient feels quite relieved. The most common duration of this diaphoretic crisis is from three to six hours, sometimes much longer. I have seen it in some cases continue for upwards of forty-eight hours.[3]

Thomas Mann, one of many distinguished creative writers to use illness as a metaphor, concluded his 1900 epic breakthrough novel *Buddenbrooks* with an account of the death of the sole heir to the family dynasty, Hanno, from typhoid. His narrative echoes Dr. Patterson's description of the crisis of a disease, and brings to mind the "decision" inherent in the definition: "If [the patient] hears the voice of life and shies from it, fearful and reticent, if the memories awakened by its lusty challenge only make him shake his head and stretch out his hand to ward them off, if he flees farther down the path that opens before him now as a route of escape—no, it is clear, he will die."[4] In *The Magic Mountain,* Mann presented a tuberculosis sanatorium in the Swiss alps as a metaphor for a decaying European society on the brink of the First World War; later in the twentieth century, Susan Sontag would see the use of cancer as a metaphor as itself an indictment of the ills of American society. The disease was "a ruthless, secret invasion." Cancer, like tuberculosis in the nineteenth century, had been described as a process in which the body was consumed by "a sign of an inward burning."[5] But neither tuberculosis nor cancer, the great metaphors of the nineteenth and twentieth centuries, respectively, were diseases whose devastating progress contained a crisis.

In the aftermath of the Renaissance and the Reformation, the medical analogy began to be more widely applied, at first mainly in terms of spiritual crises, to describe transformations of people's souls that might lead to redemption or destruction. By the eighteenth century, the political application began to be contagious. In the transformative year 1776, Tom Paine in his *American Crisis* described how crises "produce as much good as hurt. Their duration is always short; the mind soon grows through them, and acquires a firmer habit than before. But their peculiar advantage is, that they are touchstones of sincerity and bring things and men to light which might otherwise have lain forever undiscovered. . . . They sift out the hidden thoughts of men, and hold them up in public to the world."[6]

Crises of course did not always or necessarily produce a good outcome. The charismatic actress Théroigne de Méricourt, who had led the triumphant march of the market women on the king's palace in Versailles in 1789, was later in the course of the French Revolution stripped naked and beaten by more radical revolutionaries. In the hospital, she was diagnosed as suffering from "revolutionary fever," and died demented in the asylum of Charenton.[7]

Crisis was an essential part of nineteenth-century culture, which wanted to celebrate its more optimistic variant. The great national histories of that age by Macaulay, Ranke, Sybel, Michelet, Thiers, and Taine were tales of how a nation was tested and then emerged triumphant.[8] Macaulay provided a model with his *History of England,* published in the revolutionary year 1848. The five volumes began with a discussion of "errors which, in a few months, alienated a loyal gentry and priesthood from the House of Stuart," and went on to describe a new settlement, or how "from the auspicious union of order and freedom, sprang a prosperity of which the annals of human affairs had furnished no example."[9]

By the middle of the nineteenth century, it was common to see the medical metaphor applied also to financial emergencies. Finance was obviously a system that depended on circulation, just like the human body. Thus 1847–1848 was interpreted as a financial crisis (one that produced social and political revolution) triggered by crop failures.[10] And there were lessons to be learned. The British civil servant Charles Trevelyan, who bore a heavy responsibility for the mass deaths of the Irish famine, wrote an attempted defense of his actions as assistant secretary to the British Treasury titled *The Irish Crisis:*

Unless we are much deceived, posterity will trace up to that famine the commencement of a salutary revolution in the habits of a nation long singularly unfortunate, and will acknowledge that on this, as on many other occasions, Supreme Wisdom has educed permanent good out of transient evil. If, a few months ago, an enlightened man had been asked what he thought the most discouraging circumstance in the state of Ireland, we do not imagine that he would have pitched upon Absenteeism, or Protestant bigotry, or Roman Catholic bigotry, or Orangeism, or Ribbandism, or the Repeal cry, or even the system of threatening notices and midday assassinations. These things, he would have said, are evils; but some of them are curable; and others are merely symptomatic. They do not make the case desperate. But what hope is there for a nation which lives on potatoes?[11]

At a very early point, then, the discussion of crisis merged with an interpretation—drawn from the medical analogy—that a crisis could present a learning experience or even an opportunity for redemption, and that politicians needed to use a crisis skillfully in order to accomplish their policy objectives. In normal times, reform would be blocked; during crises, new approaches may well be welcomed. This point is so obvious to modern observers of the political scene that they are impelled to project it backward. Many apparently reliable academic texts quote Britain's heroic wartime leader Winston Churchill, perhaps on the eve of the 1945 Yalta conference that divided Europe into East and West, giving the advice "Never waste a good crisis." This is an entirely fabricated urban legend: Churchill never said anything like this (nor did he regard the result of Yalta as something to celebrate).[12] The dictum is correctly attributed to Rahm Emanuel, the prospective chief of staff to President Barack Obama in 2008, who in discussions with the Bush administration over the financial crisis commented: "You never want a serious crisis to go to waste. And what I mean by that is an opportunity to do things that you think you could not do before."[13] Emanuel held out in particular the example of the 1970s oil price explosion, which in his view had not been correctly used to manage a transition to a more sustainable energy policy. He also pointed out how ideas needed to be drawn from both political parties.

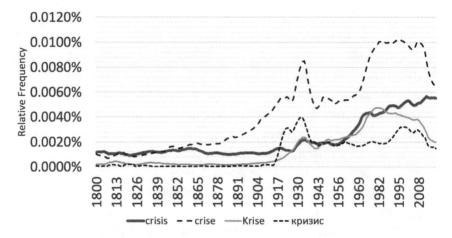

Figure 8. Frequency of the word *crisis* in printed books, 1800–2020, calculated for books published in English (crisis), French (*crise*), German (*Krise*), and Russian (*krizis*). Created from Google NGram Viewer.

The great economic crises of the past centuries prompted a much more intense discussion of the term *crisis*. An easy way of measuring the intensity of discussion is to take the frequency of the word in different languages, as measured by Google's NGram Viewer (see Figure 8). In every country, the Great Depression led to an intense preoccupation with the links between economic and financial crises on the one hand and political breakdowns on the other. The most explicit was the Soviet discussion of the Great Depression as a final crisis of capitalism—an idea that then took hold in many different languages.

Crisis as a way of understanding the world flared up again in the 1970s, with the breakdown of the par value system of Bretton Woods and the two oil shocks. Remarkably, in France, Germany, and Russia, use of the term *crisis* faded, while in English-speaking countries, it remained a powerful way of understanding the world. But crisis then became a permanent omnipresent preoccupation, and it couldn't any longer be the dramatic turning point of policy as in the original medical formulation. Koselleck explained how in the wake of crises in the 1960s and 1970s, the term "which once had the power to pose unavoidable, harsh and non-negotiable alternatives, has been transformed to fit the uncertainties of whatever might be favored at a given moment."[14]

Crises always produced inflections in the course of globalization. When Krugman was thinking about crises and globalization, he also reckoned that "integration may solve the problems it initially creates."[15] Capitalism and crises were also considered to be inseparable. Marxists famously analyzed capitalism as producing constant crises, but so did almost everyone else: no one thought that capitalism produced stability. Conventional liberal (that is, conservative) economists from the nineteenth century saw capitalism as moving through very regular business cycles, in which a crisis phase led to a cleanup and then new lending and a continuation of growth, but in new business areas. Not having crises would make capitalism undynamic. Joseph Schumpeter systematized that view in his theory of capitalism as a continuous process of creative destruction.

There have been, from time to time, bigger and more all-encompassing crises that have damaged far more than inefficient businesses; they have destroyed political and social order. Some major crises, above all the Great Depression, prompted widespread deglobalization. But many other crises, especially those that involved major supply shocks, with widespread scarcities and rocketing prices, highlighted the need for increased global contacts, with access to resources provided from great distances, as a way of alleviating distress. Thus the 1848 crisis launched what historians generally refer to as the first era of modern globalization, and the 1970s drove a new sort of globalization, with an extensive dismantling of barriers to capital mobility, as well as increased trade.

During the 1840s, the world experienced a powerful negative supply shock. The middle of the decade looked both like a classical hunger or subsistence crisis of the ancien régime, as well as a modern business-cycle downturn coupled with a financial and banking crisis. In this sense, it was both an eighteenth-century crisis and a twentieth-century crisis, which has led Jonathan Sperber to call it a "crisis of transition."[16] The food crisis followed from bad weather and poor harvests, with the weather leading additionally to crop diseases, most famously the potato blight. Most people were spending from two-thirds to three-quarters of their income on food. From 1845 to 1847 prices soared, especially in central Europe and France. In Ireland, some 80 percent of the 1846 potato crop was destroyed by *Phytophthora infestans*. There was thus a quite generalized supply shock. The financial crisis came as speculators bet on continually rising prices in 1847, and were then surprised both by the actual harvest (which was abundant) and by grain imports.

Policy measures augmented the severity of the shock, providing a powerful illustration of the Nobel Prize–winning economist Amartya Sen's proposition that famines are man- (or policy-) made.[17] The most stunning example was in Ireland, where the historical consensus is that British doctrinaire laissez-faire liberalism led to the disaster.[18] Charles Trevelyan was a perfect embodiment of the British official mindset. The Whig "ideologue" (Cormac O'Grada's term) Charles Wood, chancellor of the Exchequer, thought that "Providence and foresight" ought to have been exercised by all classes in Ireland, including "those who have to suffer the most." But in the view of the British officials, the greatest evil of all was the neglect of the destitute by "those who in their several neighbourhoods" were given the duty to "alleviate the sufferings of the poor."[19] A new twist to that story was recently given by the historian Charles Read, who showed that the fiscal stance of the British government, with higher taxes on small and medium farmers and above all traders, gave the final push: driven into bankruptcy, these entrepreneurs emigrated, and the supply chain broke down.[20] An Irish patriot who emigrated to the United States concluded: "No sack of Magdeburg, or ravage of the Palatinate, ever approached in horror and desolation to the slaughters done in Ireland by mere official red tape and stationery, and the principles of political economy."[21]

The economic and social breakdown led to a political flashpoint, with contagious revolutionary movements spreading from Paris and Palermo all over central Europe in 1848, after the worst effects of the food crisis had ended. The combination of the economic crisis and the failure of the political reform movement generated a new wave of emigration from Europe (which also helped to raise living standards there). German-speaking central Europe experienced especially high rates of migration. In poor areas such as Scandinavia with high levels of emigration, living standards rose more quickly than in poor areas with little emigration: in making this observation, the economic historians Kevin O'Rourke and Jeffrey Williamson contrasted Sweden with Portugal.[22]

The crisis was also followed by a wave of monetary expansion, pushed to some extent by the discovery of gold (the Californian gold rush of 1849) and in part by financial innovation, as France and central Europe experimented with new banks on the model of the French *crédit mobilier.* In consequence, very quickly, Europe looked much less likely to experience again the simultaneous shift to political revolution.

Trade liberalization—which was given a model in the form of the 1860 Anglo-French agreement (the Cobden-Chevalier pact)—as well as international capital movements and migration, all took off after the political revolutions of 1848, although trade had already grown substantially before 1860.[23] In particular, events of the 1840s had laid the foundation for a wave of institutional adaptations that would help to coordinate the many small states' efforts to deal with flows of money and people. These events included the creation of nation-states in Europe, with new constitutions, notably in Germany and in Italy; the administrative reform of the Habsburg Empire culminating in the *Ausgleich* (compromise) of 1867 between Austria and Hungary; and the establishment of the Austro-Hungarian Dual Monarchy. The US Civil War and the opening of Japan with the Meiji restoration can also be seen in this context of nation-building. Indeed there are linkages with the European crisis. In 1854 emigration from Germany surged to a peak (250,000) in precisely the year that Kansas had been declared open to free settlement. The surge of German and Scandinavian immigration into Kansas ensured that Kansas would become a free and not a slave-owning state. In this way migration undid the careful constitutional compromise of the Kansas-Nebraska Act, and helped set the stage for the US Civil War.

Friedrich Engels in his 1895 foreword to Marx's *Class Struggles in France* wrote how it had become clear to Marx in 1850 that "the world trade crisis of 1847 had been the true mother of the February and March revolutions, and that the industrial prosperity which had been returning gradually since the middle of 1848 and attained full bloom in 1849 and 1850 was the revitalising force of a restrengthened European reaction."[24] It's not clear that "reaction" is really the best way of describing the new and quite revolutionary form of governance that emerged in the 1850s and 1860s. The original reactionaries—like Radowitz, the garderobier of King Friedrich Wilhelm IV's "medieval fantasies"—faded.[25] They were replaced by ambiguous figures like Louis Napoleon (Napoleon III) or Otto von Bismarck: modernizers who built a world in conformity with a new logic, one implied by the word *crisis.*

Fast-forward about 120 years, to the 1970s. The trigger of the 1970s Great Inflation was a negative supply shock emanating from (mostly Middle Eastern) oil-producing countries. It occurred against a background of currency disorder: the par value system collapsed in August 1971, and the attempt to restore it in December at the Smithsonian conference was unconvincing. Since petroleum prices were conventionally quoted in dollars, oil producers at first wanted to protect the real value of their exports, and then—by 1973—realized that increasing oil prices could be an economic as well as a political weapon. There was thus a new "oil nationalism." In 1974, the oil revenues of the Organization of the Petroleum Exporting Countries (OPEC) tripled to $108 billion, accounting for an eighth of all world exports. All the major industrial countries were heavily dependent on oil imports. The higher price might be regarded as the imposition of a new (wealth- and income-reducing) tax. The industrial countries mostly decided not to adjust immediately and instead to accommodate the shock. That cushioning response pushed inflation higher. It rose to 11.0 percent in the United States in 1974 (and then, after a second oil shock, to 12.0 percent in 1980), and to higher levels in some other countries: in the United Kingdom, consumer price index (CPI) inflation in 1975 was 24.2 percent, and in 1980, 18.0 percent.

The outcome altered the attitudes of governments toward capital mobility, which had been seen with distrust in the postwar settlement (as a legacy of the 1930s). In fact, the international financial system was the key to the strategy designed by Henry Kissinger to contain the oil producers: if they could be encouraged to deposit their surpluses through international banks, they would be brought into the system. That argument was made explicitly at the first international summit of what was then the G5 in Rambouillet in 1975.[26]

The experience of the 1970s also altered the stance of major governments toward traditional Keynesianism and interventionism. It appeared that the traditional Keynesian framework of the Phillips curve was wrong, and that higher levels of inflation (if anticipated or expected) would simply produce price increases but no output gains or reductions in unemployment. The first to move in this direction were center-left governments, the UK Labour government of James Callaghan, Jimmy Carter's Democratic administration, and especially Helmut Schmidt's SPD-liberal coalition in Germany.

The legacy was inherited—and considerably expanded—by center-right governments, above all those of Reagan and Thatcher. James Callaghan's 1976 Labour Party conference speech was subsequently described as the "words which effectively buried Keynes."[27] He set out a radically new doctrine, in words that had in fact largely been penned by his son-in-law, the London *Times* journalist Peter Jay, and which Jay himself then wrote of as "the most breathtakingly frank public pronouncement since St Paul's First Epistle to the Corinthians." As he put it, "Britain has lived for too long on borrowed time, borrowed money, borrowed ideas. . . . We used to think that you could spend your way out of a recession, and increase employment by cutting taxes and boosting Government spending. I tell you in all candour that that option no longer exists, and that in so far as it ever did exist, it only worked on each occasion since the war by injecting a bigger dose of inflation into the economy, followed by a higher level of unemployment as the next step."[28] That was the story of stagflation. The British retreat marked a recognition that the state was not in a good position to decide the relative merits of the pay claims of various competing groups (teachers versus nurses versus police officers).

The late 1970s constitute the hinge of the twentieth century, the moment when the world moved decisively into a new phase of globalization. In China, Deng Xiaoping began a series of reforms that introduced the principles of the market. The year 1979 began the Iranian Revolution, when the shah was overthrown and fled Teheran on January 16. In March 1979, some members of the European Community (without the participation of the United Kingdom) launched the European Monetary System, a stepping stone on what would be the road to the most problematic aspect of European integration: the creation of a monetary union. On October 6, 1979, the chair of the US Federal Reserve Board, Paul Volcker, announced a dramatic interest-rate hike in a bid to kill inflation. And on May 3, in a general election in the United Kingdom, the Conservatives won a forty-three-seat majority, ousted the Labour government of James Callaghan, and installed Margaret Thatcher as prime minister.

The supply shock of the 1970s thus gave a dramatic fillip to the notion of global opening, or globalization, and to a challenging of state capacity (but not to any substantive rollback in the size of the state as measured by the public sector's share of national income). International migration increased, trade expanded with the formation of complex supply chains, and financial intermediation exploded. The crisis had a transformative impact.

But all these crises—especially the profound transformations—also engendered a sense of bewilderment. The proliferation of the language of crisis itself constituted a crisis. The original clear meaning of a medical point of decision had been replaced by uncertainty, multiplicity of choice, and indecision. A French sociologist, Edgar Morin, the major theorist of complexity, concluded that in the twentieth century, every domain was haunted by the idea of crisis: capitalism, society, the couple, the family, values, youth, science, law, civilization, and humanity.[29] As Koselleck describes the trajectory of the term: "Such a tendency towards imprecision and vagueness, however, may itself be viewed as the symptom of a historical crisis that cannot as yet be fully gauged."[30] Crises might well still produce new or productive responses, but as a term of analysis, *crisis* had metastasized.

14

Recoining the Words in Our Lexicon

States (and political institutions) are continually challenged, and are sometimes overwhelmed. Trust erodes. And terms reach the limit of their usefulness. Globalization always threatened to push such a corrosion of language, and the coronavirus pandemic is just the latest manifestation of a global challenge that has made us rethink the fundamentals. Today we need quick and radical rethinking about how states can be—will be—reconfigured or recoined.

Humans use particular words to describe the phenomena they observe, but at the same time they are hardwired to look for rules that are generalizable, preferably global or universal. Those attempting to cope with an evolving global society in the early nineteenth century tried to find such universal rules, only to realize that their goals could be achieved only in a national setting. A great deal of the discussion about globalization, then, became about what could be done nationally, and what protective mechanisms might be powerful enough in the face of vast external trends, forces, and threats. Socialism was a rejection of international capitalism, but it turned out—whether it was concerned with redistribution or with planning—to be also heavily dependent on a national setting, and as a result obliged to renounce its internationalist heritage. The problem of universalizability of rules thus remains, and looks even more acute: how will we organize ourselves across borders in a world that is ever more complex and interconnected, but where there are also increasing complaints related to globalism, technocracy, neoliberalism, or capitalism?

For a few decades, after the middle of the twentieth century, it appeared as if some rich countries in western Europe, North America, and Japan had reached a dynamic but stable equilibrium. Starting in the 1970s, however, that rather complacent and self-satisfied world has been torn apart by a new wave of globalization. The pandemic of 2020 has given a final push to demands for a new ordering. Globalization has now changed. There are more restrictions on the movement of physical factors—goods and people—but immaterial factors now flow through a rapidly growing "weightless economy" in a process of informational globalization.

Languages of globalization, in particular, use terms to make comparisons between societies and advance or block institutional adaptations. The languages are also about money, which becomes a ubiquitous translator, transforming goods, services, and promises into new and changing variants. Thinking about the history of terms, then, may be the equivalent of using modern distributed-ledger technology (Bitcoin is perhaps the best-known example) to verify transactions and secure both the value and the liquidity of our conceptual assets.

The twin antagonists of capitalism and socialism are now merging or converging. Both originally were conceived as helping people to give inputs, information, in a decentralized system of allocation in which spontaneous needs and wishes could be fulfilled. Both turned destructive when they produced concentrations of power—concentrations that governmental systems were supposed to regulate and control, but in practice often made only more oppressive. The search for a deconcentrated and decentralized framework for interaction looks like a reversion to an earlier dream—such as that offered in the early nineteenth century by Henri de Saint-Simon, who was simultaneously the ur-socialist and the ur-capitalist.

Here then is a manifesto, a guide to the post-coronavirus world, with a roadmap for how new social and political networks will form, largely spurred on by a radical change in the way we think of economic relations and the use of money. It might now be possible to realize parts of an old dream. Let's call the modern version *socapitalism*.

The Potential of Socapitalism

Much of the discussion about national versus global turns out to be a reflection on what can be done with money. Money is much more central to the debate about how globalization is managed than we usually think. Over the past two centuries—in other words, in the modern age of globalization—money has been a way of establishing national economic systems subject to some public control. But in the second half of the twentieth century a new order was established in which the money and the payments system of one country—the United States—were the center of international linkages. The position of the dollar became the key driver of the impression that money is unfair, and a tool of hegemony, and that genuine multilateralism is consequently impossible.

The most obvious problems highlighted by the pandemic are rising inequality in many countries, exacerbated by lack of confidence in public authority on both the national and global levels. Mistrust is coupled with bewilderment and often skepticism about fundamental facts and theories about how the world is connected and interconnected. There is an urgent need to understand why inequalities arise. But we have the technology to know more, learn more, and do more. The challenge is to harness those possibilities by creating new connections and an extended and unconventional sociability. These questions of unfairness have haunted every political debate of the past millennia. None of the issues debated here are fundamentally new—can there be new answers?

As I discussed earlier, the story of globalization is a story punctuated by dramatic conceptual changes, with periodic additions to and modifications of the lexicon of terms used to describe these ideas. The surge of new concepts at the beginning of the nineteenth century, and a further surge in the early twentieth century, are now being repeated. A striking feature of the current world is that there is an ever-increasing amount of global communication, but it is surprisingly harder (rather than easier) to obtain accurate information on many issues central to policy dilemmas. Thomas Piketty's 2020 book following up on his best-selling *Capital in the Twenty-First Century* highlights the remarkable fact that for all their statistical techniques and computational resources, modern governments and central banks are less good at collecting data on the distribution of wealth and on inequality than they were before the 1970s: authorities have not developed "the tools needed to follow the internationalization of wealth."[1] The United States is still one of the world's richest and most innovative societies, but has failed miserably in handling the informational challenges needed to tackle, say, the COVID-19 pandemic.

The major initial economic shocks that have followed from the COVID-19 pandemic have been traumatic: unemployment quickly rising to levels unknown since the Great Depression, businesses closing, disruptions of supply chains, food scarcities even as farmers do not know what to do with their crops, artists without audiences and incomes, bankrupt colleges and universities, hospitals shutting, and cities and local governments collapsing because of tax shortfalls. The globalized world is vanishing as poor countries dependent on an export-led development model see their markets disappear. Every traditional assumption about work no longer makes sense. Uncertainty is pervasive: even when a solution, a vaccine or an anti-viral drug, is found for this particular virus, we will long live in fear of a new sort of pandemic and new contagions.

This most recent crisis has shone a harsh analytical light on inequalities—not only in income, but also in access to medical facilities, food, and housing that is not cramped and (in a pandemic) unsafe. More fundamentally, it highlighted a skills divide, in which skilled workers could mostly function effectively (and be paid) in remote home offices, while unskilled workers (often migrants or ethnic minorities) were laid off or required to work in hospitals, public transportation, supermarkets, meat-processing plants, and other places where social distancing was difficult or impossible to achieve.

Optimists see a new tech-based dynamism working over a longer term: schools and universities that are more accessible because of remote learning that can be scaled up; or telemedicine delivering a better quality of care in a more evenly and equitably distributed way. But even the optimism just adds to our bewilderment, because we do not know how to bridge the gap between the dismal present and any kind of future hope.

The answer to increasing inequality is often held to lie in more, or more effective, taxation to allow a greater measure of redistribution. Fiscal needs in the wake of the coronavirus give this argument additional force. But that solution only tackles one part of the problem: the greater and underlying issue has to do with the provision of opportunities and skills, and integration of diverse populations with differing cultures, where individuals and groups often have more in common with people thousands of miles away than those in their own neighborhood.

How can a political process that is everywhere already under severe strain respond to the challenge? Before the virus, four starkly opposed binary choices set the terms of every debate: globalization or return to the nation-state; capitalism or socialism; technocracy or populism; multilateralism or geopolitics. These debates are now outdated. In each case, there is a need to move to something else. Perhaps the increasingly popular prefix *post* helps: *post-globalization* rather than *deglobalization; post-national* rather than *renationalization; post-capitalist* in combating large concentrations of capital; *post-socialist* in escaping from the limits of the nation-state inherent in traditional socialism; *post-technocratic* in allowing everyone to be a technocrat; and *post-populist* in the sense that the elevation of "the people," or "the real people," seems surreal and destructive to everyone else (who is unreal)? Technology, too, allows new connections that can build a new multilateralism, one that won't founder on the rocks of geopolitics.

The beginnings of a societal shift are already present, and may be traced in particular to new attitudes toward money, set in motion by an information-technology revolution and the application of artificial intelligence. For a long time, money seemed to be simply something created and regulated by the state, and used by people for trade, and to hedge against future uncertainty. Now we are beginning to see quasi-currencies that we ourselves are creating through selling information. It seems clear that money is going to be emancipated from the state. There is a financial revolution already in the works that is upending many conventional theories about how money and banks work, a revolution that promises to play a transformative, emancipatory role. Citizens of the world, unite: you have nothing to lose but your change. Or, as Shakespeare's proto-populist Jack Cade put it: "I thank you, good people:—there shall be no money."[2]

Reinventing the State by Rethinking Money

Money has always been a problem.[3] Conventionally, we understand money as having different functions, a jack of all trades. Economics textbooks tell us that it is a means of exchange, a unit of account, and a store of value. It is worth picking apart these elements. We are used to multi-purpose tools in our daily life that do not accomplish all the jobs with the same measure of effectiveness and efficiency—though perhaps the iPhone, capable of doing a multitude of tasks, from photography and recording to a vast range of digital services, marks a new departure. Alarm clocks connected to coffee makers never did make very good coffee, and couldn't be carried around easily when traveling. Economists have a rule that formalized this insight, named after the Dutch economist Jan Tinbergen, who said that each target required its own instrument. If money is supposed to have three targets, it may not be surprising that it does not accomplish all of them equally well.

Dissatisfaction with existing money—an inevitable consequence of imperfect multifunctionality—has prompted innovation. At the moment, we are living through a process of very rapid technological transformation, with artificial intelligence and big-data analysis being implemented in many different areas of life. It would be unrealistic to expect these transformations not to affect something as ubiquitous and problematic as money.

Money also has an inherently contentious relationship with government activity. Very often, governments have taken on themselves the task of standardizing units of measurement, or as economists would describe it, laying the basis for a currency's "unit of account" role. This may be because money represents a wonderful fiscal mechanism, or way of extracting revenue from a population. The origins of modern coins in Europe are often attributed to the organization of the military adventures of Philip of Macedon and his son Alexander the Great. In order to feed large armies moving across occupied territories, the rulers gave the troops tokens with an intrinsic value that could be exchanged for provisions, while at the same time imposing a tax on the occupied peoples that had to be paid in those tokens—thereby forcing the occupied peoples to use them for trade.

Governments with liabilities had and have a powerful motive to alter the relationship of the unit of account and make the currency that they had to pay out more valuable. *Crying down,* or debasing the coinage, was standard practice for rulers in early modern Europe.

From a very early period, money also played a role in cross-border transactions. Gold coins struck by Roman emperors, for example, can be found in archaeological sites as far away as Sri Lanka, Vietnam, and coastal

China. Money traveled long distances and into utterly unfamiliar cultures. So a crucial part of cross-border negotiation has always been the exchange rate, the equivalence of two different units of account.

Finally, money is a store of value. Indeed, it can be thought of as a kind of memory: a way of recording that I have a claim on something. But valuable objects don't always stay valuable. The New Testament famously instructs the disciples not to "lay up for yourselves treasures on earth, where moth and rust destroy and where thieves break in and steal; but lay up for yourselves treasures in heaven, where neither moth nor rust destroys and where thieves do not break in and steal. For where your treasure is, there your heart will be also" (Matthew 6:19–21). This may be both prudent and prudential advice, on the superiority of internalized claims.

After the economic shock of the coronavirus pandemic, money was expected to do even more. Some Federal Reserve officials, for instance, began to wonder whether monetary policy should not be repurposed to tackle social and racial inequality.[4]

There are thus differing dimensions of the monetary problem: some political or fiscal, some commercial, and some property-related. The strains that inevitably result from these various uses means that there is an incentive to innovate, and to think of new ways in which different functions can usefully be bundled together, combined, or even synthesized. So far, we've seen a replacement of banks as intermediaries with new and more open (more democratic) payment platforms. This shift will have major consequences for the way we approach politics, because money has long been intricately involved in constructing the language of the modern state and its politics.

Some previous episodes in monetary history may give a sense of the way in which innovation disrupts and requires new forms of organization. In a small community, the provision of goods and services to other members of the community is often treated as a sort of gift-giving exercise, in which there are very clear, but also usually not explicitly formulated, rules of reciprocity. If I give someone a piece of meat, I may hope that he will shoe my horse. Or if I ask someone to grind or mill my grain, she may expect to keep part of it. By contrast, money as a means of exchange is indispensable when it comes to payments over long distances. It is about fixing remote relationships—we could call that *functional memory*—between people who have no natural or immediate relationship with each other. It is a language that tries to remove distance.

In Europe, in the late Middle Ages, the four-party bill of exchange was introduced as a way of making payments over long distances. It seemed such an ingenious instrument that at some point, weird conspiracy theories surfaced about its origins. But the classic four-party bill depended on some degree of familiarity with the other parties, and in particular on the existence of trust over long distance. A merchant in Venice would present an instrument of obligation bought in Venice from someone with whom he regularly did business and payable in London by a correspondent of the Venetian issuer of the instrument. That correspondent would look at the paper presented and also at the presenter: he would need to assure himself both that the document was genuine, and that the instrument had not been stolen in the course of the long journey by someone who was not permitted to use it.

Such bill exchanges would have been rather limited operations, and actually not much of an improvement on a barter transaction, if it had not been possible to develop a market in which bills were traded. The bill really needed a platform in order to become a truly powerful financial instrument. Trade fairs were a way of bundling and clearing the transactions involved in the existing bills, and they developed into enormous affairs. The Spanish fair, at Medina del Campo, operated from 1421 to 1606. As Spain declined economically, the central coordinating function was increasingly taken over by the Lyons fair, and then by the one in Geneva. These fairs were a platform for transactions. Business was conducted publicly, and the reputations of individual merchants would be exposed to intense and general scrutiny.

Central banking as it is conceived in the modern world developed out of a need to provide support at the time of panic. The idea was that a large institution, with a special mandate from the government, could take a longer-term view and discount or buy assets—bills—for which there existed no market liquidity, but for which there was some confidence in the assets' long-term value. The new function was taken on in the nineteenth century by two institutions in particular, the Banque de France and the Bank of England, institutions originally established to manage the government's debt (the debt was in effect sold to the shareholders of these banks, who were compensated by a license to do other kinds of business). At the beginning, it is not clear that the Bank of England knew what it was doing. In the panic of 1825, it had been exceptionally enterprising, but the directors of the bank did not consider their action a long-term model. In 1866, after the collapse of a very large and reputable London bank, Overend, Gurney, and Company, the Bank of England repeated that sort of instinctive market support. The influential liberal periodical the *Economist* then set out a theory of how the bank was underpinning the whole London market. A bank director wrote to the *Economist* to argue that he did not consider the bank to be acting in that way. But the *Economist*'s editor, Walter Bagehot, who had written the original article (he wrote much of the content of the paper), fired back with an extensive treatment—one that quickly became a manual of central banking. It was adopted as a guide by Germans thinking about how to manage money in the newly established German Empire, and then by other monetary reformers, including the designers of the Federal Reserve system.

In the new world of banks, and then of central banks that acted as a kind of support, the operations of the bill market were no longer visible. The central bank was designed to be in a position to know the secrets of the banks without divulging them. There was no longer a platform, but instead hidden operations in a black box that operated on confidence.

Eventually, an awareness grew that the information that was embedded in the bill of exchange constituted a valuable resource in itself. Individual bills were meaningless, but an overview of the aggregation of exchanges could give an accurate picture of what goods and in what quantities were imported and exported by a particular country.

The Bank of England survived by keeping its promise to convert currency into gold. But was that promise really needed for the operation of a monetary system? Of course not, as intelligent critics began to point out. The most brilliant of those economic writers, the Scot John Law, persuaded the French monarchy to adopt a paper currency scheme that he thought superior to the Bank of England's model at a moment when France was financially depleted by war. The experiments in paper money were accompanied by an emphasis on the overall public good of providing a stable currency to meet a general need for secure and transparent payments. They ended by looking like diabolic manipulations, which Goethe then attributed to his demon Mephistopheles.

Discussion of paper currency was overshadowed by its failures; only in the later years of the twentieth century did an institutional system emerge that secured price stability.[5] During the twentieth century, the most iconic inflationary event was not the most severe or extreme hyper-inflation that occurred in Hungary after the Second World War, but the hyper-inflation that crippled Germany following the First World War. There is an irony in that the inflation began with the financing of wartime debt under a treasury secretary, Karl Helfferich, who was an economist and Germany's foremost expert on money. His textbook on money, *Das Geld*, went through many editions. At the heart of the argument of this pre-war book was the idea that paper money was in theory more stable than a metal-based commodity currency, but that it would lead to increased political conflict as debtors who would benefit from increased amounts of money in circulation (because their debts would be worth less in real terms) fought creditors who wanted a stable or restricted money supply. Helfferich concluded that "the fight over monetary value would more than any other clash of economic interests lead to a demoralization of economic and social life."[6] Helfferich's prediction played out with uncanny accuracy.

Paper money became associated with fiscal management because it was issued by governments or by central banks that held government debt as a backing for their liabilities. It was in effect nationalized, even though cross-border payments remained an important function of money. Because abuse was easy, paper money only worked effectively if it existed in a clearly defined territorial framework in which states could enforce penalties on counterfeiters or forgers, but also manage the money as part of a fiscal regime.

The precise identification of a currency with a country is a relatively recent phenomenon, dating to the establishment of nation-states in the nineteenth century. At the same time as a doctrine of ethno-linguistic nationalism started to be popular—in the wake of Johann Gottfried Herder's influential 1772 essay "Treatise on the Origin of Language"—its advocates started to see that money as well as language was a way of tying together a people.

In the nineteenth century, many governments pushed to establish national currencies.[7] The innovation was so successful that by the late twentieth century, everyone assumed that this was simply the natural order of things. But the move initially aroused a formidable pushback. In France, all kinds of coinage—mostly from the ancien régime, but also foreign coins—were circulating promiscuously until the early 1840s. Then the government tried to drive out the non-national money and make the franc central to the state. The numismatist Édouard Lelièvre de Lagrange described the action as "the war of Paris, which wants to absorb everything, against the departments wishing to preserve the little they have left."[8]

Coins and their diversity were also a mark of social division. The poor dealt with a miscellany of poor-quality coins, often with copper and silver mixtures, while the rich exchanged beautifully minted gold and silver. Poor people giving change in their own poor coins became a favorite trope of authors who wanted to point out the severity of class divisions. There was no or little interoperability of the monetary exchanges between social classes. Advocates of a nation based on popular or democratic consensus saw a unified coinage system as a way of promoting social cohesion within the nation's political framework.

The piece of information that was bundled together with money in this era was about national identity, and about social coherence within the nation. All of that, in turn, was associated with the idea that ultimately the payments promised in a monetary system depend on some fiscal capacity—an ability to raise future taxes. Otherwise the bundling becomes incredible, and people can no longer rely on their monetary promises. In the midst of the European debt crisis, the Belgian economist Paul de Grauwe stated the traditional case quite simply as a critique of the European monetary integration project: "The Euro is a currency without a country. To make it sustainable a European country has to be created."[9]

By the end of the twentieth century, non-national money looked as if it was making a comeback. First, the US dollar had become a near universal currency, with the overwhelming majority of international trade conducted in dollars. Central banks, too, held primarily dollar reserves. Then Europe, in part because of worries about the consequences of dollar preeminence, developed its own version of a cross-border currency.

The national era in money was drawing to a close at the same time as a technological revolution gave rise to radically new methods of addressing the problem of a cross-border language or memory. This insight offers a key to understanding financial evolution after the crisis of 2007–2008.

One consequence is the unbundling of the apparently solid historical link between money, on the one hand, and monetary stability and government fiscal management, on the other. Experiments to tackle the economic fallout from the coronavirus pandemic through large central bank stimulus programs, promised for long time periods, risk a new vulnerability and an oscillation between deflationary and inflationary dangers. It is likely that the world will demand a new monetary revolution.

As money is unbundled into different functions, with new platforms of exchange, where is innovation most likely to occur? One prediction: where states are weak and not trusted, and consequently state promises are not seen as highly credible. In those cases, it is much more attractive, and much more urgent, to unbundle fiscal and monetary action. By such criteria, the revolution is likely to occur fastest in quite poor countries—in Africa, or in former Soviet republics. The new technical developments offer a new possibility for leapfrogging ahead, from poverty and institutional under-development to institutional complexity and the chance for innovation and prosperity.

Another prediction looks at already well-developed industrial societies. It is in that environment where society is most divided into communities of interest that do not need to exchange much across groups, and perhaps do not want to associate with groups that have different social or cultural values. In highly modernized and individualized societies, where the promise of social cohesion means less, being able to separate peacefully into different groups may become a way of avoiding clashes and conflict. Currencies will establish communities, bound together by exchanges of information. We will unbundle different aspects of our lives: thus Starbucks cards might be used as an international currency for luxury food products, or music coins for buying or selling sounds. But the new digital ecosystems might also be rebundled in new ways: excessive consumption of coffee or of sugars might be linked to alerts to medical service providers. And the willingness to have those alerts sent might be linked to reduced health and life insurance premiums—while correspondingly, an unwillingness would be penalized.

So far, many experiments in localized currencies as a kind of barter (say, for neighborhood baby-sitting) have failed, because of a hoarding of claims and the inability consequently to realize the demand for services as the currency is in practice debased by those hoarded claims. Those limitations can be transcended by the ability to conduct exchanges between digital ecosystems: in other words, by the equivalent of a foreign exchange market (converting babysitting money into gas coupons, for example, or local theater tickets). The ease of immediate electronic marketplaces makes it much easier to do this today than it was for nineteenth-century Europeans to juggle between thalers and Louis d'or.

In each of the cases of newly created digital exchange communities, we might choose between options for how to treat the information provided. One option might be to offer a large amount of data not only to optimize choices and ensure a wider availability of services, but also to suggest possible new services (with "nudges"), both coming at the cost of privacy. Another option would protect privacy, but at a higher price. (A user who chooses to separate platforms on which to consume coffee, sugar, and alcohol from another platform used for medical services might select that option.) The differentiation would make clear or transparent the gains and the costs of the surrender of personal information. If I use a platform that exchanges the details of my abundant purchases of alcohol and sugar, my health insurance premiums would rise. If I refrained from using such a platform, the cost of my health insurance—or of obtaining a long-term mortgage—would be less. Money might again look like Mephistopheles, promising everything as long as we trade in our soul. But if we regard the trade as a payment of information, we can choose to be Mephistopheles, or not: that is radical self-determination. Instead of repeating the nineteenth-century search for a single, worldwide currency to be reached through the application of the gold standard, we can think of moving or translating between multiple currencies, thereby creating assets that are safe and do not depend on one powerful country.

Why Taxes Matter, and How to Tax Fairly

The world that is emerging will be one of greater mobility, especially in the provision of digital services and communications. But there are obviously public goods that still need to be paid for: security and defense, as well as, crucially, access to services for those who cannot afford them.

It is easier to tax immobility than mobility, and in some ways doing so is more just. This argument dates back to classical economics. David Ricardo described the rent paid to a landlord for land use as unearned payment for a natural gift, the quality of soil. Starting with Henry George, many economists have argued that taxing the value of land is an efficient source of public revenue, because it allows for the reduction of more distortive taxes on labor and capital.[10] Land prices reflect one of two things, either the presence of natural resources (such as coal, iron ore, gold, rare earth metals, or productive soil), or the value of location (in terms of access to productive activities or amenities). Either way, landowners enjoy rents that are due to natural randomness or to the benefits resulting from externalities—which are often due to public investments in transportation systems, access to supply chains, or local schools. Taxing these rents will consequently not affect the productive capacity of the land. Piketty suggests that much of the increase in wealth inequality during the second half of the twentieth century was due to rising house prices.[11] Thus land-value taxes appear as a simple way of taxing capital gains associated with these price increases, which had not followed from any particular action or investment on the part of individual landowners.

In fact, land-value taxes have other advantages: they cannot reduce the supply of land nor distort individual investments on what is built; they are unlikely to result in fiscal optimization since plots cannot be hidden or moved to tax havens; and the land provides easy collateral for the tax authorities in case of payment default. A move to such taxation might even stimulate economic activity by ensuring that all profitable land, including high-value apartments in metropolitan centers, is used and not kept idle. It would also probably reduce housing prices in dense urban areas, thus benefiting young workers who are, on average, less well-off than their elders. A striking feature of the dysfunctional world of globalization has been how many upmarket areas in cities such as New York, Vancouver, London, and Paris are effectively deserted, as residences have been bought as an investment or as a potential refuge by rich, absentee owners. Bishops Avenue in London, widely known as "Billionaires Row," has sixty-six mansions worth an estimated combined $620 million: many of them are abandoned and crumbling. Number 53, for instance, "The Temples," was bought by the Saudi royal family during the tense circumstances of 1989.

The New York Upper East Side, or the area around the Place des Vosges in Paris, have seemed empty at times, especially during the coronavirus pandemic.

In addition, as land prices increase because investments in transport and infrastructure turn low-value farmland into high-value plots for commuters, a land tax would recover for the government part of its investment costs, rather than leaving all of the gains as a windfall to the original owners.

Information, Automation, and the Fight for Equality

The availability of new types of information offers possibilities for tackling some of the inequalities and injustices that have been highlighted by the COVID-19 crisis. More automation may mean that some of the repetitive and dangerous tasks performed by low-paid essential workers could be performed by machines: for instance, supermarket clerks could be replaced with self-serve scanners; many jobs in public transportation requiring regular contact with customers could be taken over by machines; and meat processing could follow the example of countries with higher wages, such as Denmark, where such preparation is substantially automated. There are many examples, spanning various jobs and activities, many of which demonstrate how radically the response to the coronavirus has transformed established ways of doing business.

Another area of change sparked by the coronavirus crisis is the increased popularity and acceptability of telemedicine. In this area, technology offers clear advantages. More frequent or even continuous monitoring of vital statistics—temperature, blood pressure, pulse rates, oxygenation, levels of hormones, vitamins, sugars, and so on—can trigger faster pharmaceutical or medical interventions. Diseases can be anticipated before they break out. Treatment can be more precisely targeted. There is less need for expensive diagnostic tests and long hospital stays. Medical personnel are protected from physical contacts with sick patients, and patients can avoid crowded hospitals and doctor's offices. The quick availability of information can give indicators of how infectious diseases are spreading, facilitating the implementation of highly targeted preventive methods, including quick treatment and possibly quarantine. The coronavirus experience has offered multiple lessons for dealing with future pandemic threats.

Policing is another area that could likely benefit from a careful use of new technologies. The Black Lives Matter protests in the United States in the summer of 2020 brought to light for many citizens the discriminatory and racist practices of many American police departments. But a great deal of policing can be done by machine. Traffic offenses could be recorded automatically. In the case of severe—life-endangering—offenses, car motors could be stopped remotely (as they are already in the case of lease automobiles whose lease is unpaid). Facial or iris recognition means that much policing of crowds can be done inconspicuously and at a distance. With the use of these and other technologies, there will be less need for high-visibility police presences as a deterrence, and less need for militarized police operations. There would also be less incentive for the use of racial or ethnic profiling in order to establish categories of suspects—though those setting up the technologies would have to take extraordinary care not to introduce even subtle elements of such profiling into the systems themselves.

Finance is being democratized. New businesses such as Robinhood, an apparently commission-free investment platform originally born out of the anti-capitalist Occupy Wall Street movement—are making it easier and much cheaper to undertake financial transactions.[12] Platforms have eliminated the need for traditional (and expensive) institutions: banks, insurers, asset managers.

Today, access to education is restricted, and education is expensive. The increasing restrictiveness of entry into elite institutions is usually thought to be not only a driver of inequality, but importantly also a barrier to substantial mobility. The same kinds of technologies that deliver telemedicine and remote monitoring can be applied to education, with the result that many more people can have easier and cheaper access to high-quality learning experiences. It is not just a question of making instruction available. One key ingredient of successful education is student participation: in-person classes or seminars can be productive and educationally galvanizing, but they can also be boring and lead to a loss of attention and interest. The methods of the future will rely on a substantial amount of remote learning, but also on personal interaction and student participation. Education at its best is a way of establishing communities of thought and discussion, requiring the interaction of people with different skill sets, assumptions, and backgrounds—exactly what technology, at its best, can encourage.

Bringing in new perspectives was always resisted by incumbents, as it is now. In the eighteenth century, the great figures of the Enlightenment, Edward Gibbon and Adam Smith, railed against the elite English universities of Oxford and Cambridge. Gibbon left Oxford quickly, and remembered only its futility and unproductiveness. "If I inquire into the manufactures of the monks of Magdalen, if I extend the inquiry to the other colleges of Oxford and Cambridge, a silent blush, or a scornful frown, will be the only reply. The fellows or monks of my time were decent easy men, who supinely enjoyed the gifts of the founder; their days were filled by a series of uniform employments; the chapel and the hall, the coffee-house and the common room, till they retired, weary and well satisfied, to a long slumber."[13] Smith's views of his Oxford experience sounded a similar note: "The discipline of colleges and universities is in general contrived, not for the benefit of the students, but for the interest, or more properly speaking, for the ease of the masters. Its object is, in all cases, to maintain the authority of the master, and whether he neglects or performs his duty, to oblige the students in all cases to behave to him as if he performed it with the greatest diligence and ability."[14] The enormous innovation of their day took place outside the setting of universities. Today, some, particularly in the tech fields, believe it would be a more productive use of resources to reward the innovative and talented for dropping out of university. Just as in the eighteenth century, there is a drive to bring in new perspectives, and to challenge the establishment. The educational upheavals likely to follow from the coronavirus pandemic—including the closing of many colleges and universities—are likely to accelerate this trend.

The most intriguing opportunity brought about by the coronavirus pandemic may be the possibility of establishing new communities to replace the overstretched and overburdened communities we have today. Since the early twentieth century, complaints about the erosion of *Gemeinschaft* (community) and its replacement by an anonymous *Gesellschaft* (society) became commonplace in the sociological literature. As part of this process, nuclear families replaced older, much larger groupings that might have formed around extended families but were not limited to kinship groups.

In the later years of the twentieth century, the apparently ubiquitous model of advanced societies composed of nuclear families started to erode. There was a bifurcation: for educated and more wealthy individuals, family life remained a reality, although often the realities of the family became more complex, with "patchwork" units created by the inclusion of children from former spouses, and so on. By contrast, for lower-income groups, the family broke up in a way that often led to poverty and increased inequality. One illuminating argument is that the richer and better-educated families could stay together because they bought the services—childcare, educational and psychological support—that had previously been provided by the extended communities and networks of the premodern world. Poorer would-be families could not afford that kind of support, and they more frequently disintegrated.

The educational and personal transformations held out by new technologies should not only facilitate the transfer of skills, and so increase opportunities for employment and enrichment; they will likely also draw a wider and unexpected range of people into providing informal and formal supports for each other.

A World of Personalized Experiences and Options

Utopias have radical premises: characteristically computers will do all the work, while humans will simply need to live for leisure. That is, the utopia scenario assumes that everyone will live an accomplished and fascinating life of leisure. (The dystopian version typically portrays people as deeply angry and alienated, with their violent tendencies kept in check by systematized and artificial-intelligence-coordinated force.) But utopias go wrong by describing only one potential reality. Let's consider instead more possibilities.

Instead of offering a single utopian scenario, the new age will offer individuals the ability to engage with multiple modes of existence simultaneously and seamlessly. People will use their interests and abilities to find and enter large digital communities of the like-minded, and they will be able to access as many communities as they wish. In this world, probably only a few will join only the community of Elvis enthusiasts or diehard Yankee fans.

People will not live only in virtual communities. They need to eat, sleep, socialize—they will do that in existing neighborhoods. But they will escape imaginatively: they will share interests across the world, learn and work distantly, and have long-distance as well as close-by relationships.

We might think of the new world as offering a version of neo-medievalism.[15] Life in the premodern world was intensely locally rooted, with actual and often quite oppressive and intolerant communities, but people escaped if they could into a world of imagination. In the medieval case, they saw how they were linked not only to humans in other societies, but also to communities of the past and the future.

The error of the old world of globalization twentieth-century style was to think in terms of one size fits all. The problem was most apparent in the domain of monetary relations. Since the 1960s, commentators have been insisting with ever greater urgency that a world centered around the US dollar cannot survive as the role of the United States in the world economy diminishes, and as its military power is challenged by new rivals. But the dollar remained more and more, rather than less, central for the operation of financialization. The dollar became more and more of a puzzle, and to many, an irritant.

Moving Past the Latest Crisis

A Soviet joke, especially popular a few decades ago, begins with a young man shouting in the middle of Moscow's Red Square that Leonid Brezhnev is an idiot. He is quickly arrested and sentenced to twenty-five years and a half in prison: half a year for insulting the chair of the Presidium of the Supreme Soviet, and twenty-five years for revealing state secrets. The Trump administration's reaction to the book by former national security adviser John Bolton was exactly in this league: the book was considered a danger because it insulted Trump, but above all because it released highly classified material, that is, a revelation of the incompetence and lack of strategic orientation of the president.

Aspects of the United States in the traumatic year 2020 resembled in a terrifying way the last years of the Soviet Union. Part of the Soviet-US comparison is about leadership; another part is about the source of division and ultimately fission. The Soviet Union suppressed ethnic conflicts, which then broke out and pushed the society into violence, collapse, and disintegration. The leadership of the United States fanned a longtime racial divide characterized by unequal access to physical, monetary, academic, and political resources. Slavery is now commonly referred to as the original sin of the United States, by Republican Mitch McConnell as well as Democrat Joseph Biden. The old Confederate statues are now being toppled, just as statues of Stalin and Lenin fell when the Soviet Empire collapsed.

A perhaps more astonishing comparison with the late Soviet period concerns the instruments used to control the economy. The Soviet Union had a large and complicated planning apparatus that was supposed to allocate resources efficiently, and which attracted large numbers of well-educated individuals and time-servers into unproductive and frequently destructive operations. The vast financial-services sector of the United States is not the equivalent of that Soviet planning authority, but it is appropriately part of the controversy over how resources should be allocated to their most socially productive use.

Up to the end, few really thought the Soviet system would collapse, in part because economists are generally not very good at looking into crystal balls and delivering long-term prognoses. They instead rely on a precise analysis of the current state of affairs, and extrapolations based on assumptions that nothing will change. Economists know that such projections are unrealistic, but they also, sensibly, want to avoid speculation about the kind of changes that might occur—so like medieval theologians, they dress up their uncertainty about the future in an arcane language. That is, most modern economists do not know Latin well, but they are very happy to refer to *ceteris paribus* (holding other things constant) as the foundation of their ventures into forecasting.

The circumstances that led to the long period of dollar hegemony are now changing. The COVID-19 pandemic is accelerating that transformation—as it is in many other areas of life. It is bringing about more digital globalization, more information flows, and less actual globalization: that is, less movement of people and of goods. This is the ultimate weightless economy or weightless globalization.

The dollar's centrality was prompted by the demand for a deep and liquid safe asset; and that centrality will only disappear when alternative safe assets emerge, backed in some cases by non-state providers. In the past, when precious metals were the basis for a currency issue, alternative safe assets dominated. Even in the late twentieth century, nostalgic commentators looked back to that era. The alternative is to think of currency as having a real collateral—in this particular case, information generated by the participants in a wide variety of overlapping communities.

Existing states will not disappear, but we will need to make local communities more effective and more responsive. The coronavirus has demonstrated how responses to challenges vary from country to country, region to region, even neighborhood to neighborhood. Consider France, where Normandy and Brittany had few infections, but Alsace struggled with many; or Italy, where Lombardy was an epicenter of infection and mass mortality, but the Veneto nearby was relatively spared. The experience demonstrated the contribution of effective local management and local response. But it also showed that the delivery of equipment, medicine, and other resources needs to be coordinated in a broader framework, across cities and regions, but also internationally. It is also important that different laboratories in different intellectual traditions experiment with vaccines and anti-viral treatments, and share their results, to ensure the quickest, most robust response possible.

There is thus still a need to think about the way the world can be coordinated. What sort of institutions will hold this new world together? Globalists were attacked for trying to institute world government, and this was always a vain and foolish dream, since such a government would fail very quickly in any attempt at social or cultural translation. Instead, there is a need—and the technical possibility—for connecting all kinds of local communities.

It is in regulating all those connections and rooting out abusive behavior that the major challenge for a future global network will reside. Here it may be instructive to look back at the three distinct ways in which multilateral governance institutions operated in the long era of postwar stability. The first, and probably initially most attractive, but also most uncertain in terms of its legal status, was to take a judicial or quasi-judicial role in arbitrating disputes between countries. There are many situations that seem to require arbitration: trade disputes, for instance, or—often associated with trade disputes—debates about whether currencies are unfairly valued so as to produce a subsidy for exporters. The new emphasis on sovereignty in the United States, the United Kingdom, and elsewhere in Europe where "sovereignists" confront "globalists," pushes back against this type of arbitration.

The second style of multilateralism involved institutions offering advice to governments on policy consistency and on the interplay between policies in one country and those in the rest of the world: experts would explain and analyze feedbacks and spillovers and suggest policy alternatives. The essence of this kind of advice is that it is private. It is like speaking with a priest in the confessional. The outcome may be that behavior or policy changes, but the outside world will not really understand the reason or the logic that compels better behavior.

The third approach used by institutions was to act as a public persuader with a public mission. British prime minister Gordon Brown liked to use the phrase "ruthless truth-telling" or "speaking truth to power" with regard to the advice of multilateral institutions. This approach arose due to the increasing recognition of the limits of secret diplomacy and behind-the-scenes advice. Societies cannot be moved unless there is a genuine consensus that they are moving in the right direction. The backlash against globalization is fed by a climate of suspicion: experts, economists, and international institutions are not trusted. During the 2000s, then, the G20 and the International Monetary Fund moved to make public their assessments of how policy spillovers affected the world. This public style of action continues to gain proponents in our current age of transparency, when information technologies seem less secure, when secrets leak, when WikiLeaks flourishes. Now it is unwise to assume that anything is secret. These days, former diplomats publish indiscreet memoirs while officials—and indeed heads of state and government—tweet about what they are doing in nearly real time.

The accessibility of information opens a fundamental dilemma, however. Policy advice is invariably quite complicated. Spillovers and feedbacks require a great deal of analysis and explanation and cannot easily be reduced to simple formulations. Reports produced by international institutions are complex and arcane in style, with a language that does not make them easily accessible. Should they be reformulated to reach a wider audience? Should international institutions be more like judges, or priests or psychoanalysts, or persuaders? None of the traditional roles on their own and by themselves are any longer credible. But multilateral institutions will also find it impossible to take on all three roles at the same time. Judges do not usually need to provide long explanations for their rulings. If they act only as persuaders, maintaining a hyperactive tweeting account, they will merely look self-interested and lose credibility; they also won't get much done. But if the judges are secret—like the World Bank's International Center for Settlement of Investment Disputes—they will lose legitimacy, even if they are more efficient (as measured by the general societal gains arising out of their rulings).

It is easy to see why the institutions that successfully built the stable post-1945 order might be despondent in the face of apparently insuperable challenges. But there is a way out that both harnesses the new technologies and allows for the successful mediation of disputes that threaten to divide and impoverish the world.

The post-crisis world is one in which ever larger and more updated amounts of data are available. In the past, we needed to wait for months or years before we could conclude accurate assessments of the volume of economic activity or of trade. Now real-time data on a much broader set of measurable outcomes is available, and a great deal of effort is devoted to coordinating its prompt release. Some of this data is managed by international institutions, but much is held elsewhere, by universities (Johns Hopkins in the case of COVID-19 health data), individuals (as in Raj Chetty's compilation of consumer data), companies (which keep it as a commercial secret), or governments (which try to suppress it when it is uncomfortable for them). The coronavirus crisis has shone a harsh light on the way in which health data, and health outcomes, are linked to many aspects of social and economic life. Its aftermath has also led to a politicization of other data—on the incidence of crime, say, or links between crime and other socioeconomic data (such as income and ethnic identity).

The early nineteenth-century struggles over socialism and capitalism were cast as fights over ownership of the means of production. We can now be much more specific about what that concept involves. We need a movement now for the ownership of data—one analogous to early nineteenth-century workers' demands to own their labor. The wider dissemination of data will be inherently controversial, not least because it offers the public, the citizens, an element of control. They can ask: Are governments doing well in promoting positive public outcomes? Are specific companies with substantial market power hurting and harming, or protecting and promoting, the general welfare?

Managing the supply of reliable and real-time information today opens up new possibilities not only for effective macroeconomic global coordination, but also for increased democratic legitimacy. Information technologies offer a way to meet the demand for real engagement by citizens. More data, and more freely available data, will provide a basis for more informed political choice and for more stable political systems. The struggle of the twenty-first century will then be over a new type of property: who controls an individual's data, and how it is combined with the data of others. Describing and understanding this new, transformative, and potentially dangerous development will require a vocabulary rich with meaning and grounded in historical context. It will necessitate a lexicon that promotes understanding, not confusion; community, not division. And it will require a greater appreciation that words matter: that language can empower citizens as they make decisions about their data that will protect their well-being, individual interests, privacy, and peace of mind.

Notes

Introduction

1. Ludwig Wittgenstein, *Tractatus Logicus-Philosophicus* (New York: Harcourt Brace, 1922), p. 149.

2. Genesis 11:4.

3. Alexander Solzhenitsyn, "Live Not by Lies," *Index on Censorship* 2 ([1974] 2004): 205.

4. William James, *Pragmatism: A New Name for Some Old Ways of Thinking* (1907; Portland, OR: Floating Press, 2010), p. 138.

5. John Grier Hibben, "The Test of Pragmatism," *Philosophical Review* 17, no. 4 (July 1908): 369. See also George Cotkin, "William James and the Cash-Value Metaphor," *ETC: A Review of General Semantics* 42, no. 1 (1985): 37–46.

6. For instance, see the influencer Wesley Yang's blog at https://twitter.com /wesyang/status/1130858237014794240?lang=en.

7. Harold James, *The End of Globalization: Lessons from the Great Depression* (Cambridge, MA: Harvard University Press, 2001), p. 224.

8. John Stuart Mill, *On Liberty* (1859; London: Watts, 1929), p. 52.

9. See Jan-Werner Müller, *A Dangerous Mind: Carl Schmitt in Post-War European Thought* (New Haven: Yale University Press, 2003).

10. See Carl Schmitt, *Politische Theologie: Vier Kapitel zur Lehre von der Souveränität* (Munich: Duncker & Humblot, 1922), 9; see also Hasso Hofmann, "Souverän ist, wer über den Ausnahmezustand entscheidet," *Der Staat* 44, no. 2 (2005): 171–186.

11. Ronald Steel, *Walter Lippmann and the American Century* (Boston: Little, Brown, 1980), p. 267.

12. Thomas Piketty, *Capital in the Twenty-First Century,* trans. Arthur Goldhammer (Cambridge, MA: Harvard University Press, 2014); Anthony B. Atkinson, *Inequality: What Can Be Done?* (Cambridge, MA: Harvard University Press, 2015); Branko Milanovic, *Global Inequality: A New Approach for the Age of Globalization* (Cambridge, MA: Harvard University Press, 2016).

13. Helena Rosenblatt, *The Lost History of Liberalism: From Ancient Rome to the Twenty-First Century* (Princeton, NJ: Princeton University Press, 2018), p. 6.

14. Jill Lepore, *This America: The Case for the Nation* (New York: Norton, 2019), p. 40.

15. Mill, *On Liberty,* p. 43.

1.   Capitalism

1. Pierre Bourdieu, "The Forms of Capital," in J. Richardson, ed., *Handbook of Theory and Research for the Sociology of Education* (New York: Greenwood, 1986), p. 242.

2. Joyce Appleby, *The Relentless Revolution: A History of Capitalism* (New York: Norton, 2010), p. 16.

3. Joel Mokyr, *A Culture of Growth: The Origins of the Modern Economy* (Princeton, NJ: Princeton University Press, 2017), p. 267.

4. John Paul II, *Centesimus annus,* section 41, http://www.vatican.va/holy_father /john_paul_ii/encyclicals/documents/hf_jp-ii_enc_01051991_centesimus-annus_en.html.

5. Alasdair MacIntyre, *After Virtue* (London: Bloomsbury, 1981), p. 304.

6. Elizabeth Fox-Genovese and Eugene D. Genovese, *Fruits of Merchant Capital: Slavery and Bourgeois Property in the Rise and Expansion of Capitalism* (New York: Oxford University Press, 1983), p. vii.

7. Ibid., p. 18.

8. See Barbara L. Solow, "Capitalism and Slavery in the Exceedingly Long Run," *Journal of Interdisciplinary History* 17, no. 4 (Spring 1987): 711–737; see also Celso Furtado, *Economic Growth of Brazil: A Survey from Colonial to Modern Times* (Berkeley: University of California Press, 1963).

9. Gareth Austin, "The Return of Capitalism as a Concept," in Jürgen Kocka and Marcel van der Linden, eds., *Capitalism: The Reemergence of a Historical Concept* (London: Bloomsbury, 2016), p. 211.

10. See Michel Albert, *Capitalism against Capitalism* (Chichester, UK: Whurr, 1993); Peter A. Hall and David Soskice, eds., *Varieties of Capitalism: The Institutional Foundations of Comparative Advantage* (Oxford, UK: Oxford University Press, 2001).

11. Karl Polanyi, *The Great Transformation: The Political and Economic Origins of Our Time* (1944; Boston: Beacon Press, 2001), p. 81.

12. See Austin, "Return of Capitalism," for a cogent critique of Polanyi.

13. R. H. Tawney, *Religion and the Rise of Capitalism: A Historical Study* (New York: Harcourt, Brace, 1926), p. 188.

14. Pons Louis François Villeneuve and Marquis de Villeneuve, *De l'agonie de la France: Examen de la situation morale, matérielle, politique, de la monarchie française,* vol. 2 (Paris: Périsse, 1839), p. 140.

15. See Albert Schäffle, *Kapitalismus und Sozialismus mit besonderer Rücksicht auf Geschäfts-und Vermögensformen* (Tübingen: Laupp, 1870); also see Kocka and van der Linden, *Capitalism;* and Jürgen Kocka, *Capitalism: A Short History* (Princeton, NJ: Princeton University Press, 2016).

16. Nassau William Senior, *An Outline of the Science of Political Economy* (London: W. Clowes, 1836), p. 2010.

17. Kenny Meadows, *Selections from the Heads of the People; or, Portraits of the English* (London: Robert Tyas, 1845), p. 214.

18. *The Parliamentary Debates (Authorized Edition)*, vol. 71, 1843, p. 383.

19. Philipp Ritter von Holger, *Staatswirthschafts-Chemie als Leitfaden* (Vienna: Witwe Prandel, 1843), p. 35.

20. See Gary Gorton, "Banking Panics and Business Cycles," *Oxford Economic Papers* 40, no. 4 (December 1988): 751–781; see also Charles Calomiris and Gary Gorton, "The Origins of Banking Panics," in Calomiris, ed., *US Bank Deregulation in Historical Perspective* (Cambridge, UK: Cambridge University Press, 2000), pp. 93–163.

21. Otto von Gierke, *Community in Historical Perspective: A Translation of Selections from Das Deutsche Genossenschaftsrecht*, ed. Antony Black, trans. Mary Fischer (1868; Cambridge, UK: Cambridge University Press, 1990).

22. The classic statement of this argument is Ronald H. Coase, "The Nature of the Firm," *Economica* 4, no. 16 (November 1937): 386–405.

23. Fernand Braudel, *Afterthoughts on Material Civilization and Capitalism* (Baltimore: Johns Hopkins University Press, 1977); see also, in a similar vein, Giovanni Arighi, *The Long Twentieth Century: Money, Power and the Origins of Our Times* (London: Verso, 1994).

24. Paul Kennedy, *The Rise and Fall of the Great Powers: Economic Change and Military Conflict from 1500 to 2000* (New York: Random House, 1987).

25. Antoine E. Murphy, *John Law: Economic Theorist and Policy-Maker* (Oxford, UK: Oxford University Press, 1997).

26. Quoted in Larry Neal, *Rise of Financial Capitalism: International Capital Markets in the Age of Reason* (Cambridge, UK: Cambridge University Press, 1990), p. 22.

27. See Oscar Gelderblom and Joost Jonker, "Completing a Financial Revolution: The Finance of the Dutch East India Trade and the Rise of the Amsterdam Capital Market, 1595–1612," *Journal of Economic History* 64, no. 3 (September 2004): 641–672.

28. The classic modern works are Douglass North and Barry Weingast, "Constitutions and Commitment: The Evolution of Institutions Governing Public Choice in Seventeenth-Century England," *Journal of Economic History* 49, no. 4 (December 1989): 803–832; Thomas Sargent and Francois Velde, "Macroeconomic Features of the French Revolution," *Journal of Political Economy* 103, no. 3 (June 1995): 474–518. Something of this argument is anticipated in a famous passage of Marx's *Capital*, where public debt is presented as a foundation of "primitive accumulation" and capitalism: "the modern doctrine that a nation becomes the richer the more deeply it is in debt." See Marx *Das Capital*, vol. 1 (Moscow: Progress Publishers, 1970), p. 706.

29. Charles P. Kindleberger, *A Financial History of Western Europe* (London: Allen & Unwin, 1984), p. 98.

30. Rudolf Hilferding, *Das Finanzkapital*, vol. 2, ed. Eduard März (1910; Frankfurt: Europäische Verlagsanstalt, 1968), p. 399.

31. Jan de Vries and Ad van der Woude, *The First Modern Economy: Success, Failure, and Perseverance of the Dutch Economy, 1500–1815* (Cambridge, UK: Cambridge University Press, 1997), p. 696.

32. Herman van der Wee and Monique Verbreyt, *La Générale de Banque, 1822–1997: Un Défi Permanent* (Bruxelles: Racine, 1997).

33. Klaus J. Mattheier, "Autobiographie Franz Haniel," in Bodo Herzog and Klaus J. Mattheier, eds., *Franz Haniel, 1779–1868: Materialien, Dokumente und Untersuchungen zu Leben und Werk des Industriepioniers Franz Haniel* (Bonn: Ludwig Röhrscheid, 1979), p. 109.

34. Krupp to Ernst Waldthausen, March 28, 1857; Krupp archive, WA 4/III; also Wilhelm Berdrow, ed., *Alfred Krupp Briefe: 1826–1887* (Berlin: Reimar Hobbing, 1928), p. 153.

35. Krupp to Prokura, July 26, 1873, in Berdrow, *Briefe*, p. 290.

36. Adam Smith, *An Inquiry into the Nature and Causes of the Wealth of Nations,* ed. Edwin Cannan, pt. 2 (1776; Chicago: University of Chicago Press, 1976), p. 279.

37. Joseph A. Schumpeter, *The Theory of Economic Development: An Inquiry into Profits, Capital, Credit, Interest, and the Business Cycle,* trans. Redvers Opie (London: Oxford University Press, 1934), p. 74. (This is a development of a book originally published in 1911.)

38. Gierke, *Community in Historical Perspective,* pp. 203–204.

39. For a fuller exposition of this argument, see Harold James, "Corporation Law and Changes in Marriage Behavior in the Nineteenth Century," in Dieter Hein, Klaus Hildebrand, and Andreas Schulz, eds., *Historie und Leben. Der Historiker als Wissenschaftler und Zeitgenosse. Festschrift für Lothar Gall* (Munich: Oldenbourg Wissenschaftsverlag, 2006).

40. Adolf A. Berle Jr. and Gardiner C. Means, *The Modern Corporation and Private Property* (New York: Macmillan, 1932).

41. Fréderic Le Play, *La Réforme Sociale en France,* vol. 2 (Paris: E. Dentu, 1867), p. 235.

42. Werner Sombart, *Die Juden und das Wirtschaftsleben* (1911; Munich: Duncker & Humblot, 1920), p. 331.

43. See Jerry Z. Muller, *The Mind and the Market: Capitalism in Western Thought* (New York: Knopf Doubleday, 2007); also Friedrich Lenger, *Werner Sombart: Eine Biographie* (Munich: Beck, 1994).

44. Schlomo Avineri, *Karl Marx: Philosophy and Revolution* (New Haven: Yale University Press, 2019), p. 47.

45. Raymond Goldsmith, *Financial Structure and Development* (New Haven: Yale University Press, 1969), p. 400.

46. Alexander Gerschenkron, *Economic Backwardness in Historical Perspective: A Book of Essays* (Cambridge, MA: Belknap Press of Harvard University Press, 1962).

47. For recent examples, see Volker Wellhöner, *Grossbanken und Grossindustrie im Kaiserreich* (Göttingen, Germany: Vandenhoeck & Ruprecht, 1989); the more theoretical work Jeremy Edwards and Klaus Fischer, *Banks, Finance and Investment in*

Germany (Cambridge, UK: Cambridge University Press, 1994); and Caroline Fohlin, *Finance Capitalism and Germany's Rise to Industrial Power* (Cambridge, UK: Cambridge University Press, 2007).

48. Antonio Confalionieri, *Banca e Industria, 1894–1906* (Milano: Banca Commerciale Italiana Distribuzione Cisalpino–La Goliardica, 1974).

49. C. W. von Wieser, *Der finanzielle Aufbau der englischen Industrie* (Jena, Ger.: Gustav Fischer, 1919), p. vi.

50. For a political scientist's viewpoint, see Jonathan Kirshner, *Appeasing Bankers: Financial Caution on the Road to War* (Princeton, NJ: Princeton University Press, 2007).

51. Dieter Stiefel, *Camillo Castiglioni oder Die Metaphysik der Haifische* (Vienna: Böhlau, 2012).

52. *Verhandlungen des VII. Allgemeinen Deutschen Bankiertages zu Köln am Rhein am 9., 10., und 11. September 1928* [Proceedings of the seventh German bankers' convention in Cologne, September 9, 10, and 11] (Berlin: de Gruyter, 1928), pp. 135, 141, 146, 149–150.

53. Friedrich A. Hayek, *Prices and Production* (London: Routledge & Kegan Paul, 1935), p. 125.

54. John Maynard Keynes, *A Treatise on Money,* in Keynes, *Collected Writings,* vol. 5 (London: Macmillan, 1971), p. 42; See also Robert Skidelsky, *John Maynard Keynes,* vol. 2: *The Economist as Saviour, 1920–1937* (London: Macmillan, 1994), p. 320.

55. Keynes, *Collected Writings,* vol. 6, p. 337.

56. Skidelsky, *Keynes,* vol. 2, p. 317.

57. McKinsey Global Institute, *Financial Globalization: Retreat or Reset?,* March 2013, p. 4, https://www.mckinsey.com/~/media/McKinsey/Featured%20Insights/Global%20Capital%20Markets/Financial%20globalization/MGI_Financial_globalization_Executive_Summary_Mar2013.pdf.

58. Oliver Stone, director, *Wall Street,* 20th Century Fox, 1987.

59. James Tobin, "Review of Hyman P. Minsky's *Stabilizing an Unstable Economy,*" *Journal of Economic Literature* 27, no. 1 (March 1989): 106.

60. Ben S. Bernanke, "Nonmonetary Effects of the Financial Crisis in Propagation of the Great Depression," *American Economic Review* 73, no. 3 (1983): 257–276; Ben S. Bernanke and Alan S. Blinder, "Credit, Money, and Aggregate Demand," *American Economic Review* 78, no. 2 (1988): 435–439; Ben Bernanke and Mark Gertler, "Financial Fragility and Economic Performance," *Quarterly Journal of Economics* 105, no. 1 (1990): 87–114, quotation on p. 105; Ben Bernanke and Harold James, "The Gold Standard, Deflation, and Financial Crisis in the Great Depression: An International Comparison," in R. Glenn Hubbard, ed., *Financial Markets and Financial Crises* (Chicago: University of Chicago Press, 1991), pp. 33–68.

61. Tim Congdon, *Money in a Free Society: Keynes, Friedman and the New Crisis in Capitalism* (New York: Encounter Books, 2011), p. 399.

62. Claudio Borio and Philip Lowe, "Imbalances or Bubbles? Implications for Monetary and Financial Stability," in William Curt Hunter, George G. Kaufman, and Michael

Pomerleano, eds., *Asset Price Bubbles: The Implications for Monetary, Regulatory, and International Policies* (Cambridge, MA: MIT Press, 2005), pp. 247–270.

63. Hans Werner Sinn, *Casino Capitalism: How the Financial Crisis Came About and What Needs to Be Done Now* (New York: Oxford University Press, 2010).

2.   Socialism

1. Jacob Pramuk, "Here Are the Key Moments from President Trump's Republican National Convention Speech," CNBC.com, August 28, 2020, https://www.cnbc.com/2020/08/28/trump-rnc-speech-highlights.html.

2. Quoted in Joshua B. Freeman, *Behemoth: The History of the Factory and the Making of the Modern World* (New York: Norton, 2018), p. 25.

3. Robert Owen, *A New View of Society*, ed. Vic Gatrell (1816; Harmondsworth, UK: Penguin, 1970).

4. Henri Saint-Simon, *Du système industriel* (Paris: Chez A.-A. Renouard, 1821), p. 44.

5. See Riccardo Soliani, "Claude-Henri de Saint-Simon: Hierarchical Socialism?," *History of Economic Ideas* 17, no. 2 (2009): 21–39.

6. Karl Marx and Friedrich Engels, *Collected Works*, vol. 8: *The Magyar Struggle*, January 13, 1849 (London: Lawrence & Wishart, 1975), p. 238.

7. See Ernst Engelberg, *Bismarck: Urpreuße und Reichsgründer* (Berlin: Siedler, 1985), p. 656.

8. Roman Szporluk, *Communism and Nationalism: Karl Marx versus Friedrich List* (New York: Oxford University Press, 1988), p. 32.

9. Karl Marx and Friedrich Engels, *The German Ideology* (Moscow: Progress Publishers, 1964), p. 75.

10. Joseph A. Petrus, "Marx and Engels on the National Question," *Journal of Politics* 33, no. 3 (August 1971): 797–824, quotation on 801.

11. Karl Marx, *A Contribution to the Critique of Political Economy* (Chicago: Charles H. Kerr & Co., 1904), p. 207.

12. Karl Marx and Friedrich Engels, *The Communist Manifesto*, trans. Samuel Moore (1848; London: Pluto Press, 2017), pp. 51, 54–55.

13. Jonathan Sperber in David E. Barclay and Eric D. Weitz, eds., *Between Reform and Revolution: German Socialism and Communism from 1840 to 1990* (New York: Berghahn Books, 1998), pp. 167–194.

14. Lawrence H. Simon, ed., *Selected Writings by Karl Marx* (Indianapolis: Hackett, 1994), pp. 323–324.

15. Karl Marx, *Critique of the Gotha Program*, 1875, pt. 1, https://www.marxists.org/archive/marx/works/1875/gotha/ch01.htm.

16. Rudolf Hilferding, "Probleme der Zeit," *Die Gesellschaft* 1, no. 1 (1924): 1–15.

17. *Reichstagsprotokolle* [German Reichstag session reports] 1907/1909 (April 25, 1907): 1098.

18. Institut für Zeitgeschichte archive, ED93/48, 9. August 1954: Erinnerungen an Ernst Trendelenburg (Hans Schäffer).

19. Klaus Braun, *Konservatismus und Gemeinwirtschaft: Eine Studie über Wichard von Moellendorff* (Duisburg, Ger.: Duisburger Hochschulbeiträge, 1978), pp. 101, 155.

20. Hagen Schulze, ed., *Akten der Reichskanzlei. Weimarer Republik (ARWR), Das Kabinett Scheidemann: 13. Februar bis 20. Juni 1919* [Reich Chancellery files, Weimar Republic (ARWR), Scheidemann cabinet, February 13–June 20, 1919] (Boppard am Rhein: H. Boldt, 1971), p. 272.

21. Vladimir Sorokin, *The Queue*, trans. Sally Laird (1983; New York: New York Review of Books, 2008); see also Elena Osokina, *Our Daily Bread: Socialist Distribution and the Art of Survival in Stalin's Russia, 1927–1941*, trans. Kate Transchel and Greta Bucher (Armonk, NY: M. E. Sharpe, 2000); Karl Schlögel, *Das sowjetische Jahrhundert: Archäologie einer Untergegangenen Welt* (Munich: Beck, 2017), pp. 554–555, 561.

22. Eugene Zaleski, *Stalinist Planning for Economic Growth, 1933–1952* (Chapel Hill: University of North Carolina Press, 1980), p. 484.

23. Oskar Lange, "The Role of Planning in Socialist Economies," in Morris Bornstein, ed., *Comparative Economic Systems* (Homewood, IL: R. D. Irwin, 1965), p. 207.

24. Moshe Lewin, *Political Undercurrents in Soviet Economic Debates* (London: Pluto, 1975), p. 101.

25. Joseph Stalin, Joint Plenum of the C.C. and C.C.C., C.P.S.U.(B.) 1, January 7–12, 1933, The Results of the First Five-Year Plan, Report Delivered on January 7, 1933, in *Works*, vol. 13, 1930–January 1934 (Moscow: Foreign Languages Publishing House, 1954).

26. Oskar Lange, "Marxian Economics and Modern Economic Theory," *Review of Economic Studies* 2, no. 3 (June 1935): 189.

27. Oskar Lange, *On the Economic Theory of Socialism*, ed. Benjamin E. Lippincott (Minneapolis: University of Minnesota Press, 1938), p. 89.

28. Friedrich Hayek, *Collectivist Economic Planning: Critical Studies on the Possibilities of Socialism* (London: Routledge, 1935), p. 14.

29. Oskar Lange, "On the Economic Theory of Socialism," *Review of Economic Studies* 4, no. 1 (October 1936): 53–71.

30. V. B. Singh, ed., "Nehru on Socialism," Government of India Publications Division, New Delhi, 1977, pp. 50–51; see also Ozay Mehmet, *Westernizing the Third World: The Eurocentricity of Economic Development Theories* (New York: Routledge, 1999), p. 61.

31. See Bruce Caldwell, "Hayek and Socialism," *Journal of Economic Literature* 35, no. 4 (December 1997): 1856–1890.

32. Oskar Lange, "The Computer and the Market," in Alec Nove and D. M. Nuti, eds., *Socialist Economics* (London: Penguin, 1972), pp. 401–402.

33. Francis Sejersted, *The Age of Social Democracy: Norway and Sweden in the Twentieth Century*, trans. Madeleine B. Adams (Princeton, NJ: Princeton University Press, 2011), p. 388.

34. Hjalmar Branting, Nobel Lecture, June 19, 1922, https://www.nobelprize.org/prizes/peace/1921/branting/lecture.

35. Alva Myrdal and Gunnar Myrdal, *Kris i befolkningsfrågan* (Nora, Sweden: Nya Doxa, 1934), pp. 203–204; Sejersted, *Age of Social Democracy*, pp. 102–103.

36. Sheri Berman, *The Social Democratic Moment: Ideas and Politics in the Making of Interwar Europe* (Cambridge, MA: Harvard University Press, 1998), p. 161.

37. C. A. R. Crosland, *The Future of Socialism* (1956; New York: Schocken, 1963), pp. 31, 33.

38. Heinrich August Winkler, *Der Weg in die Katastrophe: Arbeiter und Arbeiterbewegung in der Weimarer Republik 1930 bis 1933* (Berlin: J. H. W. Dietz, 1987), 324–326.

39. William E. Paterson, *The SPD and European Integration* (Farnborough, UK: Saxon House, 1974), p. 2.

40. Ibid., p. 8.

41. In *Encounter* (February 1962): 65.

42. Sejersted, *Age of Social Democracy*, p. 445.

43. Roy Harrod, *The Life of John Maynard Keynes* (1951; Harmondsworth: Pelican, 1972), p. 764.

44. Rudolf Hilferding, "Das Historische Problem," *Zeitschrift für Politik*, n.s. vol. 1, no. 4 (December 1954): 295.

45. Raya Dunayevskaya, "The Case of Eugene Varga," in the supplement to the Raya Dunayevskaya Collection, microfilm nos. 12456–12462, 1949, signed "by F. Forest," https://www.marxists.org/archive/dunayevskaya/works/1949/varga.htm.

46. Geoffrey Wheatcroft, "The Paradoxical Case of Tony Blair," *The Atlantic* (June 1996), https://www.theatlantic.com/magazine/archive/1996/06/the-paradoxical-case-of-tony-blair/376602.

47. Colin MacCabe, "Blair Will Be Remembered for Betraying Labour's Values," *The Guardian*, September 24, 2006, https://www.theguardian.com/commentisfree/2006/sep/24/comment.politics1.

48. Pierre Péan, *Une jeunesse française: François Mitterrand, 1934–1947* (Paris: Fayard, 1994).

3.   Democracy, the Nation-State, and Nationalism

1. Yascha Mounk, *The People vs. Democracy* (Cambridge, MA: Harvard University Press, 2018).

2. Joseph A. Schumpeter, *Capitalism, Socialism and Democracy* (1942; New York: Harper & Row, 1976), p. 296.

3. Edward Baumstark, *Kameralistische Encyclopädie: Handbuch der Kameralwissenschaften und ihrer Literatur für Rechts-und Verwaltungsbeamte* (Heidelberg: Karl Groos, 1835), p. 64; Erik Grimmer-Solem, *Learning Empire: Globalization and the German Quest for World Status, 1875–1919* (Princeton, NJ: Princeton University Press, 2019), p. 8.

4. Dani Rodrik, *The Globalization Paradox: Democracy and the Future of the World Economy* (New York: Norton, 2011).

5. Schumpeter, *Capitalism*, p. 267.

6. US Department of State, *Country Reports on Human Rights Practices—2000*, Bureau of Democracy, Human Rights and Labor, February 2001, https://2009-2017 .state.gov/j/drl/rls/hrrpt/2000/648.htm.

7. Freedom House, Freedom in the World, 2019: Democracy in Retreat, https:// freedomhouse.org/report/freedom-world/2019/democracy-retreat.

8. Translation from University of Minnesota, Human Rights Library, "Thucydides: Pericles' Funeral Oration," http://hrlibrary.umn.edu/education/thucydides.html.

9. "Une nation est une âme, un principe spirituel. Deux choses qui, à vrai dire, n'en font qu'une, constituent cette âme, ce principe spirituel. L'une est dans le passé, l'autre dans le présent. L'une est la possession en commun d'un riche legs de souvenirs; l'autre est le consentement actuel, le désir de vivre ensemble, la volonté de continuer à faire valoir l'héritage qu'on a reçu indivis." See Ernest Renan, *Discours et conférences* (Paris: Calmann Lévy, 1887), which includes the text of the Sorbonne lecture, "Qu'est-ce qu'une nation?," from 1882.

10. Eugene Weber, *Peasants into Frenchmen: The Modernization of Rural France, 1870–1914* (Stanford, CA: Stanford University Press, 1976).

11. Wilhelm Freiherr von Humboldt, *Wilhelm von Humboldts gesammelte Schriften,* vol. 10 (Berlin: B. Behr's Verlag, 1903), p. 205.

12. Schumpeter, *Capitalism,* p. 284.

13. Max Weber, *Economy and Society: An Outline of Interpretive Sociology* (Berkeley: University of California Press, 1978), p. 291.

14. Václav Havel, *Living in Truth: 22 Essays Published on the Occasion of the Award of the Erasmus Prize to Václav Havel,* ed. Jan Vladislav (London: Faber and Faber, 1989), pp. 70–71.

15. This is the theme of an extensive argument presented in Liah Greenfeld, *Nationalism: Five Roads to Modernity* (Cambridge, MA: Harvard University Press, 1992).

16. Ludwig August von Rochau, *Grundsätze der Realpolitik, angewendet auf die staatlichen Zustände Deutschlands Theil II* (Heidelberg: J. C. B. Mohr, 1869), p. 25.

17. Karl Marx, preface to the first German edition of *Das Capital* (1867; London: Lawrence and Wishart, 1970), p. 19.

18. Hans Rothfels, *Bismarck Briefe* (Göttingen: Vandenhoeck & Ruprecht, 1955), p. 345.

19. Ibid., p. 347.

20. Harold James, *Krupp: A History of the Legendary German Firm* (Princeton, NJ: Princeton University Press, 2012), p. 60.

21. Charles Beard and Mary Beard, *The Rise of American Civilization,* vol. 2 (New York: Macmillan, 1927), pp. 53–54.

22. Quoted in Allen C. Guelzo, *Lincoln* (Oxford, UK: Oxford University Press, 2009), p. 120.

23. Friedrich Naumann, in *Verhandlungen der Verfassunggebenden Deutschen National-versammlung* [Negotiations of the constituent German national assembly], vol. 336: *Anlage zu den stenographischen Berichten* [Supplement to the shorthand reports] (Berlin: Druck und Verlag der Norddeutschen Buchdruckerei und Verlags-Anstalt, 1919), p. 242.

24. *Verhandlungen des Deutschen Reichstages* [Negotiations of the German Reichstag], electoral term 1920, vol. 236, meeting on June 25, 1922 (Berlin: Druck und Verlag der Norddeutschen Buchdruckerei und Verlags-Anstalt, 1922), p. 3058.

25. Eliza Relman, "Steve Bannon Says Ivanka Trump Is 'Dumb as a Brick,' " *Business Insider*, January 3, 2018, https://www.businessinsider.com/steve-bannon-says-ivanka-trump-is-dumb-as-a-brick-2018-1; Maureen Dowd, "He Went to Jared," *New York Times*, April 4, 2020, https://www.nytimes.com/2020/04/04/opinion/sunday/coronavirus-trump-jared-kushner.html.

26. Andrew Moravcsik, *The Choice for Europe: Social Purpose and State Power from Messina to Maastricht* (Ithaca, NY: Cornell University Press, 1998).

27. Jean Monnet, *Memoirs*, trans. Richard Mayne (London: Collins, 1978), p. 371.

28. Václav Havel, "How Europe Could Fail," *New York Review of Books* (November 18, 1993).

29. Monnet, *Memoirs*, p. 339.

30. Hans Peter Schwarz, *Helmut Kohl: Eine politische Biographie* (München: Deutsche Verlags Anstalt, 2012).

31. Martin Wolf, "Failing Elites Threaten Our Future," *Financial Times*, January 15, 2014, https://www.ft.com/content/cfc1eb1c-76d8-11e3-807e-00144feabdc0.

32. Per Jacobsson diary, 1958, cited in Harold James, *International Monetary Cooperation since Bretton Woods* (New York: Oxford University Press, 1995), p. 107.

4. Hegemony

1. J. A. O. Larsen, "Representative Government in the Panhellenic Leagues," *Classical Philology* 20, no. 4 (October 1925): 313–329; J. A. O. Larsen, "Representative Government in the Panhellenic Leagues II," *Classical Philology* 21, no. 1 (January 1926): 52–71.

2. Robert O. Keohane, *After Hegemony: Cooperation and Discord in the World Political Economy* (Princeton, NJ: Princeton University Press, 1984).

3. Ibid., pp. 31–32.

4. Stuart Schrader, *Badges without Borders: How Global Counterinsurgency Transformed American Policing* (Berkeley: University of California Press, 2019).

5. Kathrin Hille, Edward White, Primrose Riordan, and John Reed, "The Trump Factor: Asian Allies Question America's Reliability," *Financial Times*, June 15, 2020, https://www.ft.com/content/74576c3a-6303-4ba0-bbe3-15b563ce6019.

6. David Forgacs, *The Gramsci Reader: Selected Writings, 1916–1935* (New York: New York University Press, 2000), p. 192.

7. Perry Anderson, *The H-Word: The Peripeteia of Hegemony* (London: Verso, 2017), p. 96.

8. Theodor Mommsen, in *Schleswig-Holsteinische Zeitung*, May 16 and August 28, 1848, quoted in Anderson, *H-Word*, p. 7.

9. A modern account is Richard Little, *The Balance of Power in International Relations: Metaphors, Myths and Models* (Cambridge, UK: Cambridge University Press, 2007), for the Italian Renaissance discussion, see p. 43; see also M. S. Anderson, *The Rise of Modern Diplomacy, 1450–1919* (London: Longman, 1993), p. 151.

10. Walter Bagehot, *Lombard Street: A Description of the Money Market* (London: H. S. King & Co., 1873), pp. 4, 15.

11. An earlier but less stable transoceanic cable had been laid in 1858.

12. See the highly original book by Nicholas Lambert, *Planning Armageddon: British Economic Warfare and the First World War* (Cambridge, MA: Harvard University Press, 2012).

13. See ibid.

14. *Stenographische Protokolle des Hauses der Abgeordneten des Österreichischen Reichsrathes im Jahre 1897*, 13th sess., tape 2, p. 1363 (November 17, 1897).

15. Alfred T. Mahan, *The Interest of America in International Conditions* (Boston: Little, Brown, 1910), pp. 27–28.

16. Ibid., p. 36.

17. E. H. Carr, *The Twenty Years' Crisis, 1919–1939: An Introduction to the Study of International Relations* (London: Macmillan, 1939), p. 53.

18. Ibid., pp. 155, 164.

19. Ibid., p. 293.

20. Ibid., p. 282.

21. Ibid., p. 300. There is an echo of this argument in modern works, notably Adam Tooze's *The Wages of Destruction: The Making and Breaking of the Nazi Economy* (London: Allen Lane, 2006); and Brendan Simms, *Hitler: Only the World Was Enough* (London: Allen Lane, 2019).

22. Carr, *Twenty Years' Crisis*, p. 297.

23. Charles P. Kindleberger, *The World in Depression, 1929–1939*, 2nd ed. (Berkeley: University of California Press, 1986), p. 289.

24. Nikolas Busse, "Wir sind nicht Europas Hegemon," *FAZ*, April 25, 2020, https://www.faz.net/aktuell/politik/solidaritaet-deutschland-kann-die-eu-nicht-allein-tragen-16741944.html.

25. Simon Bulmer and William E. Paterson, *Germany and the European Union: Europe's Reluctant Hegemon?* (London: Red Globe Press, 2019).

26. For instance, Dirk Kurbjuweit, "America Has Abdicated Its Leadership of the West," *Spiegel*, November 14, 2016, https://www.spiegel.de/international/world/trump-election-means-europe-must-now-lead-west-a-1120929.html.

27. Alison Smale and Steven Erlanger, "As Obama Exits World Stage, Angela Merkel May Be the Liberal West's Last Defender," *New York Times*, November 12, 2016, https://www.nytimes.com/2016/11/13/world/europe/germany-merkel-trump-election.html.

28. Alison Smale and Steven Erlanger, "Merkel, After Discordant G-7 Meeting, Is Looking Past Trump," *New York Times*, May 28, 2017, "https://www.nytimes.com/2017/05/28/world/europe/angela-merkel-trump-alliances-g7-leaders.html.

29. Budget speech of November 23, 2016, in https://www.bundesregierung.de/Content/DE/Bulletin/2016/11/138-1-bkin-bt.html;jsessionid=E662DD61835F9BF54B7A7AC024CEA914.s5t1.

30. See Wade Jacoby and Sophie Meunier, "Europe and the Management of Globalization," *Journal of European Public Policy* 17, no. 3 (2010): 299–317.

31. Xi Jinping, "President Xi's Speech to Davos in Full," World Economic Forum, January 17, 2017, https://www.weforum.org/agenda/2017/01/full-text-of-xi-jinping-keynote-at-the-world-economic-forum.

32. Kwok-sing Li, *A Glossary of Political Terms of the People's Republic of China* (Hong Kong: Chinese University of Hong Kong Press, 1995), p. 403; Deng Xiaoping at United Nations General Assembly, April 10, 1974, sixth special session, https://www.marxists.org/reference/archive/deng-xiaoping/1974/04/10.htm.

33. This was the focus of Robert Shiller's presidential address to the American Economic Association, "Narrative Economics," *American Economic Review* 107, no. 4 (April 2017): 967–1004.

34. Roland Bénabou, "Groupthink: Collective Delusions in Organization and Markets," *Review of Economic Studies* 80, no. 2 (April 2013): 429–462.

35. See Emily Palmer, "A Fake Heiress," *New York Times,* May 10, 2019, https://www.nytimes.com/2019/05/10/nyregion/anna-delvey-sorokin.html.

36. Nick Paton Walsh, "A Guide to the Kremlin: Sex, Booze, Kidnap," *Guardian,* March 11, 2006, https://www.theguardian.com/world/2006/mar/11/russia.nickpatonwalsh.

37. Peter Pomerantsev, *Nothing Is True and Everything Is Possible: The Surreal Heart of the New Russia* (New York: Public Affairs, 2014), p. 47.

38. Timothy Snyder, *The Road to Unfreedom: Russia, Europe, America* (New York: Tim Duggan Books, 2018), p. 195.

39. Sheera Frenkel, "Meet Fancy Bear, The Russian Group Hacking the US Election," *Buzzfeed,* October 15, 2016, https://www.buzzfeednews.com/article/sheerafrenkel/meet-fancy-bear-the-russian-group-hacking-the-us-election.

40. Vladimir Putin, Security Conference, Munich, speech, February 2007, in *Vladimir Putin: Munich, Valdai, Sochi* (Kuala Lumpur: Institut Terjemahan & Buku Malaysia, 2014), p. 24.

41. Vladimir Putin, speech, Sochi, October 24, 2014, https://www.worldsecuritynetwork.com/Russia/no_author/Putins-World-Vision.

42. Kathy Lally, "Putin's Remarks Raise Fears of Future Moves against Ukraine," *Washington Post,* April 17, 2014, https://www.washingtonpost.com/world/putin-changes-course-admits-russian-troops-were-in-crimea-before-vote/2014/04/17/b3300a54-c617-11e3-bf7a-be01a9b69cf1_story.html.

43. Frenkel, "Meet Fancy Bear."

44. Zi Zhongyun, translated and annotated by Geremie R. Barmé, "An Old Anxiety in a New Era: 1900 & 2020," *China Heritage,* drafted on April 13, 2020, revised on April 23, 2020, http://chinaheritage.net/journal/1900–2020-an-old-anxiety-in-a-new-era.

5. Multilateralism

1. Jacob Viner, *The United States in a Multi-National Economy* (New York: Council on Foreign Relations, 1945), p. 153.

2. G. John Ikenberry, *After Victory: Institutions, Strategic Restraint, and the Rebuilding of Order after Major Wars* (Princeton, NJ: Princeton University Press, 2001).

3. Louis W. Pauly, *The League of Nations and the Foreshadowing of the International Monetary Fund*, Princeton University Essays in International Finance, no. 201, December 1996; Michel Fior, *Institution globale et marchés financiers: La Société des Nations face à la reconstruction de l'Europe, 1918–1931* (Bern: Peter Lang, 2008).

4. Sheryl Gay Stolberg, "As Leaders Wrestle with Downturn, Developing Nations Get Ringside Seats," *New York Times*, November 6, 2008.

5. Daniel Dombey, Krishna Guha, and Andrew Ward, "Talks Challenge Club of Rich Countries," *Financial Times*, November 17, 2008, https://www.ft.com/content/d2190e16-b434-11dd-8e35-0000779fd18c.

6. *United Nations Yearbook, 1971* (New York: United Nations, 1971), p. 126.

7. US Department of State, *Monetary and Financial Conference, Bretton Woods, New Hampshire, July 1 to July 22, 1944, Final Act and Related Documents*, 1944, p. 4.

8. E. E. Schattschneider, *Politics, Pressures and the Tariff; A Study of Free Private Enterprise in Pressure Politics, as Shown in the 1929–1930 Revision of the Tariff* (New York: Prentice-Hall, 1935); Mancur Olson, *The Logic of Collective Action: Public Goods and the Theory of Groups* (Cambridge, MA: Harvard University Press, 1971).

9. John G. Ruggie, *Winning the Peace: America and World Order in the New Era* (New York: Columbia University Press, 1996); G. John Ikenberry, "A World Economy Restored: Expert Consensus and the Anglo-American Postwar Settlement," *International Organization* 46, no. 1 (1992): 289–321.

10. A. Van Dormael, *Bretton Woods: Birth of a Monetary System* (New York: Holmes and Meier, 1978), p. 211.

11. John Maynard Keynes, The *Economic Consequences of the Peace* (London: Macmillan, 1919), pp. 263–264.

12. Keith Horsefield, *The International Monetary Fund, 1945–1965: Twenty Years of International Monetary Cooperation*, vol. 3 (Washington, DC: International Monetary Fund, 1969), p. 13.

13. Harold James, *International Cooperation since Bretton Woods* (New York: Oxford University Press, 1996), p. 37.

14. Van Dormael, *Bretton Woods*, pp. 6–7; Joseph Gold, *Legal and Institutional Aspects of the International Monetary System: Selected Essays*, vol. 2 (Washington, DC: International Monetary Fund, 1984), p. 19; Donald Moggridge, *Maynard Keynes: An Economist's Biography* (London: Routledge, 1992), p. 654.

15. There is a possibility that Keynes imagined a world in which there would be more exchange-rate alterations as the major adjustment mechanism for the international monetary system, with deficit countries depreciating and surplus countries appreciating. See David Vines, "John Maynard Keynes 1937–1946: The Creation of International Macroeconomics; a Review Article on 'John Maynard Keynes 1937–1946: Fighting for Britain, by Robert Skidelsky,' " *Economic Journal* 113 (June 2003): 338–361. The practice of the Bretton Woods system was remarkably different, however, with only two (contentious) appreciations of surplus currencies, in 1961 and 1969, and it would have been difficult in 1944–1945 to envisage the circumstances in which the United States, where the surpluses were likely to persist for the foreseeable future, would have agreed to an appreciation of the dollar.

16. Horsefield, *International Monetary Fund*, p. 6.

17. Samuel Brittan, *A Restatement of Economic Liberalism* (London: Macmillan, 1988), p. 87.

18. Proposals for a Clearing Union, in *Foreign Relations of the United States 1942*, vol. 1 (Washington, DC: US Government Printing Office, 1960), p. 204.

19. World Trade Organization, The Doha Round, https://www.wto.org/english/tratop_e/dda_e/dda_e.htm, accessed December 28, 2020.

20. World Bank data are at https://data.worldbank.org/indicator/TM.TAX.MRCH.WM.FN.ZS, accessed December 28, 2020.

21. European Commission, *Global Europe: Competing in the World: A Contribution to the EU's Growth and Jobs Strategy, 2006* (Brussels: European Commission, 2006), p. 567.

22. Office of the US Trade Representative, *2017 Trade Policy Agenda and 2016 Annual Report*, p. 1.

23. Andrew Walker, "US Adviser Hints at Evicting China from WTO," November 21, 2018, https://www.bbc.com/news/business-46280318.

24. Office of the US Trade Representative, *2017 Trade Policy*, p. 5.

25. Ibid., p. 6.

26. See Mark Zandi, Jesse Rogers, and Maria Cosma, "Trade War Chicken: The Tariffs and the Damage Done," Moody's Analytics, September 2019, https://www.economy.com/economicview/analysis/376236/Trade-War-Chicken-The-Tariffs-and-the-Damage-Done; Federal Reserve Board, "Disentangling the Effects of the 2018–2019 Tariffs on a Globally Connected U.S. Manufacturing Sector," December 23, 2019, https://www.federalreserve.gov/econres/feds/files/2019086pap.pdf; Ryan Hass and Abraham Denmark, "More Pain Than Gain: How the US-China Trade War Hurt America," Brookings blog, August 7, 2020, https://www.brookings.edu/blog/order-from-chaos/2020/08/07/more-pain-than-gain-how-the-us-china-trade-war-hurt-america.

27. See Robert Mundell, "The International Monetary System and the European Region," in Alexander Swoboda, ed., *L'Union Monétaire en Europe* (Geneva: HEI, 1971).

28. Michael P. Dooley, David Folkerts-Landau, and Peter Garber, "An Essay on the Revived Bretton Woods System," National Bureau of Economic Research, working paper 9971, September 2003.

29. Matthew Klein and Michael Pettis, *Trade Wars Are Class Wars: How Rising Inequality Distorts the Global Economy and Threatens International Peace* (New Haven: Yale University Press, 2020); Jean-Noël Barrot et al., *Import Competition and Household Debt*, Federal Reserve Bank of New York Staff Reports, no. 281, 2017.

30. European Central Bank, *The International Role of the Euro*, June 2020, https://www.ecb.europa.eu/pub/ire/html/ecb.ire202006~81495c263a.en.html.

31. Juan Zarate, *Treasury's War: The Unleashing of a New Era of Financial Warfare* (New York: PublicAffairs, 2013).

6.   The Frightening German *Politik* Terms

1. "Die Politik ist in der neueren Zeit die freyeste Kunst und Wissenschaft geworden" (p. 201); "So will aus dem Gemeinschaftlichen der Vorstellungen der Gedanke, und aus dem Gemeinschaftlichen in diesen der allgemeine Gedanke hervorgeht: so muss man in der Politik von den einzelnen Gegenständen und ihren Verhältnissen zu dem was dem Staate und von diesem zu dem was der Welt gemeinschaftlich ist, übergehen, wenn man sich vor Träumereien und Schwärmereien bewahren, und allgemeine Gedanken aus lebendigem Quell schöpfen will. So verfuhr Aristoteles und nach ihm jeder dem es um die Wissenschaft zu tun war," *Allgemeine Literatur-Zeitung* 3 (October 1814): 203.

2. See Urs App, *Richard Wagner and Buddhism* (Rorschach, Switz.: UniversityMedia, 2011).

3. Ludwig August von Rochau, *Grundsätze der Realpolitik,* ed. Hans-Ulrich Wehler (1853; Frankfurt: Ullstein, 1972), pp. 13, 21.

4. Ludwig August von Rochau, *Grundsätze der Realpolitik, angewendet auf die staatlichen Zustände Deutschlands Theil II* (Heidelberg: J.C.B. Mohr, 1869), pp. 18–19.

5. Rochau, *Grundsätze der Realpolitik* (1853), pp. 25, 191. See also John Bew, *Realpolitik: A History* (Oxford, UK: Oxford University Press, 2016), p. 43.

6. Otto von Bismarck, *Bismarck: Die gesammelten Werke Band 10: Reden 1847–1869,* ed. Wilhelm Schüßler (Berlin: Otto Stolberg, 1928), pp. 139–140.

7. Gustav Schmoller, "Die wirtschaftliche Zukunft: Deutschland und die Flottenvorlage," in Gustav von Schmoller, Max Sering, and Adolph Wagner, *Handels-und Machtpolitik: Reden und Aufsätze im Auftrage der Freien Vereinigung für Flottenvorträge* (Stuttgart: Cotta, 1900), p. 19.

8. "Mit einem Worte: wir wollen niemand in den Schatten stellen, aber wir verlangen auch unseren Platz an der Sonne," in *Fürst Bülows Reden nebst urkundlichen Beiträgen zu seiner Politik,* ed. Johannes Penzler, vol. 1, tape 1897–1903 (Berlin: Georg Reimer, 1907), pp. 6–8.

9. Friedrich von Holstein, *The Holstein Papers,* ed. Norman Rich and M. H. Fisher, vol. 4: *Correspondence 1897–1909* (Cambridge, UK: Cambridge University Press, 1963), p. 245.

10. Ian F. D. Morrow, "The Foreign Policy of Prince von Bülow, 1898–1909," *Cambridge Historical Journal* 4, no. 1 (1932): 64.

11. Karl Haushofer, Erich Obst, Hermann Lautensach, and Otto Maull, *Bausteine zur Geopolitik* (Berlin-Grunewald: Kurt Vowinckel, 1928), pp. 17, 27.

12. See Brian W. Blouet, "The Imperial Vision of Halford Mackinder," *Geographical Journal* 170, no. 4 (2004): 322–329.

13. H. J. Mackinder, "The Geographical Pivot of History," *Geographical Journal* 23, no. 4 (1904): 422, 433.

14. Holger H. Herwig, *The Demon of Geopolitics: How Karl Haushofer "Educated" Hitler and Hess* (New York: Rowman & Littlefield, 2016), p. 17.

15. Karl Haushofer to Rudolf Pechel, reprinted in Hans-Adolf Jacobsen, ed., *Karl Haushofer: Leben und Werk,* vol. 2 (Boppard am Rhein: Boldt, 1979), p. 3.

16. "Hitler's World Revolution," *New Statesman and Nation* 444 (August 26, 1939): 301.

17. Frederic Sondern, "Hitler's Scientists," *Current History and Forum* 53, no. 1 (June 1, 1941): 10.

18. Jacobsen, *Haushofer,* vol. 2, p. 509; also Herwig, *Demon,* p. xi.

19. Hans-Adolf Jacobsen, ed., *Karl Haushofer: Leben und Werk,* vol. 1 (Boppard am Rhein: Boldt, 1979), pp. 438, 644.

20. Patrick J. McNamara, "'The Argument of Strength Justly and Righteously Employed': Edmund A. Walsh, Catholic Anticommunism, and American Foreign Policy, 1945–1952," *US Catholic Historian* 22, no. 4 (2004): 65, 70; also Brian W. Blouet, *Geopolitics and Globalization in the Twentieth Century* (London: Reaktion Books, 2001), pp. 133–134.

21. E. Gnedin, *Iz istorii otnosheniy mezhdu SSSR i fashistskoi Germaniey* (New York: Khronika Press, 1977).

22. See A. Radó, "Geopolitika," in *Bolshaya Sovetskaya Entsiklopediya,* vol. 15 (Moscow: State Publishing House, 1929), 389–392, p. 390. On Radó, see Leonid Ivashov, *Razmyshleniya russkogo generala* (Moscow: LitRes, 2019).

23. Nicholas J. Spykman, "Geography and Foreign Policy, II," *American Political Science Review* 32, no. 2 (1938): 236.

24. Col. Charles A. Lindbergh's Radio Address, September 15, 1939, *World Affairs* 102, no. 3 (1939): 165.

25. Bew, *Realpolitik,* p. 241.

26. Ibid., p. 258.

27. See G. John Ikenberry, *A World Safe for Democracy: Liberal Internationalism and the Crises of Global Order* (New Haven: Yale University Press, 2020), p. 235.

28. Brian W. Blouet, *Geopolitics and Globalization in the Twentieth Century* (London: Reaktion Books, 2001), p. 177.

29. Colin Gray, "In Defence of the Heartland: Sir Halford Mackinder and His Critics a Hundred Years On," *Comparative Strategy* 23 (2004): 17.

30. George Kennan, [Moscow, n.d., May 1945?]: "Russia's International Position at the Close of the War with Germany," from *Foreign Relations of the United States 1945,* vol. 5, https://history.state.gov/historicaldocuments/frus1945v05/d643; John Lewis Gaddis, *George F. Kennan: An American Life* (New York: Penguin, 2011), p. 166.

31. Winston Churchill, "We Will Deal in Performances, Not Promises," radio address of October 1, 1939, in *The War Speeches of the Rt. Hon. Winston S. Churchill,* vol. 1 (London: Cassell, 1952), p. 109.

32. Thomas L. Friedman, "Now a Word from X," *New York Times,* May 2, 1998, https://www.nytimes.com/1998/05/02/opinion/foreign-affairs-now-a-word-from-x.html.

33. Bew, *Realpolitik,* p. 222.

34. Ibid., p. 218.

35. John J. Mearsheimer, *The Great Delusion: Liberal Dreams and International Realities* (New Haven: Yale University Press, 2018), p. 3.

36. Ibid., p. 150.

37. Ibid., p. 171.

38. Edward Luttwak, *Turbo-Capitalism: Winners and Losers in the Global Economy*, New York: HarperCollins, 1999, pp. 141, 135.

39. Pascal Lorot, *De la géopolitique à la géoéconomie* (1999; Paris: Éditions Choiseul, 2009), p. 14.

40. Quoted in Kelly Hooper, "Fantasy World," *Politico*, November 24, 2020, https://www.politico.com/news/2020/11/24/pompeo-biden-administration-foreign-policy-440469.

41. "Prezhde vsego priznat', chto krusheniye Sovetskogo Soyuza bylo krupneyshey geopoliticheskoy katastrofoy veka . . . Epidemiya raspada k tomu zhe perekinulas' na samu Rossiyu," http://kremlin.ru/events/president/transcripts/22931; the official Russian translation into English gives the phrase as "the collapse of the Soviet Union was a major geopolitical disaster of the century."

42. "Radical Object: The Necro-Ontology of Dark Enlightenment (Negarestani's Philosophy," Geopolitica.ru, September 19, 2019: https://www.geopolitica.ru/en/article/radical-object-necro-ontology-dark-enlightenment-negarestanis-philosophy.

43. See Marlene Ruelle, "Scared of Putin's Shadow: In Sanctioning Dugin, Washington Got the Wrong Man," *Foreign Affairs*, March 25, 2015, https://www.foreignaffairs.com/articles/russian-federation/2015-03-25/scared-putins-shadow.

44. Andreas Umland, "Das eurasische Reich Dugins und Putins: Ähnlichkeiten und Unterschiede," *Kritiknetz: Zeitschrift für Kritische Theorie der Gesellschaft*, June 26, 2014, available at http://www.kritiknetz.de/images/stories/texte/ Umland_Dugin_Putin.pdf.

45. Francis P. Sempa, "Surviving the Future: Looking Back at the Toynbee-Wakaizumi Dialogue of 1970," *The Diplomat*, January 4, 2018, https://thediplomat.com/2018/01/surviving-the-future-looking-back-at-the-toynbee-wakaizumi-dialogue-of-1970.

46. Agata Wierzbowska-Miazga, "Russia Goes on the Offensive ahead of the Eastern Partnership Summit in Vilnius," Center for Eastern Studies Commentary, Warsaw, no. 115, September 30, 2013, https://www.osw.waw.pl/en/publikacje/osw-commentary/2013-10-01/russia-goes-offensive-ahead-eastern-partnership-summit-vilnius.

47. For documentary materials, see the work of a group of filmmakers called Babylon '13, including the films *Generation Maidan: A Year of Revolution and War* (2015), *Brothers in Arms* (2015) directed by Konstiantyn Mohylnyk, and *Winter on Fire: Ukraine's Fight for Freedom* (2015) directed by Evgeny Afineevsky.

48. Andrew Wilson, *Ukraine Crisis: What It Means for the West* (New Haven: Yale University Press, 2014), p. 94; see also *Crimea, The Way Back Home,* a documentary film that premiered on Channel One of Russian TV on March 15, 2015, and was produced by Andrey Kondrashov from the geopolitical perspective of the Russian state.

49. "Statement by Ambassador Sergiy Kyslytsya," May 28, 2020, http://ukraineun.org/en/press-center/431-statement-by-ambassador-sergiy-kyslytsya-permanent-representative-of-ukraine-to-the-un-on-the-occasion-of-commemoration-of-the-signing-of-the-un-charter.

50. Vladimir Putin, "Crimean Speech," speech by President Vladimir Putin to both chambers of the Federal Assembly of the Russian Federation, March 18, 2014, http://en.kremlin.ru/events/president/news/20603.

51. Statement of Vassily Nebenzia, permanent representative of Russia to the United Nations, May 28, 2020, https://russiaun.ru/en/news/un_eu280520.

52. Putin, "Crimean Speech."

53. Ibid.

54. Vladimir Putin, "Address to the Nation," June 23, 2020, http://en.kremlin.ru/events/president/news/63548.

55. Henry Kissinger, *World Order* (New York: Penguin, 2014), p. 364.

56. Henry Kissinger, "Opinion: To Settle the Ukraine Crisis, Start at the End," *Washington Post,* March 5, 2014, https://www.washingtonpost.com/opinions/henry-kissinger-to-settle-the-ukraine-crisis-start-at-the-end/2014/03/05/46dad868-a496-11e3-8466-d34c451760b9_story.html.

57. Henry Kissinger: "Do We Achieve World Order through Chaos or Insight? Interview with Henry Kissinger," *Der Spiegel,* November 13, 2014, https://www.spiegel.de/international/world/interview-with-henry-kissinger-on-state-of-global-politics-a-1002073.html.

58. Robert Cooper, *The Post-Modern State and the World Order* (London: Demos, 2000); Robert Kagan, *Of Paradise and Power: America and Europe in the New World Order* (New York: Random House, 2003).

59. Alan S. Milward, *The European Rescue of the Nation-State* (Berkeley: University of California Press, 1992).

60. Josep Borrell, "Embracing Europe's Power," Project Syndicate, February 8, 2020, https://www.neweurope.eu/article/embracing-europes-power.

7. Debt

1. William Shakespeare, *Henry VI, Part 2,* act 4, scene 2.

2. The most influential recent account is David Graeber, *Debt: The First 5000 Years* (New York: Melville, 2011).

3. See Melissa Lane, *The Birth of Politics: Eight Greek and Roman Political Ideas and Why They Matter* (Princeton, NJ: Princeton University Press, 2015).

4. Felix Salmon, "Shrinking Banks," Reuters, August 26, 2009, http://blogs.reuters.com/felix-salmon/2009/08/26/shrinking-banks; Timur Kuran, *Islam and Mammon: The Economic Predicaments of Islamism* (Princeton, NJ: Princeton University Press, 2004).

5. Carlo Taviani, "An Ancient Scheme: The Mississippi Company, Machiavelli, and the Casa di San Giorgio (1407–1720)," *Political Power and Social Theory* 29 (August 2015): 239–256.

6. William Paterson, *A Brief Account of the Intended Bank of England* (London: Randal Taylor, 1694), p. 8.

7. The most influential account is Douglass North and Barry Weingast, "Constitutions and Commitment: The Evolution of Institutions Governing Public Choice in

Seventeenth-Century England," *Journal of Economic History* 49, no. 4 (December 1989): 803–832.

8. See Thomas Sargent, Nobel Prize acceptance speech, 2011, https://www.nobelprize.org/prizes/economic-sciences/2011/sargent/lecture.

9. My translation, from *Faust*, Part 2, in *Goethe's Werke*, vol. 41 (Stuttgart: J. G. Cotta, 1832), pp. 65, 67.

10. Jens Weidmann, "Money Creation and Responsibility," speech at the 18th Colloquium of the Institute for Bank-Historical Research (IBF), Frankfurt, September 18, 2012.

11. Honoré de Balzac, *Old Goriot [Père Goriot]*, trans. Ellen Marriage (London: Dent, 1907), pp. 15, 88, 254.

12. Charles Dickens, *Little Dorrit* (1857; New York: Carleton, 1880), chap. 6, p. 66.

13. For the Friedman quotation, see Chestnut Street, citing Luistorras, November 2, 2015, https://chesnutstreet.wordpress.com/2015/06/16/a-predictable-pathology-benjamin-m-friedman-11022015.

14. Henry Roseveare, *The Treasury: The Evolution of a British Institution* (Harmondsworth, UK: Allen Lane, 1969), p. 118.

15. Stuart Holland, "Debt, Guilt, and Human History: A Reply to Wolfgang Schäuble," July 26, 2013, https://www.yanisvaroufakis.eu/2013/07/26/debt-guilt-and-german-history-a-reply-to-wolfgang-schauble-by-stuart-holland; Yanis Varoufakis, "The Annotated Wolfgang Schäuble: Commentary on His *Guardian* Article, July 19, 2013," July 21, 2013, https://www.yanisvaroufakis.eu/2013/07/21/the-annotated-wolfgang-schauble-commentary-on-his-guardian-article-19th-july-2013.

16. Matthew 18:32–34.

17. Patricia Nilsson and Emiko Terazano, "Can Fast Fashion's $2.5tn Supply Chain Be Stitched Back Together?," *Financial Times*, May 16, 2020, https://www.ft.com/content/62dc687e-d15f-46e7-96df-ed7d00f8ca55.

18. See Adair Turner, *Between Debt and the Devil: Money, Credit, and Fixing Global Finance* (Princeton, NJ: Princeton University Press, 2016), p. 191.

19. Franco Modigliani and Merton H. Miller, "The Cost of Capital, Corporation Finance and the Theory of Investment," *American Economic Review* 48, no. 3 (June 1958): 261–297.

20. Tobias Adrian and Hyun Song Shin, "Financial Intermediary Balance Sheet Management," Federal Reserve Bank of New York Staff Report no. 532, December 2011, https://www.newyorkfed.org/medialibrary/media/research/staff_reports/sr532.pdf.

21. Douglas Irwin, *Clashing over Commerce: A History of US Trade Policy* (Chicago: University of Chicago Press, 2017), pp. 288–289; Steven A. Bank, *From Sword to Shield: The Transformation of the Corporate Income Tax, 1861* (Oxford, UK: Oxford University Press, 2010), p. 44.

22. Sheldon D. Pollack, "Origins of the Modern Income Tax, 1894–1913," *Tax Lawyer* 66 (Winter 2013): 205. An income tax had been a major goal of populist forces for at least two decades: "from 1874 to 1894, no fewer than sixty-eight bills were

introduced in Congress to enact a progressive income tax." Sheldon D. Pollack, *War, Revenue, and State Building: Financing the Development of the American State* (Ithaca, NY: Cornell University Press, 2009), p. 238.

23. I owe this interpretation to the excellent senior thesis of Charles Ughetta: "Myths, Markets and Power: Taxing Interest; Credit as Political Capital's Source and Target," Princeton University, 2019.

24. Henry Cabot Lodge, "Results of Democratic Victory," *North American Review* 159, no. 454 (September 1894): 268–277, quotation on p. 274.

25. *Congressional Record* 1673 (1894).

26. Steven A. Bank, "Historical Perspective on the Corporate Interest Deduction," *Chapman Law Review* 18, no. 1 (2014): 20.

27. Paul Marsh, "The Choice between Equity and Debt: An Empirical Study," *Journal of Finance* 37, no. 1 (1982): 126.

28. "Taft Plan for Tax Splits Committee," *New York Times*, June 19, 1909, p. 5; Bank, "Historical Perspective," p. 36.

29. Alvin C. Warren Jr., "The Corporate Interest Deduction: A Policy Evaluation," *Yale Law Journal* 83 (1974): 1584.

30. BIS figures, Statistics Table F4, updated continually, https://stats.bis.org/statx/srs/table/f4.1.

31. Emma Rothschild, *Economic Sentiments: Adam Smith, Condorcet, and the Enlightenment* (Cambridge, MA: Harvard University Press, 2001), p. 245.

32. Emma Rothschild, "Globalization and the Return of History," *Foreign Policy* 115 (Summer 1999): 110.

33. Carlos Marichal, *A Century of Debt Crises in Latin America: From Independence to the Great Depression, 1820–1930* (Princeton, NJ: Princeton University Press, 1989); Marc Flandreau and Frederic Zumer, *The Making of Global Finance, 1880–1913* (Paris: OECD, 2004); Gerardo della Paolera and Alan M. Taylor, "Sovereign Debt in Latin America, 1820–1913," NBER working paper no. 18363, September 2012.

34. Carmen M. Reinhart and Christoph Trebesch, "The Pitfalls of External Dependence: Greece, 1829–2015," Brookings Papers on Economic Activity, Fall 2015.

35. Niall Ferguson and Moritz Schularick, "The Empire Effect: The Determinants of Country Risk in the First Age of Globalization, 1880–1913," *Journal of Economic History* 66, no. 2 (June 2006): 283–312.

36. Jennifer Siegel, *For Peace and Money: French and British Finance in the Service of Tsars and Commissars* (Oxford, UK: Oxford University Press, 2014).

37. Theodore H. von Laue, *Sergei Witte and the Industrialization of Russia* (New York: Columbia University Press, 1963).

38. Olga Crisp, *Studies in the Russian Economy before 1914* (London: Macmillan, Crisp, 1976).

39. Siegel, *For Peace and Money*.

40. Adolf Weber, *Reparationen Youngplan Volkswirtschaft* (Berlin: Junker und Dünnhaupt, 1929), p. 14. There is a similar sentiment in O. Wingen, *Weltverschuldung und Deutschlands Reparationslast* (Berlin: Zentral-Verlag, 1928), p. 55.

41. For the protection provisions of the Young Plan and the Hague Agreement, see *Deutsches Reichsgesetzblatt 1930*, vol. 2, p. 514. In general on this theme, see Albrecht Ritschl, "Reparation Transfers, the Borchardt Hypothesis, and the Great Depression in Germany, 1929–32: A Guided Tour for Hard-Headed Keynesians," *European Review of Economic History* 2, no. 1 (1998): 49–72.

42. Section 32 of Report of the Committee of Experts on Reparations (Young Committee report) (London: Her Majesty's Stationery Office, 1929).

43. There is a voluminous literature on these defaults: see, for example, Harold James, *The End of Globalization: Lessons from the Great Depression* (Cambridge, MA: Harvard University Press, 2001); Michael Tomz, *Reputation and International Cooperation: Sovereign Debt across Three Centuries* (Princeton, NJ: Princeton University Press, 2012).

44. See the recent book Jerome Roos, *Why Not Default? The Political Economy of Sovereign Debt* (Princeton, NJ: Princeton University Press, 2019). What constitutes default is a very complicated and contested question: see S. Ali Abbas, Alex Pienkowski, and Kenneth Rogoff, eds., *Sovereign Debt: A Guide for Economists and Practitioners* (New York: Oxford University Press, 2019).

45. Anne O. Krueger, *A New Approach to Sovereign Debt Restructuring* (Washington, DC: International Monetary Fund, 2002).

46. Sebastian Horn, Carmen M. Reinhart, and Christoph Trebesch, "China's Overseas Lending," NBER working paper no. 26050, July 2019, revised April 2020.

47. Niall Ferguson and Moritz Schularick, "The End of Chimerica," Harvard Business School BGIE Unit, working paper no. 10–037, 2009.

48. Centre for Economic Policy Research, policy note 103, "Born Out of Necessity: A Debt Standstill for COVID-19," April 2020.

8.   Technocracy

1. William Henry Smyth, "Technocracy: National Industrial Management," *Industrial Management* 57 (March 1919): 211.

2. Ibid., p. 212.

3. Quoted in Richard Kuisel, *Capitalism and the State in Modern France: Renovation and Economic Management in the Twentieth Century* (Cambridge, UK: Cambridge University Press, 1981), p. 40.

4. Vannevar Bush, director of the Office of Scientific Research and Development, *Science: The Endless Frontier*, July 1945, https://www.nsf.gov/od/lpa/nsf50/vbush1945.htm#ch1.3; for the pushback, see Donald E. Stokes, *Pasteur's Quadrant: Basic Science and Technological Innovation* (Washington, DC: Brookings, 1997).

. 5. Warren Weaver, "Science and Complexity," *American Scientist* 36, no. 4 (October 1948): 537, 542.

6. James Burnham, *The Managerial Revolution* (London: Putnam, 1942), pp. 172 and 178.

7. Carl von Clausewitz, *On War*, ed. Michael Howard and Peter Paret (Princeton, NJ: Princeton University Press, 1976), p. 144.

8. Ibid., pp. 119–120.

9. Ibid., p. 117.

10. Ibid., p. 583.

11. Carl von Clausewitz, *Vom Kriege* (Berlin: Hohenberg, 2016), p. 487.

12. Richard Taylor Stevenson, *Missions versus Militarism* (New York: Abingdon Press, 1916), p. 78.

13. Thomas MacKinnon Wood and Arthur Henderson, *British Finance and Prussian Militarism: Two Interviews* (London: Hodder and Stoughton, 1917), p. 14.

14. Manfred Halpern, *The Politics of Social Change in the Middle East and North Africa* (Princeton, NJ: Princeton Legacy Library, 1963), p. 253.

15. James A. Bill, "The Military and Modernization in the Middle East," *Comparative Politics* 2, no. 1 (October 1969): 41–62.

16. See, for instance, the tweets of Hendrick Hertzberg of the *New Yorker,* at https://twitter.com/RickHertzberg/status/1254509734838841344.

17. N. Gregory Mankiw, "The Macroeconomist as Scientist and Engineer," NBER working paper no. 12349, June 2006.

18. Obituary of Charles Kindleberger, *MIT News,* July 7, 2003, http://news.mit.edu/2003/kindleberger.

19. Robert E. Lucas Jr. and Thomas J. Sargent, "After Keynesian Macroeconomics," *Federal Reserve Bank of Minneapolis Quarterly Review* 3, no. 2 (Spring 1979): 1–16.

20. Michael D. Bordo, "The Contribution of *A Monetary History of the United States, 1867–1960* to Monetary History," in Michael D. Bordo, ed., *Money, History and International Finance: Essays in Honor of Anna J. Schwartz* (Chicago: University of Chicago Press for the National Bureau of Economic Research, 1989), p. 51.

21. Statement by Paul A. Volcker, chair, Board of Governors of the Federal Reserve System, before the Joint Economic Committee of the US Congress, February 1, 1980, *Federal Reserve Bulletin,* February 1980, p. 140.

22. Jesper Lindé, "DSGE Models: Still Useful in Policy Analysis?," *Oxford Review of Economic Policy* 34, nos. 1–2 (Spring–Summer 2018): 269–286; Paul M. Romer, "Mathiness in the Theory of Economic Growth," *American Economic Review* 105, no. 5 (May 2015): 89–93.

23. Mankiw, "Macroeconomist as Scientist and Engineer"; see also Paul Romer, "The Trouble with Macroeconomics," September 2016, https://paulromer.net/the-trouble-with-macro.

24. James H. Stock and Mark W. Watson, "Has the Business Cycle Changed? Evidence and Explanations," FRB Kansas City Symposium, Jackson Hole, WY, August 28–30, 2003, p. 40.

25. Anna J. Schwartz, "Why Financial Stability Depends on Price Stability," *Economic Affairs* 4, no. 15 (September 1995): 21–25, quotation on p. 21; Michael D. Bordo and David C. Wheelock, "Price Stability and Financial Stability: The Historical Record," *Federal Reserve Bank of St. Louis Review* 80, no. 5 (September/October 1998): 41–62 (concentrating on disruptions caused by disinflation).

26. Eddie George, "The Pursuit of Financial Stability," speech delivered November 18, 1993, Bank of England archive, 16A32/2.

27. Claudio Borio and Philip Lowe, "Asset Prices, Financial and Monetary Stability: Exploring the Nexus," BIS working papers 114, July 2, 2002.

28. Andrew Pierce, "The Queen Asks Why No One Saw the Credit Crunch Coming," *Daily Telegraph*, November 5, 2008, https://www.telegraph.co.uk/news/uknews/theroyalfamily/3386353/The-Queen-asks-why-no-one-saw-the-credit-crunch-coming.html.

29. Helena Smith, "Lucas Papademos to Lead Greece's Interim Coalition Government," *The Guardian*, November 10, 2011, https://www.theguardian.com/world/2011/nov/10/lucas-papademos-greece-interim-coalition.

30. See Margaret Thatcher, "Speech to the Royal Society," September 27, 1988, https://www.margaretthatcher.org/document/107346.

31. Quoted in Associated Press, "Germany Plans to Abandon Nuclear Energy by 2022," CBS News, May 30, 2011, https://www.cbsnews.com/news/germany-plans-to-abandon-nuclear-energy-by-2022.

32. See Stanley Jevons, *The Coal Question; An Enquiry Concerning the Progress of the Nation, and the Probable Exhaustion of Our Coal-Mines* (London: Macmillan, 1865), pp. vii, 253, 349.

33. Quoted in Shellen Xiao Wu, *Empires of Coal: Fueling China's Entry into the Modern World Order, 1860–1920* (Stanford, CA: Stanford University Press, 2015), p. 173.

34. *The Diaries of Xue Fucheng,* quoted in ibid., p. 172.

35. *Scientific American* 261, no. 3, special issue "Managing Planet Earth" (September 1989).

36. See Environmental Investigation Agency, "Happy UN Ozone Day: Celebrating 30 Years of Ozone and Climate Protection," https://eia-international.org/news/happy-un-ozone-day-celebrating-30-years-ozone-climate-protection.

37. William C. Clark, "Managing Planet Earth," *Scientific American* 261, no. 3 (September 1989): 54.

38. See Daniel Yergin, *The Quest: Energy, Security, and the Remaking of the Modern World* (New York: Penguin, 2011), p. 401.

39. "Russia's Vladimir Putin Doubts Man-Made Climate Change, Backs Trump," *DW*, December 19, 2019, https://www.dw.com/en/russias-vladimir-putin-doubts-man-made-climate-change-backs-trump/a-51736903.

40. Helier Cheung, "What Does Trump Actually Believe on Climate Change?," *BBC News,* January 23, 2020, https://www.bbc.com/news/world-us-canada-51213003.

41. Kate Forrester, "BBC under Fire for Allowing Climate Change Denier Nigel Lawson on Radio 4," *Huffington Post UK,* August 10, 2017, https://www.huffingtonpost.co.uk/entry/bbc-under-fire-for-allowing-climate-change-denier-nigel-lawson-on-radio-4_uk_598c5f6be4b0449ed5083815.

42. Richard Collett-White and Tom Ritchie, "Brexit Party Candidates' Climate Change Denial Exposed," *London Economic,* November 22, 2019, https://www.the londoneconomic.com/news/environment/brexit-party-candidates-climate-change-denial-exposed/22/11.

43. Vera Deleja-Hotko, Ann-Katrin Müller, and Gerald Traufetter, "AfD Hopes to Win Votes by Opposing Climate Protection," *Der Spiegel,* May 6, 2019, https://www.spiegel.de/international/germany/afd-seeks-votes-by-opposing-climate-protection-a-1265494.html.

44. Beth Gardiner, "For Europe's Far-Right Parties, Climate Is a New Battleground," *Yale Environment 360,* October 29, 2019, https://e360.yale.edu/features/for-europes-far-right-parties-climate-is-a-new-battleground.

45. Arthur Neslen, "Far-Right MEPs Could Threaten EU Climate Policy, Experts Warn," *The Guardian,* May 21, 2019, https://www.theguardian.com/politics/2019/may/21/far-right-meps-could-threaten-eu-climate-policy-experts-warn.

46. Pallab Ghosh, "Mass Culling for Foot-and-Mouth 'May Be Unnecessary,' " *BBC News,* May 6, 2011, https://www.bbc.com/news/science-environment-13299666; Daniel Haydon, Rowland Kao, and R. Kitching, "The UK Foot-and-Mouth Disease Outbreak—The Aftermath," *Nature Reviews Microbiology* 2, no. 8 (September 2004): 675–681.

47. Jonathan Ford, "The Battle at the Heart of British Science over Coronavirus," *Financial Times,* April 15, 2020, https://www.ft.com/content/1e390ac6-7e2c-11ea-8fdb-7ec06edeef84.

48. Clive Cookson, "Coronavirus May Have Infected Half of UK Population—Oxford Study," *Financial Times,* March 24, 2020, https://www.ft.com/content/5ff6469a-6dd8-11ea-89df-41bea055720b.

49. US White House Press Briefings, "Remarks by President Trump, Vice President Pence, and Members of the Coronavirus Task Force in Press Briefing," April 1, 2020, https://www.whitehouse.gov/briefings-statements/remarks-president-trump-vice-president-pence-members-coronavirus-task-force-press-briefing-15.

50. Christopher Avery, William Bossert, Adam Clark, Glenn Ellison, and Sara Fisher Ellison, "Policy Implications of Models of the Spread of Coronavirus: Perspectives and Opportunities for Economists," NBER working paper no. 27007, April 2020.

51. Andrew Wilson, *Ukraine Crisis: What It Means for the West* (New Haven: Yale University Press, 2014), pp. 22–23.

52. Sasha Issenberg, "How Obama's Team Used Big Data to Rally Voters," *MIT Technology Review,* December 19, 2012, https://www.technologyreview.com/2012/12/19/114510/how-obamas-team-used-big-data-to-rally-voters.

53. Jim Rutenberg, "Data You Can Believe In," *New York Times Magazine,* June 23, 2013, https://www.nytimes.com/2013/06/23/magazine/the-obama-campaigns-digital-masterminds-cash-in.html.

54. Robert Peston, "Corbyn 2.0," *The Spectator,* November 18, 2017, https://www.spectator.co.uk/article/corbyn-2-0.

55. Richard McGregor, "US Political Marketing: Tailored Message," *Financial Times,* October 8, 2014, https://www.ft.com/content/8a9b65d8-4d68-11e4-bf60-00144feab7de.

56. Chris Hables Gray, Steven Mentor, and Heidi Figueroa-Sarriera, *Cyborg Handbook* (London: Routledge, 1995), p. 47; Caroline Gerschlager, ed., *Expanding the*

Economic Concept of Exchange: Deception, Self-Deception and Illusions (Dordrecht: Springer Science + Business Media, 2001), p. 107.

57. Alasdair MacIntyre, *After Virtue* (London: Bloomsbury, 1981), p. 90.

9. Populism

1. David Goodhart, *The Road to Somewhere: The Populist Revolt and the Future of Politics* (London: C. Hurst, 2017).

2. Barry Eichengreen, *The Populist Temptation: Economic Grievance and Political Reaction in the Modern Era* (New York: Oxford University Press, 2018), p. 1.

3. "A Close Look at President Trump's Assertion of 'Absolute' Authority over States," *NPR*, April 14, 2020, https://www.npr.org/2020/04/14/834460063/a-close-look-at-president-trumps-assertion-of-absolute-authority-over-states.

4. Josephine Harvey, "Trump Declares He Has 'Total' Authority as President in Defiant Press Briefing," *Huffington Post*, April 13, 2020, https://www.huffpost.com/entry/trump-total-authority-president_n_5e94f544c5b606109f5ea92b?ri18n=true.

5. For Prime Minister Chan-o-cha's comment, see "Prime Minister Announces Nationwide Curfew," *Thai Enquirer*, April 2, 2020, https://www.thaienquirer.com/10519/prime-minister-announces-nationwide-curfew-additional-measures.

6. Joe Hagan, "'Dishonesty . . . Is Always an Indicator of Weakness': Tucker Carlson on How He Brought His Coronavirus Message to Mar-a-Lago," March 17, 2020, https://www.vanityfair.com/news/2020/03/tucker-carlson-on-how-he-brought-coronavirus-message-to-mar-a-lago.

7. William Shakespeare, *Hamlet*, act 4, scene 1.

8. Robert Sedlaczek, "Wenn das gesunde Volksempfinden entscheidet," *Wiener Zeitung*, November 29, 2011, https://www.wienerzeitung.at/meinung/glossen/414939_Wenn-das-gesunde-Volksempfinden-entscheidet.html.

9. Irving Berlin, "Doin' What Comes Naturally," from the musical *Annie Get Your Gun*, 1948.

10. Brett Samuels, "Trump Promotes Use of Drug for Coronovirus: 'I'm Not a Doctor. But I Have Common Sense," The Hill, April 5, 2020, https://thehill.com/homenews/administration/491277-trump-promotes-use-of-drug-for-coronavirus-im-not-a-doctor-but-i-have.

11. Lionel Barber, Henry Foy, and Alex Barker, "Vladimir Putin Says Liberalism Has 'Become Obsolete,' " *Financial Times*, June 27, 2019, https://www.ft.com/content/670039ec-98f3-11e9-9573-ee5cbb98ed36.

12. Fareed Zakaria, "The Rise of Illiberal Democracy," *Foreign Affairs* 76, no. 6 (November/December 1997): 22–43.

13. Ibid., p. 23.

14. Dani Rodrick and Sharun Mukand, "Why Illiberal Democracies Are on the Rise," *Huffington Post*, May 18, 2015, http://www.huffingtonpost.com/dani-rodrik/illiberal-democracies-on-therise_b_7302374.html.

15. Csaba Tóth, "Full Text of Victor Orbán's Speech at Băile Tuşnad Tusnádfürdő of July 26, 2014," *Budapest Beacon*, July 29, 2014, https://budapestbeacon.com/full-text-of-viktor-orbans-speech-at-baile-tusnad-tusnadfurdo-of-26-july-2014.

16. Barber, Foy, and Barker, "Vladimir Putin."

17. AFP, "Erdogan Says Turkey Has Given World 'Lesson in Democracy' as He Sweeps to Election Victory," *The Journal*, June 25, 2018, https://www.thejournal.ie/erdogan-turkey-democracy-4089936-Jun2018.

18. H. E. Recep Tayyip Erdoğan, Prime Minister of Turkey, "Democracy in the Middle East, Pluralism in Europe: Turkish View," address given at Harvard University, Kennedy School of Government, January 30, 2003.

19. Jenny White, "Democracy Is Like a Tram," commentary, Turkey Institute, July 14, 2016, https://www.turkeyinstitute.org.uk/commentary/democracy-like-tram.

20. Presidency of the Republic of Turkey, Speech at the Opening of Parliament, October 1, 2014, https://www.tccb.gov.tr/en/speeches-statements/558/3192/opening-remarks-on-the-occasion-of-the-24th-term-of-the-5th-legislative-year-of-the-turkish-grand-national-assembly.

21. Norman Pollack, *The Populist Response to Industrial America: Midwestern Populist Thought* (Cambridge, MA: Harvard University Press, 1962), p. 37.

22. Richard Hofstadter, *The Paranoid Style in American Politics* (New York: Knopf, 1965), p. 8.

23. Seymour Martin Lipset and Earl Raab, *The Politics of Unreason: Right-Wing Extremism in America, 1790–1970* (New York: Harper & Row, 1970), pp. 94–95.

24. *US Congressional Record*, Senate, 57th Cong., 3rd sess., January 15, 1895, pp. 973, 976, 981.

25. For instance, Michael Kazin, *Populist Persuasion: An American History* (Ithaca, NY: Cornell University Press, 1997), and Charles Postel, *The Populist Vision* (New York: Oxford University Press, 2007).

26. Rudiger Dornbusch and Sebastian Edwards, eds., *The Macroeconomics of Populism in Latin America* (Chicago: University of Chicago Press, 1991), pp. 9, 12.

27. William Shakespeare, *Henry VI, Part 2*, act 5, scene 2.

28. Stephen Greenblatt, *Tyrant: Shakespeare on Politics* (New York: Norton, 2018), p. 35.

29. David Marsh, *The Euro: The Battle for the New Global Currency* (New Haven: Yale University Press, 2011), p. 269.

30. Olivier Meiler, "Als Erstes lebt der Streit wieder auf," *Süddeutsche Zeitung*, May 2, 2020, https://www.sueddeutsche.de/politik/coronavirus-italien-parlament-konflikt-1.4894124.

31. Margaret Canovan, "Trust the People! Populism and the Two Faces of Democracy," *Political Studies* 47, no. 1 (1999): 2–16.

32. Fintan O'Toole, *Heroic Failure: Brexit and the Politics of Pain* (New York: Apollo Books, 2018).

33. David Salsburg, *The Lady Tasting Tea: How Statistics Revolutionized Science in the Twentieth Century* (New York: Henry Holt, 2001), p. 87.

10.   Globalism

1. Julian Borger, "Donald Trump Denounces 'Globalism' in Nationalist Address to UN," *The Guardian*, September 24, 2019, https://www.theguardian.com/us-news/2019/sep/24/donald-trump-un-address-denounces-globalism.

2. Danny Hakim and Sui-Lee Wee, "From Trump the Nationalist, a Trail of Global Trademarks," *New York Times*, February 22, 2017, https://www.nytimes.com/2017/02/21/business/donald-trump-trademarks-china.html.

3. "Speech: Donald Trump Holds a Political Rally in Houston, Texas, October 22, 2018," Factbase, https://factba.se/transcript/donald-trump-speech-maga-rally-houston-tx-october-22-2018.

4. Peter Baker, "'Use That Word!' Trump Embraces the 'Nationalist' Label," *New York Times*, October 23, 2018, https://www.nytimes.com/2018/10/23/us/politics/nationalist-president-trump.html.

5. Peter Beinart, "What Trump Means When He Calls Gary Cohn a 'Globalist,' " *The Atlantic*, March 9, 2018, https://www.theatlantic.com/politics/archive/2018/03/trump-globalist-cohn/555269.

6. US Holocaust Memorial Museum, "Hitler at Siemens Factory," video clip, https://collections.ushmm.org/search/catalog/irn1000378.

7. Ernst Jäckh, *The War for Man's Soul* (New York: Farrar & Rinehart, 1943), pp. 7, 139.

8. See Rainer Eisfeld, *Ausgebürgert und doch angebräunt: Deutsche Politikwissenschaft, 1920–1945* (Baden-Baden: Nomos, 1991).

9. Speech at the Seventh Party Congress, quoted in E. H. Carr, *The Bolshevik Revolution, 1917–1923*, vol. 3 (Harmondsworth, UK: Penguin, 1966), p. 63.

10. Clare Boothe Luce, "America in the Post-War Air World," speech delivered in the US House of Representatives, February 9, 1943, in *Vital Speeches of the Day*, vol. 19 (New York: City News, 1943), p. 334.

11. Wendell L. Wilkie, *One World* (New York: Simon and Schuster Pocket Book, 1943), p. 176.

12. Wang Jianlang, *Unequal Treaties and China*, vol. 2 (Hong Kong: Silkroad Press, 2016), p. 70.

13. Ben Zimmer, "The Origins of the Globalist Slur," *The Atlantic*, March 14, 2018, https://www.theatlantic.com/politics/archive/2018/03/the-origins-of-the-globalist-slur/555479.

14. See the blurb on the cover of Wilkie, *One World*.

15. Walter Lippmann, "The Rivalry of Nations," *Atlantic Monthly* 181, no. 2 (February 1948): 19.

16. Hans Morgenthau, *Politics among Nations: The Struggle for Power and Peace*, 3rd ed. (New York: Knopf, 1960), pp. 256–257.

17. Hans Morgenthau, *Vietnam and the United States* (New York: Public Affairs Press, 1965), p. 82.

18. Morgenthau, *Politics among Nations*, p. 93.

19. Ronald Steel, *Walter Lippmann and the American Century* (Boston: Little, Brown, 1980), p. 586.

20. Hans Morgenthau, "The Moral Dilemmas of Political Action," 1950, in Hans Morgenthau, *The Decline of Democratic Politics* (Chicago: University of Chicago Press, 1962), pp. 318–327, quotation on p. 326.

21. Hans Morgenthau, *The Purpose of American Politics* (New York: Knopf, 1960), p. 8; see also Udi Greenberg, *The Weimar Century: German Émigrés and the Ideological Foundations of the Cold War* (Princeton, NJ: Princeton University Press, 2014), pp. 211–255.

22. Hans Morgenthau, *A New Foreign Policy for the United States* (New York: Frederick A. Prager, 1969), p. 84.

23. See also Jack Snyder, *Myths of Empire: Domestic Politics and International Ambition* (Ithaca, NY: Cornell University Press, 1991), p. 256.

24. Charles Gati, "Review: Another Grand Debate?: The Limitationist Critique of American Foreign Policy," *World Politics* 21, no. 1 (October 1968): 133–151.

25. "The Enduring Relevance of Reinhold Niebuhr," *BU Today,* January 31, 2008, http://www.bu.edu/articles/2008/the-enduring-relevance-of-reinhold-niebuhr.

26. Andrew Bacevich, *The Limits of Power: The End of American Exceptionalism* (New York: Henry Holt, 2008), pp. 2, 55.

27. Andrew Bacevich, "'Saving 'America First': What Responsible Nationalism Looks Like," *Foreign Affairs* (September/October 2017): 59, 61; also Bacevich, *Twilight of the American Century* (South Bend, IN: University of Notre Dame Press, 2018).

28. Russell R. Reno, *Return of the Strong Gods: Nationalism, Populism, and the Future of the West* (Washington, DC: Regnery, 2019).

29. Russell R. Reno, *Resurrecting the Idea of a Christian Society* (Washington, DC: Regnery, 2016), p. 39.

30. R. R. Reno, "Goodbye, Left and Right," *First Things,* May 8, 2017, https://www.firstthings.com/web-exclusives/2017/05/goodbye-left-and-right.

31. R. R. Reno, "Republicans Are Now the 'America First' Party," *New York Times,* April 28, 2017, https://www.nytimes.com/2017/04/28/opinion/sunday/republicans-are-now-the-america-first-party.html.

32. Liam Stack, "Globalism: A Far-Right Conspiracy Theory Buoyed by Trump," *New York Times,* November 14, 2016, https://www.nytimes.com/2016/11/15/us/politics/globalism-right-trump.html.

33. *The Alex Jones Show,* March 28, 2018, Genesis Communications.

34. Lauren Southern, "What Is a Globalist?" YouTube video posted September 16, 2016, https://www.youtube.com/watch?v=XumrD3ET3Sg&feature=emb_title.

35. Twitter post, @Lauren_Southern, November 14, 2018, 4:36 p.m.

11.   Globalization and Its Neologisms

1. Justin Wise, "Trump Adviser Says 'Globalization of Production' Caused Medical Equipment Shortages," *The Hill,* April 13, 2020, https://thehill.com/homenews/

administration/492469-trump-adviser-says-globalization-of-production-caused-medical.

2. Sebastian Conrad, *What Is Global History?* (Princeton, NJ: Princeton University Press, 2016), p. 45.

3. John Gray, *False Dawn: The Delusions of Global Capitalism* (London: Granta, 1998).

4. John G. Ruggie, "International Regimes, Transactions, and Change: Embedded Liberalism in the Postwar Economic Order," *International Organization* 36, no. 2 (Spring 1982): 379–415.

5. G. John Ikenberry, *After Victory: Institutions, Strategic Restraint, and the Rebuilding of Order after Major Wars* (Princeton, NJ: Princeton University Press, 2001).

6. Ivan Krastev and Stephen Holmes, *The Light That Failed: Why the West Is Losing the Fight for Democracy* (New York: Pegasus Books, 2020), p. 35.

7. Nick Squires, "Matteo Salvini Wades into Culture Wars as Populist Is Chased around Italy by 'Sardines,' " *Daily Telegraph,* December 14, 2019, https://www.telegraph.co.uk/news/2019/12/14/matteo-salvini-wades-culture-wars-populist-chased-around-italy.

8. Craig Willy, "Eurosceptics' Policies: Divided in Diversity," *Deutsche Presse-Agentur,* May 28, 2014.

9. Christopher Lorenz, "Management: The Risks of Simplistic Global Strategies," *Financial Times,* September 4, 1985.

10. Christian Thomasius, *Deutsche Schriften* (Stuttgart: Reclam, 1970), p. 8.

11. Giovanni Federico, "How Much Do We Know about Market Integration in Europe?" *Economic History Review* 65, no. 2 (2012): 470–497.

12. Cornelius Torp, *Die Herausforderung der Globalisierung: Wirtschaft und Politik in Deutschland, 1860–1914* (Göttingen: Vandenhoeck & Ruprecht, 2005).

13. Dani Rodrik, *The Globalization Paradox* (New York: Norton, 2011).

14. Charles P. Kindleberger, *The World in Depression* (Berkeley: University of California Press, 1973).

15. Douglas A. Irwin, *Peddling Protectionism: Smoot-Hawley and the Great Depression* (Princeton, NJ: Princeton University Press, 2011).

16. Barry Eichengreen and Kevin H. O'Rourke, "What Do the New Data Tell Us?," *VoxEU,* March 8, 2010, https://voxeu.org/article/tale-two-depressions-what-do-new-data-tell-us-february-2010-update.

17. On supply chains, see Richard Baldwin, *The Great Convergence: Information Technology and the New Globalization* (Cambridge, MA: Harvard University Press, 2016).

18. Eric Brynjolfsson and Andrew McAfee, *The Second Machine Age: Work, Progress, and Prosperity in a Time of Brilliant Technologies* (New York: Norton, 2014).

19. Ian Tomb and Kamakshya Trivedi, "'Peak Trade' Is Premature," *VoxEU,* January 6, 2017, https://voxeu.org/article/peak-trade-premature.

20. *Global Information Technology Report,* World Economic Forum, 2016, https://www.weforum.org/reports/the-global-information-technology-report-2016.

21. Susan Lund, James Manyika, and Jacques Bughin, "Globalization Is Becoming More about Data and Less about Stuff," *Harvard Business Review,* March 14, 2016, https://hbr.org/2016/03/globalization-is-becoming-more-about-data-and-less-about-stuff.

22. David Autor, David Dorn, and Gordon H. Hanson, "The China Syndrome: Local Labor Market Effects of Import Competition in the United States," *American Economic Review* 103, no. 6 (October 2013): 2121–2168.

23. Italo Colantone and Piero Stanig, "Global Competition and Brexit," *American Political Science Review* 112, no. 2 (May 2018): 201–218.

24. Reuters staff, "Trump Tweets: Trade Wars Are Good, and Easy to Win," *Reuters Business News,* March 2, 2018, https://www.reuters.com/article/us-usa-trade-trump/trump-tweets-trade-wars-are-good-and-easy-to-win-idUSKCN1GE1E9.

25. Douglas Irwin, *Clashing over Commerce: A History of US Trade Policy* (Chicago: University of Chicago Press, 2017).

26. Arnaud Costinot and Andrés Rodríguez-Clare, "Trade Theory with Numbers: Quantifying the Consequences of Globalization," in E. H. Gita Gopinath and Kenneth Rogoff, eds., *Handbook of International Economics,* vol. 4 (Amsterdam: Elsevier, 2014), 197–261; Pablo D. Fajgelbaum and Amit K. Khandelwal, "Measuring the Unequal Gains from Trade," *Quarterly Journal of Economics* 131, no. 3 (August 2016): 1113–1180.

27. See Baldwin, *Great Convergence.*

28. Max Weber, *Max Weber-Gesamtausgabe,* vol. 1, 4.1: *Landarbeiterfrage, Nationalstaat Und Volkswirtschaftspolitik. Schriften Und Reden 1892–1899,* ed. Wolfgang J. Mommsen and Rita Aldenhoff (Tübigen: Mohr Siebeck, 1993), p. 183.

29. Julie Schindall, "Switzerland's Non-EU Immigrants: Their Integration and Swiss Attitudes," *Migration Policy Institute,* June 9, 2009, http://www.migrationpolicy.org/article/switzerlands-non-eu-immigrants-their-integration-and-swiss-attitudes.

30. Sascha O. Becker, Thiemo Fetzer, and Dennis Novy, "Who Voted for Brexit? A Comprehensive District-Level Analysis," *Economic Policy* 32, no. 92 (October 2017): 601–650.

31. Luca Einaudi, *Le politiche dell'immigrazione in Italia dall'Unità a oggi* (Rome: Laterza, 2007); Douglas Massey and Jorge Durand, *Crossing the Border: Research from the Mexican Migration Project* (New York: Russell Sage, 2004).

32. Michael D. Bordo, Barry Eichengreen, Daniela Klingebiel, and Maria Soledad Martínez-Pería, "Is the Crisis Problem Growing More Severe?," *Economic Policy* 16, no. 32 (April 2001): 51–82; Michael D. Bordo and Barry Eichengreen, "Crises Now and Then: What Lessons from the Last Era of Financial Globalization," NBER working paper no. 8716, 2002; Moritz Schularick and Alan M. Taylor, "Credit Booms Gone Bust: Monetary Policy, Leverage Cycles, and Financial Crises, 1870–2008," *American Economic Review* 102, no. 2 (April 2012): 1029–1061.

33. "The Money Market," *The Economist,* December 28, 1907, 2285–2286.

34. J. Lawrence Broz, *The International Origins of the Federal Reserve System* (Ithaca, NY: Cornell University Press, 1997).

35. Paul Warburg, "Defects and Needs of Our Banking System," *New York Times,* January 6, 1907.

36. Paul Warburg, "The Reserve Problem and the Future of the Federal Reserve System, Address of Hon. Paul M. Warburg before the Convention of the American Bankers Association, Kansas City, Mo., September 29, 1916," http://fraser.stlouisfed.org/docs/historical/federal%20reserve%20history/bog_members_statements/Warburg_19160929.pdf.

37. Ben S. Bernanke, *The Courage to Act: A Memoir of a Crisis and Its Aftermath* (New York: Norton, 2015).

38. Ivan T. Berend, *An Economic History of Twentieth-Century Europe: Economic Regimes from Laissez-Faire to Globalization* (Cambridge, UK: Cambridge University Press, 2016).

39. Lionel Robbins, *The Great Depression* (London: Macmillan, 1935), p. 114.

40. "Howard S. Ellis, Bilateralism and the Future of International Trade," Princeton International Finance Section, Essays in International Finance no. 5, 1945, p. 8.

41. Kristin Forbes, "Financial 'Deglobalization'?: Capital Flows, Banks, and the Beatles," speech at Queen Mary University, London, November 18, 2014, https://www.bankofengland.co.uk/speech/2014/financial-deglobalization-capital-flows-banks-and-the-beatles.

42. Kristin Forbes, Dennis Reinhardt, and Tomasz Wieladek, "The Spillovers, Interactions, and (Un)intended Consequences of Monetary and Regulatory Policies," *Journal of Monetary Economics* 85 (2017): 1–22.

43. Patrick Hennessy, "80 Per Cent of Bank Lending 'Went Overseas,' " *Daily Telegraph,* January 17, 2009, https://www.telegraph.co.uk/finance/financialcrisis/4278583/80-per-cent-of-bank-lending-went-overseas.html.

44. Robert McCauley, Agustín S. Bénétrix, Patrick M. McGuire, and Goetz von Peter, "Financial Deglobalisation in Banking?," BIS Working Papers 650, June 2017.

45. Gideon Rachman, *Zero-Sum Future: American Power in an Age of Anxiety* (New York: Simon and Schuster, 2011).

46. Daniel Drezner, *The System Worked: How the World Stopped Another Great Depression* (Oxford, UK: Oxford University Press, 2014).

47. Patrick Donahue, "Merkel, Li Hail Trade Ties as Trump Pursues Protectionism," *Bloomberg,* January 26, 2017, https://www.bloomberg.com/news/articles/2017-01-26/merkel-li-push-eu-china-trade-ties-as-trump-lauds-protectionism.

48. Xi Jinping, "President Xi's Speech to Davos in Full," World Economic Forum, January 17, 2017, http://www.scio.gov.cn/32618/Document/1540505/1540505.htm.

49. Alison Smale and Steven Erlanger, "As Obama Exits World Stage, Angela Merkel May Be the Liberal West's Last Defender," *New York Times,* November 12, 2016, https://www.nytimes.com/2016/11/13/world/europe/germany-merkel-trump-election.html.

50. Angela Merkel, Budget speech of November 23, 2016, https://www.bundesregierung.de/breg-en/search/-strengthening-our-shared-values-390856.

51. Zi Zhongyun, translated and annotated by Geremie R. Barmé, "An Old Anxiety in a New Era: 1900 & 2020," *China Heritage,* drafted April 13, 2020, revised April 23, 2020, http://chinaheritage.net/journal/1900–2020-an-old-anxiety-in-a-new-era.

52. Reuters staff, "Ex-Fed's Volcker: Govt Should Do More to End Crisis," *Reuters Business News,* April 8, 2008, https://www.reuters.com/article/us-economy-volcker-idUSN0843904220080408.

53. Scott J. Hammond, Howard Leslie Lubert, and Kevin R. Hardwick, eds., *Classics of American Political and Constitutional Thought,* vol. 1 (Indianapolis, IN: Hackett Publishing, 2017), p. 184.

54. See Jesús Fernández-Villaverde and Tano Santos, "Institutions and Political Party Systems: The Euro Case," NBER working paper no. w23599, July 2017.

55. Ryan Teague Beckwith, "Read Steve Bannon and Reince Priebus' Joint Interview at CPAC," *Time,* February 23, 2017, https://time.com/4681094/reince-priebus-steve-bannon-cpac-interview-transcript.

56. Madeleine Albright, *Fascism: A Warning* (New York: Harper, 2018); Jason Stanley, *How Fascism Works: The Politics of Us and Them* (New York: Penguin, 2018).

57. Benito Mussolini, "The Doctrine of Fascism," 1932, in Michael J. Oakeshott, *The Social and Political Doctrines of Contemporary Europe* (Cambridge, UK: Cambridge University Press, 1939), pp. 164–168.

58. The term was used by an obscure Nazi functionary Werner Willikens, state secretary in the Ministry of Food, in 1934, and used as the key to interpreting Hitler's authority by Hitler's authoritative biographer, Ian Kershaw, in his book *Hitler: 1889–1936 Hubris* (New York: Norton, 1998).

59. Masha Gessen, "Trump's Fascist Performance," *New Yorker,* June 3, 2020, https://www.newyorker.com/news/our-columnists/donald-trumps-fascist-performance.

12.   Neoliberalism

1. See Peter Steinfels, *The Neoconservatives: The Men Who Are Changing America's Politics* (New York: Simon and Schuster, 1979); see also David Laidler, *Fabricating the Keynesian Revolution: Studies of the Inter-War Literature on Money, the Cycle, and Unemployment* (Cambridge, UK: Cambridge University Press, 1999); Robert O. Keohane, *Neorealism and Its Critics* (New York: Columbia University Press, 1986); and Walter Laqueur, "The Many Faces of Neo-Marxism," *National Interest* 125 (May/June 2013): 88–96.

2. As in Michael Lind, *The New Class War: Saving Democracy from the Managerial Elite* (New York: Portfolio Penguin, 2020).

3. Perhaps one exception is the Adam Smith Institute: see Sam Bowman, "Coming Out as Neoliberals," Adam Smith Institute, October 11, 2016, https://www.adamsmith.org/blog/coming-out-as-neoliberals.

4. See Jurgen Reinhoudt and Serge Audier, eds., *The Walter Lippmann Colloquium: The Birth of Neo-Liberalism* (Cham, Switz.: Palgrave Macmillan, 2018). There were earlier uses of the term "neoliberalism," which Sébastien Charléty has traced back to the early nineteenth century in vol. 4 of Ernest Lavisse's *Histoire de France Contemporaine* (Paris: Hachette, 1920). But it never provided a basis for any coherent doctrine until the late 1930s. Indeed, Charléty describes the romantic and skeptical neoliberals of Restoration France as engaged simply in a "negation of received faith" (*négation de la foi reçu*) (Lavisse, 200).

5. Joseph E. Stiglitz, "The End of Neoliberalism and the Rebirth of History," *Project Syndicate*, November 4, 2019, https://www.project-syndicate.org/commentary/end-of-neoliberalism-unfettered-markets-fail-by-joseph-e-stiglitz-2019-11.

6. George Monbiot, "Neoliberalism—The Ideology at the Root of All Our Problems," *The Guardian*, April 15, 2016, https://www.theguardian.com/books/2016/apr/15/neoliberalism-ideology-problem-george-monbiot.

7. "Theresa May's Conference Speech in Full," *The Telegraph*, October 5, 2016, https://www.telegraph.co.uk/news/2016/10/05/theresa-mays-conference-speech-in-full.

8. Nick Timothy, "It's Time for Boris Johnson to Take on Britain's Cult of Liberal Technocrats," *The Telegraph*, December 29, 2019, https://www.telegraph.co.uk/politics/2019/12/29/time-boris-johnson-take-britains-cult-liberal-technocrats.

9. Ian Schwartz, "Tucker Carlson: We Are Ruled by Mercenaries Who Feel No Long-Term Obligation to the People They Rule," *RealClearPolitics*, January 3, 2019, https://www.realclearpolitics.com/video/2019/01/03/tucker_carlson_we_are_ruled_by_mercenaries_who_feel_no_long-term_obligation_to_the_people_they_rule.html.

10. Erwan Bruckert, Sébastien Le Fol, and Marc Vignaud, "Bruno Le Maire: 'Le capitalisme est dans une impasse,' " *Le Point*, July 24, 2019, https://www.lepoint.fr/politique/bruno-le-maire-le-capitalisme-est-dans-une-impasse-24-07-2019-2326620_20.php.

11. See Gordon Brown, *My Life, Our Times* (London: Bodley Head, 2017), p. 23.

12. Jörg Hackhausen, "'Der Kapitalismus ist gescheitert,' " *Die Zeit*, July 13, 2009, https://www.zeit.de/online/2009/29/kapitalismus-malik-finanzkrise.

13. See David Harvey, *A Brief History of Neoliberalism* (Oxford, UK: Oxford University Press, 2007); see also Philip Mirowski and Dieter Plehwe, *The Road from Mont Pèlerin: The Making of the Neoliberal Thought Collective* (Cambridge, MA: Harvard University Press, 2009); Daniel Stedman Jones, *Masters of the Universe: Hayek, Friedman, and the Birth of Neoliberal Politics* (Princeton, NJ: Princeton University Press, 2012); Angus Burgin, *The Great Persuasion: Reinventing Free Markets since the Depression* (Cambridge, MA: Harvard University Press, 2012); Laurent Warlouzet, *Governing Europe in a Globalizing World: Neoliberalism and Its Alternatives Following the 1973 Oil Crisis* (London: Routledge, 2018); and Arnaud Brennetot, "The Geographical and Ethical Origins of Neoliberalism: The Walter Lippmann Colloquium and the Foundations of a New Geopolitical Order," *Political Geography* 49 (November 2015): 30–39.

14. See Bruce Caldwell, "Mont Pèlerin 1947," in *From the Past to the Future: Ideas and Actions for a Free Society,* ed. John B. Taylor (Stanford, CA: Hoover Institution and the Mont Pèlerin Society, 2020), 32–84, and the volume in which it appears more generally https://www.hoover.org/research/past-future-ideas-and-actions-free-society-mont-pelerin-society.

15. "Full Text of Xi Jinping's Report at 19th CPC National Congress, delivered at the Nineteenth National Congress of the Communist Party of China," *Xinhua*, October 18, 2017, updated November 4, 2017, https://www.chinadaily.com.cn/china/19thcpcnationalcongress/2017-11/04/content_34115212.htm.

16. See Lionel Barber, Henry Foy, and Alex Barker, "Vladimir Putin Says Liberalism Has 'Become Obsolete,' " *Financial Times,* June 27, 2019, https://www.ft.com/content/670039ec-98f3-11e9-9573-ee5cbb98ed36.

17. See Jonathan D. Ostry, Prakash Loungani, and Davide Furceri, "Neoliberalism: Oversold?," *Finance & Development* 53, no. 2 (June 2016): 38–41.

18. Shawn Donnan, "IMF Economists Put 'Neoliberalism' under the Spotlight," *Financial Times,* May 26, 2016, https://www.ft.com/content/4b98c052-238a-11e6-9d4d-c11776a5124d.

19. Julia Ott, "Words Can't Do the Work for Us," *Dissent* blog, January 22, 2018, https://www.dissentmagazine.org/blog/neoliberalism-forum-julia-ott. See also Daniel Rodgers, "The Uses and Abuses of 'Neoliberalism,' " *Dissent* (Winter 2018), https://www.dissentmagazine.org/article/uses-and-abuses-neoliberalism-debate.

20. For the 1980s French policymakers, see Rawi Abdelal, *Capital Rules: The Construction of Global Finance* (Cambridge, MA: Harvard University Press, 2007). For the Geneva thinkers, see Quinn Slobodian, *Globalists: The End of Empire and the Birth of Neoliberalism* (Cambridge, MA: Harvard University Press, 2017), a development of the ideas of Michel Fior, *Institution globale et marchés financiers: La Société des Nations face à la reconstruction de l'Europe, 1918–1931* (Bern: Peter Lang, 2008); and Louis W. Pauly, *Who Elected the Bankers? Surveillance and Control in the World Economy* (Ithaca, NY: Cornell University Press, 1997).

21. Rougier quickly moved away from the anti-fascism of 1938, and in 1940 worked for Marshal Pétain.

22. Reinhoudt and Audier, *Walter Lippmann Colloquium*, p. 98.

23. Ibid., p. 119.

24. Ibid., p. 124.

25. See Ralf Ptak, *Vom Ordoliberalismus zur Sozialen Marktwirtschaft: Stationen des Neoliberalismus in Deutschland* (Opladen, Ger.: Leske-Budrich, 2004); see also Wolfgang Streeck, *How Will Capitalism End? Essays on a Failing System* (London: Verso, 2016), p. 151.

26. See Henry Calvert Simons, *A Positive Program for Laissez Faire: Some Proposals for a Liberal Economic Policy,* Public Policy Pamphlet 15 (Chicago: University of Chicago Press, 1934), p. 4.

27. See Milton Friedman, "Neo-Liberalism and Its Prospects," *Farmand,* February 17, 1951, 89–93, https://miltonfriedman.hoover.org/friedman_images/Collections/2016c21/Farmand_02_17_1951.pdf.

28. See Henry C. Simons, "Economic Stability and Antitrust Policy," *University of Chicago Law Review* 12, no. 4 (1944): 338–348, quotations on pp. 343, 347.

29. See, for instance, Jaromir Benes and Michael Kumhof, "The Chicago Plan Revisited," IMF Working Paper WP/12/202, 2012, https://www.imf.org/external/pubs/ft/wp/2012/wp12202.pdf.

30. See Friedrich A. Hayek, *Prices and Production* (New York: Augustus M. Kelley, 1931), 117–118.

31. Reinhoudt and Audier, *Walter Lippmann Colloquium*, p. 170.

32. This line of argument is implicit in Wilhelm Röpke, *Die Deutsche Frage* (Zurich: Eugen Rentsch, 1945).

33. Quoted in Honoré de Balzac, *Œuvres complètes de H. de Balzac,* vol. 17 (Paris: A. Houssiaux, 1874), p. 259: "Tout le monde fait valoir son argent et le tripote de son mieux. Vous vous abusez, cher ange, si vous croyez que c'est le roi Louis-Philippe qui règne, et il ne s'abuse pas là-dessus. Il sait comme nous tous, qu'au-dessus de la Charte, il y a la sainte, la vénérée, la solide, l'aimable, la gracieuse, la belle, la noble, la jeune, la toute-puissante pièce de cent sous! or, mon bel ange, l'argent exige des intérêts, et il est toujours occupé à les percevoir!"

34. See Paul H. Douglas and Aaron Director, *The Problem of Unemployment* (New York: Macmillan, 1931); see also George S. Tavlas, "'The Initiated': Aaron Director and the Chicago Monetary Tradition," Hoover Institution Paper, 2020, https://www.hoover.org/research/initiated-aaron-director-and-chicago-monetary-tradition.

35. This is in part the argument in Harold James, *The German Slump: Policies and Economics, 1924–1936* (Oxford, UK: Oxford University Press, 1986).

36. Quoted in Friedrich A. Hayek, *The Road to Serfdom* (Chicago: University of Chicago Press, 1944), p. 31.

37. Ibid., p. 55.

38. Ibid., p. 94.

39. James, *German Slump*, p. 353.

40. Hayek, *Road to Serfdom*, p. 170.

41. See Helen Junz, "Report on the Wealth Position of the Jewish Population in Nazi-Occupied Countries, Germany and Austria," in *Independent Committee of Eminent Persons, Report on Dormant Accounts of Victims of Nazi Persecution in Swiss Banks* (Bern: Staempfli, 1999).

42. See Peter Lindseth, *Power and Legitimacy: Reconciling Europe and the Nation-State* (Oxford, UK: Oxford University Press, 2010).

43. See Tony Allan Freyer, *Antitrust and Global Capitalism, 1930–2004* (New York: Cambridge University Press, 2006).

44. See, for instance, Hayek's 1984 speech in Paris, published in *Le Figaro*, March 10, 1984. I owe this reference to Jurgen Reinhoudt.

45. Quoted in *CQ Guide to Current American Government* (Fall 1985): 80.

46. Quoted in New York (State) and A. Barton Hepburn, *Report of the Special Committee on Railroads* (Albany: Weed, Parsons and Company, 1879), p. 45; see also *Standard Oil Company of New Jersey et al., Appellants, against United States of America, Appellee*, https://www.law.cornell.edu/supremecourt/text/221/1. I owe these references to Charles Ughetta.

47. Quoted in Robert H. Bork, *The Antitrust Paradox: A Policy at War with Itself* (New York: Basic Books, 1978), p. 8. This development in antitrust thinking is neglected in most of the recent writing on the genealogy of neoliberalism; a commendable exception is Mirowski and Plehwe, *Road from Mont Pèlerin*.

48. See Michel Foucault, *The Birth of Biopolitics* (Houndsmills, UK: Palgrave Macmillan, 2008).

49. Quoted in Jason Read, "A Genealogy of Homo-Economicus: Foucault, Neoliberalism, and the Production of Subjectivity," *Foucault Studies* 6 (February 2009): 25–36, quotation on p. 28; see also Paul Michael Garrett, "Revisiting 'The Birth of Biopolitics': Foucault's Account of Neoliberalism and the Remaking of Social Policy," *Journal of Social Policy* 48, no. 3 (July 2019): 469–487.

50. See Grégoire Chamayou, *La société ingouvernable: Une généalogie du libéralisme autoritaire* (Paris: La Fabrique, 2018).

51. "Bananen für Alle," *Der Spiegel*, October 6, 2008, https://www.spiegel.de/spiegel/print/d-60883210.html.

52. Lind, *New Class War*, p. 65.

53. See Skinner quoted in Shoshana Zuboff, *The Age of Surveillance Capitalism: The Fight for a Human Future at the New Frontier of Power* (New York: Public Affairs, 2019), p. 271.

54. Simons, *Positive Program*, p. 32.

55. See the biting criticism in Atif Mian and Amir Sufi, *House of Debt: How They (and You) Caused the Great Recession, and How We Can Prevent It from Happening Again* (Chicago: University of Chicago Press, 2014).

56. See Joseph E. Stiglitz, "After Neoliberalism," *Project Syndicate*, May 30, 2019, https://www.project-syndicate.org/commentary/after-neoliberalism-progressive-capitalism-by-joseph-e-stiglitz-2019-05.

57. See Climate Leadership Council, "Former Federal Reserve Chairs and Nobel Economists Solidify Support for a Price on Carbon," *Carbon Pricing Leadership Coalition*, January 17, 2019, https://www.carbonpricingleadership.org/news/2019/1/17/former-federal-reserve-chairs-and-nobel-economists-solidify-support-for-a-price-on-carbon.

58. See Dani Rodrik, *The Globalization Paradox: Democracy and the Future of the World Economy* (New York: W.W. Norton, 2011); see also Michael D. Bordo and Harold James, "The Trade-Offs between Macroeconomics, Political Economy and International Relations," *Financial History Review* 26, no. 3 (December 2019): 247–266.

59. Quoted in Friedrich A. Hayek, "The Confusion of Language in Political Thought," in *New Studies in Philosophy, Politics, Economics, and the History of Ideas* (London: Routledge, 1978), p. 72.

13.   Crisis

1. Reinhart Koselleck, "Crisis," trans. Michaela W. Richter, *Journal of the History of Ideas* 67, no. 2 (2006): 372.

2. Paul Krugman, "Crises: The Price of Globalization?" in Federal Reserve Bank of Kansas City, *Global Economic Integration: Opportunities and Challenges*, August 24–26, 2000, pp. 75–106.

3. Robert Patterson, "An Account of Epidemic Fever of 1847–48," *Edinburgh Medical and Surgical Journal* 70 (1848): 372–373.

4. Thomas Mann, *Buddenbrooks: The Decline of a Family*, trans. John E. Woods (New York: Knopf, 1993), pp. 725–726.

5. Susan Sontag, "Illness as Metaphor," *New York Review of Books,* January 26, 1978.

6. Thomas Paine, *The American Crisis* (London: R. Carlile, 1812), p. 41.

7. See Simon Schama, *Citizens: A Chronicle of the French Revolution* (New York: Knopf, 1989), p. 874.

8. See Randolph Starn, "Historians and 'Crisis,' " *Past and Present* 52 (1971): 3–22.

9. Thomas Babington Macaulay, *The Complete Works of Thomas Babington Macaulay,* vol. 1: *The History of England from the Accession of James II* (1848; New York: Houghton Mifflin, 1899), p. 1.

10. For instance, *Die Gegenwart: Eine encylopädische Darstellung der neuesten Zeitgeschichte* (Leipzig: Brochhaus, 1849).

11. Charles Trevelyan, *The Irish Crisis* (London: Longman, Brown, Green, 1848), pp. 1–2.

12. I thank Andrew Roberts and Richard Langworth for corroboration.

13. Gerald F. Seib, "Crisis, Opportunity for Obama," from the November 2008 *Wall Street Journal* Conference, *Wall Street Journal,* November 21, 2008, https://www.wsj.com/articles/SB122721278056345271, also https://www.youtube.com/watch?v=_mzcbXiiTkk.

14. Koselleck, "Crisis," p. 399.

15. Krugman, "Crises," p. 76.

16. See Jonathan Sperber, *The European Revolutions, 1848–1851* (Cambridge, UK: Cambridge University Press, 2005); see also Mark Spoerer and Helge Berger, "Economic Crises and the European Revolutions of 1848," *Journal of Economic History* 61, no. 2 (June 2001): 293–326.

17. See Amartya Sen, *Poverty and Famines: An Essay on Entitlement and Deprivation* (Oxford, UK: Oxford University Press, 1983).

18. See Cormac O'Grada, *The Great Irish Famine* (Cambridge, UK: Cambridge University Press, 1995).

19. Quoted in Robin Haines, *Charles Trevelyan and the Great Irish Famine* (Dublin: Four Courts, 2004), p. 240.

20. See Charles Read, "Laissez-Faire, the Irish Famine, and British Financial Crisis," *Economic History Review* 69, no. 2 (May 2016): 411–434.

21. Quoted in John Mitchel, *The Last Conquest of Ireland* (Dublin: University College Dublin Press, 2005), p. 218; see also Christophe Gillissen, "Charles Trevelyan, John Mitchel and the Historiography of the Great Famine," *Revue française de civilisation britannique* 19, no. 2 (2014): 195–212.

22. Kevin O'Rourke and Jeffrey Williamson, *Globalization and History: The Evolution of a Nineteenth-Century Atlantic Economy* (Cambridge, MA: MIT Press, 1999).

23. Olivier Accominotti and Marc Flandreau, "Bilateral Treaties and the Most-Favored-Nation Clause: The Myth of Trade Liberalization in the Nineteenth Century," *World Politics* 60, no. 2 (January 2008): 147–188.

24. Karl Marx, *Die Klassenkämpfe in Frankreich, 1848 bis 1850* (Berlin: Vorwärts, 1895).

25. Herman von Petersdorff, *König Friedrich Wilhelm der Vierte* (Stuttgart: Cotta, 1900), p. 11.

26. See Harold James, *Rambouillet, 15. November 1975. Die Globalisierung der Wirtschaft* (Munich: DTV, 1997).

27. Quoted in Peter Jenkins, *Mrs. Thatcher's Revolution: The Ending of the Socialist Era* (London: Jonathan Cape, 1987), p. 18.

28. James Callaghan, Leader's Speech, Blackpool, Eng., September 28, 1976, http://www.britishpoliticalspeech.org/speech-archive.htm?speech=174.

29. Edgar Morin, "Pour une crisologie," *Communications* 25 (1976): 149–163.

30. Koselleck, "Crisis," p. 399.

14.   Recoining the Words in Our Lexicon

1. Quoted in Thomas Piketty, *Capital and Ideology,* trans. Arthur Goldhammer (Cambridge, MA: Harvard University Press, 2020), p. 672.

2. William Shakespeare, *Henry VI, Part 2,* act 4, scene 2.

3. For the following arguments, see Markus K. Brunnermeier, Harold James, and Jean-Pierre Landau, "The Digitalization of Money," NBER working paper no. 26300, 2019.

4. See James Politi, "How the Federal Reserve Came to Focus on Racial Justice," *Financial Times,* June 19, 2020, https://www.ft.com/content/7fba09e7-85b6-4abe-9c17-a1e5ab141bb9.

5. See Harold James, *Making a Modern Central Bank: The Bank of England, 1979–2003* (Cambridge, UK: Cambridge University Press, 2020).

6. Karl Helfferich, *Das Geld* (Leipzig: C. L. Hirschfeld, 1903), p. 530.

7. See Eric Helleiner, *The Making of National Money: Territorial Currencies in Historical Perspective* (Ithaca, NY: Cornell University Press, 2003).

8. Quoted in Rebecca L. Spang, *Stuff and Money in the Time of the French Revolution* (Cambridge, MA: Harvard University Press, 2015), p. 266.

9. Paul de Grauwe, "The Eurozone's Design Failures: Can They Be Corrected?," LSE lecture, 2012, https://www.lse.ac.uk/assets/richmedia/channels/publicLecturesAndEvents/slides/20121128_1830_theEurozonesDesignFailures_sl.pdf.

10. The classic text is Henry George, *Progress and Poverty* (New York: Appleton, 1879).

11. Piketty, *Capital and Ideology.*

12. Richard Henderson and Miles Kruppa, "Robinhood Upstarts Who Ambushed the Financial Establishment," *Financial Times,* August 21, 2020.

13. See Edward Gibbon, *Memoirs of My Life and Writings* (1796; New York: Funk & Wagnalls, 1969), p. 52.

14. See Adam Smith, *An Inquiry into the Nature and Causes of the Wealth of Nations,* ed. Edwin Cannan (1776; Chicago: University of Chicago Press, 1976), p. 287.

15. This was a concept applied to the European Union in particular in Jan Zielonka, *Europe as Empire: The Nature of the Enlarged European Union* (Oxford, UK: Oxford University Press, 2006).

Index